SMOKING
RISK, PERCEPTION, & POLICY

PAUL SLOVIC, EDITOR

Sage Publications
International Educational and Professional Publisher
Thousand Oaks ▪ London ▪ New Delhi

For information:

Sage Publications, Inc.
2455 Teller Road
Thousand Oaks, California 91320
E-mail: order@sagepub.com

Sage Publications Ltd.
6 Bonhill Street
London EC2A 4PU
United Kingdom

Sage Publications India Pvt. Ltd.
M-32 Market
Greater Kailash I
New Delhi 110 048 India

Printed in the United States of America

Library of Congress Cataloging-in-Publication Data

Main entry under title:

Smoking: risk, perception & policy / editor, Paul Slovic.
    p. cm.
  Includes bibliographical references and index.
  ISBN 0-7619-2380-2 (cloth: acid-free paper)
  ISBN 0-7619-2381-0 (pbk.: acid-free paper)
  1. Smoking-Health aspects. 2. Nicotine habit. 3. Cigarette smokers-Attitudes.
4. Cigarette smokers-Health risk assessment. 5. Risk perception.
6. Smoking-Government policy. I. Title: Smoking: risk, perception, and policy.
II. Slovic, Paul, 1938-
  RC567.R56 2001
  362.29'6—dc21

00-012865

01 02 03 04 05 06 10 9 8 7 6 5 4 3 2

Acquiring Editor:	Rolf Janke
Production Editor:	Claudia A. Hoffman
Editorial Assistant:	Candice Crosetti
Copy Editor:	Judy Selhorst
Typesetter/Designer:	Janelle LeMaster
Indexer:	Molly Hall
Cover Designer:	Ravi Balasuriya

Contents

III. Media Influence on Smoking

IV. Addiction

V. Legal and Policy Perspectives

Preface

American smokers consume about 500 billion cigarettes every year. More than 400,000 deaths annually are attributed to this consumption, making smoking the single most preventable cause of premature mortality in the United States. According to statistics from the World Health Organization, the picture is similar worldwide, where approximately 4 million people die annually from tobacco use, a figure that is predicted to rise to 10 million by 2030 if current trends continue. The majority of smokers start young, before age 18. In the United States, some 3,000 children and young people begin to smoke each day.

The past decade has witnessed a stream of important new developments in our understanding of cigarette smoking and its harmful consequences. There has been growing appreciation of the health effects of breathing secondhand smoke and of the effects on the fetus when a pregnant woman smokes. Most recently, a study has observed effects of nicotine dependence in 12- and 13-year-olds after only days or weeks of light smoking, a very surprising and disturbing finding (DiFranza et al., 2000). Also in the past decade, release of heretofore confidential documents of the tobacco companies has revealed a long history of attempts to attract young people to cigarettes, promote nicotine dependence, and conceal the risks (Glantz, Slade, Bero, Hanauer, & Barnes, 1996).

Another important change in regard to tobacco use in recent years has been in our understanding of the ways in which the risks of smoking are perceived by young people on the threshold of deciding whether or not to smoke and by adults who do and do not smoke. An influential book by economist Kip Viscusi (1992b) has raised the key question pertaining to youth: "At the time when individuals initiate their smoking activity, do they understand the consequences of their actions and make rational decisions?" (p. 11).

Viscusi's book, titled *Smoking: Making the Risky Decision,* addressed this question. After examining the responses from a national survey of more than 3,000 persons, he concluded that people greatly overestimate the risks posed by smoking, a finding he attributed to the large volume of information about these risks communicated by the government and the news media.

Viscusi argued that his data support a rational learning model in which consumers respond appropriately to information and make trade-offs between the risks and benefits of smoking. With respect to youth, he asserted that his findings "strongly contradict the models of individuals being lured into smoking at an early age without any cognizance of the risks" (p. 143). He further concluded that young people are so well-informed that there is no justification for informational campaigns designed to boost their awareness. Finally, Viscusi observed that social policies that allow smoking at age 18 "run little risk of exposing uninformed decision makers to the potential hazards of smoking" (p. 149). Viscusi's data and conclusions thus appear to lend support to the defense used by cigarette companies in lawsuits brought against them by diseased smokers: "These people knew the risks and made informed, rational decisions to smoke."

Viscusi's conclusions did not ring true to me. Several deficiencies in his methodology came immediately to mind. First, the principal question he relied upon asks about risks to smokers in general, not to the respondent as smoker. Weinstein (1987) and other researchers have shown repeatedly that people see themselves as being less at risk from hazards than they see other people, a phenomenon referred to as *optimism bias.*

Second, Viscusi did not consider the repetitive nature of cigarette smoking and the cumulative nature of its risks. Smoking takes place one cigarette at a time, and it seems likely that smokers perceive little or no risk from smoking individual cigarettes despite acknowledging the cumulative risks as very high. A third problem, related to the second, is Viscusi's failure to assess young people's perceptions of the risks of becoming addicted to smoking and thus smoking more cigarettes than they ever intended to consume.

Prompted by a research paper by Patrick Jamieson, Kathleen Hall Jamieson, Dean of the Annenberg School for Communication at the University of Pennsylvania and director of the Public Policy Center at the Annenberg School, had similar doubts and concerns about the knowledge base of adolescent smokers and presmokers. Seeing a need for the development and communication of better messages regarding the dangers of smoking, Dean Jamieson enlisted Daniel Romer and Patrick Jamieson of the Annenberg School, along with Neil Weinstein and myself, in a research project aimed at improving our understanding of the attitudes, beliefs, feelings, and perceptions of risk that young people and adults associate with smoking. We designed two extensive surveys and conducted them by telephone in 1999 and 2000. More than 4,000 persons ages 14 and older were interviewed. The findings from these new surveys, presented in Chapters 2, 3, 4, 6, 7, and 10, form the core of this book.

In Chapter 2, Patrick Jamieson and Daniel Romer describe the methodology for the two surveys and present demographic profiles and smoking patterns of the respondents. Between ages 14 and 22, reported use of cigarettes increased greatly. Of particular interest is the finding that, across all age categories, respondents in Survey 2 could name only about one or two of the many illnesses that result from smoking.

In Chapter 3, Jamieson and Romer examine risk perceptions of individuals aged 14-22 who participated in Survey 1. They did not find any clear or consistent pattern of risk overestimation, in contrast to Viscusi's earlier conclusions. Although some risks of smoking were recognized, many were not. There was no consistent and realistic sense of the addictive nature of smoking among these respondents, and there was a failure to appreciate how risky smoking is when compared with risks from guns, car accidents, alcohol, and drugs.

In Chapter 4, Romer and Jamieson explore in depth the role of risk perception in initiation of smoking and progression toward regular use of tobacco. Data from Survey 2 indicate that heightened perception of risk does not deter young people in the 14-22 age range from starting or continuing smoking. Perceived health risks were found to play a much greater role for adult smokers. Overall, risk perception played a larger role in decisions to stop smoking than in decisions to start. Adults' decisions to quit appeared to be more sensitive to immediate or short-term risks than were young persons' decisions to quit. Concerns about the risks of second-hand smoke influenced decisions about quitting for both young people and adults.

The analyses in Chapter 4 also confirm the central role of affective feelings in determining risk perception. Among survey respondents, positive images and feelings were associated with lower risk perceptions and increased belief in the ease of quitting. Risk perception did not influence smoking initiation apart from feelings. In other words, the decision to try smoking appeared to be driven primarily by the degree to which feelings toward smoking were favorable.

In Chapter 6, I use data from Survey 2 to define further the importance of feelings identified in the earlier chapters by Romer and Jamieson. I introduce a theoretical framework to guide analyses about the role of affect (e.g., favorable and unfavorable feelings) in determining judgment and decisions. I then use this framework, in concert with the survey data, to argue that smokers' decisions are based upon intuitive affect-based thinking, rather than upon the kind of analytic model of reasoning assumed by Viscusi. The individuals surveyed claimed they were not thinking about how smoking might affect their health when they began to smoke; instead, they were focused on trying something new and exciting. Very few smokers originally expected to be smoking for very long, even those who currently have been smoking for many years. A substantial majority of smokers planned to quit and expected to do so during the coming year, regardless of how many times they had unsuccessfully attempted to quit in the past. A high percentage of adult and youth smokers characterized themselves as addicted to cigarettes. When asked, "If you had it to do over again, would you start smoking?" more than 80% of the smokers said that they would not.

"At the time when individuals initiate their smoking activity, do they understand the consequences of their actions and make rational decisions?" The results presented in Chapter 6 lead me to argue that the answer to this central question of Viscusi's is no. When individuals decide to begin smoking, they rely on their feelings and not on analytic thinking. As a result, they do not understand the consequences of their actions and do not make decisions that are true to their future preferences. Reliance on affective feelings is typically a powerful form of rationality. However, it leads people astray when they make decisions about smoking. Borrowing from Amartya Sen's (1977) critique of economic theory, I thus characterize smokers as "rational fools."

The importance of affect is further demonstrated in Chapter 7 by Romer and Jamieson, who use data from Survey 2 to examine the influence of cigarette advertising on adolescents' decisions to start smoking. Reported exposure to advertising was found to be linked to the prevalence of two images of smoking: popularity and relaxation. Persons for whom relaxation images were more favorable exhibited lower perceptions of smoking risks. These findings suggest that, by creating favorable imagery and positive affect toward smoking in young people, advertising lays the groundwork for the subsequent initiation of smoking behavior. As these favorable images become shared in peer groups, social support is built for smoking. Exposure to antismoking messages does not seem to be successful in countering the favorable images of smoking cultivated by cigarette advertising and does not prevent the initiation of smoking.

In Chapter 10, Romer, Jamieson, and R. Kirkland Ahern use data from both surveys to demonstrate a paradox that they term the "catch-22 of smoking and quitting." This paradox results from the incompatible consequences of the belief that one can quit smoking at any time. This optimistic belief motivates smokers to attempt to quit. However, the presumption that it is easy to quit helps young people start smoking, which all too often leads to addiction, which undermines their goal of quitting. Romer and colleagues point out the challenges this belief pattern presents for anyone attempting to design communication programs that will both reduce the likelihood that nonsmokers will start and motivate current smokers to quit.

The remaining chapters place the Annenberg survey results in context and explore their implications for smoking-control policies. In Chapter 1, Jonathan Samet presents a thorough overview of the vast amount of data on the risks of tobacco smoking. He describes the risks to both active and passive smokers—including the fetus, infants, and children—as well as risks to adults.

What is known as *optimism bias* plays an important role in smokers' risk perceptions, and Neil Weinstein reviews the literature on this topic in Chapter 5. He shows that the apparent underestimation or overestimation of risk depends on how risk perceptions are assessed. There is no consistent pattern in the accuracy of smokers' numerical estimates of risk magnitudes; accuracy with this type of question depends entirely on the health outcome rated (e.g., lung cancer cases versus all deaths due to smoking). Some of these numerical judgments are overestimates and some are underestimates. Responses to other types of risk questions show that smokers do acknowledge that smokers face increased health risks. However, they judge the size of the increase in risks to be smaller and less well established than do nonsmokers. Finally, smokers resist acknowledging the personal relevance of the risks: They tend to believe that, compared with other smokers, they themselves are less at risk of becoming addicted or suffering health effects, and they claim that their own risks are only slightly greater than those of the average person. The accumulated data indicate that, despite public attention to the hazards of smoking, smokers minimize the magnitude of their personal vulnerability.

Cigarettes and other forms of tobacco are addicting. In Chapter 8, Neal L. Benowitz reviews the general aspects of nicotine dependence. He also relates this dependence to the progression of tobacco use among young people. He observes that young people underestimate the addictive nature of tobacco and the risk that they will become addicted, and thus underestimate the risk that they will incur tobacco-related disease. Thus children and teenagers become addicted to nicotine before they are able to appreciate fully the consequences of their behavior.

Benowitz's observations are placed in theoretical perspective by George Loewenstein in Chapter 9. Loewenstein views addiction as an extreme example of a wide range of behaviors that are controlled by "visceral factors" such as hunger, thirst, sexual desire, pain, and, with addiction, craving for a drug. Of particular importance is the fact that people underestimate the impact on their own behavior of visceral factors they will experience in the future. Thus, with smoking, it is difficult if not impossible to anticipate the motivational force of the craving for cigarettes that one will experience once one is addicted to cigarettes. I draw heavily on this visceral account in my analysis of the rationality of smoking decisions in Chapter 6.

The final section of this book looks at the legal and policy implications of what we have learned about smoking attitudes, perceptions, and behaviors. In Chapter 11, Jon D. Hanson and Douglas A. Kysar describe the problem of market manipulation that emerges as a result of nonrational cognitive tendencies among individuals and self-interested economic behavior among tobacco companies. They argue that tobacco firms' marketing, promotional, and public relations efforts have led to countless manipulative strategies to lower consumer risk perceptions and elevate product demand. They further contend that legal regulatory efforts that ignore or discount the effects of market manipulation fail to result in socially desirable levels of tobacco use. They propose that a crucial first step toward effective legal regulation of smoking would be the creation of an "enterprise liability" mechanism that would force cigarette manufacturers to incorporate the health costs of smoking into product prices.

In the final chapter, Richard Bonnie draws on findings from Survey 2 and a 1994 Institute of Medicine report titled *Growing Up Tobacco Free* (Lynch & Bonnie, 1994) to argue for a youth-centered strategy for preventing tobacco-related disease and death. To be successful, such a strategy must encompass measures for reducing the accessibility of tobacco products to young people and increasing their cost. It must also alter the social factors that encourage consumption. Bonnie reviews a number of actions recommended in the Institute of Medicine Report, such as raising cigarette prices, allowing state and local governments to regulate promotion and advertising of tobacco products, and improving enforcement of restrictions on youth access. He also calls upon the U.S. Congress to enact a specific regulatory statute for tobacco products, as recommended in the Institute of Medicine report.

In summary, the data and arguments presented in this book paint a portrait of cigarette smokers that is far different from the one created by Viscusi in 1992. It is hard to defend the view of the beginning smoker as well-informed and rational. Reliance upon feelings of the moment, rather than understanding and analysis of the risks, leads young people to make decisions that they view later as mistakes. Law and policy should give careful consideration to the implications of this new portrayal.

Paul Slovic

Acknowledgments

Patrick Jamieson and Dan Romer gratefully acknowledge support from the Robert Wood Johnson Foundation for the first tobacco survey. Thanks also go to the following persons for their advice and assistance in the design and execution of the surveys: Chris Adasiewicz, Dr. Suzanne Fegley, Dr. Martin Fishbein, Dr. Loretta Jemmott, Dr. Mary McIntosh, and Andy Weiss. In addition, the following staff at the Annenberg School and Public Policy Center are gratefully acknowledged for their help in completing the project: Sharon Black, Josh Gesell, Steve Hocker, Janna Robbins, and Deborah Stinnett. We also thank Judy Selhorst for her careful editing and assistance in finalizing the manuscript.

At Decision Research, statistical analysis for Chapter 6 was performed by C. K. Mertz. Invaluable secretarial assistance with the entire volume manuscript was provided by Leisha Wharfield, Janet Douglas, Janet Kershner, and Mona Bronson.

Part I

INTRODUCTION

∾ Chapter 1

The Risks of Active and Passive Smoking

Jonathan M. Samet

Evidence on the health effects of tobacco smoking, both active and passive, and of using smokeless tobacco has been central in driving initiatives to control tobacco use. This chapter provides an overview and introduction to the now-vast data on the risks of tobacco smoking, covering the risks to active smokers, including both children and adults, as well as the risks to passive smokers, including the fetus, infants and children, and adults. All persons who are concerned with tobacco control need to have an understanding of this evidence, as it represents the principal impetus for initiating tobacco control measures, and tracking the occurrence of tobacco-caused diseases is a critical element of surveillance.

Although writings on the dangers to health of tobacco use can be found dating from past centuries, the body of research evidence that constitutes the foundation of our present understanding of tobacco as a cause of disease dates to approximately the mid-20th century. Even earlier, case reports and case studies had called attention to the likely role of smoking and chewing tobacco as a cause of cancer. The rise of diseases that had once been uncommon, such as lung cancer and coronary heart disease, was noticed early in the 20th century and motivated clinical and pathological studies to determine if these increases were "real" or an artifact of changing methods of detection. By midcentury, there was no doubt that the increases were real, and the focus of research shifted to the causes of the new epidemics of "chronic diseases" such as lung cancer and coronary heart disease.

Smoking was among the postulated causes of the epidemics, although other possible causal factors were also considered: air pollution for lung cancer and the chronic lung diseases, and diet for coronary heart disease. In initiating their pioneering case-control study of lung cancer, Doll and Hill (1950; Doll, 1998) gave equal footing to smoking and air pollution as causes of lung cancer. Smoking was not widely considered as a cause of obstructive lung disease until the 1950s. Even by the 1940s, however, there was substantial evidence suggesting that smoking causes disease and premature death. Astute clinicians, such as the surgeons Ochsner and DeBakey (1939), noted the preponderance of smokers among persons receiving treatment for certain diseases, including lung cancer, and postulated a causal role for cigarette smoking. Based on his follow-up of families living in Baltimore in 1938, Pearl reported that smokers did not live as long as nonsmokers. In the 1930s and into the 1940s, Nazi scientists carried out an active program of research on smoking and health, including epidemiological studies showing the role of smoking as a cause of lung cancer. Hitler viewed smoking as a threat to the vitality of the German people, and his government carried out a vigorous antitobacco campaign (Proctor, 1995).

Key initial observations were made in epidemiological studies carried out to examine changing patterns of disease, particularly the rise of lung cancer, coronary heart disease and stroke, and chronic obstructive lung disease, including chronic bronchitis and emphysema. These studies and their success in establishing smoking as a cause of multiple diseases are widely cited as one of the great triumphs of epidemiological research. Epidemiology constitutes the scientific methods used to study determinants of disease in the population. These epidemiological studies used three principal designs: cross-sectional, case-control, and cohort.

In a cross-sectional design, often referred to as a survey, observations are made at a single point in time, and health and disease status is examined in relation to smoking. This design has been widely used in investigating the effects of smoking on lung function and respiratory symptoms. For example, in surveys of respiratory disease and smoking, lung function is measured and the level of lung function is examined in relation to current and cumulative smoking.

In a case-control study, smoking by persons having the disease of interest (e.g., lung cancer) is compared to smoking by appropriate persons not having the disease of interest; with this seemingly indirect approach, the risk of disease associated with smoking can be estimated. This design was used in the early studies of lung cancer because it could be readily implemented using hospitals as the venue for identifying cases and controls; it has since been widely used for studying other types of cancers. The cohort design involves tracking smokers and nonsmokers to assess the incidence or mortality from various diseases. In one early cohort study, Doll and Hill (1954) enrolled about 40,000 physicians in the United Kingdom and then charted their mortality in relation to smoking, which was assessed periodically. Follow-up has been sustained since 1951, and results for the first 40 years have been reported (Doll, Peto, Wheatley, Gray, & Sutherland, 1994). A 1996 National Cancer Institute (NCI) report provides a summary of findings from key recent cohort studies of smoking and disease, examining changing risks over time.

There have been many landmark investigations of smoking and disease, such as the early case-control studies of lung cancer (Doll & Hill, 1950; Levin, Goldstein, & Gerhardt, 1950; Wynder & Graham, 1950) and the large cohort studies, including the Framingham study (Dawber, 1980), the British physicians study (Doll & Hill, 1954), and the cohort studies initiated by the American Cancer Society, two of which involved one million Americans each (NCI, 1997). These initial observations quickly sparked complementary laboratory studies on the mechanisms by which tobacco smoking causes disease. The multidisciplinary approach to research on tobacco has been key in linking smoking to various diseases; the observational evidence has been supported by an understanding of the mechanisms through which smoking causes disease. By the early 1950s, for example, Wynder, Graham, and Croninger (1953) had shown that painting the skin of mice with the condensate of cigarette smoke caused tumors. In combination with the emerging epidemiological evidence on smoking and lung cancer, this observation was sufficiently powerful to be followed by the tobacco industry's dramatic response of establishing the Tobacco Industry Research Committee, later to become the Tobacco Research Council.

By the late 1950s and early 1960s, the mounting evidence received formal review and evaluation by government committees, leading to definitive conclusions in the early 1960s. In the United Kingdom, a report of the Royal College of Physicians of London concluded that smoking is a cause of lung cancer and bronchitis and a contributing factor to coronary heart disease (Scientific Committee on Tobacco and Health, 1962). In the United States, the 1964 report of the Advisory Committee to the Surgeon General concluded that smoking was a cause of lung cancer in men and of chronic bronchitis (U.S. Department of Health, Education, and Welfare [U.S. DHEW], 1964). By law, a U.S. surgeon general's report was subsequently required annually and new conclusions have been reached periodically with regard to the diseases caused by smoking. The Royal College of Physicians has also continued to release periodic reports. These reports and other expert syntheses of the evidence have proved to be an effective tool for translating the findings on smoking and disease into policy.

The systematic review process in the United States, involving evaluation of the evidence and application of criteria for causality, has resulted in an unassailable series of conclusions on the causal associations of active smoking with specific diseases and other adverse health effects (Table 1.1). As set out in the 1964 surgeon general's report, review of evidence proceeds at three sequential levels: (a) assessment of the validity of individual scientific reports, (b) judgment as to the validity of the interpretations and conclusions reached by investigators, and (c) judgments needed to formulate overall conclusions. The report commented on the need to evaluate all relevant lines of evidence, including not only epidemiological studies but clinical, pathological, and experimental evidence.

In 1964, the Advisory Committee to the Surgeon General set out criteria for judging the causal significance of an association, including the association's consistency, strength, specificity, temporal relationship, and coherence. *Consistency* refers to the similarity of findings in separate studies involving different populations. Comparability of findings across studies of different groups, using different methods, argues for causality. Stronger associations are more likely to reflect an underlying causal link, as the possibility that bias from uncontrolled confounding or other sources is responsible becomes less tenable with increasing *strength* of association. Because *specificity,* which refers to a unique exposure-disease association, is not applicable to most chronic diseases caused by smoking, this criterion has generally been set aside. Of course, smoking precedes disease onset, meeting the criterion offered for the proper *temporal relationship*—that is, exposure should come before the disease. Finally, *coherence* refers to the overall cohesion of the evidence, including the fit between population patterns of smoking and disease occurrence and the biological plausibility of the claim that an association reflects an underlying causal relationship. Assessment of coherence involves the evaluation of all relevant data, including experimental evidence, as well as consideration of mechanisms.

In offering these criteria, the 1964 committee both recognized that they were not rigid guidelines for interpretation of evidence and commented on the complexity of defining *cause* for multifactorial complex diseases. The committee summarized its definition as follows: "The word *cause* is the one in general usage in connection with matters considered in this study and it is capable of conveying the notion of a significant, effectual, relationship between an agent and an associated disorder or disease in the host" (U.S. DHEW, 1964). The principles set forth in the 1964 surgeon general's report have continued to guide the evaluation of evidence on tobacco use and health, in subsequent surgeon generals' reports and elsewhere.

The issue of passive smoking and health has a much briefer history. Some of the first epidemiological studies on secondhand smoke or environmental tobacco smoke (ETS) and health were reported in the late 1960s (Cameron, 1967; Cameron et al., 1969; Colley & Holland, 1967). Prior to that point, there had been scattered case reports, the Nazis had campaigned against smoking in public, and one German physician, Fritz Lickint, used the term *passive smoking* in a 1939 book on smoking (see Proctor, 1995). In the 1960s, the initial investigations focused on parental smoking and lower respiratory illnesses in infants; studies of lung func-

TABLE 1.1   Report Conclusions of Causal Associations of Active Smoking With Specific Diseases and Other Adverse Health Effects

Disease	Statement[a]	Surgeon General's Report
Atherosclerosis/ aortic aneurysm	Cigarette smoking is *the most powerful risk factor* predisposing to atherosclerotic peripheral vascular disease.	1983
	[Cigarette smoking is] *a cause and most important risk factor* for atherosclerotic peripheral vascular disease.	1989
Bladder cancer	Smoking is a *cause* of bladder cancer; cessation reduces risk by about 50% after only a few years, in comparison with continued smoking.	1990 (also IARC, 1986)
Cerebrovascular disease	Cigarette smoking is a *major cause* of cerebrovascular disease (stroke), the third leading cause of death in the United States.	1989
Chronic obstructive pulmonary disease[b]	Cigarette smoking *is the most important of the causes* of chronic bronchitis in the United States, and *increases the risk of dying* from chronic bronchitis.	1964
	Cigarette smoking is *the most important of the causes* of chronic non-neoplastic bronchopulmonary diseases in the United States. It *greatly increases the risk of dying* not only from both chronic bronchitis, but also from pulmonary emphysema.	1967-1979
Coronary heart disease	Additional evidence not only confirms the fact that cigarette smokers have higher death rates from coronary heart disease, but also suggests how these deaths may be *caused* by cigarette smoking. There is an increasing convergence of many types of evidence concerning cigarette smoking and coronary heart disease which strongly suggests that cigarette smoking *can cause death* from coronary heart disease.	1967
Esophageal cancer	Cigarette smoking is a *major cause* of esophageal cancer in the United States.	1982
Kidney cancer	The occurrence of malignant tumors of the . . . renal pelvis . . . is *causally related* to the smoking of cigarettes.	IARC, 1986
Laryngeal cancer	Cigarette smoking is *causally associated* with cancer of the lung, larynx, oral cavity, and esophagus in women as well as in men.	1980
Lung cancer	Cigarette smoking is *causally related* to lung cancer in men; the magnitude of the effect of cigarette smoking *far outweighs all other factors*. The data for women, though less extensive, point in the same direction.	1964

(continued)

TABLE 1.1   Continued

Disease	Statement[a]	Surgeon General's Report
	Additional epidemiological, pathological, and experimental data not only confirm the conclusion of the Surgeon General's 1964 Report regarding lung cancer in men but strengthen the *causal relationship* of smoking to lung cancer in women.	1967
Oral cancer	Epidemiological studies indicate that smoking is a *significant causal factor* in the development of oral cancer.	1979
	Cigarette smoking is *causally associated* with cancer of the . . . oral cavity . . . in women as well as in men.	1980
	Cigarette smoking is a *major cause* of cancers of the oral cavity in the United States.	1982
Pancreatic cancer	Cigarette smoking is a *contributory factor* in the development of pancreatic cancer in the United States. The term "contributory factor" *by no means excludes* the possibility of a *causal role* for smoking in cancers of this site.	1982
	The occurrence of malignant tumors of the . . . pancreas is *causally related* to the smoking of cigarettes.	IARC, 1986
Peptic ulcer disease	The *relationship* between cigarette smoking and death rates from peptic ulcer, especially gastric ulcer, *is confirmed.* In addition, morbidity data suggest a similar relationship exists with the prevalence of reported disease from this cause.	1967
	The finding of a *significant dose-related excess mortality* from gastric ulcers among both male and female Japanese cigarette smokers, in a large prospective study, and in the context of the genetic and cultural differences between the Japanese and previously investigated Western populations, *confirms and extends the association* between cigarette smoking and gastric ulcer mortality.	1973-1990
Diminished health status/ respiratory morbidity	Relationships between smoking and cough or phlegm are *strong and consistent;* they have been amply documented and are judged to be *causal.*	1984
	Consideration of evidence from many different studies has led to the conclusion that cigarette smoking is *the overwhelmingly most important cause* of cough, sputum, chronic bronchitis, and mucus hypersecretion.	1984

a. Emphases added.
b. Chronic obstructive pulmonary disease has been known by several different names over the years. These include chronic bronchitis, emphysema, chronic obstructive lung disease, and chronic obstructive bronchopulmonary disease.

tion and respiratory symptoms in children soon followed (Samet & Wang, 2000; U.S. Department of Health and Human Services [U.S. DHHS], 1986). The first major studies on passive smoking and lung cancer in nonsmokers were reported in 1981 (Hirayama, 1981; Trichopoulos, Kalandidi, Sparros, & MacMahon, 1981), and by 1986 the evidence supported the conclusion that passive smoking is a cause of lung cancer in nonsmokers, a conclusion reached by the International Agency for Research on Cancer (IARC, 1986), the U.S. surgeon general (U.S. DHHS, 1986), and the National Research Council (1986) in the United States. The evidence on child health and passive smoking was also reviewed in 1986 by the U.S. surgeon general and the National Research Council (see Table 1.2). A now-substantial body of evidence has continued to identify new diseases and other adverse effects of passive smoking, including increased risk for coronary heart disease (California Environmental Protection Agency, 1997; Samet & Wang, 2000; Scientific Committee on Tobacco and Health, 1998; World Health Organization, 1999).

๑๑ Toxicology of Tobacco Smoke

Tobacco smoke is generated by the burning of a complex organic material, tobacco, along with various additives and paper, at a high temperature, reaching about 1,000 degrees centigrade in the burning coal of the cigarette (U.S. DHEW, 1964). The resulting smoke, comprising numerous gases and also particles, includes myriad toxic components that can cause injury through inflammation and irritation, asphyxiation, carcinogenesis, and other mechanisms (see Table 1.3). Active smokers inhale mainstream smoke (MS), the smoke that is drawn directly through the end of the cigarette. Passive smokers inhale smoke that is often referred to as environmental tobacco smoke, which comprises a mixture of mostly sidestream smoke (SS) given off by the smoldering cigarette and some exhaled MS. Concentrations of tobacco smoke components in ETS are far below the levels of MS inhaled by the active smoker, but there are qualitative similarities between ETS and MS (Peterson & Stewart, 1970).

Both active and passive smokers absorb tobacco smoke components through the lungs' airways and alveoli, and many of these components, such as the gas carbon monoxide, then enter into the circulation and are distributed generally. There is also uptake of such components as benzo(a)pyrene directly into the cells that line the upper airway and the lungs' airways. Some of the carcinogens undergo metabolic transformation into their active forms, and some evidence now indicates that metabolism-determining genes may affect susceptibility to tobacco

TABLE 1.2   Adverse Effects From Exposure to Tobacco Smoke

Health Effect	Surgeon General 1984[a]	Surgeon General 1986[b]	EPA 1992[c]	California EPA 1997[d]	United Kingdom 1998[e]	WHO 1999[f]
Increased prevalence of respiratory illnesses	Yes/association	Yes/association	Yes/cause	Yes/cause	Yes/cause	Yes/cause
Decrement in pulmonary function	Yes/association	Yes/association	Yes/association	Yes/association		Yes/cause
Increased frequency of bronchitis, pneumonia	Yes/association	Yes/association	Yes/association	Yes/cause		Yes/cause
Increase in chronic cough, phlegm		Yes/association				Yes/cause
Increased frequency of middle ear effusion		Yes/association	Yes/cause	Yes/cause	Yes/cause	Yes/cause
Increased severity of asthma episodes and symptoms		Yes/cause	Yes/cause		Yes/cause	
Risk factor for new asthma			Yes/association	Yes/cause	Yes/association	
Risk factor for SIDS				Yes/cause		Yes/cause
Risk factor for lung cancer in adults		Yes/cause	Yes/cause	Yes/cause	Yes/cause	Not addressed
Risk factor for heart disease in adults				Yes/cause	Yes/cause	Yes/association

a. U.S. Department of Health and Human Services (1984).
b. U.S. Department of Health and Human Services (1986).
c. U.S. Environmental Protection Agency (1992).
d. California Environmental Protection Agency (1997).
e. Scientific Committee on Tobacco and Health (1998).
f. World Health Organization (1999).

TABLE 1.3   Concentrations of Selected Active Agents in Nonfilter Cigarette
Mainstream Smoke

Smoke Constituent	Concentration/Cigarette
Total particulate matter	15 - 40 mg
Carbon monoxide	10 - 23 mg
Nicotine	1.0 - 2.3 mg
Acetaldehyde	0.5 - 1.2 mg
Hydrogen cyanide	110 - 300 mg
Benzene	20 - 50 mg
N'-nitrosonornicotine	200 - 3000 ng
N'-nitrosopyrrolidine	0 - 110 ng
Vinyl chloride	1.3 - 16 ng
Benzo(a)pyre	20 - 40 ng
4-aminobiphenyl	2.4 - 4.6 mg

smoke (Nelkin, Mabry, & Baylin, 1998). The genitourinary system is exposed to toxins in tobacco smoke through the excretion of compounds in the urine, including carcinogens. The gastrointestinal tract is exposed through direct deposition of smoke in the upper airway and the clearance of smoke-containing mucus from the trachea through the glottis into the esophagus. Not surprisingly, tobacco smoking has proved to be a multisystem cause of disease.

There is a substantial scientific literature on the mechanisms by which tobacco smoking causes disease. This body of research includes characterization of the many components in smoke (see Table 1.3), some having well-established toxicity, such as hydrogen cyanide, benzo(a)pyrene, carbon monoxide, and nitrogen oxides. Researchers have studied the toxicity of smoke by exposing animals to tobacco smoke and smoke condensate, in cellular and other laboratory systems for evaluating toxicity, and by assessing smokers for evidence of injury by tobacco smoke, using biomarkers such as tissue changes and levels of damaging enzymes and cytokines. The data from these studies amply document the powerful toxicity of tobacco smoke. Young smokers in their 20s, for example, have been found to show evidence of permanent damage to the small airways of the lungs and to their arteries (Niewoehner, Kleinerman, & Donald, 1974; PDAY Research Group, 1990), and fluid from the lungs of smokers shows increased numbers of inflammatory cells and higher levels of markers of injury in comparison with the lungs of nonsmokers (U.S. DHHS, 1990a). With the new tools of molecular and cellular biology, we now have evidence at the molecular level of changes specific to tobacco smoke carcinogens (Denissenko, Pao, Tang, & Pfeifer, 1996; Hussain & Harris, 1998).

ᕫ Health Effects of Active Smoking

The U.S. surgeon general (U.S. DHHS, 1990b), the Royal College of Physicians of London (Scientific Committee on Tobacco and Health, 1962), the International Agency for Research on Cancer (1986), the United Kingdom's Scientific Committee on Tobacco and Health (1998), and other expert groups have identified causal associations of smoking with various diseases and other adverse effects (see Table 1.1). These associations can be grouped into the broad categories of cancer, cardiovascular disease, chronic respiratory diseases, and adverse effects on reproduction. For each of these associations, the evidence is extensive and reviewed comprehensively in the key reports. Other recent reports that provide valuable compilations of the epidemiological and other data include monographs in a series prepared in the United States by the National Cancer Institute (1996, 1997) and a 1996 issue of the *British Medical Bulletin* (Doll, 1996). In this section I address the diseases caused by active smoking, covering general issues and then focusing on specific diseases.

Studies have also shown that children who smoke are affected adversely, although without the development of specific, smoking-caused diseases (Centers for Disease Control and Prevention, 1994a). The focus of the 1994 report of the U.S. surgeon general was smoking and youth. Adolescents who smoke regularly report chronic respiratory symptoms more often than do nonsmokers and also have evidence of subtle, adverse changes in lung function. By early adulthood, smokers have greater evidence of atherosclerosis as well, as shown in studies of trauma victims who were smokers (Centers for Disease Control and Prevention, 1994a). I cover the evidence on youth and smoking in a subsection below.

For many of the diseases caused by smoking, the increases in risk in adult smokers are dramatic. Table 1.4 displays data on relative risks for dying from major smoking-caused diseases obtained in two studies, the American Cancer Society's Cancer Prevention Studies (CPS) I and II, each of which involved a sample of one million persons (Thun, Day-Lally, Calle, Flanders, & Heath, 1995). A wide range of relative risk values reflects the strength of smoking as a cause of the different diseases and the relative strengths of other causal factors; for some diseases, such as lung cancer, the relative risks are extremely high, whereas relative risk values are lower for cardiovascular diseases and some other cancers, although still in a range of medical and public health concern. For the principal chronic diseases associated with smoking, the effect on disease risk is usually manifest only after a substantial latent period, which represents the time needed for the injury to be sufficient to cause disease and for the underlying process to come to completion, such as the transformation of a normal cell to a malignant cell. For smoking

TABLE 1.4   Changes in Cigarette-Related Mortality Risks Between
Cancer Prevention Study I (1959 Through 1965) and
Cancer Prevention Study II (1982 Through 1988) and
Percentage of Deaths Attributable to Active Cigarette Smoking

	CPS I		CPS II	
	Relative Risk	*%*	*Relative Risk*	*%*
Males				
Overall mortality	1.7	42.2	2.3	57.1
Lung cancer	11.9	91.6	23.2	95.7
Coronary heart disease	1.7	41.5	1.9	46.2
Chronic obstructive pulmonary disease	9.3	89.2	11.7	91.4
Stroke	1.3	21.9	1.9	46.8
Other smoking-related cancers[a]	2.7	63.4	3.5	71.2
Females				
Overall mortality	1.2	18.7	1.9	47.9
Lung cancer	2.7	63.4	12.8	92.2
Coronary heart disease	1.4	27.0	1.8	45.1
Chronic obstructive pulmonary disease	6.7	85.0	12.8	92.2
Stroke	1.2	15.2	1.8	45.7
Other smoking-related cancers[a]	1.8	45.0	2.6	60.8

NOTE: Percentages refer to the proportions of the total cases of each cause of death attributable to smoking. For overall mortality, percentages refer to the proportion of deaths attributable to smoking.
a. Sites include larynx, oral cavity, esophagus, bladder, kidney, other urinary, and pancreas.

and lung cancer, for example, incidence rates rise after about 20 years of active smoking (Burns, Garfinkel, & Samet, 1997).

The relative risk values generally rise with indicators of exposure to tobacco smoke, including numbers of cigarettes smoked and the duration of smoking, and fall after successful cessation. Figures 1.1A and 1.1B illustrate these dose-response relationships with the number of cigarettes smoked for coronary heart disease among female participants in the Nurses Health Study (Willett et al., 1987). For the cancers caused by smoking, the relative risks tend to decline slowly as the number of years since quitting increases (U.S. DHHS, 1990b); by contrast, there is an immediate decline in the relative risk for cardiovascular disease, and the levels of former smokers tend to reach those of people who have never smoked after 5 to 10 years of abstinence. Chronic obstructive pulmonary disease

14

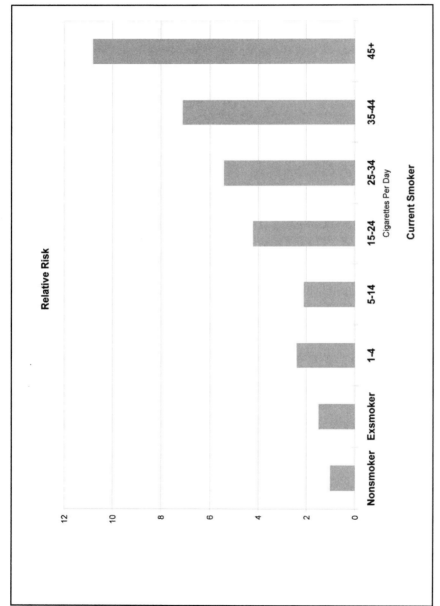

Figure 1.1A. Dose-response relationships with the number of cigarettes smoked for coronary heart disease among female participants in the Nurses Health Study (Willett et al., 1987). This figure shows the relative risk for former and current smokers compared to those who have never smoked who have a value of 1 by definition.

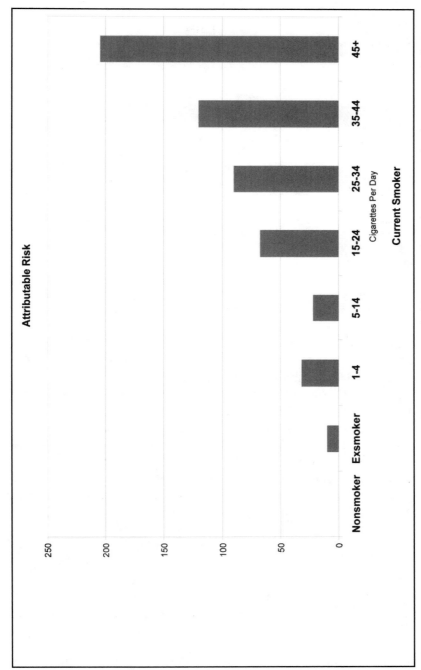

Figure 1.1B. Dose-response relationships with the number of cigarettes smoked for coronary heart disease among female participants in the Nurses Health Study (Willett et al., 1987).

15

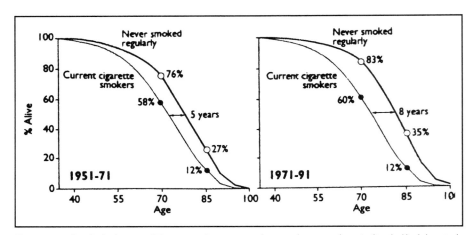

Figure 1.2. Survival after age 35 among cigarette smokers and nonsmokers in first half of the study (left) and second half of the study (right). For ages 35-44, rates for the whole study are used in both halves, because little information on these is available from the second half.
SOURCE: Doll et al. (1994). Copyright 1994 by BMJ Publishing Group. Reprinted by permission.

(COPD) results from sustained excessive loss of lung function in smokers. Fortunately, after cessation, the rate of decline quickly returns to the rate of persons who have never smoked (U.S. DHHS, 1990b).

Cigarettes have changed substantially over the past 50 years (NCI, 1996; U.S. DHHS, 1981). Filter cigarettes dominate the market, and tar and nicotine yields, as assessed by smoking machines, have declined substantially. However, actual inhaled tar and nicotine deliveries to smokers have little relationship to the machine levels (Benowitz, 1996). Epidemiological evidence shows slight reduction in risk for some cancers, particularly lung cancer, and for total mortality, comparing smokers of lower-delivery and higher-delivery products, but no reduction for myocardial infarction or COPD (Samet, 1996). In fact, rising relative risks of smoking have been documented across the recent decades, when the lower-delivery products came into widespread usage (Burns et al., 1997; Doll et al., 1994). In the cohort study of British doctors, there was a substantial increase in mortality for smokers, comparing the second 20 years of follow-up with the first (see Figure 1.2) (Doll et al., 1994). Reviewing the two Cancer Prevention Studies of the American Cancer Society, we see that relative risks increased for males and females from the first to the second study, even after changing smoking patterns are taken into consideration (Thun et al., 1995).

Although cigarette smoking causes many of the principal chronic diseases, and smokers have reduced life expectancy compared with nonsmokers, active cigarette smoking has been associated with reduced risk for selected diseases and conditions (Baron, 1996; Scientific Committee on Tobacco and Health, 1998).

These inverse associations include Parkinson's disease, endometrial carcinoma, ulcerative colitis, and extrinsic allergic alveolitis. There is also evidence that is suggestive of an inverse association for Alzheimer's disease. Although these inverse associations are of little public health consequence, they do indicate opportunities for exploring disease pathogenesis and seeking therapeutic approaches. Nicotine has been examined as a therapy for ulcerative colitis, and antiestrogenic effects of smoking have been considered as the likely explanation for the reduced risk of endometrial carcinoma.

Effects on Reproduction

Smoking during pregnancy adversely affects reproduction. It has been shown to reduce birth weight by approximately 200 grams on average (U.S. DHHS, 1990b); the degree of reduction is related to the amount smoked. If a pregnant woman who smokes gives up this behavior by the third trimester, much of this weight reduction can be avoided. Smoking also increases rates of spontaneous abortion, placenta previa, and perinatal mortality, and smoking during pregnancy is now considered to be a cause of sudden infant death syndrome (SIDS). There is more limited evidence suggesting that smoking by pregnant women may increase the incidence in their offspring of childhood cancer and congenital defects (Charlton, 1996; Scientific Committee on Tobacco and Health, 1998).

Cardiovascular Diseases

The cardiovascular diseases caused by smoking include coronary heart disease (CHD), arteriosclerotic peripheral vascular disease or atherosclerosis, and cerebral vascular disease (stroke) (U.S. DHHS, 1984, 1990a). CHD has the clinical manifestations of myocardial infarction (heart attack), angina pectoris (chest pain attributable to inadequate oxygen delivery to the heart muscle), and sudden cardiac death. These conditions have in common the narrowing of the coronary arteries, the blood vessels that carry blood to the heart. Most cases of myocardial infarction result from blockage of the narrowed coronary arteries by thrombus or blood clot. Smoking is not only a cause of the atherosclerosis that tends to narrow the coronary arteries, it also increases the tendency of the blood to clot. Myocardial infarction occurs when oxygen delivery to the heart muscle is compromised and the heart muscle is damaged. Angina pectoris is the name given to pain arising from a lack of oxygen without permanent damage to the heart muscle (ischemia).

Atherosclerosis also affects the arteries of the body, compromising blood flow. Symptoms of atherosclerosis arise when blood flow delivers insufficient oxygen for the demands of the muscle it serves or complete blockage occurs, leading to tissue damage. The aorta is the major artery of the body, coursing from the heart down the thoracic and abdominal cavities before dividing. Aortic aneurysm is an abnormal dilatation of the aorta, from which rupture and death may occur.

Stroke and *cerebrovascular accident* are general terms that refer to the clinical consequences of bleeding within the brain or brain tissue death resulting from inadequate oxygen delivery. Stroke can occur if a blood vessel is occluded by a blood clot that has arisen locally or moved from a distant site, or from bleeding within the brain. The mechanisms by which smoking causes stroke are similar to those that lead to myocardial infarction.

The epidemiological evidence on the relationship of smoking to cardiovascular diseases is massive, coming from case-control studies and a number of cohort studies, including the renowned Framingham study (U.S. DHHS, 1990b). Risk for the cardiovascular diseases increases with the number of cigarettes smoked per day and with the duration of smoking. Smoking cessation reduces the risk of the cardiovascular diseases. For coronary heart disease, the risk tends to decline rapidly immediately following cessation. After a year of not smoking, the risk to the former smoker has been reduced by about half from the risk to the current smoker. Smoking cessation also reduces risk for stroke. For the cardiovascular diseases, smoking cigarettes that are lower in tar and nicotine has not been shown to affect risk. The cardiovascular diseases have causes other than smoking, including hypertension and elevated cholesterol. After taking these factors into account, the epidemiological studies still have identified an independent effect of smoking on disease risk; thus the increased risk for cardiovascular disease in smokers does not reflect confounding by some aspect of lifestyle.

Respiratory Diseases

Chronic Obstructive Pulmonary Disease

Chronic obstructive pulmonary disease is a clinically used diagnostic label that refers to the permanent loss of lung function that affects some cigarette smokers, resulting in shortness of breath, impaired exercise capacity, and, frequently, a need for oxygen therapy. In the past, the term *emphysema* was often the diagnostic label for the same disease, but *COPD* is the term more widely applied today. COPD is characterized by slowed emptying of the lung, reflecting underlying narrowing of the airways of the lung and a loss of elasticity, reflecting the development of emphysema. *Emphysema* properly refers to permanent destruction of the alveoli, the air sacs of the lung. COPD is currently a rising cause of mortality in the United States, accounting for approximately 80,000 deaths annually. The current increase likely reflects past patterns of smoking and also the declining rates of mortality from cardiovascular disease, which have left a larger pool of persons with COPD at risk for respiratory death.

This disease develops progressively in a minority of smokers (U.S. DHHS, 1984, 1990a). Its appearance reflects an acceleration of the usual age-related loss of lung function (Fletcher & Peto, 1977). In some smokers, this loss is accelerated, and eventually lung capacity becomes reduced to a level at which functioning is affected and the symptoms of COPD occur. Cigarette smoking causes inflammation of the lungs, with the migration of inflammatory cells into the lungs and release of enzymes that can destroy the lungs' delicate structure. Smoking activates the inflammatory process and reduces the efficacy of defenses against inflammation. Unchecked inflammation, sustained over many years, underlies the development of COPD.

Relevant epidemiological evidence comes from research on the level of lung function in smokers and nonsmokers and on the change of level of lung function over time in relation to smoking; mortality from COPD has been described in cohort studies as well (U.S. DHHS, 1984, 1990a). The studies of lung function show that smokers, in comparison with nonsmokers, have a lower level of function on average and that the level of lung function in smokers declines as the number of cigarettes smoked per day increases. Smokers, followed over time, have a faster decline of lung function, on average, than nonsmokers. The rate of decline in smokers reverts to that of nonsmokers following successful quitting. Unfortunately, the damage prior to cessation is mostly irreversible. Mortality rates for COPD are approximately 10 times higher in smokers compared with nonsmokers. There is no consistent evidence that risk for this disease is associated with the tar and nicotine yield of the cigarettes smoked.

Only a few of the factors that place smokers at increased risk for COPD have been identified. One relatively uncommon genetic disorder, alpha-1-antitrypsin deficiency, markedly increases risk for early development of COPD in homozygotes. Occupational exposure may heighten risk by also accelerating decline of lung function.

Respiratory Morbidity

Respiratory infections remain a leading cause of morbidity and mortality. The scope of respiratory infections extends from the common cold, caused by viruses, to fatal pneumonias, sometimes caused by exotic organisms. The most common types of respiratory infections, colds and the lower respiratory infections (laryngitis, bronchitis, and pneumonia), are primarily caused by various respiratory viruses, but bacteria and other types of organisms can also cause pneumonia, particularly in the elderly. Persons with the smoking-caused conditions of COPD and CHD are particularly susceptible to the development of more severe respiratory infections. Moreover, respiratory infections are often the cause of death in persons with underlying COPD and in older people generally. Respiratory infections are also one of the most frequent causes of morbidity in the general population, and even healthy persons have several respiratory infections per year.

There is voluminous epidemiological evidence on respiratory health and health status in relation to smoking. Many studies have described the association of smoking with respiratory symptoms, respiratory infections, and several indicators of reduced health status generally. Epidemiological data from cross-sectional and cohort studies provide convincing evidence that smoking causes increased occurrence of the cardinal respiratory symptoms: cough (i.e., "smoker's cough"), sputum production, wheezing, and dyspnea (shortness of breath). Symptom rates are substantially higher in smokers in comparison with those who have never smoked and tend to increase in frequency with the numbers of cigarettes smoked per day. The surgeon generals' reports have repeatedly commented on these associations and have described the relationship between smoking and cough and phlegm as causal (see Table 1.1).

There is also mounting and consistent evidence that smoking increases risk for respiratory infection. In a number of the prospective cohort studies, mortality from respiratory infections has been found to be higher in smokers than in those who never smoked. Other studies have shown increased incidence of respiratory infections in smokers as well. Smokers have thus been shown to have more respiratory infections than nonsmokers and possibly more severe respiratory infections as well.

This increased risk for respiratory infections in smokers may partially explain the generally poorer health status of smokers in comparison with nonsmokers. In comparison with nonsmokers, smokers have higher rates of utilization of health care services, higher rates of absenteeism from work, and poorer self-reported health status. There is evidence of improvement in these indicators with smoking cessation. The 1990 U.S. surgeon general's report (U.S. DHHS, 1990a) comments on the better health status of former smokers in comparison with current ones (see Table 1.1).

Considered in its entirety, there is a substantial body of epidemiological evidence on respiratory morbidity and respiratory infections, as well as on morbidity and health status generally in smokers. Because respiratory infections are a principal cause of morbidity and mortality at all ages, the complementary sets of evidence on respiratory morbidity and mortality and impaired health status generally can be considered together. The extensive and consistent evidence shows increased risk for respiratory infections and morbidity and for poorer health status generally in smokers compared with nonsmokers. Dose-response relationships have been demonstrated between these outcomes and numbers of cigarettes smoked per day. The biological basis for these associations appears to lie in the diverse effects of smoking on the lungs and on defenses against respiratory pathogens. The surgeon generals' reports have repeatedly commented on respiratory morbidity in smokers as well as on the poorer health status of smokers.

Cancer

Lung Cancer

Lung cancer is the label given to primary carcinomas arising in the lung, including the four principal histologic types (squamous cell carcinoma, small cell carcinoma, adenocarcinoma, and large cell carcinoma) and several other less frequent types. These cancers arise in the airways and alveoli (air sacs) of the lung, causing symptoms as they grow and compromise the surrounding lung or spread to distant sites. Survival is poor, with only approximately 13% of lung cancer patients in the United States surviving 5 years following diagnosis (Miller, Ries, & Hankey, 1993). The lung is the principal site for deposit of the carcinogens in smoke. As inhaled smoke contacts the airways and alveoli of the lung, these carcinogens are deposited. Some require metabolic transformation by enzymes before taking a carcinogenic form; others are inherently carcinogenic. We now have evidence supporting the long-held hypothesis that cancer results from a multistep process involving multiple injuries to the genes that control the growth and differentiation of cells, including tumor suppressor genes, such as *p53*, and oncogenes, such as *ras*. Cells of the airways of smokers show changes indicating that the cells have been affected and are moving from normal toward being cancerous (Auerbach, Hammond, & Garfinkel, 1970, 1979). These changes are visible under the microscope but can now also be confirmed with more sophisticated techniques of molecular and cellular biology. Specific patterns of mutation have been found in the lung cells of smokers in comparison with nonsmokers (Wistuba et al., 1997). Additionally, a recent study showed the binding of benzo(*a*)pyrene, an active tobacco smoke carcinogen, to sites on the *p53* gene that are typically mutated in lung cancers found in smokers (Denissenko et al., 1996). This result offers an insight at the molecular level into the mechanisms by which the deposited components of tobacco smoke cause disease.

The epidemiological evidence on smoking and lung cancer is now voluminous, having accumulated across the past century. Several case-control studies were carried out in Germany before 1950. However, the most prominent and most-often cited early reports were published in 1950: three landmark case-control studies, by Doll and Hill (1950), Levin et al. (1950), and Wynder and Graham (1950), all showing strong associations of lung cancer with cigarette smoking. The U.S. study by Wynder and Graham and the British study of Doll and Hill showed that smokers experienced approximately a tenfold increased risk for lung cancer when compared to lifelong nonsmokers. Across the 1950s, additional case-control studies were conducted, and the results of the first cohort studies of smoking and disease also became available. For men, the evidence uniformly showed increased risk of lung cancer in smokers; the data for women were similar, although the degree of elevation of risk in smokers was not as great as that found in men. The epidemiological evidence has also shown consistent dose-response relations between lung cancer risk and numbers of cigarettes smoked per day and the duration of smoking. The relative risk of lung cancer falls following smoking cessation, although the absolute risk does not appear to reach that of persons who never smoked (U.S. DHHS, 1990a).

Laryngeal Cancer

Laryngeal cancers arise from the vocal cords, the fibrous structures that generate speech. Typical symptoms of laryngeal cancer include cough, coughing blood, and hoarseness. These symptoms often occur at early stages of the disease, and the majority of cases can be treated by surgery, often combined with radiation. The underlying mechanisms for lung cancer and laryngeal cancer are likely to be similar. The larynx is lined with a cellular membrane similar to that of the lungs, and carcinogens are deposited in both during smoking.

As in the case of lung cancer, the evidence on laryngeal cancer derives from case-control and cohort studies. The 1964 report of the Advisory Committee to the Surgeon General listed 10 case-control studies and 7 cohort studies on cancer of the larynx. That report concludes that "cigarette smoking is a significant factor in the causation of laryngeal cancer in the male" (U.S. DHEW, 1964, p. 212). Subsequent evidence has strengthened this conclusion, showing that risk for laryngeal cancer increases with amount and duration of smoking and falls with successful smoking cessation. Together, alcohol and cigarette smoking are synergistic in increasing risk, which means that those with heavy alcohol intake are more susceptible to cigarette smoke as a cause of laryngeal cancer.

Oral Cancer

Oral cancers are squamous cell cancers that arise in the mouth and throat. The surfaces of the oral cavity are lined with a cellular membrane that undergoes changes related to smoking. Nonmalignant lesions termed leukoplakia are associated with smoking, and as genetic damage continues, oral cancers may result.

Typically, oral cancers are detected as lumps, often with symptoms of pain or bleeding, and surgical removal may lead to cure, although at the cost of disfigurement. The oral cavity is a site of direct deposition of the particles and gases in tobacco smoke. Presumably, this direct exposure and the resulting uptake of carcinogens by the exposed cells lead to cancer. As in the case of laryngeal cancer, smoking and alcohol intake are synergistic for oral cancer.

Esophageal Cancer

Esophageal cancers, predominantly squamous carcinomas, arise in the esophagus, which links the oral cavity to the stomach. These cancers arise from the lining of the surface of this organ and cause symptoms from blockage of the esophagus by the cancer and pain as cancers spread into surrounding tissues. Survival is poor. Epidemiological studies show that the risk of esophageal cancer is elevated by approximately fivefold in smokers compared with those who have never smoked. At the time of the 1964 surgeon general's report, the evidence was not sufficient to result in a causal conclusion. However, the data were judged to meet the criteria for causality in the 1979 surgeon general's report (U.S. DHEW, 1979). At present, there is an unexplained shift in patterns of esophageal cancer, with a rise in adenocarcinoma of the distal esophagus.

Pancreatic Cancer

The pancreas is a secretory organ situated at the rear of the abdominal cavity, behind the stomach. It secretes digestive enzymes, which travel in the pancreatic duct to be released into the intestine. The pancreas also secretes insulin and other hormones into the blood. Adenocarcinoma, a cancer of the glandular cells, is the principal type of cancer that occurs in the pancreas. Because of its location and the symptom picture of typical cases, most pancreatic cancer is detected at an advanced stage and survival is poor.

A number of cohort and case-control studies show increased risk for pancreatic cancer in smokers. The risk tends to rise with the number of cigarettes smoked per day and to fall with smoking cessation. Pancreatic cancer has not been reviewed comprehensively in the surgeon generals' reports since the 1982 report, which, citing rising pancreatic cancer mortality and data from cohort and case-control studies, concludes that "cigarette smoking is a contributory factor in the development of pancreatic cancer in the U.S." (U.S. DHHS, 1982, p. 132). A 1986 study by the IARC's Working Group on Cancer reviewed 10 reports from cohort studies and 7 case-control studies. The IARC report notes that the single case-control study that did not show increased risk in smokers included persons with smoking-related diseases in the control group. The report concludes that "cigarette smoking is an important cause of pancreatic cancer" (p. 313).

Kidney Cancer

Kidney cancers arise from the body of the kidney itself (adenocarcinoma of the kidney) and from the renal pelvis, the collecting funnel for the urine formed in the tubules of the kidney. The clinical pictures of these two types of cancers are somewhat distinct, with adenocarcinomas tending to spread early and cancers of the renal pelvis causing symptoms primarily through blockage of urine and bleeding. The kidney, as a major excretory organ, is bathed in the tobacco smoke carcinogens, which are in the blood and then concentrated in the urine.

The major cohort studies show evidence of increased mortality from kidney cancer, as do case-control studies. The increase in risk for smokers, compared with those who have never smoked, is modest and there is little evidence on change in risk following smoking cessation. Nonetheless, the data have been judged as showing a causal association between smoking and cancer of the renal pelvis and body. As mentioned above, the 1986 IARC monograph concludes that smoking causes cancer of the renal pelvis, and Doll (1996) has extended the causal association to take in adenocarcinoma as well.

Cancer of the Urinary Bladder

Cancers of the bladder arise from the cells that cover the bladder's surface. Bleeding is one of the earliest symptoms of bladder cancer. If metastasis (spread) occurs, the disease can be fatal. The bladder, of course, is the site for storage of urine, which contains carcinogens that have been absorbed, metabolized, and excreted by the kidneys. The urine of smokers has been shown to contain tobacco-specific carcinogens and also to have a generally higher level of mutagenic activity, an indicator of the potential to cause genetic damage to cells. Both cohort and case-control studies show increased risk of bladder cancer in smokers compared with nonsmokers. Risks generally tend to increase with the number of cigarettes smoked per day and to fall with cessation. The 1990 report of the surgeon general concludes that smoking causes bladder cancer (U.S. DHHS, 1990a), as does the earlier 1986 report of the International Agency for Research on Cancer.

Peptic Ulcer Disease

Peptic ulcers are disruptions (ulcers) of the lining of the stomach and the duodenum (the first part of the small intestine). Peptic ulcers are usually characterized by abdominal pain and bleeding. Although peptic ulcers are a relatively uncommon cause of death, they remain a substantial source of morbidity. For uncertain reasons, morbidity and mortality from peptic ulcer disease have declined sharply in the past few decades.

Smoking has multiple effects on the gastrointestinal tract that may be relevant to peptic ulcer disease. The 1990 report of the surgeon general reviews the effects of smoking on gastrointestinal physiology (U.S. DHHS, 1990a). Smoking increases gastric acid secretion and tends to increase duodenogastric reflux (reflux of bile from the duodenum into the stomach). *Helicobacter pylori,* a bacterium, is now recognized to be a cause of peptic ulcer disease. The 1990 report notes that smoking is associated with peptic ulcer disease in persons with gastritis caused by this organism.

The association of smoking with peptic ulcer disease has been thoroughly documented in the reports of the surgeon general, and smoking is considered to be a cause of peptic ulcer disease. The evidence also indicates that smoking retards the healing of peptic ulcers, and the 1990 report of the surgeon general concludes that smokers who stop smoking may improve the clinical course of peptic ulcer disease, in comparison with those who continue to smoke following the diagnosis.

Effects on Children

The 1994 surgeon general's report considers the epidemiological findings on active smoking and respiratory health of children, covering respiratory symptoms, lung function, and general respiratory morbidity (Centers for Disease Control and Prevention, 1994a). These studies document increased respiratory symptoms in children who smoke actively in comparison with those who do not smoke. Symptoms included increased respiratory morbidity and adverse effects on lung function—effects similar to those in adults, but COPD is not observed in children, as many years of sustained smoking are generally needed to cause the disease. Evidence cited in the 1994 report and a more recent study by Gold et al. (1996) shows that active smoking slows the rate of lung growth during adolescence. The evidence also indicates less favorable lipid profiles in children who smoke.

∾ Health Effects of Passive Smoking

Evidence on the health risks of passive smoking comes from epidemiological studies that have directly assessed the associations of ETS exposure with disease outcomes and from knowledge of the components of ETS and their toxicities. Judgments as to the causality of association between ETS exposure and health outcomes are based not only on this epidemiological evidence but also on the extensive evidence derived from epidemiological and toxicological investigation of active smoking. Additionally, studies using biomarkers of exposure and dose, including the nicotine metabolite cotinine and white cell adducts, document the absorption of ETS components by exposed nonsmokers, adding to the plausibility of the observed associations of ETS with adverse effects.

ETS exposure has adverse effects on infants' and children's respiratory health, including increased risk for more severe lower respiratory infections, middle ear disease, chronic respiratory symptoms, and asthma and reduction in the rate of lung function growth during childhood (see Table 1.2). There is more limited evidence suggesting that ETS exposure during pregnancy reduces birth weight and that child development and behavior are adversely affected by parental smoking (Eskenazi & Castorina, 1999; World Health Organization, 1999). There is no strong evidence at present that ETS exposure increases childhood cancer risk.

In adults, ETS exposure has been causally associated with lung cancer and with ischemic heart disease. The association of ETS with lung cancer has now been evaluated in about 40 epidemiological studies. The most recent meta-analysis combined evidence from 37 published studies and estimated the excess lung cancer risk for nonsmokers married to smokers as 24% (95% CI 13%, 36%). Since 1986, when the U.S. surgeon general and the National Research Council of the National Academy of Sciences concluded that passive smoking causally increases the risk of lung cancer in nonsmokers, other expert groups have also found ETS to be a cause of lung cancer in nonsmokers (Australian National Health and Medical Research Council, 1997; California Environmental Protection Agency, 1997; Scientific Committee on Tobacco and Health, 1998; U.S. Environmental Protection Agency, 1992).

Coronary heart disease has also been causally associated with ETS exposure, based on observational and experimental evidence (California Environmental Protection Agency, 1997; Glantz & Parmley, 1995; Scientific Committee on Tobacco and Health, 1998; Taylor, Johnson, & Kazemi, 1992). In a meta-analysis, Law and Hackshaw (1997) estimated the excess risk from ETS exposure as 30% (95% CI 22%, 38%) at age 65. There is also evidence linking ETS to other adverse effects in adults, including exacerbation of asthma, reduced lung function, and respiratory symptoms, but the associations have not yet been judged to be causal (California Environmental Protection Agency, 1997; Samet & Wang, 2000; Scientific Committee on Tobacco and Health, 1998).

ᦕ Cigar Smoking

Rates of cigar smoking have risen substantially since the early 1990s, driven by aggressive marketing (NCI, 1998). Like cigarette smoke, cigar smoke is generated by tobacco consumption and consequently has the same injurious components. Cigar smoke differs from cigarette smoke in that it has a more alkaline pH, so that nicotine in cigar smoke is absorbed across the oral mucosa. Consequently, cigar smokers do not need to inhale smoke into the lungs in order to obtain nicotine. Cigarette smokers who switch to cigars are, however, likely to inhale more deeply than those who have smoked only cigars.

Because of the pattern of less deep inhalation by cigar smokers, the smoke exposure is heaviest in the mouth, throat, and esophagus, and cigar smokers have lesser exposure of their lungs and less systemic absorption of smoke than do cigarette smokers. Evidence on the health effects of cigar smoking has been limited because only a small proportion of smokers have used cigars only. A 1998 monograph in the National Cancer Institute's Smoking and Tobacco Control series summarizes the evidence, including new analyses of CPS I 12-year follow-up data. Relative risks for death were calculated separately for male primary cigar smokers, cigarette smokers, and persons who had never smoked cigarettes or pipes regularly (see Figure 1.3). Risks were found to be significantly increased for the cigar smokers for each category except COPD. For cancers of the upper airway and digestive tract, the relative risks were closest to those of the cigarette smokers. Much of the evidence reviewed in the monograph came from case-control studies.

In its overall conclusions, the NCI monograph identifies cigar smoking as a cause of oral, esophageal, laryngeal, and lung cancers and also notes increased risk for coronary heart disease and COPD in cigar smokers. The risks vary with reported inhalation. As noted above, cigarette smokers who switch to cigars tend to inhale more smoke than those who have smoked cigars only. Consequently, the benefits of smoking cessation are attenuated for those former cigarette smokers who change to cigar smoking. For cigar smokers, relative risks are comparable to those for cigarette smokers for cancers of the oral cavity and esophagus but are lower for cancers of the larynx and lung, for CHD, and for COPD.

❦ Summary

Tobacco smoking, particularly cigarette smoking, is a remarkably powerful cause of disease. The toxic components of tobacco smoke have been linked to cancer, heart and lung disease, and adverse effects on reproduction and the fetus. Even nonsmokers inadvertently exposed to tobacco smoke are harmed. The burden of disease caused by smoking is immense, with 1 in 10 adults worldwide currently dying of a tobacco-related disease. By 2030, tobacco is expected to be the single biggest cause of death worldwide, accounting for about 10 million deaths per year

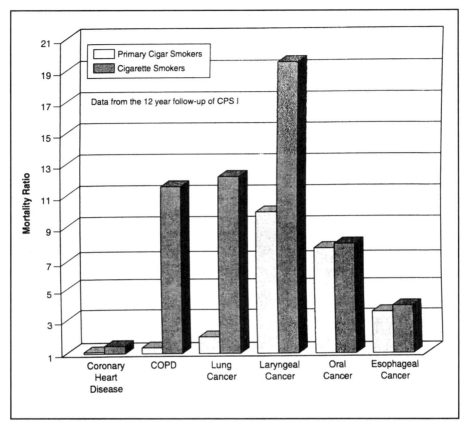

Figure 1.3. Mortality ratios for tobacco-induced diseases among male cigar and cigarette smokers in comparison with persons who have never smoked.
SOURCE: National Cancer Institute (1998).

(World Bank, 1999). Smoking is a principal cause of lost life for middle-aged persons. The strong scientific evidence on smoking as a cause of disease and the enormous adverse impact of tobacco use on global public health provide sufficient rationale for giving high priority and adequate resources to tobacco control programs.

Chapter 2

A Profile of Smokers and Smoking

Patrick Jamieson
Daniel Romer

arried from the New World to Europe, tobacco was first prescribed as a cure for the "Pockes" (Wagner, 1971, p. 11). In 1604, writing in a treatise titled *A Counter-Blaste to Tobacco*, England's King James I dismissed claims about tobacco's curative powers and instead condemned the smoking of tobacco as "a custom loathsome to the eye, hateful to the nose, harmful to the brain, dangerous to the lung, and the black stinking fume thereof, nearest resembling the horribly Stygian smoke of the pit that is bottomless" (quoted in Kluger, 1996, p. 15). In an effort to discourage smoking, he taxed tobacco heavily (Miller, 1992, p. 4).

The effects of tobacco have long attracted the attention of scientists. In 1665, for instance, Samuel Pepys was present at an experiment at the Royal Society in which a cat was fed "a drop of the distilled oil of tobacco" and promptly died (Wagner, 1971, p. 63). Many of the early claims about the harms of tobacco use were based in the experiences of physicians. Writing in 1798 in his *Essays, Literary, Moral and Philosophical*, Dr. Benjamin Rush, one of the signers of the Declaration of Independence, "objected to tobacco on grounds that it had disastrous effects on the stomach, the nerves, and the oral cavity. The use of tobacco, furthermore, he thought, tended to idleness, uncleanliness, and poor manners" (Wagner, 1971, p. 26).

In 1856-1857, the British medical journal the *Lancet* debated "the great tobacco question." "It is a popular opinion amongst sailors," wrote Dr. John Gallagher, "that tobacco smoke is a disinfectant in fevers, cholera, and other epidemics on board ship. I need hardly say this is erroneous, but I believe the use of tobacco soothes the system, like other sedatives, and renders it more able to resist the influence of disease on these occasions." "One of the morbid results of smoking," wrote Samuel Booth, a medical examiner for life assurance companies, "is an inflammatory condition of the mucous membrane of the lips, tongue, and fauces [*sic*]. The tonsils and pharynx suffer, they become dry and congested. . . . The heart and lungs are often impaired by it, and the morbid state of the larynx, trachea, bronchiae, and lungs results from the action of the narcotic upon the mucous membranes of those parts." After recounting the views of 50 doctors, the *Lancet* editorialized that "the use of tobacco is widely spread, more widely than any one custom, form of worship, or religious belief, and that therefore it must have some good or at least pleasurable effects; that, if its evil effects were so dreadful as stated, the human race would have ceased to exist" (all quotes from the *Lancet* as quoted in Wagner, 1971, p. 31).

By the early 20th century, the notion that cigarette smoking is an indicator of degenerate behavior had taken hold among those crusading against the practice. "If you will study the history of almost any criminal you will find that he is an inveterate cigarette smoker," wrote Henry Ford in 1914 (quoted in Brandt, 1990, p. 158). In 1922 Alice Tanton, a student at Michigan State Normal College, was expelled for smoking, and in 1924 the Michigan Supreme Court upheld the expulsion (Wagner, 1971, p. 46). Inviting young women such as Tanton to smoke were print ads that showed attractive women offering men cigarettes, waiting in anticipation for a man to light their cigarettes, or asking a man to blow some smoke their way. "Reach for a Lucky Instead of a Sweet," said one ad targeting women.

In 1938, two and a half centuries after Pepys witnessed the demise of the cat, Dr. Raymond Pearl of Johns Hopkins Medical School compared the longevity of smokers and nonsmokers in a study reported in *Science* that concluded that "smoking is associated with a definite impairment of longevity" (cited in Wagner, 1971, p. 69). In 1950, the U.S. Federal Trade Commission "issued cease and desist orders against Camels for claims about aiding digestion and relieving fatigue and against Old Golds for their 'Not a Cough in a Carload' campaign" (Miller, 1992, p. 8). In the same year, Wynder and Graham published a retrospective study linking cancer and smoking. Graham quit smoking in 1952; in 1957 he died of lung cancer ("Ernst L. Wynder," 1999). (In Chapter 1 of this volume, Samet presents a synoptic history of the scientific study of smoking and health from the 1950s to the present.) In 1964, a report of the U.S. surgeon general "causally" related smoking to lung cancer in men (U.S. Department of Health, Education, and Welfare, 1964,

p. 3). A year later, the Cigarette Labeling and Advertising Act, which required the placement of warning labels on cigarette packs, was approved by Congress.

More than a hundred years before Graham's death, scientists had identified the active ingredients in tobacco. In the early 1800s, Louis Nicolas Vauquelin tagged the active ingredient *nicotianine* in honor of the Frenchman who had brought the product to the French court more than two centuries earlier (Wagner, 1971, p. 65). Where the 1964 report of the Advisory Committee to the Surgeon General titled *Smoking and Health* (U.S. Department of Health, Education, and Welfare, 1964) identified smoking tobacco as habituating, in 1988 a surgeon general's report titled *The Health Consequences of Smoking: Nicotine Addiction* showed that, like cocaine and heroin, nicotine is an addictive drug (Centers for Disease Control, 1988).

Three decades after the release of the first U.S. surgeon general's report, a lawsuit by the state of Minnesota against the tobacco industry resulted in the public release of millions of pages of industry documents. A review of these documents revealed that "for decades, the industry knew and internally acknowledged that nicotine is an addictive drug and cigarettes are the ultimate nicotine delivery device; that nicotine addiction can be perpetuated and even enhanced through cigarette design alterations and manipulations; and that 'health-conscious' smokers could be captured by low-tar, low-nicotine products, all the while ensuring the marketplace viability of their products" (Hurt & Robertson, 1998, p. 1173).

Whereas "during the first decades of the 20th century, lung cancer was rare . . . as cigarette smoking became increasingly popular, first among men and later among women, the incidence of lung cancer became epidemic" ("Achievements," 1999, p. 986). As Samet notes in Chapter 1 of this volume, use of tobacco can cause heart disease, atherosclerotic peripheral vascular disease, laryngeal cancer, oral cancer, esophageal cancer, chronic obstructive pulmonary disease, intrauterine growth retardation, and low birth weight.

The average number of cigarettes smoked per person in the United States has varied dramatically across the 20th century. "Annual per capita cigarette consumption increased from 54 cigarettes in 1900 to 4345 cigarettes in 1963 and then decreased to 2261 in 1998" ("Achievements," 1999, p. 988). In 1939, 61% of adults reported smoking; by 1998, the proportion had dropped to 28% ("Smoking," 1998, p. 7). A Gallup survey conducted in 1954 found that "90% of the public . . . had heard or read about reports that cigarettes 'may be one of the causes' of lung cancer" (Saad, 1998, p. 2). Three and a half decades later, in 1990, 94% of those surveyed agreed with the stronger claim that "smoking is one of the causes of cancer" (Saad, 1998, p. 3).

Roughly 48 million adults in the United States smoke cigarettes, and more than 430,000 of them die of smoking-related causes each year ("Achievements,"

1999, p. 990). Of those who continue to smoke, about 50% will die of smoking-related causes ("Achievements," p. 990). Smoking "has resulted in more than 10 million deaths since the first Surgeon General's report in 1964" ("Smoking-Attributable Mortality," 1999, p. 137). It has been estimated that "if current tobacco-use patterns persist, an estimated 5 million persons who were aged 0-17 years in 1995 will die prematurely from a smoking-related illness" ("Projected," 1996, p. 971). The most preventable cause of early death in the United States is cigarette smoking (Centers for Disease Control, 1989). Globally, if current patterns persist, more than 200 million individuals who are currently children and teens will die of smoking-related illnesses (Peto, Lopez, Boreham, Thun, & Heath, 1994).

To understand more fully the relationships among perception of the risk of smoking, feelings about smoking, images associated with smoking, and decisions to smoke or quit, the Annenberg Public Policy Center, with partial support from the Robert Wood Johnson Foundation, sponsored two surveys. Both surveys were approved by the Institutional Review Board of the University of Pennsylvania. In this chapter, we report the methodology employed in each and summarize what we have learned about smoking and the climate in which it occurs.

∽ Survey 1

Methodology

Smoking usually begins in adolescence. The school-based Youth Risk Behavior Surveillance System found in 1997 that "nationwide, one fourth (24.8%) of students had smoked a whole cigarette before 13 years of age" (Kann et al., 1998, p. 15). Furthermore, 91% of the adults in the United States who have ever been daily smokers tried their first cigarette before age 20, and 77% had become daily smokers by that age (Centers for Disease Control and Prevention, 1994a). In order to understand the next generation of smokers, we focused in Survey 1 on young people in the age range of 14 to 22 years old. Individuals 18 to 22 years old were included in this survey because smoking among college students, which had "remained steady from 1986 through 1990," then "increased, reaching 27% in 1995" (Wechsler, Rigotti, Gledhill-Hoyt, & Lee, 1998, p. 1673). More than "one quarter of college students who smoked in 1997 reported starting to smoke regularly in college and half of current smokers in college tried to quit in the preceding year" (p. 1678).

We begin with the methods and findings of Survey 1 that set the stage for many of the results reported in this book. The survey itself is reproduced in Appendix A. This survey was administered by Princeton Survey Research Associates (PSRA) from May 27 through July 12, 1999, to a nationally representative sample of young adults, ages 14 to 22, living in telephone households in the continental United States. The survey sample included 300 14- to 22-year-olds who smoked cigarettes at least once in the 30 days preceding the date of interview (smokers) and 300 who did not smoke cigarettes during this period (nonsmokers).

More than 13,000 households were identified using random-digit dialing procedures. Within these households, 67.5% were successfully contacted by an interviewer and 76.2% agreed to provide the needed screening information to identify a person aged 14 to 22. Approximately 8.5% of these cooperating households contained an eligible English-speaking respondent. Nearly all eligible respondents (99.3%) were successfully interviewed. In each qualifying household with more than one member age 14 to 22, the respondent was selected randomly using the "most recent birthday" method. Respondent selection was conducted with an adult age 18 or older, and parental permission was obtained before any respondent age 14 or 15 was interviewed. Because nonsmokers outnumber smokers by roughly 2 to 1 in this age range, only a random half of nonsmoking respondents was interviewed. Selecting nonsmokers at random throughout the field period reduced biases that would have occurred if only the first 300 nonsmokers had been interviewed. This design ensured that smoker and nonsmoker interviews were distributed roughly equally across the field period. The overall response rate, taking into account the households that were not reached for screening purposes, was 51%.

A smoker was identified as a person who reported smoking at least one cigarette in the past 30 days. Of those who had not smoked in the past 30 days, 38% indicated that they had once smoked a cigarette, at least one or two puffs. This group was classed with nonsmokers.

PSRA managed the fieldwork and processed the data according to the specifications of Patrick Jamieson. Sampling was subcontracted to Survey Sampling, Inc., of Westport, Connecticut, and interviewing was subcontracted to Schulman, Ronca & Bucuvalas, Inc., of New York.

Using the prevalence of smokers obtained in the screener to the survey (32%), we weighted the data to adjust the proportion of smokers in the 14-22 age range to approximate more closely their true representation in the national population. We also weighted the data to correspond to U.S. Census Current Population Survey estimates for gender, race, age, and census region.

As Table 2.1 indicates, we found in Survey 1 that smokers tended to be older than nonsmokers, to be more likely to be racially white and less likely to be black,

TABLE 2.1   Demographic Profile of Survey 1

Characteristic	Smokers (weighted N = 183)	Nonsmokers (weighted N = 417)	Weighted Total (N = 600)
Age**			
14-15	8.7	29.3	23.0
16-17	16.8	26.1	23.3
18-19	27.2	19.4	21.8
20-22	47.3	25.2	31.9
Gender			
Male	52.2	51.1	51.4
Female	47.8	48.9	48.6
Region			
Northeast	20.8	16.8	18.0
Midwest	25.7	23.6	24.2
South	38.3	35.6	36.4
West	15.3	24.0	21.4
Race/ethnicity*			
White	80.1	68.0	71.7
Black	7.2	15.4	12.9
Hispanic	9.4	13.2	12.1
Other	3.3	3.3	3.3
Currently in school**			
Yes	47.5	73.6	65.6
No	52.5	26.4	34.4
Education completed**			
Less than 9th grade	6.6	23.1	18.0
9th-11th grades	29.6	35.8	34.0
High school	34.1	15.9	21.4
Post high school	28.0	21.2	23.2
College degree	1.1	3.8	3.0
Postgraduate degree	0.5	0.2	0.3
Parents/adults smoke**			
Yes	62.3	32.4	41.5
No	37.2	67.6	58.3

NOTE: All entries are percentages of column total. Characteristics that differ significantly between smokers and nonsmokers are indicated by *$p < .05$; **$p < .01$.

and to be both more likely to be out of school and to have a smoker in the family. Smokers had completed more schooling, but this was because they were older.

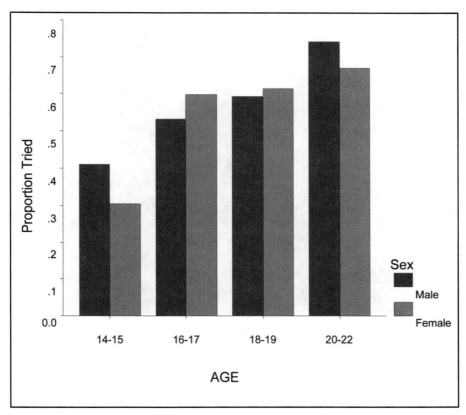

Figure 2.1. Reported trial of cigarettes by age and sex of respondent in Survey 1.

Smoking Prevalence

Figures 2.1 and 2.2 show the data from Survey 1 on the prevalence of ever having tried a cigarette and current smoking by age and gender. Consistent with other recent surveys of young people ("Tobacco Use," 2000), a dramatic rise in cigarette trial can be seen during this age period. Trial in young men goes from just above 40% to more than 70%, and in women it goes from about 30% to nearly 70%.

These rapid increases in trial are accompanied by increases in reports of current smoking (past 30 days). As Figure 2.2 indicates, young men's current smoking levels rise from just under 10% to nearly 50%, and young women's smoking levels rise from just over 10% to more than 40%. These findings are comparable to those of the recently reported National Youth Tobacco Survey (NYTS), which was conducted in schools in the fall of 1999 ("Tobacco Use," 2000). That survey found that

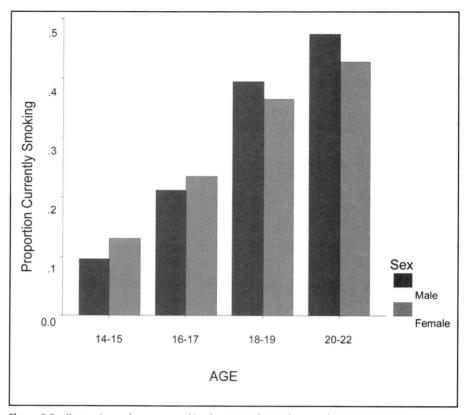

Figure 2.2　Proportions of current smoking by age and sex of respondent in Survey 1.

about 28% of high school students were currently smoking cigarettes (past 30 days). A comparison of the NYTS with our survey by grade level is somewhat problematic because our survey was conducted during the spring and summer months, when students were either making the transition between grades or on break. However, respondents in the survey between the ages of 15 and 18 reported current use at a level of approximately 24%, somewhat below the levels reported in the NYTS. This discrepancy is potentially attributable to our use of a phone survey as opposed to the school-based survey used by the NYTS. It is not surprising that young people in their homes would report somewhat lower levels of smoking than they report in school settings. Nevertheless, both survey results are of the same order of magnitude and display the dramatic increase in smoking that has alarmed health authorities. We are confident, therefore, that the results of Survey 1 can be used for the purpose for which the survey was designed—namely, to help us understand the risk perceptions and other predictors that are associated with uptake and cessation of smoking in young people within this age range.

໑໐ Survey 2

Methodology

Survey 2 was conducted with two separate samples simultaneously. Interviewing was conducted from November 11, 1999, to February 15, 2000. One sample of young people ages 14 to 22 was drawn using the same procedures as in Survey 1. However, nonsmokers were not excluded from interviewing. This survey is reproduced in Appendix B. The resulting sample of 2,002 persons ages 14 to 22 contained 487 current smokers (23.9%). The other sample for Survey 2 was drawn using similar procedures but targeted persons ages 23 and older. This adult sample contained 1,504 persons ages 23 to 95, with 310 current smokers (20.6%). The response rate for the youth sample was 51%, just as in Survey 1; the rate for the adult sample was 38%. These rates include failures to reach households that might be eligible but either could not be contacted or refused to cooperate.

Survey 2 was conducted by Schulman, Ronca & Bucuvalas, Inc., of New York, which managed the fieldwork and processed the data according to the specifications of Paul Slovic, Neil Weinstein, Daniel Romer, and Patrick Jamieson.

In addition to our focus on risk, Survey 2 also contained questions about other influences on smoking experienced by those in the 14-22 age group. These questions focused on exposure to both cigarette advertising and antismoking advertising, imagery associated with smoking, feelings associated with smoking, and peer-group smoking and approval of smoking. Although Survey 2 was longer than Survey 1, it required only 20 minutes of interviewing time on average.

Demographic Characteristics

Table 2.2 shows the demographic characteristics of the segment of the sample aged 14 to 22, and Table 2.3 displays the characteristics of the segment aged 23 and older. Data were weighted as for Survey 1 to match the demographic profiles of the Current Population Survey for age, gender, race, and census region. The demographic profile of smokers in the 14-22 age group matches that of the sample in Survey 1, which was conducted 6 months earlier. One major difference between these samples is the greater proportion of respondents reporting that they were in school at the time of the Survey 2 (75.9% versus 65.6%). Given that Survey 1 was conducted at the end of the school year and during the summer, this difference was expected. Survey 2 also had a smaller proportion of respondents who had finished high school (10.2% versus 21.4%), a result again attributable to the time of the survey in relation to the school year.

TABLE 2.2   Demographic Characteristics of the 14- to 22-Year-Old Sample in Survey 2

Characteristic	Smokers (weighted N = 510)	Nonsmokers (weighted N = 1,492)	Weighted Total (N = 2,002)
Age**			
14-15	7.3	28.7	23.2
16-17	16.5	25.0	22.8
18-19	29.8	22.0	24.0
20-22	46.5	24.3	30.0
Gender**			
Male	55.7	49.3	50.9
Female	44.3	50.7	49.1
Region			
Northeast	20.7	17.2	18.1
Midwest	23.7	24.3	24.1
South	32.7	37.7	36.4
West	22.9	20.9	21.4
Race/ethnicity**			
White	82.0	68.3	71.8
Black	4.3	17.0	13.7
Hispanic	11.4	12.3	12.0
Other	2.3	2.5	2.4
Currently in school**			
Yes	56.9	75.9	75.9
No	43.1	24.1	24.1
Education completed			
Less than 9th grade	7.5	22.2	18.4
9th-11th grades	38.4	43.5	42.2
High school	18.2	7.5	10.2
Post high school	33.1	21.0	24.1
College degree	1.4	4.2	3.4
Postgraduate degree	0.4	1.0	0.8
Parents/adults smoke**			
Yes	52.0	33.9	38.5
No	47.5	65.4	60.8

NOTE: All entries are percentages of column total. Characteristics that differ significantly between smokers and nonsmokers are indicated by $*p < .05$; $**p < .01$.

The demographic characteristics of respondents in the adult sample (Table 2.3) indicate that in this age range, smokers tended to be younger and less well edu-

TABLE 2.3   Characteristics of the Adult Sample (Age 23 and Older) in Survey 2

Characteristic	Smokers (weighted N = 306)	Nonsmokers (weighted N = 1,198)	Weighted Total (N = 1,504)
Age**			
23-29	19.6	12.5	14.0
30-39	27.8	21.4	22.7
40-49	23.2	22.5	22.6
50-59	16.3	16.8	16.6
60-69	7.8	12.4	11.6
70+	5.2	14.4	12.6
Gender			
Male	51.6	46.7	47.7
Female	48.4	53.3	52.3
Region			
Northeast	18.4	20.1	19.7
Midwest	27.9	22.7	23.8
South	39.3	34.3	35.3
West	14.4	23.0	21.2
Race/ethnicity			
White	83.0	81.1	81.4
Black	9.2	10.7	10.4
Hispanic	4.3	5.6	5.3
Other	3.6	2.6	2.9
Education completed*			
Less than 9th grade	3.6	2.2	2.5
9th-11th grades	15.7	9.9	11.1
High school	26.5	21.2	22.3
Post high school	32.7	27.5	28.5
College degree	11.1	19.6	17.8
Postgraduate degree	10.1	18.7	17.0

NOTE: All entries are percentages of column total. Characteristics that differ significantly between smokers and nonsmokers are indicated by *$p < .05$; **$p < .01$.

cated than nonsmokers. In addition, smokers in the older sample were less differentiated from nonsmokers by race and ethnicity than in the 14-22 age sample. These patterns match the profiles obtained by other recent national surveys of adults ("Cigarette Smoking," 1999).

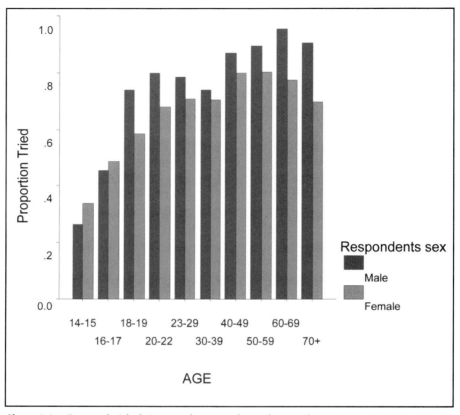

Figure 2.3.   Reported trial of cigarettes by age and sex of respondent in Survey 2.

Smoking Prevalence

Survey 2 confirmed the rapid increase in both trial and current smoking levels found in Survey 1. Figure 2.3 shows the results for reported trial and Figure 2.4 presents the results for current smoking across both surveys. The most striking pattern in the trial results is the high level of trial among persons ages 20 to 22. This confirms the findings of other recent national surveys of persons ages 18 and older that those in their early 20s report very high rates of cigarette use ("Cigarette Smoking," 1999). This increased use is consistent with the upward trend among high school students that has been documented by the Monitoring the Future Studies since 1992 (Johnston, O'Malley, & Bachman, 1999b).

The dramatic increase in recent smoking is also apparent in Figure 2.4, which shows levels of current smoking (past 30 days) by age and gender. Here again, the 20-22 age group reports higher levels of current smoking than does the slightly older 23-29 age group. Older age groups report even less smoking despite high

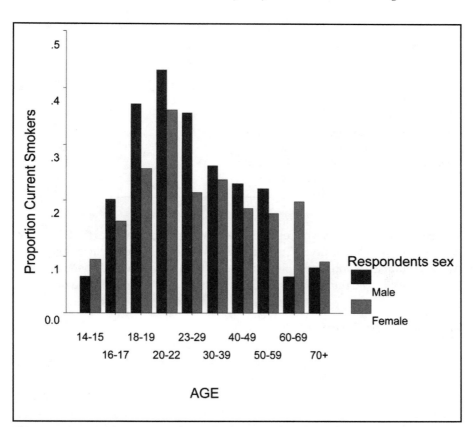

Figure 2.4. Reported current use of cigarettes by age and gender in Survey 2.

levels of reported trial. This probably reflects the success of antismoking efforts during the past 20 years ("Tobacco Use," 2000; Warner, 1989).

The results of Survey 2 are not directly comparable to other surveys with adults because the definition of current smoking commonly used in adult surveys screens for those who have smoked at least 100 cigarettes in their lives. In addition, current smokers are defined as those who say they "smoke cigarettes every day or some days," with no time frame specified. However, the decline in current smoking across older age cohorts is consistent with those surveys ("Achievements," 1999). As noted earlier, Survey 2 was conducted during the school year, and a higher proportion of young people in the 14-22 age group reported current school attendance. In addition, whether respondents considered themselves to be in school or not, the summer months probably allow young people greater opportunity to smoke. This may explain the somewhat lower levels of current smoking (past 30 days) reported in Survey 2 (25.5% versus 30.6% in Survey 1). Although current smoking was lower, there was very little difference between

TABLE 2.4   Reported Smoking Behavior in Survey 2 (in percentages)

Current and Previous Smoking	Ages 14-22	Ages 23+
Never smoked	44.2	20.4
Tried but did not continue	21.6	40.3
Quit or do not smoke now	3.6	14.4
Smoke less than 1 cigarette per day	10.2	6.6
Smoke between 1 and 10 cigarettes per day	10.6	5.7
Smoke more than 10 cigarettes per day	9.8	12.6

surveys in the proportion who reported ever having tried cigarettes (57.2% in Survey 1 versus 55.8% in Survey 2). Nearly all of the difference in current smoking was attributable to young people in Survey 2 who said they had tried cigarettes but had not smoked them in the past 30 days (30.3% versus 26.5% in Survey 1).

Frequency of Cigarette Smoking

To assess frequency of current smoking, we asked respondents who reported smoking in the past 30 days to indicate about how many cigarettes they smoked per day during that period. For respondents who said they had smoked in the past but not in the past 30 days, we asked whether they smoked occasionally but not in the past 30 days, whether they had tried smoking but never continued, or whether they had once smoked regularly but no longer do. As Table 2.4 shows, 30.6% of respondents between the ages of 14 and 22 reported smoking at least occasionally, even if not in the past 30 days, whereas only 24.9% of older respondents reported this level of recent smoking. Nevertheless, among these two groups of smokers, only about one-third of younger smokers (9.8%) reported smoking more than 10 cigarettes per day, compared with about half of older smokers (12.6%). These differences in smoking patterns suggest that even though younger smokers consume fewer cigarettes on average than older smokers, they are clearly at risk for progressing to heavier levels of smoking. In addition, a large proportion of younger smokers already smoke at levels comparable to those of older and more established smokers.

Other Uses of Tobacco

In addition to asking respondents about their experiences with cigarettes, we asked whether they had smoked cigars of any kind, whether they had used chew-

TABLE 2.5   **Current Use of Tobacco Products (past 30 days) and Awareness and Trial of Bidis in Survey 2 and the NYTS (in percentages)**

Type of Product	Survey 2			NYTS (N = 15,058)
	Ages 14-22 (N = 2,002)	Ages 23+ (N = 1,504)	High School (N = 924)	
Cigarettes	25.3	19.9	15.0	28.4
Cigars	9.3	5.7	6.3	15.3
Chewing tobacco	4.1	4.1	3.4	6.6
Bidis				
Aware	26.9	16.6	23.1	NA
Ever tried	10.5	2.0	6.2	NA
Past 30 days	1.0	0.1	0.5	5.0
Any tobacco use	29.6	24.9	18.9	NA

NOTE: NA = not applicable. High school students in Survey 2 are shown for comparison with the NYTS.

ing tobacco of any kind, and whether they had heard of or used "flavored cigarettes called bidis." The results indicate that higher proportions of young people, ages 14 to 22, than older persons use cigarettes, cigars, and bidis, and that there is little difference between age groups in the use of chewing tobacco (see Table 2.5).

The vast majority of recent tobacco users were cigarette smokers (85.5% of young people and 79.9% of persons older than age 22). As was the case for reported smoking of cigarettes, reported recent use of cigars, chewing tobacco, and bidis by young people was lower in our telephone survey than in the school-based National Youth Tobacco Survey ("Tobacco Use," 2000). However, the rank order of reported use of the four types of products was similar in the two surveys.

Concerns About Sample Representativeness

The lower levels of recent use of tobacco products found in the Annenberg surveys compared with the school-based NYTS might be interpreted to indicate that high-risk youth are underrepresented in the Annenberg samples. Telephone surveys may reduce the tendency to report recent use of tobacco among young people. For example, more than 6% of our sample reported having tried smoking bidis; however, less than 1% claimed to have smoked them in the past 30 days.

TABLE 2.6	Reported Source of Cigarettes by Age in Survey 2 (in percentages)				
	Young People				*Adults*
Source	*14-15*	*16-17*	*18-19*	*20-22*	*23+*
Convenience stores	24.3	45.8	78.9	78.0	57.5
Supermarkets	0.0	7.2	3.3	7.6	21.6
Friends	62.2	37.3	7.9	7.2	2.6
Relatives	5.4	6.0	.7	.4	0.3
Other	8.1	2.4	9.2	6.8	16.4

Alternatively, respondents in school-based surveys may actually overstate recent use of tobacco products. This is especially likely when intact classrooms are used to conduct surveys, as was done in the NYTS. Adolescents may be more apt to say that their experimentation with tobacco was recent in the presence of their friends, even if the questionnaires are completed anonymously. Despite the differences between surveys, we are confident that the Annenberg Tobacco Surveys cover a sufficient range of smokers and nonsmokers. The wide range of smoking behaviors found in these surveys should enable us to study the role of risk perception and other major influences on smoking initiation and cessation.

How Cigarettes Are Obtained

To determine how young people obtain cigarettes, we asked respondents where they "get most of [their] cigarettes." As Table 2.6 indicates, 24.3% of 14- and 15-year-olds and 45.8% of 16- and 17-year-olds said that they purchase cigarettes at convenience stores "such as 7-11 and gas stations." Use of convenience stores increases with age in the youth sample. Most of the 14- and 15-year-olds obtain cigarettes from friends and relatives, but this tendency declines among older adolescents, who purchase cigarettes in stores. Our finding of high proportions of young people buying cigarettes is consistent with the findings of earlier surveys ("Comparison," 1992).

Effects of Promotions

To gain a better understanding of the impact of cigarette marketing, we asked several questions about cigarette promotional activities. Bars and other drinking and eating establishments constitute one avenue through which tobacco companies can reach young people. We asked respondents if they had gone to a "bar, pub, or microbrewery in the past six months." About 40% of the 14- to 22-year-old sample responded yes, only a slightly smaller proportion than in the adult sample (45%). Of those who said they had gone to such places, about 16% of the 14- to 22-year-olds said they had seen there "entertainment sponsored by a cigarette company." Only 8% of those in the adult sample reported seeing such sponsored activities in bars and other drinking establishments.

Young people may also be exposed to cigarette advertising and promotions at sports events. Evidence that such events contribute to young people's exposure to cigarette advertising comes from a national telephone survey conducted by the Annenberg Public Policy Center in 1999. That survey included interviews with 301 adolescents ages 10 to 17 as well as one parent of each adolescent. Respondents were asked if they could "name the famous cartoon animal that is associated with cigarette advertisements." Approximately 70% were able to name the Joe Camel character. Another 9% gave an incorrect name, and about 20% did not know about the character at all. In addition, 9% of respondents reported owning "a T-shirt, hat or any other item with the logo of a cigarette brand, such as Camel or Marlboro, on it."

If attendance at sports events increases exposure to cigarette brands and logos, we would expect greater awareness of Joe Camel among adolescents who attend sports events. This expectation was confirmed. Nearly three-fourths of the respondents reported attendance at a sports event in the past 6 months. Among those who attended sports events, 73% gave the correct name for Joe Camel; among those who did not attend such events, only 65% gave the correct name. This difference was statistically reliable (OR = 1.95, $p = .034$) in an analysis that controlled for the age and gender of the adolescent; the age, gender, and race of the parent; and the adolescent's perceived prevalence of smoking in his or her friendship network and ownership of cigarette promotional items.

Illnesses Associated With Smoking

We asked respondents in Survey 2 to name any "illnesses" they could that are "caused by smoking cigarettes." The dominant response was lung cancer, named by 89.6% of young people and 84.0% of persons over age 22 (Figure 2.5). The respondents' knowledge of other health effects of smoking was quite limited (especially when compared with the extensive list of adverse health outcomes discussed by Samet in Chapter 1 of this volume). On average, respondents could name only slightly more than 2 illnesses (2.2 for the youth sample and 2.3 for adults). Chapters 3, 4, 5, 6, 7, and 10 in this volume examine the significance of

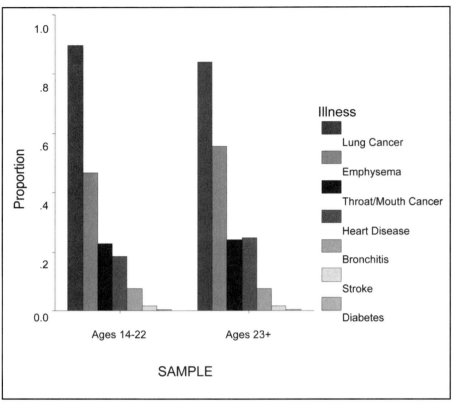

Figure 2.5. Proportions of young people ages 14 to 22 and persons over age 22 who named illnesses caused by smoking.

these and other findings from the two surveys on perceptions of the effects of smoking on health.

⟨⟩ Summary

Discussions of the supposed benefits and consequences of smoking tobacco have been ongoing since the 1600s. Proponents and opponents of smoking have clashed over such issues as whether smoking causes cancer and whether nicotine is addictive. Although per capita consumption of cigarettes in the United States has declined in recent decades, young people continue to adopt the behavior. The

14- to 22-year-olds in our surveys reported rapidly increasing use of cigarettes within this age period, a trend that is comparable to findings from other national surveys. Indeed, higher proportions of young people than adults report use of cigarettes and other tobacco products. Although young smokers as a group do not smoke as frequently as adult smokers, many already smoke at high levels and others are at risk of progressing to a more frequent habit. Young smokers appear to have little difficulty obtaining cigarettes in stores even at ages 14 and 15. They are exposed to cigarette marketing at sports events and other entertainment sites. Despite years of education about smoking risks and warning labels on tobacco products, most can name only about two illnesses that result from smoking.

Part II

PERCEPTIONS OF RISK BY ADOLESCENTS AND ADULTS

Chapter 3

What Do Young People Think They Know About the Risks of Smoking?

Patrick Jamieson
Daniel Romer

I n this chapter we examine the first Annenberg Tobacco Survey to answer the question, How well are 14- to 22-year-olds able to report the risks of smoking? Most adolescents try smoking at least once: Estimates of the proportion who experiment with cigarettes vary from 47% to 90%. Many who experiment smoke only a few cigarettes. Those who smoke three or more cigarettes are likely to become regular smokers (Lynch & Bonnie, 1994).

Determining whether adolescents actually understand the risks they take when they make the decision to smoke is important, because antismoking messages often contain information about the hazards of the activity. If, as Viscusi (1992b) has argued, young people already understand the risks, then the money spent disseminating this information would be better spent on other content.

Some researchers have found that, in general, smokers overestimate the health risks of the behavior (Kristiansen, Harding, & Eiser, 1983; Viscusi, 1992b); others have concluded the opposite (Ayanian & Cleary, 1999; Schoenbaum, 1997; Strecher, Kreuter, & Kobrin, 1995; Sutton, 1998). Viscusi (1992b) argues that his findings that young people overestimate the risk of contracting lung cancer contradict the notion "of individuals being lured into smoking at an early age without any cognizance of the risks" (p. 143). Slovic (2000b) responds that "the high percentage of people who are dissatisfied with their decision to begin smoking inval-idates Viscusi's claim that such decisions are fully informed and in the individual's best interests" (p. 276; see also Chapter 6, this volume).

The tobacco industry is quick to argue that those who choose to smoke know the risks. In October 1998, a lead attorney for the tobacco companies responded to a class action lawsuit brought by ill smokers seeking damages from the industry by saying, "The basic common sense of the American people for the most part is: You knew the risk, you took the choice, and you should be responsible" (quoted in Fields, 1998, p. A16). One reason the cigarette industry vigorously advances this claim is that when the public believes that an industry is responsible for cancer, it tends to hold the industry morally responsible to compensate for or ameliorate the harm (National Research Council, 1989, p. 58).

Unlike many other studies, ours does not assume that an individual's accurate reporting of data on risk necessarily indicates an understanding of the actual risk. In Chapter 6 of this volume, Slovic shows how many factors can influence the re-porting of quantitative answers to questions about smoking risks. Our objective is merely to determine the extent to which young people are aware of information about the risks of smoking.

Previous attempts to assess risk perception have used only a few measures of smoking risks. Viscusi (1992b) examined three: the likelihood of lung cancer at-tributable to smoking, the mortality risk of smoking, and the years of life lost as a result of smoking. Our first survey contained 12 questions about the health effects of smoking that could be compared with epidemiological evidence about the risks of smoking. After assessing our respondents' answers to these questions, we con-clude (a) that reports that young people overestimate the risks of lung cancer from smoking are problematic, (b) that young people do recognize some health risks of smoking, (c) that 14- to 22-year-olds do not have a consistent and realistic sense of the addictive nature of smoking, and (d) that 14- to 22-year-olds do not know how risky smoking is in relation to some other health risks.

Reports That Young People Overestimate the Risk of Lung Cancer From Smoking Are Problematic

Viscusi (1992b) found that adolescents as well as adults overestimate the likeli-hood that cigarette smokers will contract lung cancer and experience early death as a result of smoking. However, since he conducted his studies, epidemiological estimates of the risks of smoking have risen. Health experts now estimate that

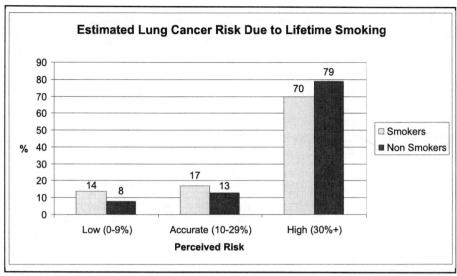

Figure 3.1. Distributions for estimates of proportion of smokers who will contract lung cancer because they smoke. Estimates are categorized as low, accurate, and high (using 10% to 29% as accurate) and by current smoking status of respondent.

50% of lifelong smokers die prematurely from the habit (Peto, Lopez, Boreham, Thun, & Heath, 1994) and that about 30% of these deaths result from lung cancer (Thun, Day-Lally, Calle, Flanders, & Heath, 1995). A reasonable estimate is that 80% of those who get lung cancer die from it (Viscusi, 1992b). As a result, if 15% of smokers die prematurely from lung cancer, then at least 20% of smokers contract lung cancer as a result of smoking.

We asked our respondents to "think about people who smoke cigarettes. Out of every 100 cigarette smokers, how many do you think will get lung cancer because they smoke? How many will die from a smoking related illness?" Consistent with Viscusi's (1992b) findings, respondents in Survey 1 overestimated the extent to which smoking increases the risk of lung cancer. Figure 3.1 shows the distribution of estimates for lung cancer risk (percentage of smokers who get lung cancer from smoking). Accurate estimates were categorized as ranging from 10% to 29%. Persons estimating the risk as below 10% and those who reported that they did not know the risk were categorized as low; those who reported the risk as greater than 29% were categorized as high. As is evident, 70% of smokers and 79% of nonsmokers in our sample overestimated the risk of lung cancer. However, their beliefs about the likelihood of dying from a smoking-related cause were more accurate (using a range of 40% to 59% as accurate in Figure 3.2). In this case, only 34% of smokers and 41% of nonsmokers overestimated the death rate from smoking. However, 41% of smokers and 27% of nonsmokers either underestimated or did not know this rate.

A critical assumption in comparing these estimates with epidemiological evidence is the comparability of the models underlying the estimates. We have analyzed several sources of noncomparability between young people's models of disease prevalence and the models used by epidemiologists (Romer & Jamieson, in press) and have found that 14- to 22-year-olds make at least two assumptions about lung cancer mortality that are not comparable to the ones made by epidemiologists when they are calculating mortality risk for smoking (Rothman, 1986) or adjusting these risks for the fatality rate of lung cancer (Viscusi, 1992b).

First, young people underestimate the fatality rate of lung cancer. Even though lung cancer is widely recognized as fatal, respondents ages 14 to 22 in Survey 1 regarded the fatality rate as lower than epidemiological estimates would suggest. As a result, their estimates of lung cancer prevalence should be higher than would be expected based on epidemiological estimates of the fatality rate of lung cancer.

Second, young people assume that lung cancer overlaps with other conditions, such as heart disease. As a result, young people's attributions of the causes of mortality due to smoking may add up to more than 100%. Because epidemiologists typically count only the primary cause of death in calculating attributed risk, only one condition gets "credit" for any death, and the sum across different conditions equals 100%. When comparing laypersons' estimates of risk to those of epidemiologists, we need to be aware that any one disease may include overlap with other diseases that are counted separately by epidemiologists.

The much higher estimates for lung cancer shown in Figure 3.1 compared with epidemiological estimates may well reflect the very different understandings underlying these two estimates. In Chapter 6 of this volume, Slovic presents further evidence that underscores the differences between estimates of single causes that must add up to 100% and those that are made without this constraint. Estimates of total mortality resulting from smoking (Figure 3.2), which may be less subject to discrepancies in definition with epidemiological analysis, suggest that many smokers either do not know or underestimate the effects of smoking on mortality. At the same time, our analysis suggests that direct comparisons between people's estimates of mortality due to single disease conditions and those based on epidemiological methods are difficult to evaluate.

ⅎ Years of Life Lost Are Not Well Understood

The Office on Smoking and Health of the Centers for Disease Control and Prevention (1996) reports, based on unpublished 1994 data, that "on average, smok-

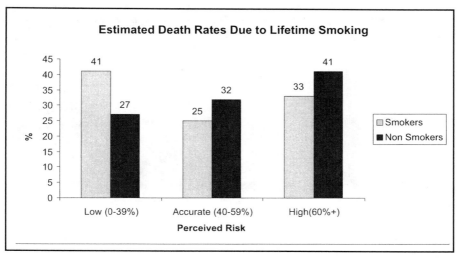

Figure 3.2. Distributions for estimates of proportion of smokers who will die because they smoke. Estimates are categorized as low, accurate, and high (using 40% to 59% as accurate) and by current smoking status of respondent.

ers die nearly seven years earlier than nonsmokers." We asked respondents two questions about years of life lost due to smoking. The first asked whether it was "true or false that smoking two or more packs of cigarettes a week will most likely shorten a person's life, or don't you know enough to say?" For those who said true, we asked them to judge "by how many years does smoking two or more packs a week shorten a person's life? Would you say a few months, one year, five to 10 years or 20 years?"

As seen in Figure 3.3, the majority of both smokers and nonsmokers in our sample believed that smoking shortens one's life. Nevertheless, the question elicited a large percentage of "don't knows." One might speculate that smokers would say they don't know as a mechanism to reduce the dissonance created in the clash between their self-images as intelligent persons and their images of themselves as engaging in a potentially life-shortening behavior. But that explanation fails to account for the 18% of nonsmokers who also gave the "don't know" answer. A more plausible explanation is that antismoking campaigns have failed to inform many young people of the extent of life potentially lost due to smoking.

Although 44% of the smokers and 48% of the nonsmokers correctly put the amount of life lost at 5 to 10 years, 26% of the nonsmokers and 21% of the smokers underestimated the effects of smoking on longevity (Figure 3.4). In sum, almost half of the smokers either underestimate or report not knowing by how

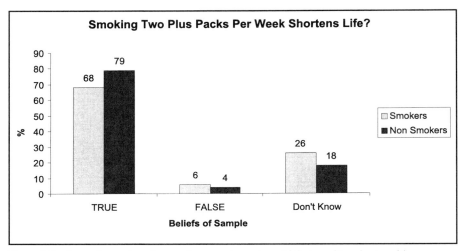

Figure 3.3. Proportions of smokers and nonsmokers who said that smoking shortens life.

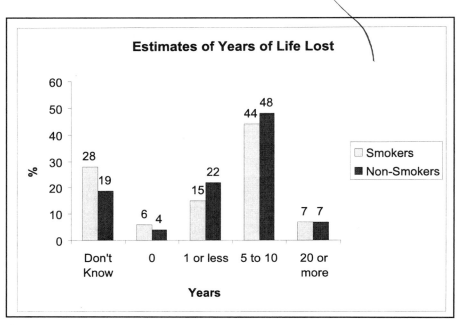

Figure 3.4. Proportions of smokers and nonsmokers who estimated each category for years of life lost due to lifetime smoking.

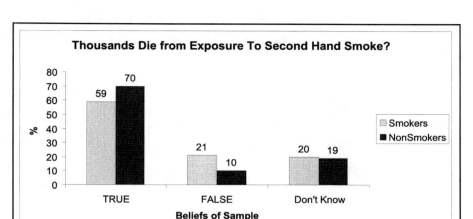

Figure 3.5. Proportions of smokers and nonsmokers who believed that exposure to secondhand smoke can be lethal.

many years on average smoking two or more packs a week will shorten a person's life. This lack of knowledge about loss of life expectancy is consistent with Slovic's analysis of similar data from the second Annenberg survey (see Chapter 6).

∞ Some Health Risks of Smoking Are Well Recognized

We asked three questions about health risks that respondents appeared to recognize. One concerned the effects of secondhand smoke ("Each year thousands of nonsmokers die from breathing other people's smoke"—true or false). According to the U.S. Environmental Protection Agency (1992), nonsmokers' exposure to secondhand smoke causes an estimated 3,000 deaths per year from lung cancer. About 70% of nonsmokers and 59% of smokers correctly reported that second-hand smoke is hazardous to nonsmokers (Figure 3.5). Nevertheless, 20% of smokers and 19% of nonsmokers said they did not know.

A second question asked: "Which statement comes closer to what you think? (A) People your age who smoke can damage their lungs from smoking for just a few years. (B) People your age cannot damage their lungs from smoking because you have to smoke for many years for that to happen." The claim that smoking for just a few years can damage the lungs of young people was more widely believed

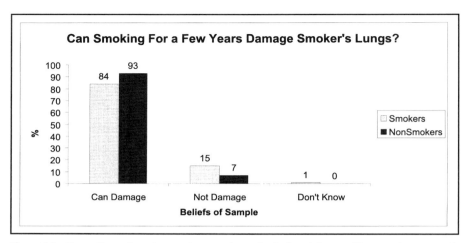

Figure 3.6. Proportions of smokers and nonsmokers who believed that smoking can damage one's lungs.

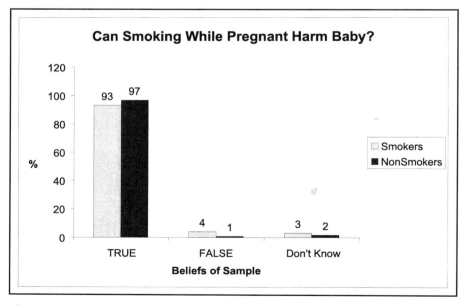

Figure 3.7. Proportions of smokers and nonsmokers who believed that the babies of pregnant women who smoke are at risk.

(Figure 3.6). More than 80% of smokers and 90% of nonsmokers agreed with this claim.

Of the three claims, the one most widely recognized was that smoking by a pregnant woman can have health consequences for her child. The true-or-false item was worded as follows: "Women who smoke while pregnant increase the chances their baby will be born with health problems." More than 90% of both smokers and nonsmokers stated that this claim is true (Figure 3.7).

∾ Young People Do Not Have Consistent and Realistic Knowledge of the Addictive Nature of Smoking

The young person who sees short-term gain in smoking but perceives that he or she will quit before becoming addicted may be surprised to learn how difficult it is to quit. The authors of the Monitoring the Future Study found that more than half of their respondents who smoked at least half a pack a day said that they had tried to quit smoking and found they could not. Of daily smokers who thought they would not be smoking in 5 years, nearly 75% were still smoking 5 to 6 years later (Centers for Disease Control and Prevention, 1994a; Johnston, O'Malley, & Bachman, 1993).

Evidence that smokers do not have consistent views of the addictive nature of smoking comes from a summary of their polled responses. We asked respondents: "In your opinion, once someone is smoking two or more packs a week, how easy or hard is it for them to quit and never smoke again? Is it . . . (A) Very easy, and anyone who wants to can. (B) Hard, but most people can do it if they really try. (C) Very difficult and most cannot do it. (D) Almost impossible, and only a few will be able to do it." Among smokers, 62% thought that quitting is either very easy or hard but doable for most people. Nonsmokers were less optimistic, with only 46% giving the same responses (Figure 3.8). Although 58% of the smokers had tried to quit at least once, that failure was not reflected in their optimism about the possibility of quitting. Figure 3.9 shows that optimism about quitting remained high among smokers despite the frequency of their previous attempts to quit.

Smokers also have relatively optimistic beliefs about the meaning of tobacco addiction. Although 82% agreed with the statement "A chemical in cigarettes makes smoking addictive," nearly 60% of these smokers still said that they believed quitting is either very easy or possible for most people if they really try. Despite the recognition that tobacco is addictive, young smokers think they can give

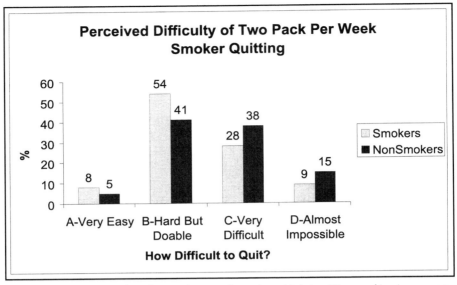

Figure 3.8. Proportions of smokers and nonsmokers who said that quitting smoking is very easy, hard but doable, very difficult, or almost impossible.

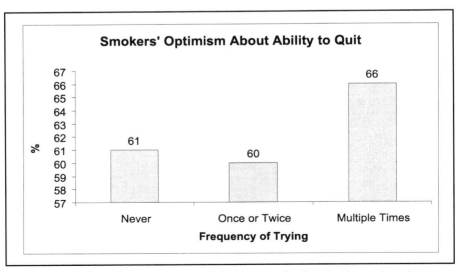

Figure 3.9. Proportions of smokers who said that it is easy or hard but doable to quit smoking given the number of times they have tried to quit in the past.

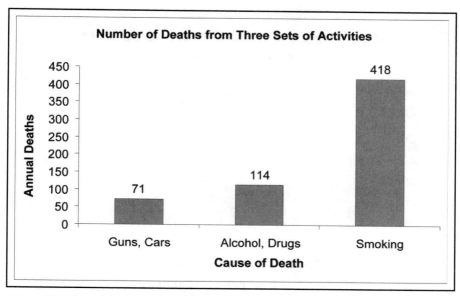

Figure 3.10. Annual deaths (in thousands) attributable to three sets of activities: guns and car accidents, alcohol and drug use, and cigarette smoking (see McGinnis & Foege, 1993).

up the habit if they so desire. The implications of this optimistic belief are examined in greater detail in Chapters 6 and 10 of this volume.

∾ Young People Do Not Know How Risky Smoking Is in Relation to Other Health Risks

Another way to assess what people know about the risks of smoking is to ask them to compare the riskiness of different behaviors. To determine what young people know about the relative risks of one behavior in relation to others, we included two questions. A true-or-false item was worded, "Each year more people die from gunshots and car accidents than die from smoking." We also asked, "Of all the deaths in one year, do you think more people die from smoking or from abusing alcohol and drugs?" The correct answer in each case (see Figure 3.10) is that smoking is the greater cause of mortality, killing more people each year than gunshots or car accidents combined and more than abuse of alcohol and drugs combined (McGinnis & Foege, 1993).

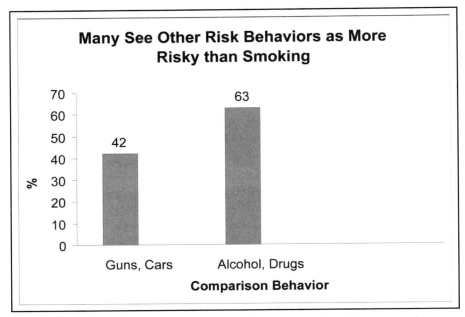

Figure 3.11. Proportions of young people who said that two sets of activities—guns and car accidents, and alcohol and drug use—are more lethal than smoking.

Figure 3.11 shows that more than 40% of the 14- to 22-year-olds in our sample mistakenly believed that more people die from gunshots and car accidents each year than die from smoking. Although smoking kills more people each year than alcohol and drugs combined, most respondents believed that the opposite was the case. The perceptions of smokers and nonsmokers did not differ.

Smokers also perceived getting drunk to be more risky than smoking. All respondents were asked to rate smoking, getting drunk regularly, and smoking marijuana regularly on the same risk scale (from *very risky* to *not at all risky*). As Figure 3.12 illustrates, smokers were less likely than nonsmokers to rate all three activities as very risky. However, smokers were least likely to downplay the risks of regular alcohol use. The heightened risk associated with alcohol may have resulted from the perception that smoking involves little immediate risk to life, whereas getting drunk, like a single act of unprotected sex with an infected partner, can create immediate risk. In addition, young people may be more salient as victims of the effects of alcohol, particularly if the victim is involved in an act of violence or drives. If respondents thought the question pertained only to comparisons between younger people, then perhaps they might be correct in believing that alcohol is a larger source of death than smoking. However, in the second Annenberg survey, we again asked whether smoking kills more people than alco-

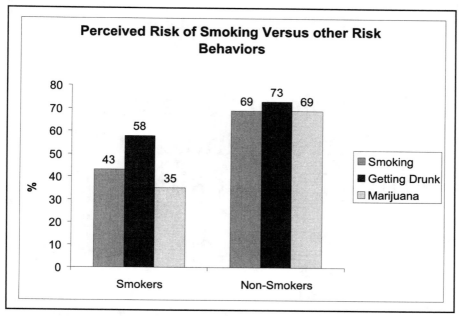

Figure 3.12. Proportions of current smokers and nonsmokers who believed that each of three activities—smoking, getting drunk, and using marijuana—is "very risky to a person's health."

hol and drugs, but added the additional qualifier that the question pertained to people of all ages. The young respondents still believed that alcohol and drugs are more deadly.

⁄ Conclusion

The results of the first Annenberg Tobacco Survey invite the conclusion that 14- to 22-year-olds are not adequately informed about the risks of smoking cigarettes. Although many appear to overestimate the extent of the increased risk of lung cancer from smoking, a sizable number underestimate the overall risk of mortality and the number of years of life lost on average due to smoking. Additionally, young people inaccurately perceive smoking to be responsible for fewer deaths than gunshots and car accidents combined, and as safer than alcohol and drug use. Finally, 14- to 22-year-old smokers express unwarranted optimism about the ability of people to quit smoking.

Chapter 4

The Role of Perceived Risk in Starting and Stopping Smoking

Daniel Romer
Patrick Jamieson

W hat role, if any, does perception that smoking is risky play in individuals' decisions to start, continue, and stop the behavior? In Chapter 3, we showed that young people do not have consistent views about the risks of smoking. They often underestimate the addictive properties of tobacco and fail to recognize that smoking causes more mortality than other risk behaviors, such as alcohol and drug consumption. In this chapter, we examine whether young people who do recognize the risks of smoking are less inclined to try smoking and to continue the behavior than those who do not appreciate the risks. We also extend our analysis to adults, whose greater experience of smoking may lead them to be more sensitive to its risks.

We explore the role of risk perception using two causal models, one for the initiation and progression to smoking and the other for intentions to quit (see Appendix C for a description of this methodology). In the initiation model (Figure 4.1), we assess the effects of a wide array of risk perceptions on smoking trial (ever having smoked a cigarette). The model also tests whether concerns about the short-term hazards of smoking (Immediate Harm) influence young people more than the longer-term risks emphasized in overall risk assessments (Risk).

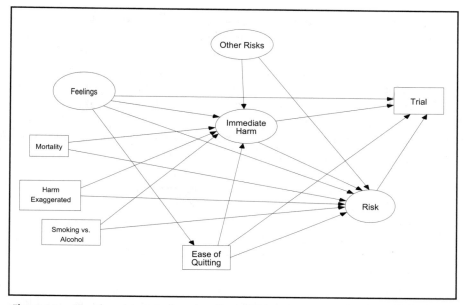

Figure 4.1. Causal model used to test the effects of risk perceptions on the initiation of smoking.

The initiation model also examines the potential effects of feelings about smoking. In Chapter 6 of this volume, Slovic discusses the importance of the affect heuristic in people's decisions about risky activities and suggests that it may play a role in smoking initiation. When people follow this heuristic, they may decide to try a risky behavior simply because their feelings about it are favorable. Furthermore, this heuristic may also lead people to underestimate the risk associated with a behavior. As a result, perceptions of smoking risk and decisions to start smoking may both be influenced by feelings associated with smoking. To control for this possibility, the model holds constant the effects of feelings as it tests for the role of risk perception in the initiation of smoking.

The initiation model also examines the effects of optimism about the ease of quitting smoking. In Chapter 10, we show that young people's optimism about the ease of quitting allows them to start smoking despite their awareness of the longer-term health risks. The initiation model allows us to ask whether this optimism influences smoking initiation apart from a wide array of beliefs related to the risk of engaging in the behavior.

Our analysis of the effects of perceived risk is based on the results of the second Annenberg Tobacco Survey. Survey 2 covered many of the same beliefs that were examined in Survey 1 (see Chapter 3) but also allowed us to assess the effects of feelings and perceptions of short-term risks of smoking. In addition, Survey 2 allowed us to study the risk perceptions of adults.

Nine of the risk measures in our analysis are shown in Table 4.1. The items are organized into six categories that resulted from a preliminary factor analysis. The first two factors were assumed to mediate people's perceptions of the more specific beliefs assessed by the remaining questions. We included two items referring to the overall risks of smoking so that both smokers and nonsmokers could report the risks they saw to themselves. We took from Slovic (1998, 2000a) two items referring more to concerns about the immediate harm of smoking. Three items that referred to other risk behaviors (marijuana use, alcohol use, and failure to use a seat belt in a car) were highly related, suggesting the presence of a general aversion to health risk behaviors. We used two items to assess Viscusi's measure of lung cancer risk perception (lung cancer mortality risk difference between smokers and nonsmokers). Another question asked whether respondents believed that the risks of smoking have been exaggerated, and we included a final item that allowed us to assess whether respondents knew that smoking results in more deaths than drinking or use of illegal drugs.

Feelings were assessed with two measures of anticipated reactions to smoking a cigarette: (a) how good or bad and (b) how relaxed or tense one would expect to feel. These items were highly correlated ($r = .54$) and strongly related to smoking initiation (see our analysis of advertising and smoker imagery in Chapter 7).

Our analysis of the effects of optimism (see Chapter 10) suggested the importance of asking smokers about their own ability to quit smoking rather than about the ability of a hypothetical smoker. In Survey 2, we asked about the perceived ease of quitting in a way we thought would personalize the question for smokers but still allow nonsmokers to answer: "If you were to smoke a pack of cigarettes a day, how difficult do you think it would be to quit?" Nevertheless, respondents' answers to this question were not as closely related to smokers' intentions to quit as were their answers when we asked them about their own ability to quit (see our analysis of Survey 1 in Chapter 10). However, we use responses to this question for all analyses in this chapter.

∽ Risk Perception and Smoking Initiation

We tested the model first with cigarette trial (any past experience of smoking) as the critical outcome and then repeated the analysis with progression to smoking as the dependent variable. The initiation model (Figure 4.2) fit the data well, yielding a comparative fit index (CFI) of .998 (Bentler, 1990). The weights next to each path represent standardized path coefficients (sp). As we found in other analyses

---

TABLE 4.1   Risk Measures by Factor

Overall risk of smoking
   A. In your opinion, is your smoking (if you were a smoker, would your smoking be) very risky for your health, somewhat risky, a little risky or not risky at all for your health?
   B. In your opinion, would your smoking every day be very risky for your health, somewhat risky, a little risky or not risky at all for your health?

Immediate harm of smoking
   Imagine someone who starts to smoke a pack of cigarettes a day at age 16.
   How much do you agree with the following statements about this person?
   A. There is usually no risk to the person at all for the first few years.
   B. Although smoking may eventually harm this person's health, there is really no harm to him or her from smoking the very next cigarette.

Risk of other behaviors
   If you _____, do you think it would be very risky for your health, somewhat risky, a little risky or not risky at all for your health?
   A. got drunk regularly
   B. smoked marijuana regularly
   C. never wore a seat belt when riding in a car

Mortality risk of smoking[a]
   A. Now I would like you to imagine 100 cigarette smokers, both men and women, who smoked cigarettes for their entire adult lives. How many of these 100 people do you think will die from lung cancer?
   B. I just asked you about smokers. Now I would like you to imagine 100 nonsmokers, both men and women, who never smoked and don't live with smokers. How many do you think will die from lung cancer?

Harm exaggerated
   The harmful effects of cigarettes have been exaggerated. Do you strongly agree, somewhat agree, somewhat disagree or strongly disagree?

Smoking versus alcohol and drugs
   Of all the deaths in one year to people of all ages, do you think more people die from smoking or abusing alcohol and drugs?

---

a. Perceived mortality risk was constructed as the difference between smoker and nonsmoker lung cancer mortality.

(see Chapter 7), feelings were strongly related to trial ($sp = .59, p < .001$). Feelings were also negatively related to overall risk perception ($sp = -.12, p < .01$). In addition, several risk-related beliefs (Mortality, Smoking versus Alcohol/Drugs, and Other Risks) influenced overall risk perception apart from their relation to feelings. Nevertheless, despite the addition of various alternative risk measures, overall risk perception was not related to cigarette trial ($sp = .03, p > .25$).

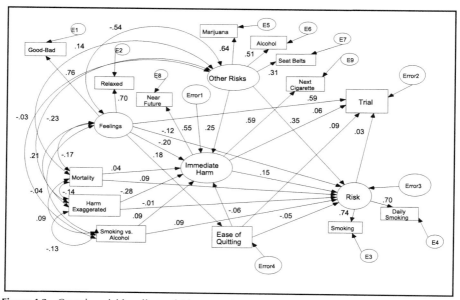

Figure 4.2. Causal model for effects of risk perception on cigarette trial. Weights next to paths represent standardized coefficients.

We tested the possibility that even if risk perceptions do not influence trial by affecting overall risk perception, they may do so by altering beliefs about the short-term harm of smoking (Immediate Harm). This factor did increase perceptions of overall risk (sp = .15, p < .02), and several risk beliefs were related to perception of immediate harm (Other Risk, Harm Exaggerated, and Smoking versus Alcohol/Drugs). Nevertheless, perceived immediate harm did not inhibit trial (sp = .06, p < .15). Perceived ease of quitting was related to trial (sp = .09, p < .001) apart from its relation to overall risk perception. Indeed, it is the only risk-related belief to predict trial in the model.

This model supports the central role of positive feelings in the determination of risk perception. Feelings were negatively related to overall risk even after various risk perceptions were controlled for (sp = –.12, p < .05). Positive feelings also reduced perceived risk by increasing belief in the ease of quitting (sp = .18, p < .01) and the belief that smoking poses little immediate harm (sp = –.20, p < .01). Nevertheless, none of the risk beliefs (with the exception of optimism about the ease of quitting) appeared to influence smoking initiation apart from its relation to feelings. This finding suggests that unless risk beliefs are related to feelings about smoking, young people disregard the risks of smoking when deciding to smoke their first cigarettes (see also Chapter 6). Some of their risk perceptions are unrealistically low (see Chapter 3), and many think that the risks have been exaggerated.

But whatever their level of risk perception, young people are driven primarily by their feelings about smoking in their decisions to try it.

That feelings play a central role is supported by our findings regarding the role of advertising in smoking initiation, which we discuss in Chapter 7 of this volume. There we note that although recent counteradvertising has influenced young people's perceptions of the risks of smoking, it has not affected their feelings about smoking and hence has not had much impact on rates of smoking initiation. In contrast, industry advertising for cigarettes introduces favorable images and feelings that promote the initiation of smoking.

∾ Risk Perception and Subsequent Smoking in Young People

Although risk perception is minimally related to smoking trial, it is possible that risk is a greater concern once young people have started smoking. To assess the effects of perceived risk once young smokers have started the habit, we developed a new model with progression toward a smoking habit as the ultimate outcome. At the low end of this outcome were those who never tried smoking (46%) followed by those who tried but did not continue (22%), those who smoke only occasionally (14%), those who currently smoke between 1 and 14 cigarettes a day (10%), and those who smoke 15 or more cigarettes a day (9%). To separate the effects of trial from current smoking levels, the model incorporated trial as a precursor to smoking progression. The trial model already established that risk perception does not predict trial. In this progression-to-smoking model, we were interested to see if risk perception influences smoking behavior following trial.

This model also differed from the initiation model in that it included the effects of addiction on subsequent perceptions of risk (Figure 4.3). In our analysis of the effects of addiction (see Chapter 10), we found that smokers who progress in their habits increasingly recognize their addiction to the behavior. This recognition increases their perception of risk and reduces their optimism about quitting. We included these feedback effects of addiction to account for the resulting positive relation that should occur between risk perception and smoking. Although we asked the addiction question only of current smokers, we coded all nonsmokers as not addicted.

The solution to this model in Figure 4.3 provided an adequate fit to the data (CFI = .992). The solution indicates that perception of overall risk did not influence the progression of the smoking habit ($sp = .00, p > .25$). Perceived addiction increased with the amount smoked ($sp = .72, p < .001$), and this influence directly

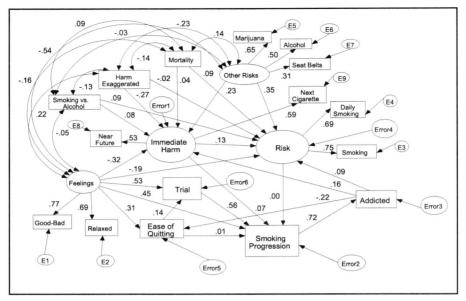

Figure 4.3.   Causal model for progression to smoking in 14- to 22-year-olds.

increased overall perceived risk ($sp = .09, p < .05$). The effect on perceptions of immediate harm was even stronger ($sp = .16, p < .001$). Although there was a small positive relation between perception of immediate harm and smoking ($sp = .07, p < .05$), this is probably a result of smoking rather than a cause of it. Our addiction measure may not be able to capture completely the feedback effects of smoking on risk perception.

There was also feedback from addiction to ease of quitting ($sp = −.22, p < .001$). As young smokers become addicted, they feel that it is less easy to quit. Although perceived ease of quitting is positively related to trial, the reduced optimism resulting from perceived addiction cannot decrease trial because smoking initiation has already occurred. Our analysis of optimism in Survey 1 (see Chapter 10) suggests that optimism about quitting should encourage less smoking. However, perceived ease of quitting was not related to the progression of smoking in Survey 2.

In summary, young people ages 14 to 22 are differentially sensitive to various risks related to smoking (e.g., mortality and smoking versus other risk behaviors). Furthermore, these risk perceptions influence their short-term and overall assessments of risk related to smoking even after their feelings toward smoking are controlled for. However, apart from their feelings toward smoking, there is no evidence that recognition of risks deters young people from trying smoking or progressing toward a smoking habit.

❧ Risk Perception Among Adults

Even though young people appear to disregard the risks of smoking, the same may not be true of adults. To examine the relation between risk perception and both trial and use in adults, we tested the same models with respondents ages 23 and older in Survey 2. The test of the initiation model produced results similar to our findings with 14- to 22-year-olds. This is not surprising, given that trial tends to occur during the adolescent years and therefore should not be determined differently for adults. However, the adult model for progression of smoking beyond trial did uncover evidence that perceived health risk is a deterrent to continued smoking (see Figure 4.4). Perception of overall risk reduces the amount smoked ($sp = -.15$, $p < .001$), although perception of immediate harm had little impact on either smoking or overall risk perception. There was evidence that addiction causes feedback to perceptions of overall risk ($sp = .11$, $p < .01$) and immediate harm ($sp = .10$, $p < .05$) and to the belief that quitting is easy ($sp = -.28$, $p < .001$). However, even after this influence is removed, perceived risk reduces the amount smoked.

In conclusion, young people in the 14-22 age range are not less likely to start or to continue to smoke even when they have a heightened perception of risk. Perceptions of health risks play a much bigger role for adults, who reduce their smoking as their perception of its risks increases. Those who choose never to smoke do so primarily because they have unfavorable feelings associated with the behavior. The one risk-related belief that can inhibit trial is the belief that quitting is difficult. Those who have this belief are less likely to start smoking. However, because of the catch-22 of smoking and quitting described in Chapter 10, there is a risk in encouraging people to believe that quitting is difficult, because for those who do start smoking, this belief ultimately inhibits the motivation to quit.

❧ Perceived Risk and Intentions to Quit Smoking

In this section we examine the role of risk perception in decisions to quit smoking. Up to this point, we have seen little evidence that risk influences young people's

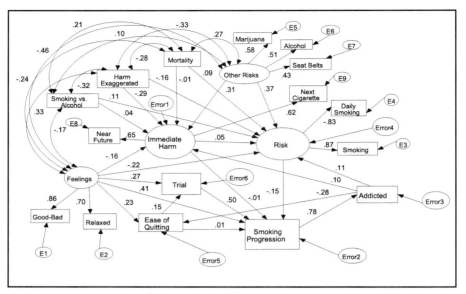

Figure 4.4. Causal model of effects of perceived risk on smoking progression in adults.

initiation or progression of smoking behavior. However, the results of both of the Annenberg surveys indicate that young smokers do consider quitting and that their intentions to do so increase the likelihood that they will quit (see Chapters 6 and 10). There are good reasons to expect risk perception to motivate decisions to quit. In Chapter 6, Slovic identifies a pattern of smoking initiation in which concerns about the risks matter less than the expected benefits of the experience. Although young people disregard the health risks when they take up smoking, they attend more and more to these risks after their smoking habit has developed.

If the benefits of smoking do not exceed the perceived risks, then young smokers should consider quitting, and they should be motivated to do so in proportion to the risks they perceive for the activity. Viscusi (1983; Viscusi & Magat, 1987) calls this phenomenon the "hazard-quitting relation." When people decide whether to undertake a potentially dangerous activity (such as a new job), they may accept the potential risks as a cost of learning more about the activity. However, after sufficient exposure to the activity, they may find that the benefits do not outweigh the risks. To the degree this is so, they are likely to express intentions to quit.

We found support for the hazard-quitting hypothesis for young smokers in Survey 1 (Romer & Jamieson, in press). As young persons' perceptions of risk increased, so did their plans to quit. Both subjective ratings of smoking risk and beliefs about the mortality effects of smoking predicted intention to quit. In the following sections, we examine the same relation with our expanded ability also to test the roles of feelings and addiction as potential deterrents to quitting.

∾ The Role of Danger to Others

In addition to the risk to the smoker, smoking endangers the health of those who are exposed to secondhand smoke. As Weinstein argues in Chapter 5 of this volume, smokers tend to be optimistic about their own risks from smoking. However, Jamieson (1999) has hypothesized that concern about risk to others (through secondhand smoke) may be a strong motivator for smokers to quit. People's disregard for risks to the self may be outweighed by their concern about risks to others. Young smokers may want to retain the right to decide whether to smoke or not, but their right to do so may be limited by the rights of others not to be exposed to the same hazard.

Two lines of research support this expectation. A phenomenon called the *third-person effect* suggests that people discount the personal effects of harmful environments while at the same time recognizing the risks to others. Research into third-person effects has focused on harmful media influences, such as libel (Cohen, Mutz, Price, & Gunther, 1988), pornography (Gunther, 1995), television news (Perloff, 1989), ads for products (Gunther & Thorson, 1992), negative political ads (Cohen & Davis, 1991), offensive print ads (Price, Tewksbury, & Huang, 1998), and televised programming (Lasorsa, 1989). In each of these instances, respondents have concluded that the harmful influences on others are greater than the influences on them. Consistent with this perception, people have also been found to be more willing to support restrictions on media that might harm others even though they deny that such content influences them (Gunther, 1995; McLeod, Eveland, & Nathanson, 1997; Price et al., 1998).

Explanations for the third-person effect focus on the desire to maintain control or self-esteem (Gunther, 1995). This explanation has also been proposed for the unrealistic optimism that Weinstein has found to characterize cigarette smokers, who tend to think they are less at risk than others for the adverse health outcomes of smoking (see Chapter 5). Perhaps the motivation to preserve the belief that one is better off than others may be used to encourage smokers to quit. If this is true, the motivation that may lead individuals to ignore or downplay their own risks of smoking may provide incentives for quitting. We tested this hypothesis by examining the effects on smokers of their knowledge that secondhand smoke is dangerous. Our findings suggest that this knowledge should motivate quitting even if smokers do not incorporate this risk into their judgments of personal risk.

ℂℂ Analysis of Intentions to Quit Smoking

Our analysis of risk and intentions to quit smoking focused on the 478 young people and 310 adults in Survey 2 who reported that they had smoked in the past 30 days. These respondents were also asked if they planned to quit smoking and, if so, whether they planned to do so within the next 6 months, between 6 months and a year from the time of the survey, or more than a year after that time. A single measure of quit intention was constructed from these answers. Those saying they would quit in the next 6 months were given the highest score (3), those saying they would quit in between 6 months and a year were given the next-highest score (2), and those saying they would not quit, would quit after the next year, or could not say when they were going to quit were given the lowest score (1).

The causal model in Figure 4.5 was designed to test the role of risk perception in decisions to quit. Both Immediate Harm and Risk were defined as in the earlier models of smoking initiation and progression (see Table 4.1 for the wording of these items). We assumed that smokers view the immediate effects of smoking differently from the overall effects, which include the long-term risks. Including both mediators in the model allows us to assess the sources of the risk that smokers consider when they make decisions about quitting.

The Immediate Harm and Risk factors were assumed to mediate the effects of various beliefs regarding the risks of smoking. These included the beliefs that smoking causes lung cancer mortality, that the harm of smoking has been exaggerated, that it is easy to quit, that secondhand smoke is harmful (Secondhand Smoke), and that the smoker may not live long enough to be concerned about the ill effects of smoking (Won't Live, asked only of respondents ages 14 to 22). A measure of concern about other risks (marijuana, alcohol, and nonuse of seat belts) was also included.

Three variables that might influence both risk perceptions and intentions to quit were included as predictors: how much the smoker felt addicted to tobacco (Addicted), how positive the smoker felt about smoking (Feelings), and how many times the smoker had tried to quit in the past (Number of Quit Attempts). The amount currently smoked should be negatively related to plans to quit but positively related to perceptions of addiction. Including these variables in the model should enable us to observe more clearly the direct effects of risk perception on plans to quit (see also Chapter 10 for a similar analysis).

The model for young smokers fits the data well (Figure 4.6). Nearly all of the goodness-of-fit variation is predicted by the model (CFI = .998). The model indicates that overall risk perception increases the intention to quit ($sp = .16$, $p < .05$),

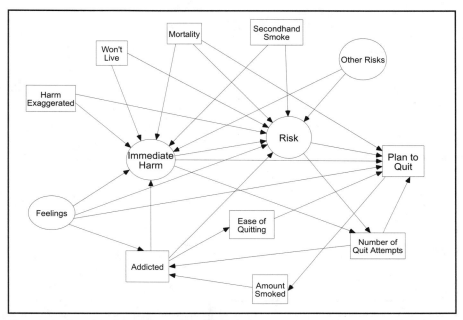

Figure 4.5. Causal model used to test the effects of risk perceptions on intentions to quit smoking.

which reduces smoking levels ($sp = -.10$, $p < .05$). Although the risk of immediate harm from smoking was related to overall risk ($sp = .24$, $p < .05$), it did not directly influence quit intention. Feelings are related to both risk perception factors, just as in the initiation and progression models tested earlier. Feelings were also directly related to plans to quit ($sp = -.20$, $p < .05$). The more favorable the smoker felt about smoking, the less he or she wanted to quit. However, feelings did not account for the influence of risk on smoking behavior as in our models for trial and subsequent smoking behavior.

Smokers who reported that they were addicted perceived greater overall risk ($sp = .15$, $p < .05$), an influence that increased their plans to quit. This finding is encouraging because it suggests that perceived addiction can help to motivate quitting. However, addicted smokers are likely to have relatively more favorable feelings toward smoking ($sp = .15$, $p < .05$), and this relation will impede their efforts to quit. In addition, addicted smokers are less likely to be optimistic about their success at quitting ($sp = -.20$, $p < .001$). Although our measure of perceived ease of quitting was not strongly related to intentions to quit in Survey 2 ($sp = .05$, $p > .25$), this influence of addiction will reduce intentions to quit and impede subsequent efforts to do so. Our analysis of this variable with data from Survey 1 (see Chapter 10) showed that a rating of the smoker's personal ability to quit ("If you were to

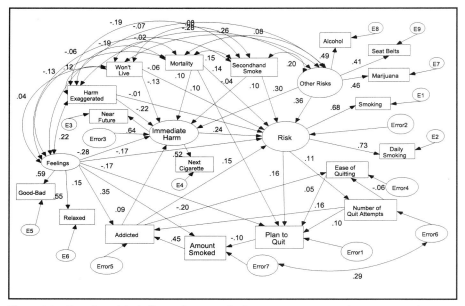

Figure 4.6. Causal model of effects of perceived risk on intentions to quit for young people ages 14 to 22.

quit, how difficult would it be for you do it?") was more closely related to intentions than was a projection for a hypothetical smoker ("If you smoked a pack of cigarettes a day, how difficult would it be for you to quit smoking?"). Unfortunately, Survey 2 did not include the same measure of ease of quitting that was used in Survey 1.

Overall perceptions of risk also motivated attempts to quit ($sp = .11$, $p < .05$), and young smokers who had tried to quit also had stronger intentions to quit in the future ($sp = .10$, $p < .05$). However, previous attempts to quit increased perceived addiction ($sp = .16$, $p < .01$), which had mixed influences on intentions. Heavier smokers were also more likely to report having tried to quit in the past, a relation that is represented by the correlation between the errors in the two variables ($sp = .29$, $p < .01$). This relation may reflect the fact that heavier smokers have had more opportunities to quit.

A large proportion of young smokers (18%) agreed that they might not live long enough for the effects of smoking to harm them. This belief reduced the perceived immediate harm of smoking ($sp = -.13$, $p < .05$). It did not affect overall risk directly ($sp = -.06$, $p > .25$). Nevertheless, this form of extreme pessimism is clearly not functional for young people, and the finding suggests that smoking cessation programs that focus on the risks of smoking may reach the limits of their effectiveness when confronted with persons who are this fatalistic about their futures.

The belief that smoking causes lung cancer mortality did increase the perceived overall risk of smoking ($sp = .14, p < .05$). It was not related to the immediate danger of smoking ($sp = .10, p > .15$), but it did increase intentions to quit apart from perceived risk ($sp = .10, p < .05$). This replicates our findings in Survey 1 (Romer & Jamieson, in press). This direct relation suggests that smokers do not fully incorporate their awareness of mortality attributable to smoking in their overall assessments of smoking risk. If they did, then their belief about mortality risk would be completely explained by one or both of the risk mediators.

We hypothesized that the belief that secondhand smoke poses harm to others should motivate quitting even among those who deny the risks to themselves (Jamieson, 1999). Knowledge about the danger of secondhand smoke is related to overall perceived risk ($sp = .10, p < .10$), and therefore intentions to quit. However, we did not find that secondhand smoke motivated quitting apart from perceived health risk. In an analysis of Survey 1, Glantz and Jamieson (2000) also found support for the relation between knowledge of secondhand smoke and intention to quit. This suggests that young smokers do recognize this hazard when evaluating the risk of smoking and are motivated to quit based on it, just as they are by beliefs about the risks of smoking to the self. Apparently, harm to others from secondhand smoke operates just as harm to the self does when young smokers consider the risks of smoking, and they disregard this harm to others just as much as they disregard the harm to themselves when initiating the smoking habit. However, the risks to others become more salient as young smokers consider the wisdom of continuing their smoking habits.

The belief that other behaviors, such as using marijuana and alcohol, are a risk to health also increases both forms of risk related to smoking. This finding may reflect personality differences in tolerance of risk. Holding it constant in the model suggests that the other risk beliefs are separable from this personality difference and are likely to be susceptible to influence through information campaigns. For example, those smokers who think that the harm of smoking has been exaggerated are likely to discount the immediate dangers of smoking ($sp = -.22, p < .01$). Information to the contrary may convince such smokers that the risks are real and should be taken seriously.

⬿ Predictors of Quitting in Adults

We tested the same model among adult smokers (see Figure 4.7). This model also fit the data well (CFI = .997). One significant difference between the adults and young people in our sample was the type of risk that motivated plans to quit.

Compared with the young people, the adults were much more concerned about the immediate harmful effects of smoking on their health ($sp = .27$, $p < .001$). Indeed, overall risk assessments did not directly influence intention to quit ($sp = .04$, $p > .25$). However, overall risk perceptions did influence quit attempts ($sp = .32$, $p < .001$), which motivated plans to quit ($sp = .17$, $p < .01$). The number of quit attempts and amount currently smoked were correlated in adults ($r = .13$, $p < .05$). However, plans to quit were only marginally related to current smoking levels ($sp = -.06$, $p > .25$).

Perceived addiction has effects for adults that are similar to those for young people, increasing perceived risk and reducing optimism about quitting. Number of quit attempts also increases perceived addiction. However, as their failures to quit built up, the adult smokers in Survey 2 became much less optimistic about their chances of quitting than did younger smokers: $sp = -.21$ ($p < .001$) versus $-.06$ ($p > .15$). This finding suggests that maintaining optimism that one can quit is a more serious obstacle for mature smokers who have not already quit the habit.

Unlike what we found with young people, feelings were not as strong determinants of immediate or overall risk assessment in adults. Neither path from feelings to these risk assessments is significant in the model ($sps = -.15$ and $-.08$, $ps > .15$). Although feelings were still inhibitors of plans to quit smoking ($sp = -.15$, $p < .05$), it appears that feelings posed less of a barrier to acting on risk perceptions in adults.

Belief in the long-term mortality effects of smoking directly affected intentions to quit in adults as well as young people ($sp = .18$, $p < .01$). However, mortality beliefs did not influence overall risk perceptions ($sp = .03$, $p > .25$), and they were slightly negatively related to the perceptions of immediate harm ($sp = -.15$, $p < .05$). However, this indirect influence on plans to quit was much weaker than the direct one ($-.04$ versus $.18$). Hence the overall effect of beliefs about mortality was to increase intentions to quit.

The belief that the harm of smoking has been exaggerated reduced both risk mediators and, as a result, inhibited the formation of intentions to quit. Concern about other risks (marijuana, alcohol, and nonuse of seat belts) was also a strong influence on both risk mediators and therefore motivated quitting. As with young people, this influence likely reflects sensitivity to health risks in general.

Finally, knowledge that secondhand smoke is dangerous was a strong determinant of overall smoking risk perception ($sp = .19$, $p < .01$). However, this mediator was not as strongly related to intentions to quit as were the immediate dangers of smoking. It appears that for adults, the danger of secondhand smoke is more strongly related to beliefs about lung cancer mortality ($r = .32$ versus $.15$) than it is for young people. In addition, concerns about other risks (marijuana, alcohol, and nonuse of seat belts) were more closely linked with concerns about secondhand smoke in adults than in young people ($r = .39$ versus $.20$). These findings suggest

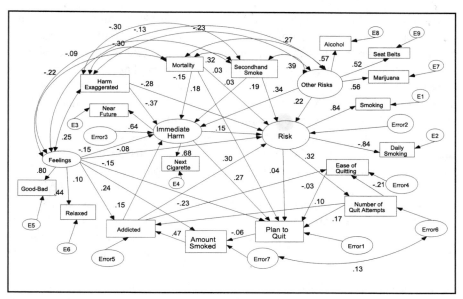

Figure 4.7. Causal model of effects of perceived risk on intentions to quit smoking in adults.

that concern about secondhand smoke is a significant motivator for quitting in adults, but its effect on quitting is closely linked with other perceptions of risk that are more strongly associated with quitting.

᧒ Summary and Conclusions

The analyses presented in this chapter show that risk perception plays a much stronger role in decisions to stop smoking than in decisions to start. Although young people do not appear to take account of the health risks of smoking when initiating the behavior, they appear more sensitive to these risks after they have developed their smoking habits. Indeed, their intentions to quit are directly influenced by perceived risk, including the risks of long-term disease. This pattern of findings supports the hypothesis of a hazard-quitting relation to potentially dangerous activities. As Viscusi (1983; Viscusi & Magat, 1987) has noted, people may experiment with such activities as a way to learn more about their risks and benefits. Unfortunately for those experimenting with smoking, the resulting addiction may make it difficult to withdraw from the activity.

Adults also exhibit a hazard-quitting relation to smoking, but for them the relation is more focused on the immediate risks. We found that adult assessments of overall risks did not influence intentions to quit as strongly as did perceptions of the immediate dangers. Adult preoccupation with immediate risks suggests that the hazards of smoking become more pressing as smokers age. Older smokers also appear more sensitive to beliefs about risk, and they are less inclined than younger smokers to base risk assessments on their feelings. Messages that focus on both the long-term and the short-term risks of smoking should be effective in motivating adults to quit. Ironically, messages that focus on long-term health risks may be more effective in motivating young people to quit.

Like young people, adults are concerned about the long-term mortality effects of smoking, and these concerns influence their intentions to quit. However, concerns about these risks are not fully incorporated into either young or adult smokers' assessments of overall health risks. We do not know whether smokers ignore them when assessing the risks of smoking or simply regard them as a different form of risk.

Concerns about the risks of secondhand smoke clearly influence the decisions about quitting made by both young people and adults. Jamieson (1999) hypothesized that concerns about secondhand smoke should motivate quitting even if smokers discount the risks of smoking to themselves. However, we found that, for the young people in our sample, the influence of secondhand smoke was completely mediated by concerns about the personal risks of smoking. This suggests that young people disregard this hazard just as they disregard risk to themselves when they begin smoking. However, concerns about this risk do surface when young people consider the decision to quit.

Adults' knowledge of the risk of secondhand smoke also influences their intentions to quit, but this knowledge appears to be more closely linked with mortality risks of smoking and concerns about other risk behaviors. For adults, the hazards of secondhand smoke become part of an entire constellation of concerns about smoking. As a result, secondhand smoke loses its uniqueness as a motivator for quitting. Nevertheless, it remains a powerful force in adults' decisions to quit.

Although we expected optimism about quitting to motivate intentions to quit, we did not observe this relation in Survey 2. Perceived ease of quitting was only somewhat positively related to quit intention for young people. It was slightly negatively related to quit intention in adults. Nevertheless, considerable research suggests that personal efficacy for quitting is a predictor of actual quitting (Borland, Owen, Hill, & Schofield, 1991; Norman, Conner, & Bell, 1999; Sargent, Mott, & Stevens, 1998), and we found evidence for this relation when we analyzed the results of Survey 1 (see Chapter 10).

⟆ Chapter 5

Smokers' Recognition of Their Vulnerability to Harm

Neil D. Weinstein

S everal authors have suggested that smokers overestimate the health risks of smoking (Kristiansen, Harding, & Eiser, 1983; Sutton, 1995a; Viscusi, 1990, 1992b). These results challenge the belief that people begin to smoke and continue to smoke in large part because they fail to appreciate the risks. Other researchers, using somewhat different questions to assess risk perceptions, have concluded that smokers either accurately estimate or underestimate the risks of smoking (Schoenbaum, 1997; Sutton, 1998).

If smokers do not recognize their vulnerability, continuing attention to this topic in antismoking programs is certainly indicated. However, if smokers overestimate their risks, one might conclude that in the interests of accuracy, attempts should be made to lower their risk perceptions. Viscusi (1992b), for example, suggests that further campaigns to convince adolescents of the risks of tobacco use are not needed.

The studies that have compared objective and perceived risks have generally been very careful about the values they have used for the former (e.g.,

AUTHOR'S NOTE: This chapter is a revision and update of an article that first appeared under the title "Accuracy of Smokers' Risk Perceptions" in the *Annals of Behavioral Medicine*, volume 20, pages 135-140, 1998. Used with permission.

Schoenbaum, 1997), but most have paid much less attention to the procedures used to assess smokers' perceptions. Often it has simply been assumed that when smokers are asked to state the percentage chance that they will contract a smoking-related illness, to estimate how many smokers out of 1,000 will develop lung cancer, to rate (on a scale of 0 to 10) the likelihood that they will live to age 75, or to generate other smoking statistics, the answers they give are meaningful to them. (For a more skeptical view, see Borland, 1997.) A further implicit assumption has been that if the estimates of risk produced by surveyed smokers agree with the epidemiological data, the smokers' understanding of their risks is adequate.

The preceding are highly questionable assumptions. Before reaching any decisions about the need to change antismoking campaigns, we should look more carefully at what it means to comprehend and accept a risk. It is the thesis of this chapter that comparing numerical risk estimates with objective statistics is not sufficient to determine whether or not smokers fully recognize the personal consequences of smoking.

⚬⚬ Problems With Reliance on Numerical Risk Estimates

A variety of studies have shown that numerical risk estimates provided by survey respondents often say little about those individuals' reactions to risk in real-life settings. Shiloh and Saxe (1989), for example, found no correlation between the probabilities provided to couples during genetic counseling and the decisions they then made about childbearing. Windschitl and Wells (1996) found that individuals' judgments of likelihood made on a scale of verbal categories predicted their subsequent actions better than did their numerical likelihood estimates.

A number of researchers have discussed the difficulties that laypersons have in generating risk estimates in terms of percentages (Black, Nease, & Tosteson, 1995; Diefenbach, Weinstein, & O'Reilly, 1993). In fact, a surprisingly large proportion of survey respondents have been found to select "50%" (Sutton, 1995a) or "50 out of 100" (Viscusi, 1992b) for their estimate of the risk of smoking. Do they really mean that the risk is exactly 50%, or do they mean to say that the outcome might or might not happen? Research suggests that many of such estimates ought to be interpreted as "don't know" responses (Bruine de Bruin, Fischhoff, Halpern-Felsher, & Millstein, 2000; Fischhoff & Bruine de Bruin, 1999).

Further demonstrating the public's difficulties with numerical risk information, Black et al. (1995) used a scale to measure differences in "numeracy" among individuals. They found that 38% of their generally well-educated sample (62%

college graduates) made such basic errors as giving a higher estimate for the like-lihood of breast cancer in the next 10 years than for the likelihood in the next 20 years and giving a higher estimate for the likelihood of dying of breast cancer than for the likelihood of developing breast cancer.

Others have reported enormous differences in how people interpret the odds associated with small probabilities (such as 1 in 1,000). Some people focus on the large denominator and are reassured, whereas others focus on the single victim and become more concerned than ever (Lippman-Hand & Fraser, 1979; Slovic, Monahan, & MacGregor, 2000). Many studies show that perceptions of risk are affected by factors other than the likelihood of harm (Slovic, 1987). For example, Sandman, Weinstein, and Miller (1994) demonstrated that by modifying the range covered by a "risk ladder," one can alter risk perceptions. A home pollution test with a stated risk of 1 in 100 that appeared one-fourth of the way up a risk lad-der was viewed as less serious than when the same risk—with the same odds—appeared three-fourths of the way up a different risk ladder.

Finally, questions about smoking risk usually refer to "smokers in general" or to the "average smoker" (Kristiansen et al., 1983; Viscusi, 1990). Individuals in these surveys are not being asked about their own risk, even though people usu-ally distinguish between their own risk and the risk of others. For most hazards, judgments of the difference between our own risk and others' risks are character-ized by "optimistic bias" or "unrealistic optimism" (Weinstein, 1987, 1998b). Re-gardless of whether respondents tend to overestimate or underestimate the risk for people in general, they tend to believe that their own personal risk is less than their peers' risk.

Taken together, the available evidence demonstrates that people in general have great difficulty using the odds and percentages that form the scientist's risk language. The ability to cite a statistic accurately does not mean that those who do so understand what the number really means, that they actually use this number in making decisions, or that they think the number applies to their own situations. This conclusion should not be surprising. Hardly ever do individuals receive, gen-erate, or make choices on the basis of numerical probability data.

∾ Evaluating Smokers' Risk Perceptions

There are clearly many different aspects to the hazards posed by smoking. To de-termine whether or not people adequately understand these risks, one should, at a minimum, examine their knowledge of the kinds and severity of the illnesses caused by smoking, of the probability that smokers will experience these ill effects, of the ways in which their own personal risks may differ from those of the average smoker, and of the difficulty of quitting after one has started smoking (Weinstein, 1999). However, most research has focused on only two of these four major topics: the perceived likelihood of harm for smokers in general and for the individual respondent as a smoker. Thus I limit the present review mainly to perceptions of illness probability, including also the small number of studies that have examined beliefs about risk factors for experiencing this harm.

Even the limited topic of risk likelihood is complex. In fact, we know little about how people normally process and remember information about the probability of harm. Are they more at ease thinking about the absolute magnitude of a risk, or do they prefer to think in terms of risk comparisons (i.e., which risks are bigger or smaller than others)? Do people attend to absolute risks at all, or do they care more whether their own risks are higher or lower than those of their peers? Given that people in general have difficulty with numerical probabilities, do they use some kind of verbal or nonverbal category system for risk? Do they experience probability and risk primarily as affective or emotional feelings (see Slovic, Chapter 6, this volume)? Do different people use different kinds of cognitive structures to understand their vulnerability? Given this uncertainty in how people actually think about risk, the elicitation of numerical risk estimates, although one way to gauge the public's recognition of smoking risks, is clearly insufficient.

The number of different types of risk judgments one could elicit is enormous. Respondents could be asked about the likelihood of smoking-related illness in general, about broad disease categories (such as cancer or cardiovascular disease), or about specific illnesses (such as lung cancer or stroke). Judgments could refer to the likelihood of an event (absolute risk) or to the relative likelihood of one group compared with another (comparative risk), and responses could be made on numerical or verbal scales. Questions could ask about the individual respondent, the respondent if he or she smoked (or did not smoke), nonsmokers in general, smokers in general, or people smoking specific numbers of cigarettes per day. It is obvious that combinations of these elements will lead to huge numbers of different risk judgments. Nevertheless, using a variety of measures will clearly provide a much better assessment of risk understanding and acceptance than could any single measurement strategy.

In the remainder of this chapter, I will review the available research literature to arrive at an appraisal of the extent to which smokers acknowledge their vulnerability to the health effects of smoking. I will not summarize the literature according to the specific judgments made, but according to the conclusions that can be drawn from these judgments. First, Table 5.1 displays a few examples of studies that compared numerical estimates of absolute risk with objective statistics. Examination of these data can reveal whether the respondents in these studies un-

TABLE 5.1   Examples of Smokers' Quantitative Risk Assessments

Study	Conclusion	Risk Variable and Scale
Borland (1997)	O, U	"Proportion of smokers [who] die from causes that are directly related to their smoking" (7-point scales: unequal intervals, fractions) tended to yield underestimates of risk. "If you continue to smoke, what . . . is the percentage chance that smoking will cause you a fatal illness?" (11-point scale: percentages) tended to yield overestimates. Took a value between 1 in 4 and 1 in 3 as the accepted correct figure at the time of the surveys (1989-1992) and a value of about 1 in 2 as correct at the time of writing (1995).
Kristiansen et al. (1983)	O, U	Given that a person died of lung cancer, "how likely . . . it is that [the person] was a smoker" (underestimated). Given that a person is a smoker/nonsmoker, "how likely . . . it is that [the person] will die of lung cancer" (overestimated) (scale: 0 = not at all likely to 100 = extremely likely). Used 90% as the true probability of smoking given lung cancer, and 22.5%/1.7% as the probability of lung cancer given smoking/not smoking.
Schoenbaum (1997)	A, U	"Chances that you will live to be 75 or more?" (11-point scale: 0 = no chance at all to 10 = absolutely certain). Light smokers approximately correct; heavy smokers overestimated survival. Used 59.4% and 74.7% as the correct values of male and female light smokers, respectively, and used 26.3% and 30.8% as the corresponding figures for heavy smokers.
Sutton (1995a)	O	"Your own chances of getting lung cancer/heart disease?" (scale: 0% to 100%). No specific value cited as correct.
Sutton (1998)	U	"Out of 1000 20-year-olds . . . who smoke . . . regularly . . . , how many . . . will be killed by smoking before the age of 70?" (scale: 0 to 1,000). Accepted "about 250" in 1,000 as proportion that will be killed by smoking before age 70.
Viscusi (1990)	O	"Among 100 cigarette smokers, how many . . . will get lung cancer because they smoke?" (scale: 0 to 100). Accepted 5-10% as the true risk.

NOTE: A = accuracy; O = overestimation of risk; U = underestimation of risk.

derestimated, accurately estimated, or overestimated risks. Next, Table 5.2 displays studies in which responses of smokers were considered to see if they

TABLE 5.2   Smokers' Acknowledgment of Increased Risk

Study	Risk Variable and Scale
Boney-McCoy et al. (1992)	"Assume that you are/are not currently a smoker: If you were to continue smoking . . . what . . . are the chances that you would develop heart disease/lung cancer/emphysema?" (scale: 0% to 100%). Smokers gave higher risk estimates for self as smoker than for self as nonsmoker.
Chapman et al. (1993)	Asked if smokers were more likely than nonsmokers to develop heart disease/poor circulation/bronchitis/stroke/lung cancer (yes or no). Approximately 50% of smokers agreed that smoking can cause the first four illnesses; 72% agreed that smoking can cause lung cancer.
Cohn et al. (1995)	"Compared to other boys/girls your age, how likely are you to get hooked on cigarettes/get cancer in later life?" (5-point scale: –2 = much less likely to to +2 = much more likely). Smokers rated their relative risk to be higher than did nonsmokers and ex-smokers. Adolescent sample and parent sample.
Eiser et al. (1995)	Gave a risk score indicating the chance of getting cancer (continuous scale without upper limit: 0 = absolutely impossible, 100 = the average level of risk for a typical 35-year-old man living in this country with no previous history of serious illness). Smokers gave higher estimates of their own risk than did nonsmokers.
Gerrard et al. (1996)	"How likely is it that you will have a smoking-related illness (for example, lung cancer)?" and "Compared to others your age, how likely is it that you will have a smoking-related illness?" (7-point scale: 1 = not at all to 7 = very much). Adolescents who began smoking during the study increased their ratings of their risk.
Grant & Job (2000)	Asked respondents to estimate the likelihood of experiencing lung cancer/heart disease/lung disease other than cancer/respiratory infections/stroke (continuous scale: 0% = the event will never happen to 100% = the event is certain to happen). Smokers rated their risk higher than did nonsmokers and ex-smokers.
Hahn et al. (1998)	"Compared to other people—the same sex and age as you— . . . chances of developing lung cancer/smoking cough?" (7-point scale: –3 = much below average to +3 = much above average). Smokers rated their risk as higher than did nonsmokers and ex-smokers. Among long-term smokers, personal risk ratings increased with cigarette consumption.
Hansen & Malotte (1986)	Rated risk for themselves/regular, 10-20 cigarettes a day smoker/themselves as 10-20 cigarettes a day smoker of getting lung cancer/heart disease/carbon monoxide in the blood/being too out of breath to run hard (11-point scale: 0 in 10 to 10 in 10). Smokers' ratings of own risk were higher than nonsmokers' ratings of own risk. Adolescent sample.

Lee (1989)	Asked respondents to "think about what is likely to happen to yourself/average Australian smoker" and give chance of developing lung cancer/heart disease/chronic lung disease other than cancer (scale: 0% = no chance to 100% = certain to happen). Smokers' ratings of own risk were higher than nonsmokers' ratings of own risk.
McKenna et al. (1993)	Rated the likelihood of heart disease/lung cancer/bronchitis/stroke for themselves/average smoker/average nonsmoker (scale: 0% = never to 100% = certain). Smokers' ratings of own risk were higher than nonsmokers' ratings of own risk.
Milam et al. (2000)	High school students rated the likelihood of experiencing trouble catching your breath/irregular heartbeat/wrinkles on your face/chronic cough in the next 15 years for themselves and for a fellow student of the same age and gender (5-point scale: 1 = not at all likely to 5 = very likely). Compared to their ratings of a fellow student, smokers rated their risk higher than did nonsmokers on all four items.
Reppucci et al. (1991)	Rated the likelihood of their getting lung cancer compared to other students in their school (7-point scale: –3 = much below average to +3 = much above average). Smokers rated their relative risk as higher than did nonsmokers. Adolescent samples.
Strecher et al. (1995)	"Compared to others your same age and sex, how would you rate your risk of . . . heart attack/cancer/stroke?" (7-point scale: –3 = much below average to +3 = much above average). Smokers rated their risk as above average more often than did nonsmokers or ex-smokers.

acknowledged that there is *any* risk to smoking. For example, smokers might have been asked to evaluate the lung cancer risks of smokers and nonsmokers, and a comparison of these two judgments shows whether the smokers acknowledged an impact of smoking on lung cancer.

Table 5.3 lists studies in which the judgments of smokers and nonsmokers were compared to see if these groups see equal amounts of risk. For instance, both groups might have been asked to rate how risky it is to smoke a pack of cigarettes a day. Finally, Table 5.4 brings together a variety of studies that investigated, without relying on numerical estimates of epidemiological statistics, whether smokers fully recognize the *magnitude* of the risk. Some of theses studies examined whether smokers tend to deny that smoking risks apply as much to themselves as they do to other smokers. Other studies reported the proportion of smoker respondents who claimed their own risk of cancer is the same as or even lower than that of the average person, or the proportion of smokers who asserted that a smoker's risk of heart disease risk is only "slightly" greater than that of nonsmokers.

TABLE 5.3   Differences Between Smokers' and Nonsmokers' Views of the Risks of Smoking

Study	Conclusion	Risk Variable and Scale
Benthin et al. (1993)	M	"If you/some other person your age engaged in this activity [smoking cigarettes]," what would be the "risk of . . . getting sick?" (7-point scale: 1 = very much at risk to 7 = not at all at risk). Smokers rated the risk of smoking to themselves or to others if they smoked as lower than did nonsmokers. Adolescent sample.
Boney-McCoy et al. (1992)	M	Rating self as smoker, smokers rated their risk lower than did former and nonsmokers.
Boyle (1968)	M	Asked respondents if they thought smoking can cause lung cancer/bronchitis/heart attack/stroke (yes or no). Smokers were less likely than nonsmokers to agree that smoking can cause lung cancer. No differences on other items. Adolescent sample.
Chapman et al. (1993)	M	Smokers were less likely than ex-smokers to agree that smoking increases the risks of five illnesses.
	M	Asked respondents if they agree with 14 risk-minimizing statements (e.g., "Most lung cancer is caused by air pollution"; "It's safe to smoke low tar cigarettes") (5-point scale: 1 = strongly agree to 5 = strongly disagree). Smokers were significantly more likely than ex-smokers to agree with 11 of 14 minimizing statements.
Eiser et al. (1979)	M	Fewer smokers than nonsmokers believed that smoking is "really as dangerous as people say" (yes or no).
Eiser et al. (1995)	M	Smokers judged the increase in cancer risk of target people who smoked over that of target people who did not smoke to be smaller than did nonsmokers.
Grant & Job (2000)	M	Smokers gave lower ratings for the likelihood of illnesses occurring to the average student who smokes than did nonsmokers and ex-smokers.
Greening & Dollinger (1991)	NM	Rated the likelihood that "someone like yourself" would die from cancer/stroke/emphysema (7-point quasi-logarithmic scale: 0 = impossible to 6 = quite likely). Smokers rated risk of smoking "for someone like yourself" the same as did nonsmokers. Adolescent sample.
Hansen & Malotte (1986)	M	Smokers rated the risk for themselves as regular smokers and for target regular smoker as lower than did nonsmokers.
Kristiansen et al. (1983)	NM	Smoking status did not affect estimates of the probability that a smoker will die from lung cancer or the probability that someone dying from lung cancer was a smoker.

Lee (1989)	M	Smokers' ratings of the average smoker's risk were lower than nonsmokers' ratings of this risk.
LoConte (1995)	M	Smokers were more likely than nonsmokers to agree with a wide range of risk-minimizing statements (5-point scale: 1 = strongly disagree to 5 = strongly agree).
Reppucci et al. (1991)	NM	"Does smoking increase or decrease the likelihood of getting lung cancer/emphysema/heart disease?" (7-point scale). Smokers rated the effects of smoking about the same as did nonsmokers. Adolescent sample.
Resnicow et al. (1999)	M	Asked high school seniors how much people risk harming themselves by using cigarettes (4-point scale). Heavy smokers rated the risk as lower than occasional smokers, who rated the risk as lower than nonsmokers.
Romer & Jamieson (Annenberg Survey 1)	M	Is smoking "risky for your personal health?" (4-point scale). Smokers rated the risk of smoking to be smaller than did nonsmokers. Adolescent sample.
Slovic (2000a)	M	Agreement with statements about the risk of smoking (e.g., "There is really no risk at all for the first few years") (4-point scale: 1 = strongly disagree to 4 = strongly agree). Smokers were less likely than nonsmokers to agree that short-term smoking is harmful. (Nearly all agreed that smoking a pack a day is eventually harmful.) Adolescent sample.
Sutton (1998)	NM	Smokers, ex-smokers, and nonsmokers gave equal estimates for the number of smokers who die before age 70 from smoking.
Viscusi (1992b, pp. 77-80)	M	"Among 100 cigarette smokers, how many . . . will die from lung cancer . . . and all other illnesses because they smoke?" Smokers gave lower estimates than did nonsmokers.
	M	"The average life expectancy for a 21-year-old male (female) is that he (she) would live for another 53 (59) years. What . . . is the life expectancy for the average male (female) smoker?" Smokers' life expectancy estimates were greater than those of nonsmokers.
Viscusi (1991a)	M	Smokers gave lower estimates of the lung cancer risk than did nonsmokers.

NOTE: M = risk-minimizing finding; NM = not risk-minimizing finding.

The tables in this chapter indicate the wordings of the questions used in the investigations (when given) as well as the types of response scales employed and the numbers of response choices offered. Once question wording and response scale information for a particular study has been given in a table, it is not repeated

TABLE 5.4   Smokers' Ratings of Their Relative Risk and Risk Factors

Study	Conclusion	Risk Variable and Scale
Annenberg Survey 2	NM	"Compared to the average smoker, do you think you are more likely to get sick from smoking, less likely to get sick from smoking, or that your chance of getting sick from smoking is about the same as the average smoker?" Almost as many smokers said they were more likely (20%) as said they were less likely (22%).
	M	"Compared to the average smoker, do you smoke more cigarettes/do you smoke cigarettes with higher tar and nicotine levels/inhale more/could you quit more easily/are you more addicted/is your lifestyle more healthy/are you more influenced by cigarette ads?" (responses: more, less, or about the same). On all seven issues, smokers judged themselves lower in risk than the average smoker.
Ayanian & Cleary (1999)	M	"Do you think your risk of heart disease/cancer is higher, lower, or about the same as other men/women your age?" Of current smokers, 71% considered their heart disease risk to be average or below average; 60% considered their cancer risk to be average or below average. Among those smoking 40 or more cigarettes a day, the corresponding figures were 61% and 51%, respectively.
Benthin et al. (1993)	NM	Smokers rated their risk from smoking the same as they rated the risk from smoking to some other person their age.[a]
Boney-McCoy et al. (1992)	M	Smokers gave slightly lower risk ratings for self as smoker (assuming they continued to smoke) than they gave for the typical smoker.
Cohn et al. (1995)	M	Adolescent smokers rated their risk of developing cancer to be about the same as the risk of the average person their age.
Grant & Job (2000)	M	Smokers rated their own risk lower than they rated the risk of the average smoker.
Hahn et al. (1998)	M	Smokers rated their own risk the same as the risk of others their age.
	M	Among short-term smokers, there was no relationship between cigarette consumption and estimates of personal risk.
Hansen & Malotte (1986)	M	Adolescent smokers rated hypothetical self as regular smoker lower in risk than target smoker even though the two were said to have the same amount and duration of smoking.
	M	Smokers rated their own risk as lower than self as regular smoker.
Lee (1989)	M	Smokers rated their own risks as lower than the risk of the average smoker.

Leventhal et al. (1987)	M	Asked respondents, if they smoked, "Would [you] be less likely, about as likely, or more likely to get sick from smoking than other people?" Of smokers, 47% said they would be less likely to get sick. Adolescent sample.
LoConte (1995)	NM	"Compared to the average smoker, what are your chances of experiencing lung cancer/heart disease/ stroke/throat cancer/hypertension?" (7-point scale: 1 = much less to 7 = much greater). College student smokers rated their risks about the same as the average smoker.
McKenna et al. (1993)	M	Smokers rated their own risk lower than they rated the average smoker's risk.
Milam et al. (2000)	M	Smokers rated their own risk lower than they rated the risk for a fellow student at their school.
Reppucci et al. (1991)	M	Smokers rated their risk of lung cancer as only slightly above average of their classmates.
	M	Smokers rated their risk of heart disease and emphysema as no different from the average risk of their classmates.
Segerstrom et al. (1993)	M	Among smokers, 53% claimed that the tar content of their cigarettes is lower than that of most cigarettes, compared to 17% who said the tar of their brand is higher; 48% of smokers claimed that their brand is less hazardous than others, compared to 17% who said their brand is more hazardous.
Strecher et al. (1995)	M	As many smokers rated their risk of smoking-related diseases to be below average as above average.
Sutton (1995a)	M	"Compared with the average . . . smoker/nonsmoker . . . your own chances of getting lung cancer/heart disease?" (7-point scale: 1 = much higher to 7 = much lower). Smokers' mean comparative risk for lung cancer and heart disease was "a bit higher" than the average person's.
	NM	Smokers perceived their risk of lung cancer as the same as the average smoker's risk. Female smokers perceived their risk of heart disease as slightly greater than the average smoker's risk.
Sutton (1995b)	M	"Your own chances of getting lung cancer at some time in your life?" (scale: 0% = no chance to 100% = certain). Heavy smokers rated their risk the same as their rating for the average smoker (light smokers rated their risk as lower).
	M, NM	Smokers were somewhat pessimistic in directly comparing their risk to the average smoker's risk but somewhat optimistic in separate ratings of their risk and the average smoker's risk.

NOTE: M = risk-minimizing finding; NM = not risk-minimizing finding.
a. This study used an unusually broad definition of *smoker*: 1 cigarette or more in the past 6 months.

in later tables. Unless otherwise indicated, the respondents in these studies were adults or college students, and the scales were intended to have equal-sized intervals between choices.

Quantitative Measures of Absolute Risk

Table 5.1 presents a small sampling of recent studies that reached conclusions about the accuracy of smokers' risk perceptions by comparing numerical judgments of absolute risk with an objective risk statistic. The studies illustrate the different questions asked and the different scales used to record estimates. It is clear from the table that different approaches lead to quite different impressions about the accuracy of smokers' risk perceptions. Depending on the outcome people are asked to rate, one can find overestimation of risk, accuracy, or underestimation of risk. There is no consistency.

Smoker's Perceptions of Differences in Risk Between Smokers and Nonsmokers, and Differences Between Smokers' and Nonsmokers' Views of Their Own Risks

Although perceptions of risk in quantitative units may have little bearing on behavior, *comparisons* between several absolute risk judgments may be more influential. For instance, if a woman estimates her risk to be 20% and the true risk is 30%, this error probably has negligible effects. But if a woman believes that her risk is 20% and that the average woman's risk is 30%, this social comparison may have important consequences for her feelings of vulnerability and her perceived need to quit smoking (Gibbons & Buunk, 1997).

Studies providing data about smokers' views of the risks of smokers and nonsmokers or agreement with statements about the riskiness of smoking are summarized in Table 5.2, which shows unequivocally that smokers acknowledge that smokers face higher risks of various health problems than do nonsmokers.

Smokers' and Nonsmokers' Views of Smoking Risks

Table 5.2, however, tells only part of the story. A different approach is to ask whether smokers and nonsmokers see smoking as equally hazardous. Table 5.3 summarizes studies examining this question. In the great majority of the studies, nonsmokers and former smokers rated smoking as riskier than did smokers. This conclusion applies not only to differences in estimates of risk probabilities but also to different rates of agreement with statements minimizing the risk of smoking. A particularly interesting finding is the observation that adolescent smokers and adolescent nonsmokers agree on the harmful effects of long-term smoking, but disagree substantially about the riskiness of short-term smoking (Slovic, 2000a).

Smokers' Comparisons of Themselves With Other Smokers and With Nonsmokers

The data in Table 5.3 do not show whether it is smokers or nonsmokers who misperceive the danger in smoking. Do smokers underestimate the danger, or do nonsmokers overestimate the danger? Similarly, although Table 5.2 shows that smokers acknowledge that their risk is at least somewhat greater than that of nonsmokers, we need to ask whether they acknowledge the full magnitude of the relative risk. In fact, Borland (1997) found that, when given a list of seven causes of death (smoking and six others with much lower probabilities) and asked, "Which cause of disease or accident caused the most deaths?" only about one-third of smokers correctly chose smoking. Similarly, Eiser, Sutton, and Wober (1979) found that only 14% of smokers realized that smoking causes more deaths than road accidents. Both these studies suggest that smokers do not recognize the amount of harm caused by smoking.

Table 5.4 provides perhaps the most direct answer to the question of whether smokers fully acknowledge their risk. The table lists studies in which smokers directly compared their own risk to the risk of other smokers or to the risk of nonsmokers. The table also includes a few studies in which smokers compared their risk factors to those of other smokers. Together, the literature is quite clear in showing that smokers substantially underestimate their own personal risk. In the great majority of studies, smokers have demonstrated unrealistic optimism: They assert that their own risk is lower than the risk faced by other smokers.

A few of these studies did not find that smokers claim to be less at risk than their fellow smokers. Several of these used data collected in face-to-face interviews (Sutton, 1995a, 1995b), and in such contexts, respondents may have felt that it was socially unacceptable to assert to interviewers that they are "better" than their peers. In two other studies (Annenberg Survey 2; LoConte, 1995), these relative risk judgments were requested of respondents only after a great many other questions about smoking were asked, and the thinking that occurred in response to these other questions may have altered smokers' comparative risk judgments (for further discussion of these exceptions, see Sutton, 1999).

Even when the *mean* response of smokers does not show an optimistic bias, one should not overlook the fact that substantial proportions of smokers in these studies did not acknowledge *any* increase in risk. For example, Ayanian and Cleary (1999) found that at least half of two-pack-a-day smokers believed that their risk of heart disease and cancer is either "average" or "below" that of the average person.

Other types of data displayed in Table 5.4 also indicate an underestimation of risk. For example, among short-term smokers, no relationship was found between the amount they smoke and their perceived risk of illness (Hahn, Renner, & Schwarzer, 1998). Smokers claimed that they smoke less, smoke cigarettes lower in tar and nicotine, have healthier lifestyles, and would be better able to quit than other smokers (Annenberg Survey 2; Segerstrom, McCarthy, & Caskey, 1993).

When smokers rate their chances of developing smoking-related illnesses, their mean response indicates that they think their chances are "equal to" or only "slightly greater than" than the chances of the "average person." The actual risk of lung cancer for smokers may be 10 times the risk of a nonsmoker, but, at most, smokers say that their own risk is "a bit higher" than average.

Other Indications of Smokers' Risk Minimization

Aside from the research on risk ratings presented in Tables 5.1-5.4, other studies have revealed a variety of mechanisms by which smoking risk is minimized. For example, both adolescents and adults believe that they are less likely than peers to become "hooked" on cigarettes (Cohn, Macfarlane, Ynez, & Imai, 1995). Smokers' estimates of the number of years of smoking needed to produce health effects increase with the number of years they have been smoking (Hahn et al., 1998).

Smokers also appear to compartmentalize their risk recognition. Grant and Job (2000) found that smokers rated their chances of experiencing five smoking-related illnesses (including four that are major causes of mortality) higher than did nonsmokers, with average risk ratings of 47% and 29%, respectively. Despite acknowledging a greater likelihood of suffering these life-threatening illnesses, these smokers were just as optimistic that they would live past 80 years of age as were nonsmokers.

Other risk-minimization mechanisms appear in longitudinal research. Gibbons, McGovern, and Lando (1991) found that when members of smoking cessation classes relapsed, they then reduced their ratings of the riskiness of smoking. Similarly, Gerrard, Gibbons, Benthin, and Hessling (1996) showed that teens who begin to smoke have a number of mechanisms for reducing internal conflict. They increase their estimates of the proportion of peers who smoke, and they decrease their ratings of how important safety issues are to them when deciding whether to smoke.

Risk-minimization and personal-exclusion tendencies apply as much to adult smokers as to adolescent smokers. The only difference between adolescents and adults uncovered in this review concerns the harmfulness of smoking. Adolescents gave lower ratings for the amount of harm caused by occasional, experimental, and regular smoking than did their parents (Cohn et al., 1995).

᥍᧖ Conclusion

The preceding review shows that conclusions about smokers' acknowledgment of smoking risks depend on the way in which risk judgments are assessed. Clearly, smokers do acknowledge some risk; nevertheless, they minimize the size of that risk and show a clear tendency to believe that the risk applies more to other smokers than to themselves. The same reluctance to recognize vulnerability is likely to be found when other hazards—such as heavy drinking, unsafe sex, and speeding in automobiles—are studied in detail. People may be quite aware of well-publicized risks and may even overestimate their numerical probability, but they still resist the idea that the risks are personally relevant (e.g., regarding breast cancer, see McCaul & O'Donnell, 1997).

The finding of a distinction between views of personal risk and views of the risk faced by the rest of the population is not surprising. People do not want to believe that they are at risk, and they are quite clever at constructing arguments to explain why their risks are lower than those of others (Hoorens, 1996; Schwarzer, 1994). In fact, attempts to reduce optimistic biases are often unsuccessful (Weinstein & Klein, 1995).

Further research on how people naturally think about risk is certainly needed. At present, no single method for assessing risk perceptions can be recommended. Instead, the best approach is to use a variety of assessment strategies: numerical and verbal measures of absolute risk, comparisons of personal risk with the risk faced by others, comparisons of personal risk with personal risk from other hazards, and agreement with a variety of statements about the risk. The data on smoking reviewed here suggest that comprehension of risk and acknowledgment of personal risk are complex topics; researchers need to apply a variety of approaches to reveal the elements within that complexity.

Also clearly needed is research on communicating risk magnitudes and on methods for overcoming unrealistic optimism. An understanding of these topics is likely to have value in many contexts. For example, better messages can help women understand the risks of breast cancer and the relative costs and benefits of hormone replacement therapy. Better messages can help people make sense of the results when they are tested for cancer-related genes. Better messages may even help government officials communicate with citizens about pesticides, hazardous waste sites, indoor air pollution, and other topics about which public responses are often far out of balance with the actual size of the risks.

Risk perception is only one of a number of factors relevant to smoking decisions. At present, perceived risk is not seen by the smoking prevention community as particularly important in smoking initiation (Flay, 1985). A common view is that efforts to prevent smoking by focusing on risk are unsuccessful because the risks are too far in the future to affect prospective smokers. The failure of health promotion programs that have focused on the riskiness of smoking seems to support this conclusion. The research summarized here suggests another possibility: that previous efforts have so far failed to get people to recognize fully the size of the risks or their own personal susceptibility. If we can develop communications that show the true magnitude of smoking damage and that thwart prospective and beginning smokers' attempts to minimize personal vulnerability, a focus on the dangers of smoking may prove more helpful in preventing and reducing smoking than it has so far.

Chapter 6

Cigarette Smokers

Rational Actors or Rational Fools?

Paul Slovic

I don't smoke and don't care to be around smoke, but I believe smokers should have the right to smoke if they choose. What I cannot comprehend, however, is why smokers are being allowed to sue tobacco companies for millions of dollars because of choices they made on their own.

No one forces anyone to smoke. We have been warned ever since I can remember about the dangers of smoking. If I choose to smoke, then I also must pay the consequences of whatever that choice leads to, whether it's lung cancer or a home that burns because I fell asleep in bed with a cigarette in my hand.

This whole thing is totally unfair to the tobacco industry. But maybe I can learn something from it. Maybe I'll start smoking so I can die rich some day and leave all my millions to my kids and grandkids.[1]

In numerous legal battles across the United States, lawyers for the cigarette industry have been relying heavily on the argument that smokers know the health risks of smoking and are making rational decisions to smoke because the benefits

AUTHOR'S NOTE: This chapter is a revised version of the following article: Paul Slovic, *Rational Actors and Rational Fools: The Influence of Affect on Judgment and Decision Making.* 6 Roger Williams University L. Rev., 167-216 (2000).

Figure 6.1. Things everybody knows.
SOURCE: Copyright © 1999 Mike Thompson. Reprinted with permission.

to them outweigh the risks. Such "informed consumers," the lawyers claim, have no cause for complaint if they become ill.

Do individuals really know and understand the risks entailed by their smoking decisions? This question is particularly important in the case of young persons, because most smokers start during childhood and adolescence. After many years of intense publicity about the hazards of smoking cigarettes, it is generally believed that every teenager and adult in the United States knows that smoking is hazardous to one's health. Apart from writers of letters to newspaper editors and editorial cartoonists (see Figure 6.1), the most enthusiastic empirical demonstration of this "fact" comes from research on perceptions of risk from smoking reported by Viscusi (1992b; see also Viscusi, 1990, 1991a).

Analyzing survey data, Viscusi concluded that young smokers are not only informed about the risks of smoking, they are overinformed in the sense that they overestimate those risks. He also concluded that, despite this overestimation, young people operate rationally on the information they have. In this chapter, I present a counterview based upon work in cognitive psychology that demonstrates the powerful influence of experiential thinking and affect on judgment and decision making. I describe some of this work in the next section. In the final section of the chapter, I examine data from the Annenberg Survey 2 that demonstrate how experiential thinking misleads smokers and, contrary to Viscusi's view, causes them to underestimate the risks of smoking.

∽ Experiential Thinking and the Affect Heuristic

This section introduces a theoretical framework that describes the importance of affect in guiding judgments and decisions. As used here, *affect* means the specific quality of "goodness" or "badness" (a) experienced as a feeling state (with or without conscious awareness) and (b) demarcating a positive or negative quality of a stimulus. Affective responses occur rapidly and automatically—note how quickly you sense the feelings associated with the word *treasure* or the word *hate*. Following Finucane, Alhakami, Slovic, and Johnson (2000), I shall argue that reliance on such feelings can be characterized as the "affect heuristic." Below, I briefly trace the development of the affect heuristic across a variety of research paths. A more extensive review can be found in Slovic, Finucane, Peters, and MacGregor (in press).

Background

A strong early proponent of the importance of affect in decision making was Zajonc (1980), who argued that affective reactions to stimuli are often the very first reactions, occurring automatically and subsequently guiding information processing and judgment. According to Zajonc, all perceptions contain some affect. "We do not just see 'a house': We see a *handsome* house, an *ugly* house, or a *pretentious* house" (p. 154). He later adds: "We sometimes delude ourselves that we proceed in a rational manner and weigh all the pros and cons of the various alternatives. But this is probably seldom the actual case. Quite often, 'I decided in favor of X' is no more than 'I liked X.' . . . We buy the cars we 'like,' choose the jobs and houses we find 'attractive,' and then justify these choices by various reasons" (p. 155).

Affect also plays a central role in what have come to be known as "dual-process theories" of thinking, knowing, and information processing. As Epstein (1994) observes, "There is no dearth of evidence in everyday life that people apprehend reality in two fundamentally different ways, one variously labeled intuitive, automatic, natural, non-verbal, narrative, and experiential, and the other analytical, deliberative, verbal, and rational" (p. 710). Table 6.1 further compares these two systems. One of the characteristics of the experiential system is its affective basis. Although analysis is certainly important in many decision-making circumstances, reliance on affect and emotion is a quicker, easier, and more efficient way to navigate in a complex, uncertain, and sometimes dangerous world. Many theo-

TABLE 6.1   Two Modes of Thinking: Comparison of the Experiential and
             Rational Systems

Experiential System	Rational System
1. Holistic	1. Analytic
2. Affective: pleasure/pain oriented	2. Logical: reason oriented (what is sensible)
3. Associationist connections	3. Logical connections
4. Behavior mediated by "vibes" from past experiences	4. Behavior mediated by conscious appraisal of events
5. Encodes reality in concrete images, metaphors, and narratives	5. Encodes reality in abstract symbols, words, and numbers
6. More rapid processing: oriented toward immediate action	6. Slower processing: oriented toward delayed action
7. Self-evidently valid: "Experiencing is believing"	7. Requires justification via logic and evidence

SOURCE: Adapted from Epstein (1994).

rists have given affect a direct and primary role in motivating behavior. Epstein's view on this is as follows:

> The experiential system is assumed to be intimately associated with the experience of affect, . . . which refer[s] to subtle feelings of which people are often unaware. When a person responds to an emotionally significant event . . . the experiential system automatically searches its memory banks for related events, including their emotional accompaniments. . . . If the activated feelings are pleasant, they motivate actions and thoughts anticipated to reproduce the feelings. If the feelings are unpleasant, they motivate actions and thoughts anticipated to avoid the feelings. (p. 716)

Also emphasizing the motivational role of affect, Mowrer (1960a) conceptualized conditioned emotional responses to images as prospective gains and losses that directly "guide and control performance in a generally sensible adaptive manner" (p. 30; see also Mowrer, 1960b). Mowrer criticized theorists who postulate purely cognitive variables such as expectancies (probabilities) intervening between stimulus and response, cautioning that we must be careful not to leave the organism at the choice point "lost in thought." Mowrer's solution was to view expectancies more dynamically (as conditioned emotions such as hopes and fears) serving as motivating states leading to action.

One of the most comprehensive and dramatic theoretical accounts of the role of affect in decision making is presented by the neurologist Antonio Damasio in his book *Descartes' Error: Emotion, Reason, and the Human Brain* (1994). Damasio's theory is derived from observations of patients with damage to the ventromedial frontal cortices of the brain that has left their basic intelligence, memory, and capacity for logical thought intact but has impaired their ability to "feel"—that is, to associate affective feelings and emotions with the anticipated consequences of their actions. Close observation of these patients combined with a number of experimental studies led Damasio to argue that this type of brain damage induces a form of sociopathy (Damasio, Tranel, & Damasio, 1990) that destroys the individual's ability to make rational decisions—that is, decisions that are in his or her best interest. Persons suffering such damage became socially dysfunctional even though they remain intellectually capable of analytic reasoning. Commenting on one particularly significant case, Damasio (1994) observes:

> The instruments usually considered necessary and sufficient for rational behavior were intact in him. He had the requisite knowledge, attention, and memory; his language was flawless; he could perform calculations; he could tackle the logic of an abstract problem. There was only one significant accompaniment to his decision-making failure: a marked alteration of the ability to experience feelings. Flawed reason and impaired feelings stood out together as the consequences of a specific brain lesion, and this correlation suggested to me that feeling was an integral component of the machinery of reason. (p. xii)

In seeking to determine "what in the brain allows humans to behave rationally," Damasio argues that thought is made largely from images, broadly construed to include sounds, smells, real or imagined visual impressions, ideas, and words. A lifetime of learning leads these images to become "marked" by positive and negative feelings linked directly or indirectly to somatic or bodily states (Mowrer and other learning theorists would call this *conditioning*): "In short, *somatic markers are . . . feelings generated from secondary emotions. These emotions and feelings have been connected, by learning, to predicted future outcomes of certain scenarios*" (Damasio, 1994, p. 174). When a negative somatic marker is linked to an image of a future outcome, it sounds an alarm. When a positive marker is associated with the outcome image, it becomes a beacon of incentive. Damasio concludes that somatic markers increase the accuracy and efficiency of the decision process, and their absence degrades performance by "compromising the rationality that makes us distinctly human and allows us to decide in consonance with a sense of personal future, social convention, and moral principle" (p. xii).

Based on ideas about affect marking images (e.g., Damasio, 1994), which in turn motivates behavior (e.g., Epstein, 1994; Mowrer, 1960a, 1960b), affect can be portrayed as an essential component in many forms of judgment and decision making. Specifically, Finucane et al. (2000) propose that people use an *affect heuristic* to make judgments. That is, representations of objects and events in people's minds are tagged to varying degrees with affect. In the process of making a judgment or decision, an individual consults or refers to an "affect pool" containing all the positive and negative tags consciously or unconsciously associated with the representations. Just as imaginability, memorability, and similarity serve as cues for probability judgments (e.g., the availability and representativeness heuristics first described by Tversky & Kahneman, 1974), affect may serve as a cue for many important judgments. Relying on an affective impression can be far easier—more efficient—than weighing the pros and cons or retrieving from memory many relevant examples, especially when the required judgment or decision is complex or mental resources are limited. This characterization of a mental shortcut leads to the labeling of the use of affect as a *heuristic.*

Empirical Evidence

This subsection presents and integrates the findings of a series of diverse studies demonstrating the operation of the affect heuristic.

Manipulating Preferences Through Controlled Exposures

The fundamental nature and importance of affect have been demonstrated repeatedly in a remarkable series of studies by Robert Zajonc and his colleagues (see, e.g., Zajonc, 1968). The concept of stimulus exposure is central to all of these studies. The central finding is that, when objects are presented to an individual repeatedly, the "mere exposure" is capable of creating a positive attitude or preference for these objects.

In a typical study, stimuli such as nonsense phrases, faces, or Chinese ideograms are presented to an individual with varying frequency. In a later session, the individual judges these stimuli on liking, familiarity, or both. The more frequent the exposure to a stimulus, the more positive the response. A meta-analysis by Bornstein (1989) of mere exposure research published between 1968 and 1987 included more than 200 experiments examining the exposure-affect relationship. Unreinforced exposures were found reliably to enhance affect toward visual, auditory, gustatory, abstract, and social stimuli.

Winkielman, Zajonc, and Schwarz (1997) have demonstrated the speed with which affect can influence judgments in studies employing a subliminal priming paradigm. A participant was "primed" through exposure to a smiling face, a frowning face, or a neutral polygon presented for 1/250 of a second, an interval so brief that there is no recognition or recall of the stimulus. Immediately following this exposure, an ideogram was presented for two seconds, following which the participant rated the ideogram on a scale of liking. Mean liking ratings were significantly higher for ideograms preceded by smiling faces. This effect was lasting. In a second session, ideograms were primed by the "other face," the one not associated with the stimulus in the first session. This second priming was ineffective because the effect of the first priming remained.

Sherman, Kim, and Zajonc (1999) tested the perseverance of induced preferences by asking participants to study Chinese characters and their English meanings. Half of the meanings were positive (e.g., beauty) and half were negative (e.g., disease). Participants were then given a test of these meanings followed by a task in which they were given pairs of characters and were asked to choose the one they preferred. Participants preferred characters with positive meaning 70% of the time. Next, the characters were presented with neutral meanings (desk, linen) and subjects were told that these were the "true" meanings. The testing procedure was repeated and, despite the participants' having learned the new meanings, preferences remained the same. Characters that had been initially paired with positive meanings still tended to be preferred.

These and many other related studies demonstrate that affect is a strong conditioner of preference, whether or not the cause of that affect is consciously perceived. They also demonstrate that affect is independent of cognition, indicating that there may be conditions of affective or emotional arousal that do not necessarily require cognitive appraisal. This affective mode of response, unburdened by cognition and hence much faster, has considerable adaptive value in many situations.

Image, Affect, and Decision Making

Consistent with the literature just reviewed, a number of nonlaboratory studies have also demonstrated strong relationships among imagery, affect, and decision making. Many of these studies have used a word-association technique to discover the affective connections that individuals have learned through life experiences. Researchers using this method present each subject with a target stimulus, usually a word or very brief phrase, and ask him or her to provide the first thought or image that comes to mind. The process is then repeated a number of times, say three to six, or until no further associations are generated. Following the elicita-

TABLE 6.2   **Images, Ratings, and Summation Scores for One Respondent**

Stimulus	Image Number	Image	Image Rating
San Diego	1	Very nice	2
San Diego	2	Good beaches	2
San Diego	3	Zoo	2
San Diego	4	Busy freeway	1
San Diego	5	Easy to find way	1
San Diego	6	Pretty town	2
Total			10
Denver	1	High	2
Denver	2	Crowded	0
Denver	3	Cool	2
Denver	4	Pretty	1
Denver	5	Busy airport	−2
Denver	6	Busy streets	−2
Total			1

SOURCE: Slovic et al. (1991).
NOTE: Based on these summation scores, this person's predicted preference for a vacation site would be San Diego.

tion of images, the subject is asked to rate each image he or she has given on a scale ranging from very positive (e.g., +2) to very negative (e.g., −2), with a neutral point in the center. Scoring consists of summing or averaging the ratings to obtain an overall index.

This method has been used successfully to measure the affective meanings that influence people's preferences for different cities and states (Slovic et al., 1991) as well as their support for or opposition to technologies such as nuclear power (Peters & Slovic, 1996). Table 6.2 illustrates the method in a task where one respondent was asked to give associations for each of two cities and, later, to rate each image affectively. The cities in this example show the clear affective superiority of San Diego over Denver for this subject. Slovic et al. (1991) showed that summed image scores such as these were highly predictive of expressed preferences for living in or visiting cities. In one study, we found that the image score predicted the location of *actual* vacations during the next 18 months.

Subsequent studies have found affect-laden imagery elicited by word associations to be predictive of preferences for investing in new companies on the stock market (MacGregor, Slovic, Dreman, & Berry, 2000) and of adolescents' decisions to take part in health-threatening and health-enhancing behaviors such as smoking and exercise (Benthin et al., 1995).

The Affect Heuristic in Judgments of Risk and Benefit

The research that, in conjunction with the sorts of findings reported above, led to recognition of the affect heuristic, had its origins in the early study of risk perception reported by Fischhoff, Slovic, Lichtenstein, Read, and Coombs (1978). One of the findings in that study and subsequent replications of it was that perception of risk and society's responses to risk were strongly linked to the degree to which a hazard evoked feelings of dread (see also Slovic, 1987). Thus activities associated with cancer (e.g., activities exposing people to radiation or toxic chemicals) are seen as riskier and more in need of regulation than activities associated with less dreaded forms of illness, injury, and death (e.g., accidents).

A second finding in the study by Fischhoff et al. (1978) has been even more instrumental in the study of the affect heuristic. This is the finding that judgments of risk and benefit are negatively correlated. For many hazards, the greater the perceived benefit, the lower the perceived risk, and vice versa. Smoking, use of alcoholic beverages, and consumption of food additives, for example, tend to be seen as very high in risk and relatively low in benefit, whereas the use of vaccines, antibiotics, and X rays tend to be seen as high in benefit and relatively low in risk. This negative relationship is noteworthy because it occurs even when the nature of the gains or benefits from an activity is distinct and qualitatively different from the nature of the risks. That the inverse relationship is generated in people's minds is suggested by the fact that risk and benefits generally tend to be positively (if at all) correlated in the world. Activities that bring great benefits may be high or low in risk, but activities that are low in benefit are unlikely to be high in risk (if they were, they would be proscribed).[2]

A study by Alhakami and Slovic (1994) found that the inverse relationship between the perceived risk and perceived benefit of an activity (e.g., using pesticides) was linked to the strength of positive or negative affect associated with that activity. This result implies that people base their judgments of an activity or a technology not only on what they *think* about it but also on what they *feel* about it. If they like an activity, they are moved to judge the risks as low and the benefits as high; if they dislike it, they tend to judge the opposite—high risk and low benefit.

These findings suggest that use of the affect heuristic guides perceptions of risk and benefit as depicted in Figure 6.2. If so, providing information about risk

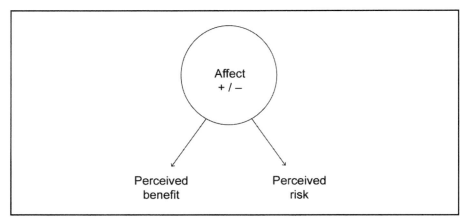

Figure 6.2. A model of the affect heuristic explaining the risk/benefit confounding observed by Alhakami and Slovic (1994). Judgments of risk and benefit are assumed to be derived by reference to an overall affective evaluation of the stimulus item.
SOURCE: "The Affect Heuristic in Judgments of Risks and Benefits," M. L. Finucane, A. Alhakami, P. Slovic, and S. M. Johnson. 2000. © John Wiley & Sons Limited. Reproduced with permission.

should change the perception of benefit and vice versa (see Figure 6.3). For example, information stating that benefit is high for some technology should lead to more positive overall affect, which would, in turn, decrease perceived risk. Indeed, Finucane et al. (2000) conducted this experiment, providing four different kinds of information designed to manipulate affect by increasing or decreasing perceived risk and increasing or decreasing perceived benefit. In each case there was no apparent logical relation between the information provided (e.g., information about risks) and the nonmanipulated variable (e.g., benefits). The predictions were confirmed. When the information that was provided changed either the perceived risk or the perceived benefit, an affectively congruent but inverse effect was observed on the nonmanipulated attribute, as depicted in Figure 6.3. These findings support the theory that risk and benefit judgments are causally determined, at least in part, by the overall affective evaluation.

The affect heuristic also predicts that using time pressure to reduce the opportunity for analytic deliberation (and thereby allowing affective considerations freer rein) should enhance the inverse relationship between perceived benefits and risks. In a second study, Finucane et al. (2000) showed that the inverse relationship between perceived risks and benefits increased under time pressure, as predicted. These two experiments with judgments of benefits and risks are important because they support Zajonc's (1980) contention that affect influences judgment directly and is not simply a response to a prior analytic evaluation.

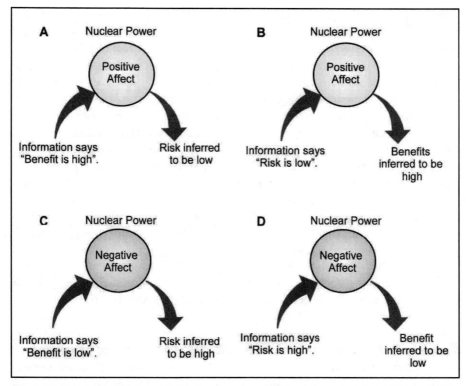

Figure 6.3. Model showing how information about benefit (A) or information about risk (B) could increase the overall affective evaluation of nuclear power and lead to inferences about risk and benefit that coincide affectively with the information given. Similarly, information could decrease the overall affective evaluation of nuclear power as in C and D, resulting in inferences that are opposite those in A and B.
SOURCE: "The Affect Heuristic in Judgments of Risks and Benefits," M. L. Finucane, A. Alhakami, P. Slovic, and S. M. Johnson. 2000. © John Wiley & Sons Limited. Reproduced with permission.

∞ Is the Decision to Smoke Informed and Rational?

Viscusi's Account and Its Shortcomings

In his book titled *Smoking: Making the Risky Decision,* Viscusi (1992b) addresses the following question: "At the time when individuals initiate their smoking activity, do they understand the consequences of their actions and make rational decisions?" (p. 11). He goes on to define the appropriate test of rationality in terms of "whether individuals are incorporating the available information about smoking risks and are making sound decisions, given their own preferences" (p. 12). Viscusi even questions whether an individual's future self may have different preferences, although he never offers information on any test of this possibility: "Does the 20-year-old smoker fully recognize how his or her future self will value health as compared with smoking?" (p. 119).

The primary data upon which Viscusi (1992b) relies come from a national survey of more than 3,000 persons ages 16 and older in which respondents were asked, "Among 100 cigarette smokers, how many do you think will get lung cancer because they smoke?" Analyzing responses to this question, Viscusi found that people greatly overestimated the risks of a smoker getting lung cancer.[3] They also overestimated overall mortality rates from smoking and loss of life expectancy from smoking. Moreover, young people (ages 16-21) overestimated these risks to an even greater extent than did older people. Viscusi also found that perceptions of risk from smoking were predictive of whether and how much people smoked, for young and old alike.

Viscusi (1992b) argues that these data support a rational learning model in which consumers respond appropriately to information and make reasonable trade-offs between the risks and benefits of smoking. With respect to youth, he concludes that his findings "strongly contradict the models of individuals being lured into smoking at an early age without any cognizance of the risks" (p. 143). Viscusi further concludes that young people are so well-informed that there is no justification for informational campaigns designed to boost their awareness. Finally, he observes that social policies that allow smoking at age 18 "run little risk of exposing uninformed decision makers to the potential hazards of smoking" (p. 149). Viscusi's data and conclusions thus appear to lend support to the defense used by cigarette companies to fend off lawsuits brought by diseased smokers: These people knew the risks and made informed, rational choices to smoke.[4]

Viscusi's arguments would seem, at first glance, to have merit from the standpoint of experiential thinking as well as from his analytic perspective. On experiential grounds, the well-known association of cigarettes with cancer, a dread disease, should create enough negative affect to stimulate a powerful drive to avoid this harmful behavior. Consistent with this view, many people do decide not to smoke or to quit smoking. The minority who initiate smoking or maintain the habit may also be doing so on the basis of informed experiential or analytic thinking that has led them to conclude that the benefits outweigh the risks.

On the other hand, there appear to be a number of ways in which reliance on experiential thinking might lead smokers to fail to appreciate risks and to act in ways that are not in their best interests. In particular, the exposure to information that Viscusi believes causes overestimation of risk cuts both ways. The major exposure comes from massive advertising campaigns designed to associate positive imagery and positive affect with cigarette smoking. A recent ad for Kool Natural

Lights, for example, featured a picture of a beautiful waterfall on the cigarette package. In addition, the word *natural* appeared 13 times in the ad.

More subtle than the content of cigarette ads is the possibility that the "mere exposure effect" that results from viewing them repeatedly (Bornstein, 1989; Zajonc, 1968) also contributes to positive affect for smoking in general and for specific brands of cigarettes in particular. Through the workings of the affect heuristic, this positive affect would be expected not only to enhance individuals' attraction to smoking but to depress the perception of risk (Finucane et al., 2000).

Within the experiential mode of thinking, "seeing is believing," and young people in particular are likely to see little or no visible harm from the smoking done by their friends or themselves. In this sense, smoking risks are not "available" (Tversky & Kahneman, 1973).

Viscusi's arguments are also lacking in a number of other respects, as I have indicated in several previous studies (Slovic, 1998, 2000a, 2000b). Here I shall focus on two failings, both of which relate to experiential thinking. The first reflects the repetitive nature of cigarette smoking and the accumulation of risk over a long period of time. The second reflects young people's failure to appreciate the risks of becoming addicted to smoking.

Cigarette smoking is a behavior that takes place one cigarette at a time. A person smoking one pack of cigarettes every day for 40 years "lights up" about 300,000 times. Although most smokers acknowledge a high degree of risk associated with many years of smoking, many believe they can get away with some lesser amount of smoking before the risk takes hold. Many young smokers, in particular, believe that smoking for only a few years poses negligible risk. They are more prone to believe in the safety of short-term smoking than are young nonsmokers (Slovic, 1998, 2000a).

Belief in the near-term safety of smoking combines in an insidious way with a tendency for young smokers to be uninformed about, or to underestimate, the difficulty of stopping smoking. Recent research indicates that adolescents begin to show evidence of nicotine dependence within days to weeks of the onset of occasional use of tobacco (DiFranza et al., 2000). Many young people regret their decision to start smoking and attempt unsuccessfully to stop. The 1989 Teenage Attitudes and Practices Survey found that 74% of adolescent smokers reported they had seriously thought about quitting, and 49% had tried to quit in the previous 6 months (Allen, Moss, Giovino, Shopland, & Pierce, 1993). A longitudinal survey conducted as part of the University of Michigan's Monitoring the Future Study found that 85% of high school seniors who smoked occasionally predicted that they probably or definitely would not be smoking in 5 years, as did 32% of those who smoked one pack of cigarettes per day. However, in a follow-up study conducted 5-6 years later, of those who had smoked at least one pack per day as seniors, only 13% had quit and 69% still smoked one pack or more per day. Of those who smoked one to five cigarettes per day as seniors, only 30% had quit (60% had expected to do so) and 44% had actually increased their cigarette consumption (Centers for Disease Control and Prevention, 1994a; Johnston, O'Malley, & Bachman, 1993).

The belief pattern that emerges from these and various other studies is one in which many young smokers perceive themselves to be at little or no risk from each cigarette smoked because they expect to stop smoking before any damage to their health occurs. In reality, a high percentage of young smokers continue to smoke over a long period of time and are certainly placed at risk by their habit.

New Data: The Dominance of Experiential Thinking

Viscusi's arguments about perceptions of risk and the informed choices made by smokers assume the preeminence of the analytic mode of thinking. Viscusi (1992b) portrays the beginning smoker as a young economist, weighing the benefits against the risks before making the fateful decision to light up: "One might expect some individuals to rationally choose to smoke if the weight they placed on the benefits derived from smoking exceeds their assessment of the expected losses stemming from risks" (p. 135). But the evidence for smokers' short-term perspectives and underestimation of the grip of addiction suggests that experiential and affective forces are leading many young people to make smoking decisions that they later regard as mistakes.

Evidence for this view comes from data collected in a national telephone survey of more than 3,500 individuals conducted on behalf of the Annenberg Public Policy Center of the University of Pennsylvania in the fall of 1999 and winter of 1999-2000. Households were selected through random-digit dialing, and within each household a resident aged 14 or older was selected randomly for the interview. Young people were oversampled. Completed interviews were obtained for 2,002 members of a "youth sample" ages 14 to 22 and 1,504 members of an adult sample ranging in age from 23 to 95. Within the youth sample there were 478 smokers and 1,524 nonsmokers; among the adults there were 310 smokers and 1,194 nonsmokers.[5]

Recall that the experiential mode is automatic, based on feelings, and not always accessible to conscious awareness. People acting experientially may not sense that they are consciously deliberating. Experiential thinking is evident throughout responses to the survey questions (see Table 6.3). Almost 80% of the adult smokers surveyed answered "not at all" when asked how much they thought about how smoking might affect their health when they first began to smoke (Question 19a). Young smokers appeared more likely to have thought

TABLE 6.3 **Perceptions and Expectations of the Beginning Smoker (in percentages)**

Questions/Responses	Adult Smokers (N = 310)	Young Smokers (N = 478)
Q19A. When you first started to smoke, how much did you think about how smoking might affect your health?		
A lot	5.8	13.8
A little	15.5	38.9
Not at all	78.4	46.9
Don't know/refused	0.3	0.4
Q19C. How much do you think about the health effects of smoking now?		
A lot	53.9	54.6
A little	32.9	36.0
Not at all	12.3	8.6
Don't know/refused	1.0	0.8
Q19D. Since you started smoking, have you heard of any health risks of smoking that you didn't know about when you started?		
Yes	54.8	33.5
No	43.9	66.3
Don't know/refused	1.3	0.2
Q19E. When you first started smoking, did you think more about how smoking would affect your future health or about how you were trying something new and exciting?		
Thought about future health	4.5	21.1
Thought about trying something new and exciting	67.4	58.0
Other	18.1	11.5
Don't know/refused	10.0	9.4
Q19F. When you first started smoking, how long did you think you would continue to smoke?		
A few days	3.9	9.4
A few months	4.5	6.5
Less than a year	3.2	7.7
1-5 years	4.8	10.2
More than 5 years	7.4	4.8
Didn't think about it	75.8	61.3
Don't know/refused	0.3	0.0

about health when they began to smoke, but their most frequent answer was still "not at all." However, now that they smoke, most of these individuals said that they do think about the health effects (Question 19c). A substantial proportion of

TABLE 6.4   Responses to Question "About How Many Times, If Any, Have You Tried to Quit Smoking?" (in percentages)

Number of Times	Adult Smokers (N = 310)	Young Smokers (N = 478)
0	21.3	38.1
1	16.8	21.8
2-4	38.4	30.1
5-9	11.6	4.0
10+	9.4	4.8
Don't know/refused	2.6	1.3

smokers also said that, since they started smoking, they have heard of health risks they did not know about when they started (Question 19d).

Most telling are the answers to Questions 19e and 19f. Far more beginning smokers were thinking about "trying something new and exciting" than were thinking about health (19e). When asked how long they thought they would continue to smoke when they first started, the majority of young and older smokers said that they did not think about it (19f).

Data from the Annenberg survey indicate that most smokers neither want to continue smoking nor expect to do so. The majority of smokers had made more than one attempt to quit (Table 6.4), and about 65% of the adults and 84% of the young people said that they planned to quit (Table 6.5, Question 29). Of those who planned to quit, about 78% of the adults and 72% of the youth planned to do so within the next year (Table 6.5, Question 29a). When asked whether the researchers would find that they had successfully quit smoking if they were called again in a year (Table 6.5, Question 29b), 78% of the adults and 83% of the young people said yes.

Tables 6.6 and 6.7 present the responses to these same three questions about quitting, conditioned by the number of past attempts to quit (Table 6.6) and by the length of time the individual had been smoking (Table 6.7). In Table 6.6 we see that, except for adults who had never tried to quit, a substantial majority of smokers planned to quit (Question 29) and planned to do so within the next year (Questions 29a and 29b), even though they had unsuccessfully attempted to quit a number of times before. Thus we see that, among youth who had attempted to quit 10 or more times, 91.3% still planned to quit, and 85.7% of those expected to do so in the first year (Question 29a). This estimated 1-year time line was lower (61.1%) when elicited in Question 29b, but it was still far greater than the "no" response (16.7%).

TABLE 6.5   Perspectives on Quitting Smoking (in percentages)

Questions/Responses	Adult Smokers (N = 310)	Young Smokers (N = 478)
Q29. Do you plan to quit smoking?		
Yes	65.5	83.7
No	30.6	13.2
Don't know/refused	3.9	3.1
Q29A. When are you planning to quit?		
Next 6 months	49.3	57.0
6 months to a year	24.1	19.5
More than a year from now	15.8	18.2
Don't know/refused	10.8	5.2
Q29B. If we called you again in a year, would you guess you would have successfully quit smoking?		
Yes	77.8	83.3
No	11.4	9.8
Don't know/refused	10.7	6.9

Similar optimism about quitting was evident among longtime smokers (Table 6.7). Even among those who had been smoking for more than 5 years, 64% of adults and 80% of young people planned to quit, and most of these individuals planned to do so within the next year. The median age of the adults who had been smoking for more than 5 years was 41, which makes it likely that they had actually been smoking for more than 20 years (more than 5 years was the longest time in the response options presented by the interviewers). It is noteworthy that these older smokers were as optimistic as young smokers about quitting within the next year.

Although we have seen above that most smokers were not thinking about health risks when they first began to smoke, some of those who were may have been reassured by the thought that there is little or no harm to smoking in the short run. I had earlier observed this in a survey of a sample of high school-age smokers (Slovic, 2000a), and the present findings replicate this result. When asked to "imagine someone who starts to smoke a pack of cigarettes a day at age 16," 29.7% of adult smokers and 26.4% of young smokers agreed with the statement "There is usually no risk to the person at all for the first few years." Agreement was lower among nonsmokers (18.8% for adults and 20.6% for youth). When asked, "How long, if ever, do you think it takes for smoking to seriously

TABLE 6.6   Plans to Quit Smoking by Number of Past Attempts to Quit (in percentages)

	Number of Attempts to Quit							
	0		1-4		5-9		10+	
Questions/Responses	AS	YS	AS	YS	AS	YS	AS	YS
Q29. Do you plan to quit smoking?								
Yes	39.4	74.7	67.8	89.5	88.9	100.0	79.3	91.3
No	54.6	22.0	28.1	7.7	11.1	0.0	20.7	8.7
Don't know	6.1	3.3	4.1	2.8	0.0	0.0	0.0	0.0
Q29A. When are you planning to quit?								
Next 6 months	38.5	56.6	46.6	55.0	62.5	57.9	52.2	76.2
6 months to a year	26.9	15.4	27.6	23.0	18.8	21.0	17.4	9.5
More than a year from now	15.4	23.5	17.2	16.3	15.6	15.8	8.7	9.5
Don't know	19.2	4.4	8.6	5.9	3.1	5.3	21.7	4.8
Q29B. If called in a year, would you have quit?								
Yes	88.2	86.7	81.4	85.0	69.2	66.7	56.2	61.1
No	0.0	7.1	9.3	9.2	19.2	26.7	25.0	16.7
Don't know	11.8	6.1	9.3	5.8	11.5	6.7	18.8	22.2

NOTE: AS = adult smokers; YS = young smokers.

harm the health of a new smoker?" 44.8% of adult smokers and 32.0% of young smokers answered 5 years or more.

Addiction

Loewenstein (1999; Chapter 9, this volume) has proposed a theoretical perspective that portrays addiction as an extreme form of a class of behaviors that are controlled by "visceral factors." Visceral factors include drive states such as hunger, thirst, sexual desire, moods and emotions, physical pain, and, for addiction, intense craving for a drug or cigarette. From the experiential perspective, it is very difficult, if not impossible, to appreciate one's own susceptibility to visceral influences. As Loewenstein observes: "Unlike currently experienced visceral factors, which have a disproportionate impact on behavior, delayed visceral factors tend to be ignored or severely underweighted in decision making. Today's pain, hunger, anger, etc. are palpable, but the same sensations anticipated in the future receive little weight" (p. 240).

TABLE 6.7   Plans to Quit Smoking by Length of Time Smoking (in percentages)

	Length of Time Smoking							
	1 Month or Less		About 1 Year		1-5 Years		More Than 5 Years	
Questions/Responses	AS	YS	AS	YS	AS	YS	AS	YS
Q29. Do you plan to quit smoking?								
Yes	—	81.4	—	82.5	74.2	87.3	63.7	80.2
No	—	15.2	—	14.3	25.8	11.0	32.2	15.9
Don't know	—	3.4	—	3.2	0.0	1.8	4.1	4.0
Q29A. When are you planning to quit?								
Next 6 months	—	85.4	—	55.8	39.1	51.8	50.0	54.5
6 months to a year	—	6.2	—	28.8	17.4	21.6	25.6	16.8
More than a year from now	—	2.1	—	7.7	17.4	22.1	15.7	23.8
Don't know	—	6.2	—	7.7	26.1	4.5	8.7	5.0
Q29B. If called in a year, would you have quit?								
Yes	—	90.9	—	86.4	92.3	81.5	75.4	80.6
No	—	6.8	—	6.8	7.7	10.3	12.3	12.5
Don't know	—	2.3	—	6.8	0.0	8.2	12.3	6.9

NOTE: AS = adult smokers; YS = young smokers.

The Annenberg survey data provide abundant evidence regarding the difficulties of stopping smoking. First, as shown earlier, in Table 6.4, the majority of the adult and young smokers had attempted to quit, usually more than once. Second, despite their lack of success in quitting, most of these individuals planned to stop smoking in the near future (Tables 6.5, 6.6, and 6.7). Another indication of the short-term perspective of smokers and their misperception of the ease of quitting comes from the finding that only 7.4% of the adult smokers and 4.8% of the young people expected to smoke for more than 5 years when they began (Table 6.3, Question 19f), yet 87.1% of these adults and 26.4% of these youth reported that they had been smoking for more than 5 years.

When asked whether they considered themselves addicted to cigarettes, 76.4% of the adult smokers and 58.8% of the young people said yes (bottom row of Table 6.8). The proportions of adults and young people who considered themselves addicted increased sharply with the number of attempts to quit and length of time smoking (Table 6.8, Questions 30 and 31).

TABLE 6.8   Responses to the Question: "Do you consider yourself addicted to cigarettes?" (in percentages)

Questions/Responses	Adult Smokers			Young Smokers		
	Yes	No	Don't Know	Yes	No	Don't Know
Q30. About how many times, if any, have you tried to quit smoking?						
0	59.1	37.9	3.0	41.2	57.7	1.1
1	76.9	23.1	0.0	56.7	43.3	0.0
2-4	78.2	21.0	0.8	75.7	24.3	0.0
5-9	91.7	8.3	0.0	73.7	26.3	0.0
10+	93.1	6.9	0.0	91.3	8.7	0.0
Q31. How long have you smoked?						
Few months or less	—	—	—	3.4	96.6	0.0
About a year	—	—	—	33.3	65.1	1.6
1-5 years	64.5	35.5	0.0	64.5	35.5	0.0
More than 5 years	79.6	19.6	0.7	88.1	11.1	0.8
All respondents	76.4	22.6	1.0	58.8	40.4	0.8

Viscusi's Quantitative Risk Estimates Are Unreliable

Viscusi (1992b) places great weight on the validity of his quantitative questions about smoking risk perceptions. However, there are a number of reasons to be suspicious about the reliability of answers to his questions about the relative frequency of lung cancer among 100 smokers. First, he asked respondents to estimate the risks to 100 smokers, not to themselves. Answers for themselves would likely be lower, as a result of optimism bias (Weinstein, 1998a). Second, Tversky and Koehler (1994) have developed and tested a theoretical model, *support theory*, that shows that respondents asked to judge the likelihood for one focal event (e.g., lung cancer) produce higher probabilities than do respondents asked for judgments of the same event in the context of other alternative events. Third, we would expect that young smokers, as experiential rather than analytic thinkers who do not expect to be smoking much longer, would not be paying careful attention to tracking lung cancer rates among smokers. Hence they would not have firm quantitative estimates in their heads.

The Annenberg survey tested these suspicions by first replicating Viscusi's line of questioning and then adding a variation in the question format along the lines suggested by Tversky and Koehler's theory. Early in the survey, respondents were

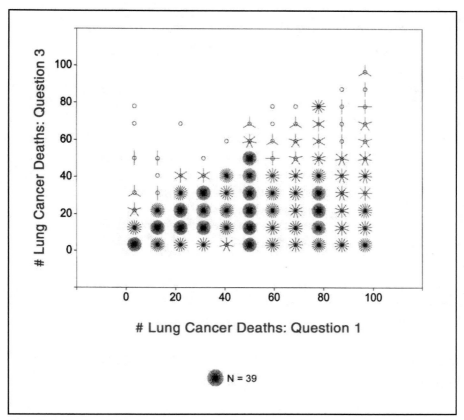

Figure 6.4. Sunflower plot showing the relationship between adult respondents' estimates of lung cancer deaths among 100 smokers. Question 1 asked only about lung cancer. Question 3 asked about lung cancer and other causes of death. Open circles represent 1 respondent. Multiple cases at a point are represented by the number of petals on the sunflower.

asked to "imagine 100 cigarette smokers, both men and women, who smoked cigarettes their entire adult lives. How many of these 100 people do you think will die from lung cancer?" This was immediately followed by a similar question asking about the number of lung cancer deaths among 100 *nonsmokers*. Next, a third question asked for respondents' estimates of the number of deaths among the same 100 smokers from (a) automobile accidents, (b) heart disease, (c) stroke, (d) lung cancer, and (e) all other causes combined (the order of a, b, and c was randomized).

Table 6.9 presents the means and standard deviations of the estimates for lung cancer among the 100 smokers inquired about in the first and third questions. The answers to the first question, about lung cancer alone, were in the range obtained in Viscusi's surveys, with estimates by the youth sample being larger than esti-

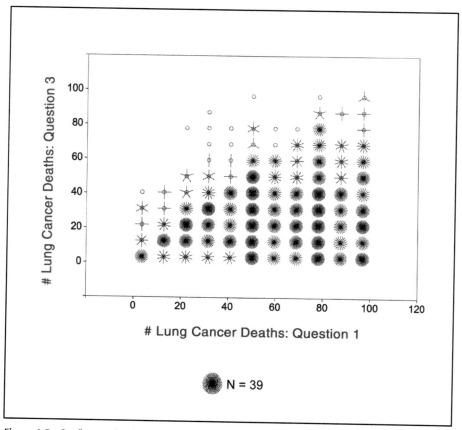

Figure 6.5. Sunflower plot showing the relationship between young respondents' estimates of lung cancer deaths among 100 smokers. Question 1 asked only about lung cancer. Question 3 asked about lung cancer and other causes of death. Open circles represent 1 respondent. Multiple cases at a point are represented by the number of petals on the sunflower.

mates by the adults (60.4 versus 48.5). However, the estimates for lung cancer decreased by more than 50% when made in the context of the other causes (Question 3). The proportions of respondents who reduced their first estimates when given a small number of alternative causes of death in Question 3 were 72.6% (adults) and 80.9% (youth). Furthermore, the correlation between the two estimates, a form of reliability, was very low, only .33 for the adults and .19 for the younger respondents (see the scatterplots in Figures 6.4 and 6.5). These results thus replicate and extend findings obtained earlier with a sample of university students (Slovic, 2000b). They demonstrate that one can get a wide range of estimates for lung cancer (or other smoking-induced causes of death) simply by varying the number of other causes respondents are also asked to judge.

TABLE 6.9	Judged Deaths From Lung Cancer Among 100 Smokers				
	Adult Sample (N = 1,416)			Youth Sample (N = 2,002)	
	Mean	SD		Mean	SD
Question 1	48.5	27.4		60.4	25.1
			$r_{13} = .33$		$r_{13} = .19$
Question 3	23.5	17.5		28.3	19.4
% Q3 < Q1	72.6			80.9	

Quantitative judgments of lung cancer risk were also elicited in other ways in the survey, but these judgments, too, were unreliable. Question 6 in the survey, also given in two forms, asked: "If you smoked a pack of cigarettes a day, how much do you think it would increase your chances of getting lung cancer?"[6] Possible responses were as follows:

Question 6, Format A	Question 6, Format B
No more likely	No more likely
Twice as likely	Twice as likely
5 times as likely	3 times as likely
10 to 20 times as likely	5 times as likely
50 times as likely	10 or more times as likely

The results from Question 6 are displayed in Table 6.10. Note that, in both versions, the estimated rates of increase in lung cancer were higher for the young smokers than for the adults. More salient is the fact that the proportion of adult smokers estimating the increase at 10 times or greater was 41.1% under Format A but only 14.6% under Format B. For young smokers, the corresponding figures were 57.1% (A) and 30.9% (B). We thus see that size of the estimated effect of smoking on lung cancer was strongly dependent on response format, much as was found with Questions 1 and 3.

Another quantitative risk response upon which Viscusi (1992b) relies was elicited by this question: "The average life expectancy for a 21-year-old male (female) is 53 (59) years. What do you believe the life expectancy is for the average male (female) smoker?" Here, too, Viscusi's respondents seemed to appreciate or even overestimate the risks. Their mean loss of life expectancy was *11.5* years.

TABLE 6.10   Response Distributions for Question 6: Increases in Lung Cancer (in percentages)

Format A	Adult Smokers (N = 153)	Young Smokers (N = 245)	Format B	Adult Smokers (N = 157)	Young Smokers (N = 233)
No more likely	9.2	2.9	No more likely	14.6	4.3
Twice as likely	28.1	24.5	Twice as likely	36.9	13.7
5 times as likely	16.3	15.5	3 times as likely	10.8	17.6
10 to 20 times as likely	25.5	35.1	5 times as likely	19.1	31.3
50 times as likely	15.6	22.0	10 or more times as likely	14.6	30.9
Don't know/refused	5.2	0.0	Don't know/refused	3.8	2.2

The Annenberg survey included two versions of a question asking about the extent to which smoking a pack of cigarettes a day "would shorten your life." Possible responses were as follows:

Question 7, Format A	Question 7, Format B
Not at all	Not at all
1 year	A few months
5 to 10 years	1 year
15 years	2 to 3 years
20 years or more	5 to 10 years

We see in Table 6.11 that, in both versions, young smokers estimated somewhat greater loss of life expectancy than did adults. More important, however, is the strong influence of response scale format. For adults, 77.0% of the sample estimated a life shortening of 5 years or more under Format A, compared with only 48.1% under Format B. Corresponding figures for young smokers were 82.7% (A) and 52% (B).

The data from nonsmokers (not shown here) reveal a pattern of format effects quite similar to those of smokers in Tables 6.10 and 6.11. Taken together, these results and those in Table 6.9 indicate that the survey respondents, young and old alike, did not have reliable quantitative knowledge about smoking risks. The judgments they provided depended on how the response options were framed. This conclusion is consistent with other theoretical and empirical research demonstrating the dependence of quantitative judgments such as these on the form of

TABLE 6.11 Response Distributions for Question 7: Shortening of Life (in percentages)

Scale Format A	Adult Smokers (N = 152)	Young Smokers (N = 230)	Scale Format B	Adult Smokers (N = 158)	Young Smokers (N = 248)
Not at all	6.6	1.7	Not at all	9.5	3.2
1 year	9.9	13.0	A few months	6.3	10.1
5 to 10 years	53.3	50.9	1 year	5.7	5.2
15 years	11.2	18.3	2 to 3 years	20.3	26.6
20 years or more	12.5	13.5	5 to 10 years	48.1	52.0
Don't know/refused	6.6	2.6	Don't know/refused	10.1	2.8

the question and response scale (e.g., Slovic, Monahan, & MacGregor, 2000; Tversky & Koehler, 1994). It is also consistent with the view that smokers do not think analytically about the risks they are taking.

The Failure of Rationality

Viscusi (1992b) argues that smokers make informed, rational decisions to smoke. Viscusi has also asserted that the key question pertaining to the failure of the rational model is one in which an individual, asked to go back in time to the moment of decision and repeat the choice, would not make the same choice again. I asked that question in a small survey of smokers at the University of Oregon and in a poll of Oregon residents (Slovic, 2000b). The Annenberg telephone survey asked it as well of all smokers: "If you had it to do over again, would you start smoking?" The results, shown in Table 6.12, are clear. More than 85% of adult smokers and about 80% of young smokers answered no. Moreover, the pattern of responses shown in the table was similar for both young and adult smokers. The more they felt addicted to cigarettes, the more often they had tried to quit, the longer they had been smoking, and the more cigarettes they were smoking per day, the more likely they were to say no.[7]

Recall Viscusi's central question: "At the time when individuals initiate their smoking activity, do they understand the consequences of their actions and make rational decisions?" The data presented here indicate that the answer to this question is no. Most beginning smokers do not appreciate how their future selves will perceive the risks from smoking and value the trade-off between health and the need to smoke.

TABLE 6.12   Smoking: Would You Start Again? (in percentages)

	Adult Smokers (N = 310)		Young Smokers (N = 478)	
Questions/Responses	Yes	No	Yes	No
Overall	11.9	85.5	17.0	80.1
Q32. Do you consider yourself addicted to cigarettes?				
Yes	11.4	86.9	13.9	84.3
No	14.3	81.4	21.8	74.6
More than average	7.7	90.4	7.1	92.9
Same as average	11.1	85.6	15.3	80.9
Less than average	16.2	83.8	20.4	77.0
Q30. Number of times tried to quit?				
0	27.3	66.7	22.5	73.1
1-4	9.4	88.3	14.5	83.9
5-9	8.3	91.7	10.5	84.2
10+	0.0	100.0	4.4	95.6
Q31. How long have you smoked?				
Few months or less	—	—	22.0	74.6
About 1 year	—	—	20.6	76.2
1-5 years	19.4	80.7	16.7	79.4
More than 5 years	11.1	86.3	13.5	86.5
Q26. Cigarettes smoked per day last 30 days?				
Less than 1	16.1	83.9	25.3	69.5
1-5	10.5	89.5	18.9	77.5
6-10	10.0	88.0	19.4	79.6
11-14	11.1	86.1	13.4	83.6
15-19	15.4	82.0	5.9	91.2
20	10.4	85.1	7.0	93.0
More than 20	11.4	86.4	12.1	87.9

This is a strong repudiation of the model of informed rational choice. It fits well with findings that indicate that smokers give little conscious thought to risk when they begin to smoke. They appear to be lured into the behavior by the prospects of fun and excitement. Most begin to think of risk only after they have started to smoke and have gained what to them is new information about health risks. The increased likelihood of smokers' repudiating their earlier decision exhibited by those who have been smoking for the longest time, those who are currently smoking the most cigarettes, those who perceive themselves at high risk from smoking, those who have tried most often to quit, and those who acknowledge their addiction, paints a sad portrait of individuals who are unable to control a behavior that they have come to recognize as harmful.

These disturbing findings underscore the distinction that behavioral decision theorists now make between decision utility and experience utility (Kahneman, 1997; Kahneman & Snell, 1992; Loewenstein & Schkade, 1999). This distinction arises from numerous studies of persons who have experienced very good outcomes, such as winning the lottery, or very bad ones, such as becoming paraplegic or testing positive for HIV. Winning the lottery leaves people much less happy than they had expected, and people adjust to being paraplegic or HIV-positive much better than they had expected (Brickman, Coates, & Janoff-Bulman, 1978). In the case of smoking, the discrepancy between decision utility and experience utility underscores the veracity of Loewenstein's visceral account of addiction.

◌◌ Cigarette Smokers: Rational Actors or Rational Fools?

Rationality is a product not only of the analytic mind but of the experiential mind. As Damasio (1994) observes:

> The strategies of human reason probably did not develop, in either evolution or any single individual, without the guiding force of the mechanisms of biological regulation, of which emotion and feeling are notable expressions. Moreover, even after reasoning strategies become established . . . their effective deployment probably depends, to a considerable extent, on a continued ability to experience feelings. (p. xii)

Ironically, the perception and integration of affective feelings, within the experiential system, is exactly the kind of high-level maximization process postulated by economic theorists since the days of Jeremy Bentham. In this sense, the affect heuristic enables us to be rational actors in many important situations—but not in all situations. It works beautifully when our experience enables us to anticipate accurately how much we will like the consequences of our decisions. It fails miserably when the consequences turn out to be much different in character from what we had anticipated. In such situations, exemplified well by the smoking of cigarettes, the rational actor becomes the rational fool.[8]

恃 Notes

1. This quote comes from a letter to the editor that was published in the *Register Guard* in Eugene, Oregon, on April 12, 2000 (p. 10a).

2. This inverse relationship is found as well when the correlation is computed across individuals judging the same activity. Thus one person may judge nuclear power to be high in risk and low in benefit, whereas another might judge it low in risk and high in benefit.

3. The mean estimate was 43 of 100, compared with an actuarial value that Viscusi (1992b) claims was only 10-15 of 100. Similar overestimation was found in subsequent studies that asked about lung cancer mortality rather than incidence (Viscusi, 1998a)

4. Viscusi (1992b) interprets his findings as follows: "There is substantial evidence that individuals make tradeoffs with respect to smoking risks and other valued attributes. This behavior is consistent with . . . models of rational behavior. . . . it is unlikely that smoking rates greatly exceed what would prevail in a fully informed market context" (p. 144). Other scholars, quoted on the dust jacket of Viscusi's book, appear to buy Viscusi's argument. A blurb from Alan Schwartz of the Yale Law School notes: "This book combines two disciplines, cognitive psychology and the economics of risk, to make an important contribution to the smoking debate. Viscusi shows that persons in all age groups overestimate smoking risks, as theory predicts, and that persons behave rationally respecting the smoking decision given their perception of the facts. After these findings, the smoking decision can justifiably be regulated only in consequence of third party effects, not because consumers make poor health choices." And Robert D. Tollison of George Mason University asserts: "Viscusi's book will provide the intellectual basis and framework for a long overdue reassessment of the role of government in protecting consumers and workers from certain types of risky behavior. It should come as no surprise that the government has once again been overzealous in their protection of consumers and workers from the dangers of smoking by mandating hazard warnings on packages, restricting television advertising and imposing restrictions on where smoking is permitted. Viscusi analyzes the government's actions and offers us some interesting routes out of the swamp of overprotection."

5. A smoker was defined as someone who said he or she had smoked at least one cigarette within the past 30 days.

6. This was not a question used by Viscusi; rather, it was selected as another way to elicit quantitative estimates of the lung cancer risk associated with smoking.

7. The perception that smoking is risky to one's health was also correlated strongly with the "no" response for both young and adult smokers.

8. I have borrowed the notion of the rational fool from Amartya Sen's (1977) penetrating critique of the behavioral foundations of economic theory.

Part III

MEDIA INFLUENCE ON SMOKING

Chapter 7

Advertising, Smoker Imagery, and the Diffusion of Smoking Behavior

Daniel Romer
Patrick Jamieson

Branding irons in hand, the denim-shirted cowboy in the brown leather chaps pauses. His eyes are concealed by the brim of his white hat. On his hands are leather gloves. He is muscular, handsome, and tan. He is also rugged and independent. Although the background is blurred, a reader can surmise from the hay at his feet that he is in a field. "Come to where the flavor is," says the print. Inset just below is a picture of a package of cigarettes with the word *Marlboro* on it. At the bottom of the page, a white box with black letters contains the surgeon general's warning: "Quitting smoking now greatly reduces serious risks to your health." The page is an ad from Philip Morris. It offers a powerful image designed to elicit positive feelings about smoking. Yet the ad also contains a warning about minimizing risk.

A lthough cigarette advertising has been widely disseminated for most of the 20th century, large-scale efforts to counter the influence of cigarette promotion began in earnest only in the late 1960s ("Achievements,"

1999). For a brief period, the Fairness Doctrine required the airing of counteradvertising on television and radio to match the advertising used by the cigarette industry. This intervention led to the voluntary removal of cigarette advertising from television and radio by the industry in 1971. Nevertheless, the tobacco industry still managed to spend several billions of dollars annually on promotions and advertising in other venues and media (Sargent, 1998). With the signing of the master settlement agreement between the industry and 46 states in 1998, billboard advertising has been further restricted ("Achievements," 1999). However, cigarette advertising still appears in print media, in stores where tobacco products are sold, and on smaller billboards. As we confirm in Chapter 2 of this volume, cigarette promotion also continues in entertainment venues, such as at sports events and in bars and other drinking establishments. However, the tobacco industry has agreed to stop the sale and distribution of clothing and other items carrying the logos of cigarette brands.

Communication programs designed to counter industry advertising and promotion have taken many forms. School-based antismoking education began to focus on more effective strategies in the 1970s (Centers for Disease Control and Prevention, 1994a). These strategies emphasized resistance to those peer and advertising pressures that encourage smoking initiation (Bruvold, 1993; Rooney & Murray, 1996). Obligatory warning labels began to appear on all tobacco products and advertising in 1965, although it was not until 1984 that these labels actually specified the health risks (Viscusi, 1992b). Some states began their own counteradvertising programs in the early 1990s, using funds raised through taxes on cigarette sales (Pechmann, 1997). The Centers for Disease Control as well as various nonprofit organizations have also sponsored campaigns. The master settlement agreement has further encouraged states to devote a portion of their revenues to counteradvertising and other educational efforts concerning tobacco use, and the American Legacy Foundation was created specifically to sponsor such efforts ("Achievements," 1999).

In this chapter, we examine the role of advertising as an influence on adolescents' decisions to start smoking. Advertising is, of course, a powerful means of shaping and reinforcing social norms. In a 1977 review, Martin Fishbein, codeveloper of the theory of reasoned action, argued that although attitudes are more central to adult decisions to smoke, social factors are more salient to those who are younger.

Cigarette advertising reaches large numbers of adolescents (Pierce et al., 1991; Tye, Warner, & Glantz, 1987). At ages as young as 6, children can recall cigarette ads (Charlton, 1986), and they show evidence of exposure to advertised images at even younger ages (Fischer, Schwartz, Richards, Goldstein, & Rojas, 1991). The rationale for use of some images was revealed when tobacco industry documents were released in a court case in Canada. One 1982 document from RJR-MacDonald (R. J. Reynolds in Canada) indicated that smokers of the Export brand "will be perceived as . . . characterized by their self-confidence, strength of character, and individuality which makes them popular and admired by their peers." Even those who lack the cognitive development to understand the reasons for ads can recall the images those ads convey (Aitken, Leathar, & Squair, 1986). When Britain outlawed "tough" images in cigarette ads, the number of young people who indicated "looks tough" as a reason for smoking declined (Charlton, 1986).

Researchers have known for decades that young people who smoke are more aware of cigarette advertising than are those who do not engage in the behavior (Chapman & Fitzgerald, 1982). Increased smoking correlates with increased awareness of cigarette ads (Goldstein, Fischer, Richards, & Creten, 1987), with more heavily advertised brands better known (Goldstein et al., 1987; Hunter et al., 1986) and more often smoked ("Changes," 1994; McNeill, Jarvis, & West, 1985). The dramatic increase in smoking by female adolescents in the late 1960s was associated with the introduction of brands targeted and advertised to young women at that time (Pierce, Lee, & Gilpin, 1994). Furthermore, cigarette brands that are popular among adolescents are more likely to be advertised in magazines that have youthful readers than are brands that are popular among adults (King, Siegel, & Celebucki, 1998). Indeed, analyses conducted by the American Legacy Foundation suggest that tobacco advertising in magazines with high teen readership has increased since the signing of the master settlement agreement.

In a study of teenagers, the perceived influence of ads for cigarettes was found to outweigh whether the teenagers' parents, siblings, or peers smoked as well as intention to smoke as a predictor of initiation of smoking behavior (Armstrong, deKlerk, Shean, Dunn, & Dolin, 1990). Data such as these support a causal link between tobacco advertising and smoking ("Cigarette Advertising," 1990; Tye et al., 1987).

Many cigarette ads focus on creating favorable images of smoking (Chapman & Fitzgerald, 1982; Klintzner, Gruenewald, & Bamberger, 1991). In this chapter, we present results from the second Annenberg Tobacco Survey to show how this imagery creates favorable feelings about smoking while dampening perceptions of health risks. Using a diffusion model, we examine the effects of advertising's influence on both the individual and the peer group. Finally, we examine the effects of anticigarette advertising on the imagery, feelings, and risk perceptions that young people associate with smoking. From this analysis, we conclude that the decline in adolescents' perceived health risk of smoking as they age is a result of the diffusion of favorable images and feelings toward the behavior. Recent counteradvertising has had little effect on imagery and feelings. It has been shown to increase the perception of risk, but because imagery and feelings contribute more heavily to smoking initiation than does perception of risk, this effect is too small to have much impact on its own.

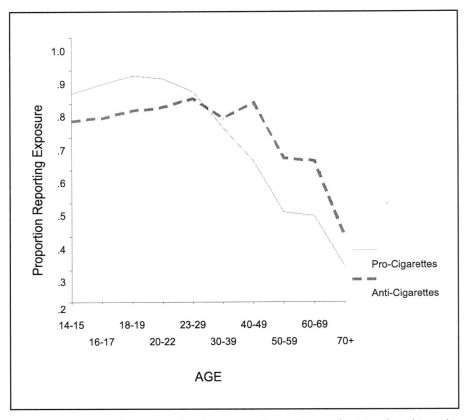

Figure 7.1. Cigarette advertising reaches the young audience. Counteradvertising also achieves this objective although with somewhat less reach.

🌀 Exposure to Cigarette Ads and Counteradvertising

We assessed exposure to cigarette advertising by asking respondents in the second Annenberg survey to name a brand of cigarettes for which they had recently seen an ad. Figure 7.1 shows the proportion of each age group that could name a recently advertised brand. Exposure was highest (about 90%) in the 14-29 age range and declined thereafter. We found that cigarette advertising was most likely to be noticed by younger people and was reported only slightly more often by smokers than by nonsmokers (data not shown). There was little difference in exposure between the ages of 14 and 29.

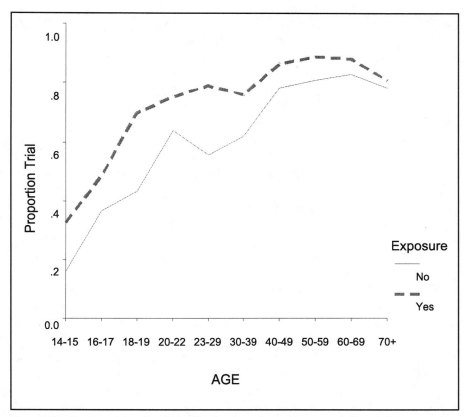

Figure 7.2. Cigarette trial reaches higher levels among those able to name a brand of cigarettes they had recently seen advertised (yes) compared with those who did not recall seeing such ads (no).

In addition to questions about cigarette industry ads, we asked respondents whether they had seen or heard any ads in the past month that "told people why they shouldn't smoke." As Figure 7.1 indicates, about 75% of young people had seen such ads. Antismoking advertising appears to be reaching the right audience. It had also reached respondents older than age 30.

∾ Diffusion of Smoking Initiation

Figure 7.2 shows cigarette trial (reports of "ever having smoked a cigarette, even one or two puffs") as a function of age and exposure to cigarette advertising. Although considerable trial occurs among young people who cannot recall the name of an advertised cigarette brand, exposure to cigarette advertising is related to younger initial age of smoking and to higher proportions of trial. Because trial among older age groups is likely to have occurred when they were younger, the figure also reflects cohort differences in the popularity of smoking at various times in the past. For example, respondents in the 23-39 age range reported virtually the same level of trial as those in the 18-22 age range. Consistent with the evidence presented in Chapter 2, this probably reflects the lower levels of smoking initiation that occurred in the 1980s, when most of this segment was first experimenting with tobacco. Older cohorts reported higher levels of trial, reflecting the greater popularity of smoking when these individuals were adolescents.

We used a diffusion model to examine the mechanisms that encourage the initiation of smoking in young people ages 14 to 22. Such models have been used to explain the diffusion of new products in marketing (Mahajan & Peterson, 1985) as well as the initiation of risk behavior in adolescents (Rodgers & Rowe, 1993), including smoking (Rowe, Chassin, Presson, Edwards, & Sherman, 1992). Diffusion resulting from advertising and the media is often found to produce a more rapid growth pattern than diffusion produced by interpersonal processes, which begin more slowly before accelerating (S-shaped growth). However, the processes can occur in tandem (Valente, 1995), with advertisers sending favorable images of smokers that diffuse rapidly while smoking initiation follows the S-shaped pattern characteristic of the diffusion of behavior through peer networks. The initiation curves in Figure 7.2 display the S-shaped pattern at the point where rapid growth in trial is just beginning to emerge. We will call this combination of diffusion patterns the *image diffusion model of smoking* (IDMS).

Table 7.1 lists the major stages in the IDMS. According to the model, the diffusion of favorable images by cigarette advertising reaches individual young people as well as their friends. As exposure to advertising builds shared images of smoking within peer networks, the favorable feelings elicited by the images make the behavior more attractive and more acceptable. When acceptance of smoking grows within peer networks, peer approval creates a climate favorable to initiation. Over time, this climate supports the diffusion of smoking behavior, as individuals most attracted to cigarettes initiate the behavior and thereby encourage others with somewhat less favorable attitudes to follow. According to this model, industry advertising promotes smoking by rapidly disseminating favorable images of smoking to young people, who become more likely to smoke as they recognize the acceptance of this behavior by their peers. Antitobacco advertising could in principle counteract the diffusion of favorable images by disseminating unfavorable images of smokers and favorable images of nonsmokers.

TABLE 7.1   Stages in the Image Diffusion Model of Smoking

1. Favorable images reach individuals and their friends.
2. Images elicit favorable feelings that increase attraction toward smoking.
3. Perceived support for smoking grows among peers.
4. Initiation of smoking occurs first for those most attracted to the behavior.
5. Initiation then diffuses to those who are somewhat less attracted.

〜 Imagery Promoted by Cigarette Advertising

Cigarette advertising tends to sell the product by showing favorable images of users and of the experience of smoking rather than by highlighting specific product attributes. Sexy, attractive users in relaxed settings are common images. To assess their effects, we examined several images associated with smoking (popularity, celebrity status, relaxation, drinking) as well as several consequences attributed to smoking (weight management, relaxation, and inability to participate in athletics) to see whether they were related to advertising exposure and whether they were motivating for young people.

After asking respondents to imagine someone smoking a cigarette, we asked them to describe the smoker along 11 dimensions. From these ratings, four images of smoking were identified using factor analysis: the *popular* smoker, who is a combination of happy, attractive, and popular; the *relaxed* smoker, who is a combination of relaxed and not anxious or sick; the *celebrity* smoker, who is alone but a celebrity; and the *drinker,* who has just done something satisfying. Figures 7.3A-7.3D (pp. 134-137) show the age patterns of the component images, and Figures 7.4A-7.4D (pp. 138-141) show the combined image scores as a function of exposure to cigarette advertising. Relaxation appears to be dominant among the four image types: That portrayal of smoking had already reached 60% of the youngest members of the adolescent sample and grew to about 70% of the 18- to 19-year-olds. As perceived relaxation increased, images of the ill smoker declined. Images of the anxious smoker remained stable in the young cohorts and increased in the older ones. As Figure 7.4A (p. 138) shows, the overall relaxation image (based on the three components) developed rapidly and to a greater extent among young people exposed to advertising. Those not exposed to advertising also received the image, but with a lag.

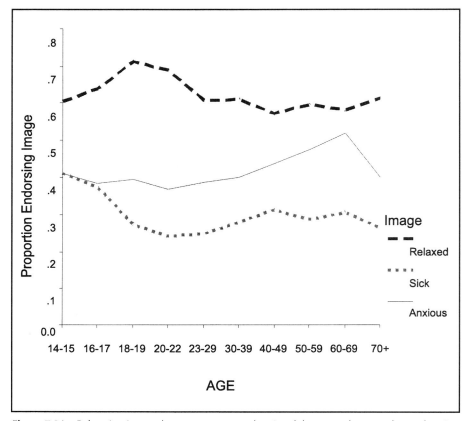

Figure 7.3A. Relaxation images become more prevalent in adolescent cohorts, and nonrelaxation images (sick and anxious) decline.

Popularity images also increased with age and were more common among those exposed to advertising (Figures 7.3B and 7.4B). Celebrity status was somewhat more salient among the younger groups (Figures 7.3C and 7.4C) and was apparently cultivated outside mainstream advertising, perhaps through films and other media (Terre, Drabman, & Speer, 1991). The concept of the smoker as drinker also grew among the young (Figures 7.3D and 7.4D), but it appeared to be more aligned with advertising among older age groups.

Exposure to cigarette advertising was strongly related to images of popularity and relaxation, especially among the young. Smokers reported these images more often than did nonsmokers (data not shown). However, in analyses presented later in this chapter, we will show that advertising is more likely to be a cause of

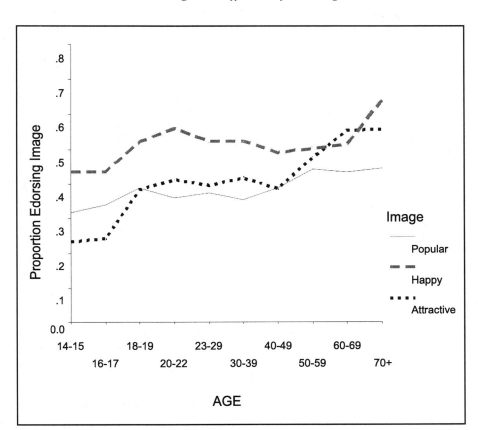

Figure 7.3B. Popularity images grow during adolescence.

imagery and feelings than a result of current smoking levels. For that reason, we present imagery results without controlling for smoking status.

We also found that the perceived benefit of relaxation from smoking increased during adolescence (Figure 7.5, p. 142). We asked respondents whether they thought it was true or false that "smoking makes (would make) it easier for me to relax and have a good time with friends." Belief that cigarettes are relaxing increased even in young people not exposed to cigarette advertising, suggesting that the associations built by advertising eventually diffuse to those not heavily exposed to ads. This diffusion process is evident in the acquisition of the relaxation image as a function of friendship-group smoker composition (Figure 7.6, p. 143). Among young people with greater proportions of friends who smoke, the relaxation image grew more rapidly. This pattern is consistent with the early stages of the IDMS.

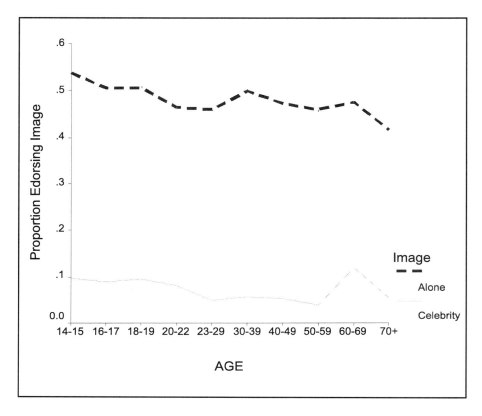

Figure 7.3C. Celebrity images tend to be stronger among the young.

We also asked respondents about two other consequences sometimes attached to smoking: weight loss and inability to participate in athletics. Neither of
these consequences was associated with exposure to advertising. Smokers appre-
ciated the expected benefit of losing weight more than did nonsmokers. However,
this perceived benefit was not as salient among men. Among women smokers
of all ages, more than 40% saw smoking as a way to control weight (Figure 7.7,
p. 144). Finally, very low proportions of young smokers said that they thought they
could smoke and still participate in athletics (Figure 7.8, p. 145). Older smokers
believed they could participate in athletics more than did younger smokers.

In summary, we found that two related images of smoking are associated with
exposure to cigarette advertising in young people: popularity and relaxation.
These images are also diffused through peer networks. Although the celebrity image is associated with youth smoking, it does not appear to be created by advertis-

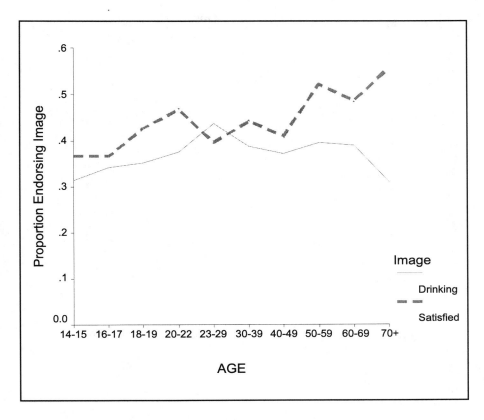

Figure 7.3D. Drinking image grows during adolescence.

ing. The drinker image is more likely to be tied to smoking in older age groups. Young people appear to be aware of the unhealthy consequences of smoking, at least as far as athletic participation is concerned. The presumed weight-control benefits of smoking are also not associated with advertising, although women appear to be more sensitive to and attracted to this benefit than are men.

∾ Feelings Associated With Smoking

The diffusion of favorable images of smoking is an effective strategy in cigarette advertising. We asked respondents how good or bad they would expect to feel if

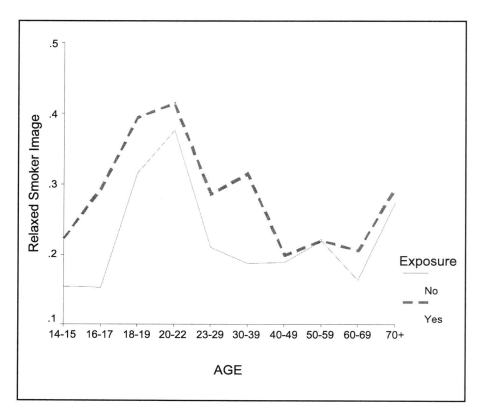

Figure 7.4A. Relaxed image of smoker (relaxation minus anxious and sick) grows rapidly during adolescence, especially among those exposed to advertising. There is a lag in the growth of the image among those not exposed.

they smoked a cigarette. We also asked them to rate how risky smoking is to the smoker's health. Figure 7.9 (p. 146) shows that feelings associated with the smoking experience in persons ages 14 to 22 were highly related to favorable relaxation images of the behavior. As relaxation images of smoking became more favorable, feelings became more positive and perceptions of the risks of smoking declined. These findings suggest that, by creating favorable imagery and affect in young people, advertising lays the groundwork for the subsequent diffusion of smoking initiation through peer networks.

An important step in the diffusion process is the creation of support for the new behavior in the peer group. Indeed, adolescents exposed to cigarette advertising reported greater prevalence of smoking in their friendship networks. As Figure 7.10 (p. 147) indicates, this reported prevalence grew with age and exposure to cigarette advertising. The perception that others in one's peer networks are en-

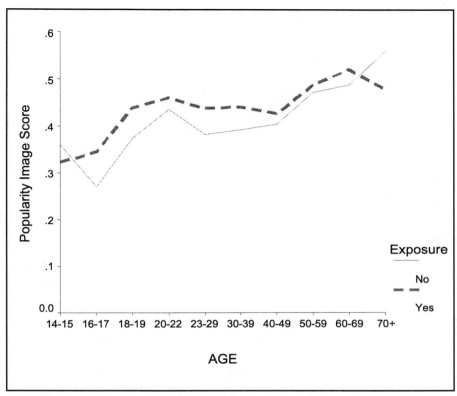

Figure 7.4B. Popular image of the smoker (popular, happy, and attractive) is stronger among those exposed to advertising during adolescence. This image is also strong among the older cohorts.

gaging in a new behavior is a primary determinant of behavioral diffusion (Mahajan & Petersen, 1985; Rodgers & Rowe, 1993). Research on successful counteradvertis- ing suggests that the belief that peers are not likely to smoke inhibits the diffusion of smoking (Flynn et al., 1994; Siegel & Biener, 2000).

๑๐ Diffusion of Smoking Through Peer Networks

The IDMS predicts that cigarette trial diffuses more rapidly through peer networks with smokers and that this process is facilitated among individuals with

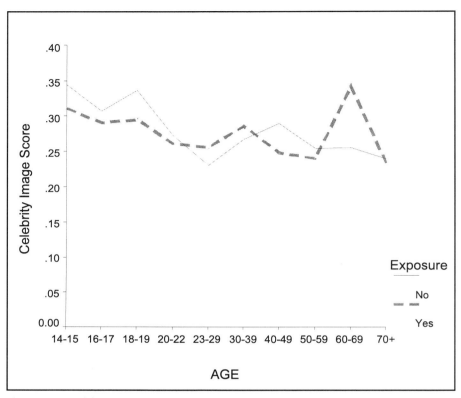

Figure 7.4C. Celebrity image (celebrity and alone) is greatest among youth. However, it is not stronger among those exposed to advertising.

more favorable feelings toward smoking. Figure 7.11 (p. 148) shows the prevalence of cigarette trial across the ages in our surveys. The proportion of adolescents ages 14 and 15 who had tried smoking was a function of the prevalence of smoking among their friends. Adolescents with friends who smoke reached higher levels of trial, and they did so at younger ages. The convergence in growth curves as age increases suggests that today's friendship groups play a smaller role in smoking trial than they did when the older cohorts were younger.

Figure 7.12 (p. 149) shows the prevalence of cigarette trial for respondents grouped by age and feelings toward smoking. In this case, young people with favorable feelings toward smoking reached higher levels of trial at younger ages. Individuals are much less susceptible to diffusion if they have unfavorable feelings about smoking. The combined influence of feelings and perceived prevalence of smoking is shown in Figure 7.13 (p. 150) for young people ages 14 to 22. The influence of friends on cigarette trial was greater the more favorable the person's feelings toward smoking. For respondents with both favorable feelings and very high

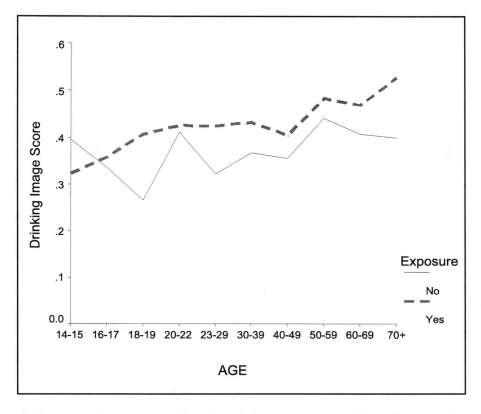

Figure 7.4D. Drinking image (drinking and satisfied) is stronger among older respondents and is more linked with advertising in older age groups.

proportions of friends who smoke, the probability of having tried cigarettes approaches 1.

In summary, cigarette advertising promotes the diffusion of smoking by facilitating the acceptance of favorable images of smoking behaviors within peer groups. This communication builds positive feelings toward smoking and encourages the diffusion of smoking behavior through peer networks.

∞ Counteradvertising and Perceived Risk

In Survey 2, self-reported exposure to anticigarette ads was also related to perceived risk of smoking, as Viscusi (1992b) has argued (Figure 7.14, p. 151). This relation was stronger for perceptions of lung cancer risk than for other health-re-

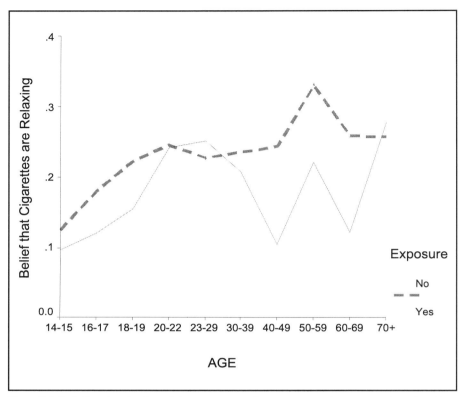

Figure 7.5. Belief in relaxation benefit is stronger at earlier ages among those exposed to advertising and remains salient in older persons exposed to advertising.

lated smoking risks (data not shown). However, the decline in risk perception that continued until about age 40 was independent of exposure to counteradvertising. This suggests that other factors are responsible for the decline in risk perception with age. Our results suggest that the rapid rise in favorable imagery, favorable feelings, and use of tobacco reduces the perceived risk associated with smoking. Indeed, Slovic, Finucane, Peters, and MacGregor (in press) have found evidence for an "affect heuristic" when people evaluate risks (see Slovic, Chapter 6, this volume). When using this heuristic, those with more positive feelings about an activity rate its risks as less threatening. According to this explanation, the decline in risk perception is related to increasingly favorable images and feelings toward smoking. To test this hypothesis, we formulated a sequence of causal models that examined the relations among advertising, imagery, feelings, cigarette trial, and risk perception in the 14-22 age group. Appendix C contains a description of the causal modeling methodology we used to study the relations among these variables.

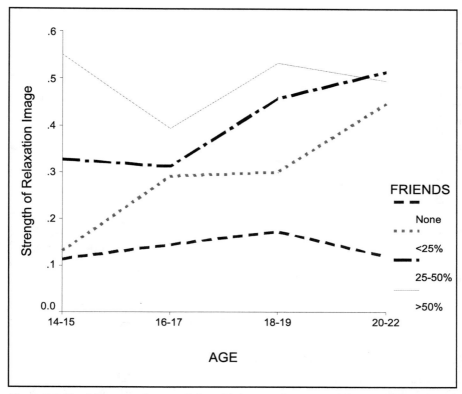

Figure 7.6. Friendship networks transmit favorable images of cigarette smoking. Young people with no friends who smoke are unlikely to have the relaxation image. Those with many friends who smoke have the image at an early age. The rest acquire the image over time.

◌ A Causal Model of Advertising Influence on Imagery, Feelings, and Smoking Trial

Our model places feelings at the center of the changes that occur during the 14-22 age period as registered in Survey 2. Imagery created by advertising directly affects feelings, and these feelings in turn affect smoking trial. In addition, positive feelings reduce risk perception, an effect that should also encourage trial. Health risk perception declines with age, an effect that is attributable to the buildup of favorable images and feelings during this adolescent period. As these images and feelings are shared in peer groups, social support is built for smoking. Smoking then

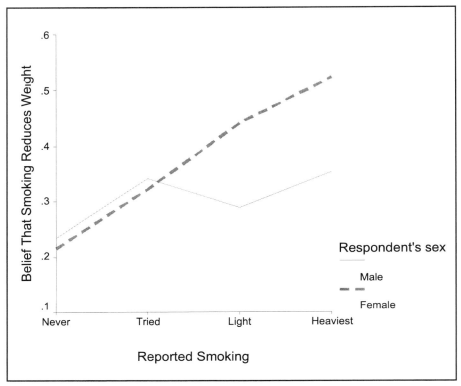

Figure 7.7. Belief that smoking can control weight is strongest in women who report currently smoking less than one cigarette per day (light) or more compared with those who never smoked or who tried but did not continue (tried).

diffuses through peer groups. Counteradvertising could influence the same factors that cigarette advertising influences. We were interested in seeing whether current counteradvertising efforts have succeeded in affecting the images, feelings, and perceptions of risk that cigarette advertising influences.

   Our first causal model is shown in Figure 7.15 on page 152. This model looks at the influence of advertising, age, and white racial identification on trial of cigarette smoking. Each causal path has a standardized path coefficient (*sp*) representing the strength of its relationship. We focus on whites because of their greater levels of cigarette smoking in the 14-22 age group (Johnston, O'Malley, & Bachman, 1999b; see also Chapter 2, this volume) and the likelihood that this will influence peer group formation and the diffusion of smoking in those groups. Health risk perception was indexed by two ratings of smoking risk, the perceived risk of smoking to the respondent's health (hypothetically for nonsmokers and current smoking for smokers) and the perceived risk of smoking every day. These ratings

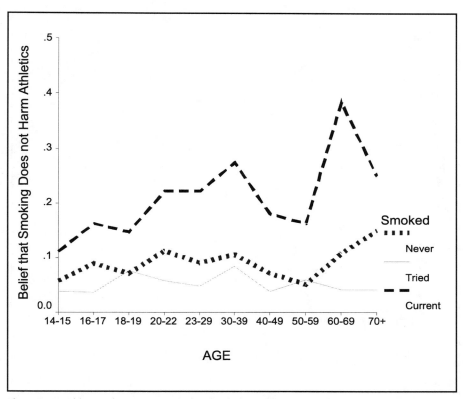

Figure 7.8. Older smokers are more inclined to believe that smoking does not interfere with athletics.

were correlated ($r = .51$) and used to create a health risk mediator in the analysis (Risk). Viscusi's measure of health risk, attributed risk for lung cancer mortality, was not included in this factor because it correlates less well with risk ratings ($r = .15$). Its exclusion does not change our conclusions. We analyze this measure in Chapter 4 of this volume, where we consider a wide range of risk indicators as predictors of trial.

Figure 7.15 shows that, as adolescents age, risk perception plays a small role in deterring cigarette trial ($sp = -.17, p < .001$). The direct relation between age and trial in our sample ($sp = .31, p < .001$) was more than 30 times greater than the relation mediated by risk ($-.07 \times -.17 = -.01$). Nevertheless, risk perception declined with age even after exposure to advertising was controlled for. Exposure to cigarette advertising was positively related to trial ($sp = .10, p < .001$) and, surprisingly, counteradvertising was as well ($sp = .07, p < .001$). Neither counteradver- tising nor cigarette advertising was related to perceived risk. The finding that whites were more likely to try smoking than other racial groups ($sp = .14, p < .001$) con-

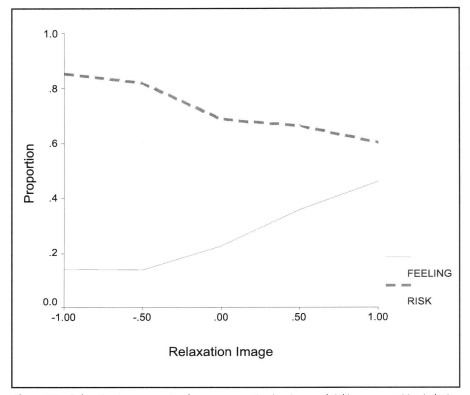

Figure 7.9. Relaxation image, ranging from very negative (anxious and sick) to very positive (relaxing but neither sick nor anxious), is associated with more favorable feelings toward smoking and less perceived risk in young people ages 14 to 22. The proportions of young people who report favorable feelings increase and the proportion who report that smoking is "very risky" decrease as imagery becomes more favorable.

firms the value of incorporating this variable into the analysis. Here again, this relation was not mediated at all by perceived risk. The model fit the data quite well. The comparative fit index (CFI) comparing the model with one in which none of the covariation in the data set is explained (Bentler, 1990) indicated that the model accounted for nearly all of the covariation (CFI = .999).

The second model shown in Figure 7.16 (p. 153) was identical to the first with the exception that peer approval of smoking was added as a predictor of trial and risk perception. Peer approval was indexed by two correlated measures: the perceived prevalence of smoking in one's friendship network and the perceived approval of smoking among friends (*r* = .34). Inclusion of this predictor eliminated the relation between age and risk perception. It also substantially reduced the relation between age and trial (from .31 to .22). The decline in these relations indicates that much of the growth in trial is attributable to peer-group influence, a

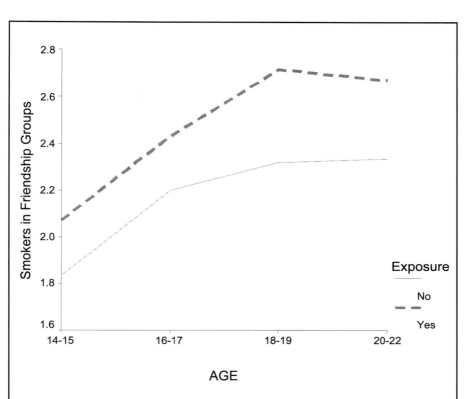

Figure 7.10. Young people's friendship groups increasingly include smokers, especially if they are exposed to advertising. Friendship scores are coded as 1 (*no friends*), 2 (<25%), 3 (25-50%), and 4 (>50%).

finding consistent with other research on smoking initiation (Conrad, Flay, & Hill, 1992). Because peer-group approval grows with age ($r = .24$) and is positively related to trial ($sp = .44$, $p < .001$), it can account for some of the influence of age on trial. Peer-group approval is also negatively related to risk perception ($sp = -.27$, $p < .001$). As a result, it accounts for the decline in risk perception with age.

Including peer approval in the model also reduced some of the impact of cigarette advertising (from .10 to .06). As the IDMS predicts, cigarette advertising influences trial in part by helping to build peer-group support for smoking. Because exposure to cigarette advertising and peer-group approval were correlated ($r = .13$), the positive impact of advertising on trial was partly mediated by peer-group influence. The positive relation between counteradvertising and trial was also eliminated (going from .07 to .03) once peer-group approval was held constant. As expected, the influence of race was also mediated by peer-group approval. The direct path between race and trial declined substantially in the second model (go-

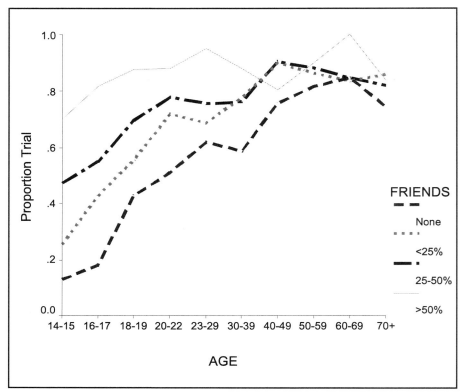

Figure 7.11. Cigarette trial reaches higher levels among young people with friends who smoke. Among those who report that more than half their friends smoke, trial has already reached 70% in the youngest age cohort. Among those with no smokers in their friendship network, trial has reached less than 20% at ages 14 and 15 and never reaches the high levels seen in the other groups.

ing from .14 to .07). The second model also accounted for nearly all of the covariation in the data set (CFI = .999).

In the second model, peer-group approval is an important mediator of trial that also accounts for the decline of risk perception as adolescents age. According to the IDMS, advertising influences trial by disseminating favorable images of and feelings about smoking. This influence helps to build peer-group support. According to this explanation, advertising influences peer approval through images and feelings received by the individual as well as by others in the peer group. To test this prediction, we added imagery and feelings as mediators of trial and risk perception. Feelings were indexed by two measures: how good or bad one would expect to feel smoking a cigarette and how relaxed or tense one would expect to feel smoking a cigarette. These items were highly correlated, $r = .54$. Imagery was

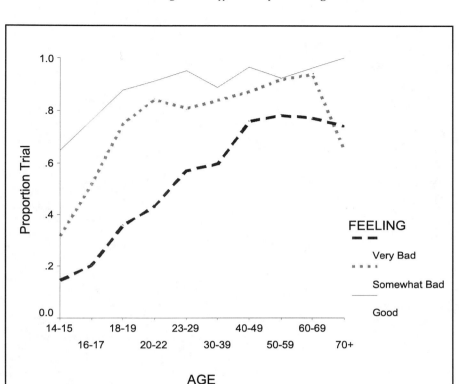

Figure 7.12. Cigarette trial reaches higher levels among young people with favorable feelings about smoking.

indexed by the two scores that were related to advertising: relaxation and popularity. These scores were also related to each other ($r = .32$).

The overall model in Figure 7.17 (p. 154) fit the data well, accounting for more than 99% of the potential goodness of fit in the data set (CFI = .998). It is noteworthy that imagery directly influenced feelings ($sp = .66$, $p < .001$), which were strongly related to both trial ($sp = .35$, $p < .001$) and risk ($sp = -.40$, $p < .001$). The more favorable one's feelings toward smoking, the lower one's perceptions of the risk of that behavior. However, risk was no longer related to trial ($sp = .04$, $p < .25$). Apparently, the negative relation between trial and risk perception is completely accounted for by the effects of feelings. Cigarette advertising increases positive imagery ($sp = .07$, $p < .05$), which then affects feelings. Advertising does not affect feelings directly ($sp = .04$, $p < .15$).

There is controversy in the peer-influence literature as to whether the peer group influences the individual's risk behavior directly or the individual selects

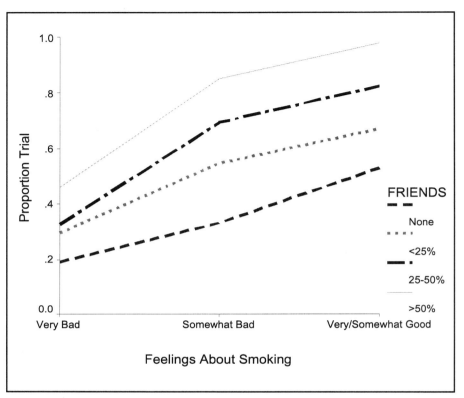

Figure 7.13. The influence of friends on cigarette trial is greater as feelings become more favorable among young people ages 14 to 22.

the peer group based on similar attitudes and preferences toward risk behavior (Ennett & Bauman, 1994; Fisher & Bauman, 1988; Sieving, Perry, & Williams, 2000). The stages outlined in the IDMS suggest that both processes occur. By disseminating favorable images of smokers, advertising encourages attraction to peers who smoke (selection). At the same time, approval of smoking by peers encourages smoking among those who have not yet started (diffusion).

The results in the model provide support for both selection and diffusion. Imagery leads to greater peer approval ($sp = .19, p < .01$), and feelings influence both trial and peer-group approval ($sp = .46, p < .001$), indicating that individuals who are predisposed to smoke are also attracted to peers who smoke. Nevertheless, peer-group approval directly affects trial apart from the influence of feelings ($sp = .29, p < .001$), indicating that smoking diffuses through peer networks. The influence of the peer group is also registered in the finding that peer-group approval mediates the greater smoking by whites than nonwhites. One of the reasons whites smoke more is that they are exposed to more smoking among their peers

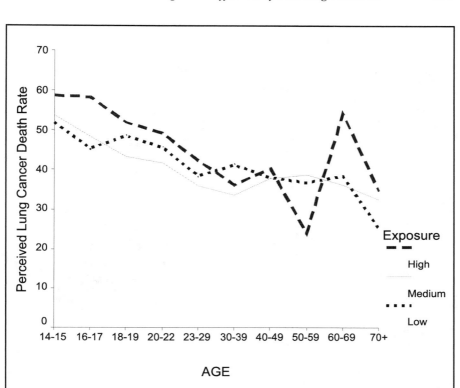

Figure 7.14. Young people exposed to heavier levels of counteradvertising report higher death rates from lung cancer among lifetime smokers. Exposure to counteradvertising was coded as high if respondents reported seeing or hearing many ads that give people reasons not to smoke, medium if they reported only some ads, and low if they reported no ads.

$(.13 \times .29 = .04)$, an effect that is separate from their stronger feelings about smoking $(.06 \times .35 = .02)$. In addition, advertising directly influences peer approval $(sp = .07, p < .01)$ apart from its influence on imagery and feelings. This influence reflects the effects that advertising has on friendship networks, which also receive images supportive of smoking.

The model indicates that counteradvertising does not influence imagery or feelings. However, it does increase perceived risk $(sp = .07, p < .05)$. Unfortunately, risk perception is no longer a significant deterrent to smoking once feelings are held constant. As a result, the counteradvertising to which our young people reported exposure had little impact on preventing the initiation of smoking.

The model in Figure 7.17 (p. 154) assumes that peer approval of smoking is in part a consequence of imagery and feelings about the behavior. An alternative interpretation is that peer approval is a cause of imagery and feelings. This view

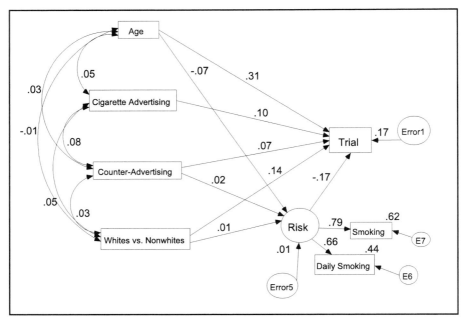

Figure 7.15. Causal model of smoking initiation (trial) in 14 to 22 age group with risk perception as a mediator. Standardized path weights indicate the magnitude of effects in the model.

gives the peer group a much stronger role in the development of favorable attitudes toward smoking. We tested this hypothesis by reversing the paths connecting imagery and feelings to peer approval. With peer approval as the cause of both imagery and feelings, the goodness of fit of the model declined (the Akaike information criterion [AIC; see Akaike, 1987] increased from 254.5 to 258.3, and the root mean square error of approximation [RMSEA] increased from .032 to .033). This comparison between models indicates that peer approval is a consequence of imagery and feelings (selection) as well as a cause of smoking.

A comparison of the results of the three models regarding the effects of age suggests that nearly half of the increase in cigarette trial over the 14-22 age range is explained by peer-group approval, imagery, and feelings. Peer-group approval (the model in Figure 7.16) reduced the direct effect from .31 to .22. The addition of imagery and feelings reduced it to .18. These reductions represent about 42% of the effect of age on trial. Other potential influences not mediated by diffusion from peers or by imagery and feelings would increase the explanatory power of the model. These influences might include family smoking as well as role models in films and other media. In addition, our causal model did not include other attitudes toward smoking based on the benefit of weight control, which may also contribute to cigarette trial, especially among young women. We did not assess

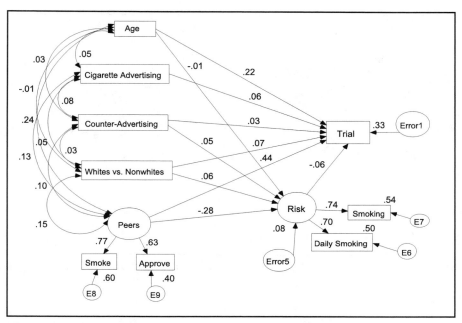

Figure 7.16. Causal model with peer approval as predictor of trial in 14 to 22 age group.

the separate impact of promotional activities such as giveaways of apparel and other items that display cigarette brand logos. Research suggests that these are potent influences on smoking behavior (Biener & Siegel, 2000; Pierce, Choi, Gilpin, Farkas, & Berry, 1998). We did not include promotional activity that occurs in bars where cigarette brands are used to sponsor entertainment. Finally, considerable cigarette promotion occurs under the aegis of sports events. We have found that young people who attend sports events are more likely to be aware of specific cigarette symbols, such as Joe Camel (see Chapter 2). We do not know whether this awareness was tapped when we asked respondents if they had seen or heard cigarette advertising.

An alternative explanation of the causal relations observed between advertising and smoking is a model in which advertising awareness is merely a consequence of individual and peer smoking behavior. To test this notion, we removed both cigarette advertising and counteradvertising from their role as causes of feelings and risk perception and made them consequences of feelings and imagery along with peer and personal smoking behavior. However, this model fit the data much less well than the advertising model (AIC increased from 253.0 to 340.9, and RMSEA increased from .032 to .040). In it, only peer smoking and trial affected advertising. Neither feelings nor imagery affected either form of advertising. In other words, the model with advertising as a cause of smoking provides a better

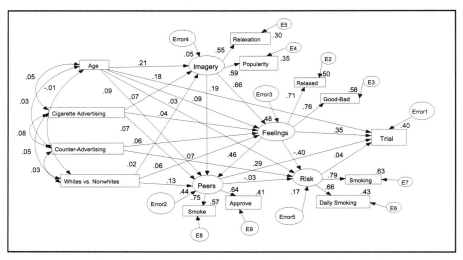

Figure 7.17. Causal model of cigarette trial with imagery, feelings, and risk as mediators in 14 to 22 age group.

explanation of the results than one in which smoking behavior drives advertising awareness.

⚭ Summary and Conclusions

The results found using the causal models indicate that, at the time of Survey 2, existing anticigarette advertising had not been successful in countering the favorable images of smoking cultivated by cigarette advertising. These campaigns have failed to increase the favorability of the nonsmoking image or to reduce the favorability of the smoking one. Although we have presented only the results of the effects of advertising on cigarette trial, tests to determine influences on current smoking revealed similar results. In Chapter 4 of this volume, we present more detailed models concerning the effects of various smoking risk beliefs on both initiation and progression to regular smoking.

One limitation of our analysis of counteradvertising is our inability to identify the source of the counteradvertising that respondents report. Some of this advertising is supported by the industry itself, and it may not be as effective as campaigns funded by states or other organizations. In addition, our sample is not large enough to identify the effects of particular statewide counteradvertising campaigns. Recent findings suggest that the early effects of the Massachusetts campaign included success in inhibiting initiation of smoking (Siegel & Biener, 2000). Evaluations of campaigns in California (Popham et al., 1994) and Florida (Bauer, Johnson, Hopkins, & Brooks, 2000) also suggest that these programs reduced smoking among young people, and the most recent surgeon general's report supports the use of mass media as part of concerted community efforts to reduce the onset and continuation of smoking (U.S. Department of Health and Human Services, 2000).

A frequent finding in studies of counteradvertising is that successful programs reduce adolescent smoking by reducing perceptions of support for smoking in peer networks (Flynn et al., 1994; Siegel & Biener, 2000). Our causal models suggest that the same process mediates the success of cigarette advertising. Unfortunately, when researchers test for the influence of cigarette advertising, they sometimes hold constant perceptions of smoking in peer groups (Biener & Siegel, 2000; Pierce et al., 1998). This procedure removes some of the effects of advertising itself and makes it look less influential than it actually is. As a result, the most potent effects of advertising appear to be restricted to young people who also report participation in promotional activities (e.g., giveaways of clothing with cigarette logos). Our results indicate that advertising has far wider effects than merely influencing the small proportion of youth who respond to such promotions (in Chapter 2, we report that about 9% of young people ages 12 to 17 have participated in such promotions).

Viscusi's (1992b) claim that anticigarette messages have been targeted to the young and have raised their perceptions of smoking risks is supported by our findings here. However, it is also clear that messages that only influence perceived risk will be relatively ineffective in influencing perceived benefits and favorable images that, even in the face of the risks of smoking, can encourage trial of smoking. These shared images can also encourage peers to influence one another's behavior. As a result, Viscusi's claim that young people reduce their smoking because of their heavy exposure to warnings about cigarette risks is not supported by our findings.

In summary, our causal models indicate that the dramatic decline in risk perception that characterizes the later adolescent period is a result of the widespread diffusion of favorable images of smoking and positive feelings about the experience. Favorable feelings associated with smoking may allow the affect heuristic suggested by Slovic (see Chapter 6) to undermine the deterrent effect of perceived risk on smoking trial. As a result, even if anticigarette advertising increases perceived risk, the overwhelming influence of tobacco industry advertising and promotion acts to increase favorable images and feelings associated with smoking. These images and feelings then reduce the perception of risk.

Part IV

ADDICTION

∾ Chapter 8

The Nature of
Nicotine Addiction

Neal L. Benowitz

Cigarettes and other forms of tobacco are addicting. Most smokers use to-bacco regularly because they are addicted to nicotine. Furthermore, most smokers find it difficult to quit using tobacco because they are addicted to nicotine. Nicotine addiction develops in the first few years of cigarette smoking —that is, for most people, during adolescence or early adulthood. Most smokers begin smoking during childhood or adolescence: 89% of daily smokers tried their first cigarette by or at age 18, and 71% of persons who have ever smoked daily began smoking daily by age 18 (see Table 8.1). Among persons under 18 years of age, more than 6,000 try their first cigarette and more than 3,000 become daily smokers each day ("Incidence," 1998). The earlier in life a child tries a cigarette, the more likely he or she is to become a regular smoker (that is, to smoke monthly or more frequently) or a daily smoker. For example, 67% of children who initiate smoking in the 6th grade become regular adult smokers, and 46% of teenagers who initiate smoking in the 11th grade become regular adult smokers (Chassin, Presson, Sherman, & Edwards, 1990). Furthermore, the earlier a young person begins smoking, the more cigarettes he or she will smoke as an adult (Tailoi & Wynder, 1991). Prevention of tobacco addiction and the related health conse-

AUTHOR'S NOTE: This is a revised version of a chapter that appeared in *Growing Up Tobacco Free: Preventing Nicotine Addiction in Children and Youths,* edited by B. S. Lynch and R. J. Bonnie. Copyright © 1994 by National Academy Press. Reprinted with permission of the National Academy Press, Washington, DC.

159

TABLE 8.1   Cumulative Percentages of Recalled Age at Which Persons Ages 30-39 First Tried a Cigarette or Began Smoking Daily

Age (years)	All Persons (N = 6,388)	Persons Who Had Ever Tried a Cigarette	Persons Who Had Ever Smoked Daily	
< 12	14.1	18.0	15.6	1.9
< 14	29.7	38.0	36.7	8.0
< 16	48.2	61.9	62.2	24.9
< 18	63.7	81.6	81.9	53.0
≤ 18	68.8	88.2	89.0	71.2
< 20	71.0	91.0	91.3	77.0

SOURCE: National Household Surveys on Drug Abuse, United States, 1991, cited in Centers for Disease Control and Prevention (1994a, p. 65).

quences, therefore, requires early intervention for children and adolescents. To understand why young people use tobacco and why prevention measures are necessary and preferable to cessation measures to deter young people's tobacco use, it is useful to understand nicotine dependence. This chapter reviews (a) the general aspects of nicotine dependence, derived from research primarily conducted with adults, and (b) the evidence concerning nicotine dependence and the factors that promote initiation and progression of tobacco use among young people.

∽ General Aspects of Nicotine Addiction

The Daily Nicotine Addiction Cycle

Given the pharmacological properties of nicotine, a daily cycle of addiction can be described as follows. The first cigarette of the day produces substantial pharmacological effects (pleasure, arousal, enhanced performance), but simultaneously the brain's chemistry changes and tolerance begins to develop. With subsequent cigarettes, nicotine accumulates in the body and is associated with the development of a greater level of tolerance. Withdrawal symptoms become more pronounced between successive cigarettes. The tolerance that develops over the day may be partially overcome by the transiently high brain levels of nicotine that occur immediately after the smoking of individual cigarettes, but the primary pleasurable effects of individual cigarettes tend to lessen throughout the day. As the day progresses, people tend to smoke more to relieve the symptoms of abstinence. Overnight abstinence allows considerable resensitization to the actions of nicotine, and the cycle begins again the next day.

What Is Addiction?

The World Health Organization describes drug dependence as "a behavioral pattern in which the use of a given psychoactive drug is given a sharply higher priority over other behaviors that once had a significantly higher value" (Edwards, Arif, & Hodgson, 1982, p. 19). In other words, the drug comes to control behavior to an extent considered detrimental to the individual or to society.

Historically, the term *drug addiction* meant that tolerance developed to the effects of a drug during repetitive use, and that after cessation of such use, withdrawal symptoms emerged (termed *physical dependence*). The prototypical addictive drug was heroin, and drug addiction has had a connotation of social deviance or criminal behavior in the United States. This historical view of addiction was revised by the 1964 Expert Committee of the World Health Organization. As discussed in detail in the 1988 surgeon general's report, such a definition is narrow and does not address addictions such as cocaine or binge alcoholism (Centers for Disease Control, 1988). A definition based on concepts of drug dependence developed by expert committees of the World Health Organization and appearing in publications of the National Institute on Drug Abuse and the American Psychiatric Association includes compulsive drug-seeking behavior, effect of the drug on the brain, and usually a need for the drug to maintain homeostasis. Specific criteria for a drug that produces dependence or addiction have been presented by the U.S. surgeon general (Centers for Disease Control, 1988; see Table 8.2), and specific criteria for diagnosing drug dependence or addiction in individuals have been presented by the American Psychiatric Association (1994; see Table 8.3).

Pharmacological Aspects of Nicotine

The pharmacological effects of nicotine are essential to sustaining cigarette smoking. Viewed another way, people use tobacco to deliver nicotine to their bodies. The primary physiological effects of nicotine (reviewed in detail in Centers for Disease Control, 1988) are as follows:

TABLE 8.2   Criteria for Drug Dependence

Primary criteria
  Highly controlled or compulsive use
  Psychoactive effects
  Drug-reinforced behavior

Additional criteria
  Addictive behavior often involves the following:
    Stereotypical patterns of use
    Use despite harmful effects
    Relapse following abstinence
    Recurrent drug cravings
  Dependence-producing drugs often manifest the following:
    Tolerance
    Physical dependence
    Pleasant (euphoric) effects

SOURCE: Adapted from Centers for Disease Control (1988).

- Electroencephalographic desynchronization
- Increased circulating levels of catecholamines, vasopressin, growth hormone, adrenocorticotropic hormone, cortisol, prolactin, and beta-endorphin
- Increased metabolic rate
- Lipolysis, increased free fatty acids
- Heart rate acceleration
- Cutaneous and coronary vasoconstriction
- Increased cardiac output
- Increased blood pressure
- Skeletal muscle relaxation

Smokers give various explanations for their smoking. Many report that smoking produces arousal, particularly with the first few cigarettes of the day, and relaxation, particularly in stressful situations. Many smokers report that smoking helps them concentrate and lifts their mood. Nicotine has been shown to increase vigilance in the performance of repetitive tasks and to enhance selective attention. Smokers commonly report pleasure and reduced anger, tension, depression, and stress after smoking a cigarette. The extent to which the enhanced performance and mood after smoking are due to the relief of symptoms of abstinence or to an intrinsic enhancement effect on the brain is unclear. A few studies do show im-

TABLE 8.3   Criteria for Substance Dependence

A maladaptive pattern of substance use, leading to clinically significant impairment or distress, as manifested by three (or more) of the following, occurring at any time in the same 12-month period:

1. Tolerance, as defined by either of the following:
   a. A need for markedly increased amounts of the substance to achieve intoxication or desired effect.
   b. Markedly diminished effect with continued use of the same amount of the substance.
2. Withdrawal, as manifested by either of the following:
   a. The characteristic withdrawal syndrome for the substance (refer to Criteria A and B of the criteria sets for withdrawal from the specific substance).
   b. The same (or a closely related) substance is taken to relieve or avoid withdrawal symptoms.
3. The substance is often taken in larger amounts or over a longer period than was intended.
4. There is a persistent desire or unsuccessful efforts to cut down or control substance use.
5. A great deal of time is spent in activities necessary to obtain the substance (e.g., visiting multiple doctors or driving long distances), use the substance (e.g., chain-smoking), or recover from its effects.
6. Important social, occupational, or recreational activities are given up or reduced because of substance abuse.
7. The substance use is continued despite knowledge of having a persistent or recurrent physical or psychological problem that is likely to have been caused or exacerbated by the substance (e.g., current cocaine use despite recognition of cocaine-induced depression, or continued drinking despite recognition that an ulcer was made worse by alcohol consumption).

SOURCE: American Psychiatric Association (1994, p. 181).

provement in the performance of nonsmoking subjects after dosing with nicotine, suggesting at least some direct enhancement.

Some of the gratifying effects of nicotine are due to the relief of the symptoms of nicotine withdrawal. When nicotine use is abruptly stopped, withdrawal symptoms emerge. The typical symptoms are as follows:

- Restlessness
- Eating more than usual
- Anxiety/tension
- Impatience
- Irritability/anger

- Difficulty concentrating
- Excessive hunger
- Depression
- Disorientation
- Loss of energy/fatigue
- Dizziness
- Stomach or bowel problems
- Headaches
- Sweating
- Insomnia
- Heart palpitations
- Tremors
- Craving cigarettes (Gritz, Carr, & Marcus, 1991)

Most withdrawal symptoms reach maximal intensity 24 to 48 hours after cessation of tobacco use and gradually diminish in intensity over several weeks. Some symptoms, such as eating more than usual, weight gain, and craving cigarettes (particularly in stressful situations) may persist for months or even years after cessation.

Actions of Nicotine on the Brain

The nicotine molecule is shaped like acetylcholine. Acetylcholine is a neurotransmitter—that is, a chemical naturally found in the body that is involved in transmitting information from one neuron to another. Receptors (specialized proteins that selectively bind drugs and initiate drug effects in the body) for acetylcholine are called cholinergic receptors. Nicotine acts on certain cholinergic receptors in the brain and other organs of the body. The receptors would normally be acted on by the body's own acetylcholine. By activating cholinergic receptors, nicotine enhances the release of other neurotransmitters and hormones, including acetylcholine, norepinephrine, dopamine, vasopressin, serotonin, and beta-endorphin. The physiological effects of nicotine include behavioral arousal and sympathetic neural activation. Release of specific neurotransmitters has been speculatively linked to particular reinforcing effects of nicotine (Pomerleau & Pomerleau, 1984). For example, enhanced release of dopamine, norepinephrine, and serotonin may be associated with pleasure as well as appetite suppression, the latter of which may contribute to lower body weight. Release of acetylcholine may be associated with improved performance on behavioral tasks and improvement of memory. Release of beta-endorphin may be associated with reduction of anxiety and tension.

Tolerance and Withdrawal

With prolonged or repetitive exposure to nicotine, the brain cells adapt in such a way as to compensate for the actions of nicotine—that is, to return brain functioning to normal. This process is called neuroadaptation. Neuroadaptation is associated with an increasing number of nicotinic receptors in the brain. Neuroadaptation results in the development of tolerance; that is, a given level of nicotine comes to have less of an effect on the body, and higher levels of nicotine are needed to produce the effects that lower doses formerly produced. Substantial tolerance develops to the behavioral arousal and cardiovascular effects of nicotine when a person smokes multiple cigarettes or uses multiple doses of smokeless tobacco, even within the course of a single day. Regular tobacco users regain sensitivity to the effects of nicotine, at least in part, after overnight abstinence from tobacco.

When the brain has adapted so as to function normally in the presence of nicotine, it also becomes dependent on the presence of nicotine for normal functioning. When nicotine is not available (such as when a smoker stops smoking), the brain function becomes disturbed, resulting in a number of withdrawal symptoms, as mentioned above.

Absorption of Nicotine From Tobacco

Nicotine from tobacco smoke is rapidly absorbed into the systemic circulation after inhalation, then is quickly carried to various body organs, including the brain. Nicotine levels in the blood rise quickly after smoking, with arterial blood levels exceeding venous levels in the first few minutes. Because nicotine is a weak base and is ionized at acid pH, there is little absorption of nicotine through the membranes of the mouth from the acidic smoke of blond (light-colored) tobacco. However, the smoke of pipes, cigars, and dark tobacco is more alkaline, so nicotine is absorbed through the mouth from these products.

Distribution and Elimination
of Nicotine From the Body

A cigarette delivers nicotine to the brain within 10 to 19 seconds from the start of a puff. The rapid passage of nicotine from the lungs to the arterial circulation to the brain provides for rapid behavioral reinforcement for smoking and for the possibility for the smoker to control levels of nicotine in the brain and to modulate pharmacological effects. Nicotine is also distributed extensively to other body tissues. Slow release from tissues explains in part the elimination half-life of 2 to 3 hours.

Nicotine is eliminated primarily by liver metabolism. The rate of metabolism is quite variable from person to person, so the same level of nicotine intake may be associated with different concentrations of nicotine in the blood of different people. The main metabolite of nicotine, cotinine, has a long half-life (on average 17 hours) and has been widely used by researchers as a biochemical marker of nicotine exposure.

Intake and Accumulation of Nicotine During Cigarette Smoking

On the average, smoking a cigarette results in the absorption into the bloodstream of about 1 mg of nicotine, but the range is from 0.5 to 3.0 mg. The elimination half-life of nicotine is 2 to 3 hours. This means that the level of nicotine in the blood decreases by one-half every 2 or 3 hours. It also means that after a single use of tobacco, nicotine remains in the body for 8 to 12 hours. With repeated smoking, nicotine levels accumulate over 6 to 8 hours, plateauing through the remainder of the day, then gradually falling overnight. Thus regular cigarette smoking results in continued exposure of the brain and body to nicotine.

Addiction and the Light or Occasional Smoker

Among adults, the light or occasional smoker (i.e., one who regularly smokes five or fewer cigarettes per day or who does not smoke every day) is in general less addicted than are daily smokers of more than five cigarettes per day (Shiffman, 1989). Smoking appears to be reinforced for light smokers by the direct pharmacological effects of nicotine, as described above, as well as by behavioral aspects of tobacco use, as described below. The use of tobacco in response to withdrawal symptoms is less of a factor in such tobacco users. Among adults, light or occasional smokers are relatively uncommon (less than 10% of adult smokers; Centers for Disease Control, 1989); they have higher success in smoking cessation than do heavier smokers, although not all light smokers are able to quit. In contrast, many more children than adults are light or occasional smokers. However, light smoking by children is often not a stable pattern; rather, it represents a stage in escalation to daily smoking.

Nicotine Compensation

The "Low-Yield" Cigarette

Some tobacco advertisements indicate that particular brands of cigarettes deliver less nicotine and tar than their competitors' brands, implying a health benefit to low-yield cigarettes. Some people switch to low-yield cigarettes in an attempt to reduce the health consequences of smoking, but that is an unlikely result. A daily smoker tends to regulate his or her nicotine intake to a specific level in order to achieve desired effects and to minimize withdrawal symptoms. This nicotine regulation influences how smokers smoke cigarettes with various nicotine yields and how they respond to cutting down on the number of cigarettes they smoke per day. When smoking lower-yield cigarettes, smokers puff more frequently or more intensely than when smoking higher-yield cigarettes, presumably to obtain their usual specific level of nicotine from each cigarette. In switching from high-yield to low-yield cigarettes, smokers consume more nicotine from the low-yield cigarette than predicted by smoking-machine tests. Conversely, smokers consume less nicotine than predicted from high-yield cigarettes.

The intake of nicotine, with blood cotinine or nicotine concentrations used as markers of nicotine intake, has been studied in large groups of people smoking their chosen brands of cigarettes (Benowitz et al., 1983). In such studies, nicotine intake has been found to correlate only weakly with the advertised yield. The slope of the regression line between advertised nicotine yields and blood nicotine or cotinine levels is shallow, suggesting only small differences of intake from cigarettes of widely different nicotine yields. Because of this compensatory smoking, having smokers switch to low-yield cigarettes reduces the risk of smoking to a much lesser degree, if at all, than suggested by the decreases in yield.

Smoking Fewer Cigarettes

The regulation of nicotine intake by daily smokers is also apparent when the number of cigarettes available to a smoker is restricted. In one study of heavy smokers, when the number of cigarettes was reduced from unlimited (average 37 per day) to 5 cigarettes per day, the average intake of nicotine per cigarette tripled (Benowitz, Jacob, Kozlowski, & Yu, 1986). As a result, reducing the number of cigarettes to 15 per day had very little effect, and reducing to 5 cigarettes per day reduced the daily exposure to tobacco toxins only by 50%. This observation explains why many smokers who are instructed to quit report cutting down to about 10 cigarettes per day, but cannot reduce their consumption to fewer than 10. At 10 cigarettes per day, smokers still can absorb adequate nicotine to maintain nicotine addiction.

Behavioral Aspects of Addiction

The behavior of smoking is maintained both by the direct pharmacological effects of nicotine (including relief of withdrawal) and by learned responses. Anticipatory responses develop as a consequence of repetitive use of tobacco, during which various kinds of gratifications from smoking occur in the presence of specific cues from the environment. For example, when a smoker encounters stressors or situational reminders of smoking, these stimuli revivify the pleasurable or other reinforcing aspects of smoking, which then generate the urge to smoke. Such recurrent anticipatory responses may persist 6 months or longer after physical dependence has been overcome, accounting for the relapses that occur beyond the first week or two after cessation of tobacco use. Such anticipatory responses probably also develop to some degree in occasional smokers.

There are various conceptualizations of the nature of the anticipatory response system. One is the conditioning model, in which learned associations between the effects of cigarette smoking and specific cues in the environment motivate smoking. Another model is self-regulation, in which high-risk situations activate cognitive processes in the form of pleasurable expectations and a reduced sense of personal control, which then increases the likelihood of smoking (Marlatt & Gordon, 1985). Examples of common anticipatory reactions include smoking after a meal, with a cup of coffee or an alcoholic beverage, during a break from work, while talking on the phone, and while with friends who smoke.

It is noteworthy that aspects of the drug-taking behavior itself often become pleasurable, in addition to the pleasure afforded by the pharmacological effects of nicotine. For example, manipulation of smoking materials or the taste, smell, or feel of tobacco smoke in the throat can become associated with the reinforcing effects of smoking and can become pleasurable in themselves. When a smoker becomes abstinent, he or she must learn to forgo not only the pharmacological pleasures afforded by the drug, but also the pleasure of engaging in those aspects of drug-taking behavior that have become pleasurable through anticipatory mechanisms.

Behavioral factors other than anticipatory mechanisms may also influence personal susceptibility to drug addiction. For example, some smokers, particularly Caucasian women, smoke as a means of maintaining lower body weight (Camp, Klesges, & Relyea, 1993). Certain characteristics of individuals appear to promote initiation of smoking and the development of nicotine addiction, as I will discuss in more detail in a later section of this chapter.

Comparison of Nicotine Addiction
With Other Drug Addictions

It is obvious that all drugs of dependence share psychoactivity, produce pleasure, and are shown to reinforce drug-taking behavior. (For a detailed review of the comparison of nicotine and other drug addictions, see Centers for Disease Control, 1988.) The nature of nicotine's psychoactivity, which is generally subtle and is consistent with high levels of cognitive performance, is considerably different from that of heroin or cocaine, which produce intense euphoria and may be disruptive to performance. The subtle psychoactive effect of nicotine is experienced hundreds of times per day (through each puff) and exerts a powerful effect on behavior over time. Although nicotine's psychoactive effect is less dramatic than that of other drugs, the strength of the addiction is as powerful or more powerful. The consequences of nicotine's addictiveness are clearly more dramatic, making tobacco use the number one health problem in the United States.

Compulsive use can be observed with all addictive drugs, but the compulsiveness is manifested in different patterns. Some drugs, such as cocaine and heroin, are used by some addicted persons only intermittently—that is, every few days or even at longer intervals—but the compulsion to use the drug does repeat. Cigarette smokers, on the other hand, rarely go more than a day without nicotine. At work or in other public places where smoking is proscribed, smokers may need to take numerous breaks throughout the day to smoke. No single physical-dependence model describes the way in which drug use is continually compelled, but these compulsive behaviors are strongly controlled by the addictive actions of the drugs.

Use despite harmful effects confirms the difficulty that many persons have in quitting drug use. This is clearly evident to clinicians who treat alcoholics with chronic liver disease, heroin addicts with infective endocarditis, and cigarette smokers. For example, only 50% of smokers who suffer acute myocardial infarction quit smoking, despite their physicians' admonitions to do so (Havik & Maeland, 1988). It has been argued that for many activities that entail risk, such as sex, sunbathing, and skiing, the individual assumes a risk and makes a free choice, and that the same is true of cigarette smoking. However, lifelong smoking results in the premature death of one in three smokers and the disability of a great number of smokers from chronic lung disease, indicating a substantially different level of risk.

Relapse rates after abstinence appear to be similar for tobacco, heroin, and alcohol; about 60% of quitters relapse within 3 months and 75% within 6 months (Hunt, Barnett, & Branch, 1971). These relapse rates have been observed in clients discharged from treatment programs. It has been argued that the relapse rate for tobacco among spontaneous quitters might be lower than these rates. Recent

data indicate that relapse rates for smokers who have undergone minimal intervention treatment in a physician's office and who have successfully abstained for
24 hours are 25% at 2 days, 50% at 1 week, and 75% at 2 months (Kottke, Brekke,
Solberg, & Hughes, 1989), whereas two-thirds of smokers who quit on their own
relapse within 2 days (Hughes et al., 1992).

Recurrent drug cravings have been described for each of the addicting drugs,
although there has been considerable debate about the use of the term *craving*. A
better term might be *strong desire* to use a drug. When desires for different drugs
were compared among polydrug abusers, most of whom smoked cigarettes, the
reported intensity of desire for cigarettes when they are not available was as high
as or higher than the intensity of desire for heroin, alcohol, or cocaine when the
latter was not available (Kozlowski et al., 1989).

Tolerance to the various drugs of abuse has been well documented, although
the time course varies. Different time courses of tolerance might influence the
pattern of drug use. For example, tolerance to many effects of nicotine develops
quickly, within the day, and there is resensitization of many responses overnight.
Intermittent high levels of nicotine in the brain from individual puffs might also
overcome tolerance to some extent, so that effects can be experienced from individual cigarettes. Presumably because of the daily cycle of tolerance and
resensitization, daily doses of nicotine tend to stabilize, and, after a period of dose
escalation in the first few years, many smokers smoke the same number of cigarettes each day. In contrast, tolerance lasts longer in an alcoholic who drinks all
day and whose brain is more or less continually exposed to alcohol throughout
the day. Tolerance likewise occurs during cocaine binges when progressively
larger doses are used in an attempt to maintain a cocaine high; however, between
binges, sensitivity to cocaine may be regained. One implication of the development of tolerance is that regular smokers are able to consume far greater amounts
of tobacco smoke and associated toxins than if they had not become tolerant.

Physical dependence has been well characterized for smokers as well as for
other drug abusers. It has been argued that a marked stereotypical syndrome occurs in a person after he or she stops use of heroin or alcohol, whereas withdrawal
symptoms after individuals stop smoking vary widely in nature and magnitude. In
one study, such symptoms were not sufficiently present in 22% of quitters to constitute a diagnosis of withdrawal (Hughes & Hatsukami, 1986). Although it is true
that smoking does not result in seizures or delirium tremens, withdrawal from
smoking can be extremely disruptive to personal life. Nicotine withdrawal may be
viewed as closer to withdrawal from other stimulants, such as cocaine: The withdrawal syndrome is not life threatening, but it profoundly affects behavior and remains a strong impetus to recurrent drug use. Conversely, some persons who are
dependent on heroin or alcohol stop their drug use abruptly without marked
withdrawal symptoms.

Agonist drug "replacement" to modify withdrawal symptoms or to facilitate cessation has been used with narcotic abuse (methadone and L-acetylmethadol) and alcoholism (benzodiazepines) as well as with tobacco addiction (nicotine gum, transdermal nicotine, and nicotine nasal spray). In all cases the agonist relieves withdrawal symptoms. Methadone and nicotine can be used over several months, with gradual tapering, to facilitate cessation. Methadone is also used in the long term to maintain abstinence. Although such use is not recommended for nicotine replacement, 6% to 38% of nicotine gum users continue to use the gum for a year or more after they stop smoking, apparently as a sort of maintenance treatment (Hajek, Jackson, & Belcher, 1988; Hughes, 1988).

Nicotine Dependence in Young People

Tobacco use begins with experimentation, often in early adolescence or in the preteen years. The immediate impetus to experiment is social, prompted by friends, family members, or role models who smoke. (Other factors involved in initiation and progression of smoking are discussed in detail in a later section of this chapter.) Estimates of the percentages of young people who experiment with smoking vary from 47% to 90%. Most who experiment smoke only a few cigarettes. Those who smoke three or more cigarettes have a high likelihood of becoming regular smokers (Russell, 1990). Once a person becomes a regular smoker, the number of cigarettes he or she smokes per day tends to escalate over several years (McNeill, Jarvis, Stapleton, West, & Bryant, 1989). Even when young people smoke only a few cigarettes per day, they inhale tobacco smoke effectively and take in as much nicotine per cigarette as do adults, as has been shown in studies measuring salivary cotinine per cigarette smoked per day.

Epidemiology and Natural History of Cigarette Smoking

Data from the Youth Risk Behavior Survey for smoking initiation by high school students in the United States are presented in Table 8.4 (1990) and Table 8.5 (1997). In 1990, by age 13, 56% of young people had tried smoking, and 9% were regular smokers (that is, they smoked on 5-15 days or more in the past 30 days). The proportion of young people trying cigarettes increases with each year of age, so that by age 17, 77% had tried smoking and 25% were regular smokers (Escobedo, Marcus, Holtzman, & Giovino, 1993). Data on the numbers of cigarettes consumed by young people of various ages are provided in Table 8.6. Younger children are less likely to be daily smokers; if they are, they smoke fewer ciga-

TABLE 8.4	Percentages of Boys and Girls Who Initiate Smoking at Specific Ages	
Age (years)	Girls	Boys
< 9	3.6	6.7
9-10	6.4	8.0
11-12	14.9	16.7
13-14	24.9	24.1
15-16	19.5	19.4
> 17	4.4	5.0

SOURCE: Data from the Youth Risk Behavior Survey, 1990, as cited in Escobedo et al. (1993).
NOTE: Sample sizes for the various age groups were the same ($n = 11,241$) because new smokers who emerged from among those who had never smoked for successive age groups were added incrementally to numerators of older age groups.

rettes per day. Thus at ages 12-13, 16.5% of adolescent smokers are daily smokers, compared with 47.5% of teen smokers between 16 and 18 years old. At ages 12-13, 11% of smokers smoke 10 or more cigarettes per day, compared with 27.2% of smokers 16-18 years old.

The development of nicotine addiction has been characterized as a series of five stages:

1. Preparatory
2. Initial trying
3. Experimentation
4. Regular use
5. Nicotine addiction (Flay, Ockene, & Tager, 1992)

The *preparatory* stage includes formation of knowledge, beliefs, and expectations about smoking. *Initial trying* refers to trials with the first two or three cigarettes (events discussed in more detail later in this section). *Experimentation* refers to repeated, irregular use over an extended period of time; such smoking may be situation specific (for example, smoking at parties). *Regular smoking* may mean smoking every weekend or in certain parts of each day (such as after school with friends). *Nicotine addiction* refers to regular smoking, usually every day, with an internally regulated need for nicotine. Thus, for individual young people, there is a progression of smoking over time from initiation to experimentation with light smoking to regular and heavy smoking. Unlike adults, in whom intermittent or

TABLE 8.5   **Percentages of High School Students Who Reported Smoking Initiation and Quitting Behaviors, United States, Youth Risk Behavior Survey, 1997**

	Lifetime Smokers[a]	Lifetime Smokers Who Have Ever Smoked Daily[b]	Ever-Daily Smokers Who Have Ever Tried To Quit Smoking[c]	Former Smokers[d]
Sex				
Male	70.9	34.7	68.7	13.0
Female	69.3	37.1	77.6	14.0
Grade				
9th	67.7	35.7	66.1	17.8
10th	70.0	34.9	77.3	14.6
11th	68.8	34.1	73.2	10.0
12th	73.7	35.5	74.4	12.4
Totals	70.2	35.8	72.9	13.5

SOURCE: Centers for Disease Control and Prevention (1994a, p. 61).
a. Ever tried cigarette smoking, even one or two puffs.
b. Ever tried cigarette smoking, even one or two puffs, and have ever smoked at least one cigarette every day for 30 days.
c. Have ever smoked at least one cigarette every day for 30 days and have ever tried to quit smoking. Excludes data from 55 students who reported that they had never tried to quit, but did not smoke on any of the 30 days preceding the survey.
d. Have ever smoked at least one cigarette every day for 30 days and did not smoke on any of the 30 days preceding the survey. Excludes data from 55 students who reported that they had never tried to quit, but did not smoke on any of the 30 days preceding the survey.

light smoking may be a stable and relatively nonaddictive pattern of smoking, children who are light smokers are often in a phase of escalation, with a typical interval from initiation to addiction of 2-3 years. The interval between initiation and addiction is based on a comparison of the cumulative prevalence curves for trying a first cigarette and smoking daily (Table 8.1) and the interval between initiation of smoking and the rise of salivary cotinine concentrations to adult levels.

The natural history of the smoking experience for an individual provides insight into the pharmacology of the addiction process. The first cigarette smoked is often perceived as aversive, producing coughing, dizziness, and/or nausea. With repeated smoking, tolerance develops to the noxious effects of cigarette smoking, and smokers tend to report positive effects of smoking. As the daily intake of nicotine increases, the development of physical dependence—that is, experiencing withdrawal symptoms between cigarettes or when cigarettes are not available—becomes established. Thus there appears to be a progression over time from

TABLE 8.6	Percentages of Current Smokers by the Number of Days Smoked in the Past Month and the Average Number of Cigarettes Smoked Daily							
	Number of Days Smoked in the Past Month [a]				Number of Cigarettes Smoked Daily [b]			
	< 5	5-9	10-29	Every Day	< 5	5-9	10-19	> 20
Overall	24.1	8.7	26.4	40.8	37.9	20.4	25.7	16.0
Gender								
Boys	23.9	8.5	26.6	41.0	33.9	19.3	27.6	19.2
Girls	24.3	8.9	26.2	40.6	42.7	21.6	23.5	12.1
Age (years)								
12-13	51.9	8.3[c]	23.3	16.5[c]	64.3	24.6[c]	11.0[c]	0.0
14-15	28.4	9.8	34.5	27.3	55.5	17.2	23.0	4.3
16-18	20.0	8.4	24.1	47.5	31.6	21.1	27.2	20.1
Race								
White	23.4	8.4	26.2	42.0	36.6	20.1	26.5	16.8
African American	37.0	15.0[c]	26.5	21.6	60.3	20.5[c]	16.3[c]	2.9[c]
Hispanic origin								
Hispanic	30.7	11.2[c]	31.9	26.3	59.2	22.5	11.6[c]	6.6[c]
Non-Hispanic	23.5	8.5	26.0	42.0	36.3	20.2	26.9	16.7

SOURCE: Teenage Attitudes and Practices Survey, United States, 1989, reported in Moss, Allen, Giovino, and Mill (1992), as cited in Centers for Disease Control and Prevention (1994a, p. 118).
a. Excludes unknown number of days smoked.
b. Excludes unknown number of cigarettes smoked daily and none smoked in the past week.
c. Estimate does not meet standards of reliability or precision (<30% relative standard error).

smoking initially for social reasons to smoking for pharmacological reasons. The latter includes both smoking for positive effects of nicotine and smoking to avoid withdrawal symptoms, as discussed above.

✤ Evidence for Nicotine Dependence in Young People

Many young people describe themselves as being dependent on tobacco, and there is evidence that nicotine dependence does become established in youthful smokers. The evidence reveals that young people (a) consume substantial levels of nicotine, (b) report subjective effects and subjective reasons for smoking, (c) experience withdrawal symptoms when they are not able to smoke, and (d) have difficulty quitting tobacco use.

That young people *consume substantial amounts* of nicotine was shown in a 3-year study of 197 London schoolgirls who entered the study between the ages of 11 and 14. Saliva cotinine concentrations in girls who were smokers throughout the 3 years were higher at each year's evaluation. Average salivary cotinine levels were 103, 158, and 208 ng/ml (McNeill et al., 1989). The level of 208 ng/ml is similar to that found in many adult daily smokers. The ratio of salivary cotinine per cigarette per day, an index of the amount of nicotine taken in per cigarette, was similar for girls with various levels of cigarette consumption, and similar to that for adults. Thus there seems to be the same intake of nicotine per cigarette among adolescent girls as among adults. Also of note in the study was that smokers who smoked at the time of all three surveys, as well as smokers who were occasional smokers or nonsmokers at the time of the first survey but who subsequently became daily smokers, showed escalation of cigarette consumption and saliva cotinine levels each year. Likewise, plasma cotinine concentrations in American adolescent smokers recruited for a smoking cessation study were similar to levels observed in adult smokers (Hurt et al., 2000).

That young people *experience pharmacological effects* of nicotine from tobacco smoke was reported in an earlier study by the same researchers (McNeill, Jarvis, & West, 1987). A smoking questionnaire asked a group of 170 British schoolgirls ages 11-17 about five subjective effects of smoking. Feeling high and feeling more alert, which are stimulant-like effects, were described by only a few respondents. Feeling calmer was the most common effect described, and was more likely to be reported by daily smokers than by occasional smokers. There was also a significant correlation between salivary cotinine concentrations and the response of feeling calmer. Feeling calmer may be a beneficial effect that is particularly desirable for young people with high levels of anxiety or depression (as I will discuss later in this chapter). Alternatively, feeling calmer could represent the reversal of nicotine withdrawal symptoms. In any case, there is clear evidence that youthful smokers do smoke for the pharmacological effects of tobacco, presumably the effects of nicotine.

That young people *experience withdrawal symptoms* when they try to give up smoking has been demonstrated as well. McNeill, West, Jarvis, Jackson, and Bryant (1986) queried 191 schoolgirls 11-17 years old who were current cigarette smokers about how they felt when they tried to stop smoking. Of this group of smokers, 71% of the daily smokers and 72% of the occasional smokers had made at least one attempt to quit and had failed. Of these subjects, the average cigarette consumption by the daily smokers (69 girls) was 6.8 cigarettes per day, with an average salivary cotinine of 182 ng/ml. The average salivary cotinine concentration

TABLE 8.7   High School Seniors' Attempts to Quit Smoking

	Percentage of Respondents Answering Yes		
Monitoring the Future Study Survey Question	1976-1979	1980-1984	1985-1989
Do you want to stop smoking now?			
Among those who smoked at all during the past 30 days	46.1	47.1	42.5
Among those who smoked 1 cigarette/ day during the past 30 days	46.1	47.6	43.9
Have you ever tried to stop smoking and found that you could not?			
Among those who smoked at all during the past 30 days	31.5	31.4	27.8
Among those who smoked > 1 cigarette/ day during the past 30 days	38.5	41.6	39.4

SOURCE: Centers for Disease Control and Prevention (1994a, p. 78).

in the occasional smokers (47 girls) was 22 ng/ml; 74% of the daily smokers and 47% of the occasional smokers experienced one or more of six symptoms of nicotine withdrawal. The withdrawal score correlated significantly with salivary cotinine concentration and with weekly cigarette consumption. Rojas, Killen, Haydel, and Robinson (1998) reported on 249 California adolescents who were current smokers but had tried to quit smoking in the past. Self-reported withdrawal symptoms included a strong need to smoke (45%), feeling nervous and tense (32%), restlessness (30%), irritability (29%), hunger (25%), being unable to concentrate (22%), feeling miserable and sad (15%), and trouble sleeping (13%). The occurrence of the symptoms was similar in males and females. These studies demonstrate that adolescent smokers experience withdrawal symptoms when they try to quit and that many have difficulty quitting. Other studies further reveal that many young smokers want to quit but have difficulty doing so. Townsend, Wilkes, Haines, and Jarvis (1991) reported that 60% of adolescent smokers evaluated in a general medical practice made an agreement with the practice doctor or nurse to give up smoking. Stone and Kristeller (1992) surveyed 10th-grade students in suburban Massachusetts: 14% of the students were daily smokers; of these, 28% reported that they continued to smoke because they were addicted. The Monitoring the Future Study, which looked at high school seniors in the United States, asked about interest in quitting smoking and prior attempts at quitting (see Table 8.7). Of smokers (1985-1989) who had smoked at all in the past 30 days, 42.5% reported a desire to stop smoking. Of this group, and of the sub-

TABLE 8.8   High School Seniors Predict Whether or Not They Will Be
             Smoking in 5 Years (in percentages)

Senior Year Smoking Status (use in past 30 days)	Definitely Will	Probably Will	Definitely Will Not	Probably Will Not	Number
None	0.4	1.3	21.0	77.3	1,926
< 1 cigarette/day	0.5	14.7	56.5	28.3	248
1-5 cigarettes/day	1.8	37.6	44.1	16.5	211
About one-half pack/day	0.6	57.7	30.3	11.3	197
≥ 1 pack/day	5.1	62.9	26.7	5.2	228
Total	0.9	14.2	27.0	58.0	2,810

SOURCE: Monitoring the Future Study, Institute for Social Research, University of Michigan, 1976-1986 senior classes (Johnston et al., 1994b). Data reprinted by permission.

group who smoked daily, 28% and 39%, respectively, stated that they had tried to stop in the past and could not (Centers for Disease Control and Prevention, 1994a, p. 78).

Dozois, Farrow, and Miser (1995) found that 72% of adolescents in a youth detention center in Seattle had made previous quit attempts, and Dappen, Schwartz, and O'Donnell (1996) reported that among vocational school students they surveyed, 72% had tried to quit at least once and 53% had attempted to quit at least three times. Both studies also found that respondents described withdrawal symptoms during quit attempts.

The observation that adolescents are motivated enough to enroll in a smoking cessation clinical trial but are still unable to quit smoking further documents the severity of nicotine addiction in youth. Hurt et al. (2000) conducted an open-label study of 110 adolescents in Minnesota and Wisconsin during which participants were treated with nicotine patches and behavioral counseling. The quit rate in the study was only 5% at 6 months, a rate that is lower than that observed in patch treatment trials in adults.

Another perspective on the difficulty of quitting involves young people's expectations regarding their future smoking behavior. Seniors in high school were asked, "Do you think you will be smoking cigarettes 5 years from now?" Among the respondents who were occasional smokers (less than one cigarette per day), 85% stated that they probably or definitely would not be smoking in 5 years, as did 32% of those who smoked one pack per day or more (see Table 8.8). However, at follow-up 5-6 years later, of those who smoked occasionally only 58% had quit and 28% had actually increased their cigarette consumption. Of those who had

TABLE 8.9   Direction of Change in Smoking Between Senior Year of
High School and 5-6 Years Later

| | Smoking Status 5-6 Years Later (%) | | | | |
Senior Year Smoking Status (use in past 30 days)	Quit	Less Use	Same Level	More Use	Number
None			85.6	14.4	9,238
< 1 cigarette/day	57.8		14.4	27.8	1,268
1-5 cigarettes/day	29.6	8.8	17.2	44.4	1,058
About one-half pack/day	18.8	13.6	21.7	46.0	1,000
> 1 pack/day	13.2	17.2	40.2	29.0	869

SOURCE: Monitoring the Future Study, Institute for Social Research, University of Michigan, 1976-1986 senior classes (Johnston et al., 1994b). Data reprinted by permission.

smoked one pack or more per day, only 13% had quit and 70% still smoked one pack or more per day. Smokers of 1-5 or about 10 cigarettes per day at the time of the initial questionnaire also were less likely to have quit than they had predicted, and on average escalated their smoking over the subsequent 5 years (Centers for Disease Control and Prevention, 1994a, p. 84; see Table 8.9).

Thus, consistent with the concept of addiction, smokers' expectations of future smoking behavior show little relationship to their actual behavior; that is, young smokers think that they will be able to quit but underestimate the power of their addiction. Even those who smoke only a few cigarettes per day during high school have a high risk of becoming heavy smokers as adults.

These data are evidence that nicotine addiction develops during adolescence, and that most adolescents who are daily cigarette smokers (as well as some who are occasional smokers) are addicted to nicotine. Once adolescents are addicted, cessation is difficult, as it is for adults; thus interventions are needed at early stages to prevent the establishment of a pattern of addiction. The likelihood of successful quitting among adolescents is greater the sooner the adolescent tries to quit after initiating tobacco use, and the fewer cigarettes he or she has smoked (Ary & Biglan, 1988; Ershler, Leventhal, Fleming, & Glynn, 1989).

Risk Factors for Smoking Initiation

Understanding why children begin to smoke is important to the planning and development of effective prevention strategies. The numerous major factors that

TABLE 8.10 Psychosocial Risk Factors in the Initiation of Tobacco Use Among Adolescents

Risk Factors	Smoking	Smokeless Tobacco
Sociodemographic factors		
Low socioeconomic status	X	
Developmental stage	X	X
Male gender		X
Environmental factors		
Accessibility	X	X
Advertising	X	X
Parental use		
Sibling use	X	
Peer use	X	X
Normative expectations	X	X
Social support	X	
Behavioral factors		
Academic achievement	X	X
Other problem behaviors	X	X
Constructive behaviors	X	
Behavioral skills	X	
Intentions	X	X
Experimentation	X	X
Personal factors		
Knowledge of consequences		X
Functional meanings	X	X
Subjective expected utility	X	
Self-esteem/self-image	X	X
Self-efficacy	X	
Personality factors	X	
Psychological well-being	X	

SOURCE: Centers for Disease Control and Prevention (1994a, p. 123).

influence or predict initiation and escalation of tobacco use are reviewed extensively in the 1994 surgeon general's report (Centers for Disease Control and Prevention, 1994a) and are listed in Table 8.10. In general, the psychosocial risk factors can be described as a continuum of proximal to distal factors. Proximal factors directly affect an individual's choice to use tobacco, whereas distal factors do so indirectly. For example, being offered a cigarette at a party is a proximal factor;

prior exposure to advertising showing young adults smoking at a party would be a distal factor influencing the decision to use tobacco. Although proximal factors may seem more influential because of their immediacy, distal factors "acquire potency if they are pervasive and provide consistent, repetitive messages across multiple channels. Distal factors are also powerful because, over time, they affect proximal factors as these influences become interpreted and internalized, particularly among adolescents as they try to shape a mature self-identity" (Centers for Disease Control and Prevention, 1994a, p. 123).

The degrees to which any of these risk factors influence smoking behavior vary among the risk factors and among research studies. Readers who are seeking a detailed discussion of the risk factors should refer to the surgeon general's report. In this subsection I provide only an overview of those issues most pertinent to the policy questions addressed in this chapter.

Initiation of cigarette smoking is influenced by several kinds of factors: environmental, behavioral, personal, and sociodemographic (Perry & Silvis, 1987). Among the *environmental* factors that influence initiation of smoking are having many friends who smoke and having a best friend who smokes. Parental smoking is more important in establishing smoking as a normative behavior and is associated with more positive and fewer negative perceptions of the health consequences of smoking. Advertising and exposure to smoking in the mass media (e.g., television, movies) and at sports events reinforces the idea that smoking is an adult, sophisticated, attractive, and sexy behavior and downplays the adverse health consequences of smoking.

Behavioral analysis indicates that cigarette smoking is often an early manifestation of problem behavior. Some schoolchildren manifest such problem behaviors as poor school performance, low aspiration for future success, school absences, and the intention to drop out of school or actually dropping out. Other problem behaviors linked to cigarette smoking include alcohol and other drug use and other risk-taking or rebellious behaviors.

A number of *personal* characteristics of adolescents have been linked to cigarette smoking: (a) low self-esteem, poor self-image, low perception of self-efficacy, and susceptibility to peer pressure; (b) sensation seeking, rebelliousness, and sense of invulnerability; (c) low knowledge level of the adverse effects of cigarette smoking; (d) depression and/or anxiety; and (e) pharmacological response. Considerable recent research has shown a high prevalence of depression among current smokers. Smokers are more likely than nonsmokers to have histories of major depression, even preceding initiation of smoking (Anda et al., 1990; Breslau, Kilbey, & Andreski, 1991; Glassman et al., 1990), and smokers with histories of depression have been found to have lower smoking cessation rates than smokers without depression.

A recent study of adolescents found that a lifetime history of major depression was a strong predictor of becoming a smoker, and, conversely, being a smoker was a predictor of developing major depression in the ensuing 12 months (Brown, Lewinsohn, Seeley, & Wagner, 1996). Adverse childhood experiences (e.g., emotional, physical, or social abuse; a battered mother; parental separation or divorce; growing up with a substance-abusing or mentally ill household member) substantially increase the likelihood of becoming a smoker (Anda et al., 1999).

Various *pharmacological* responses to smoking (presumably to nicotine) from the first cigarette may also predict the likelihood of progression to regular smoking. Hirschman, Leventhal, and Glynn (1984) found that a report of dizziness after smoking the first cigarette predicted a high rate of progression to the next cigarette, whereas reports of adverse effects, such as coughing, were not associated with progression. Although the mechanism of such a link between dizziness and smoking progression is not apparent, a pharmacological link between cigarette smoking and depression is reasonable. Nicotine is known to release dopamine, norepinephrine, and serotonin in the brain in animals. Antidepressant drugs have similar effects. Thus it is possible that pharmacological responses to nicotine promote tobacco use in people who are depressed.

Evidence from studies of twins suggests a moderate *genetic* influence on both initiation and maintenance of cigarette smoking (Carmelli, Swann, Robinette, & Fabsitz, 1992). Possible mechanisms include genetically determined differences in the pharmacological response to and/or metabolism of nicotine, differences in personality, and the presence or absence of an affective or other psychiatric disorder, particularly depression. Cigarette smoking and alcoholism are often found together, and studies in twins suggest that these addictions share, to some extent, a common generic determinant (Swann, Carmelli, Rosenman, Fabsitz, & Christian, 1990). Some proportion of the genetic predisposition to tobacco addiction thus appears to be specific, but some appears to be linked to alcoholism or to other drug addictions.

The factors that influence initiation of smoking may be predominantly of one type, and those that influence the progression of smoking may be of another type. Hirschman et al. (1984) studied 386 urban public school children, grades 2-10, to determine how many had ever tried smoking, and then how many had progressed to a second and third cigarette. The main risk factors for the 47% of children who had tried at least one cigarette were grade level in school (that is, the higher the grade level and the older the child, the higher the likelihood of having tried a cigarette), having a best friend who is a smoker, and risk-taking behavior (reported on a questionnaire). Progression to a second cigarette (32% of those who smoked one cigarette) was predicted by life stress (predicted rapid progression), friends who smoke (predicted slow progression), lack of negative attitudes toward smoking, and an experience of dizziness when smoking the first cigarette. Progression to a third cigarette (in 77% of those who had smoked two cigarettes) was predicted by best friend being a smoker, feelings of helplessness, and rapid progression to the second cigarette. These analyses support the idea that initiation of cigarette smoking is primarily a consequence of environmental factors, whereas progression appears to be influenced more by personal and pharmacological factors.

Concern about body weight and a prior history of dieting have been reported to be related to both the prevalence of smoking and smoking initiation in Minnesota girls in grades 7-10 (French, Perry, Leon, & Fulkerson, 1994). This observation suggests that both attitudes and pharmacology are operative on adolescent smoking related to body weight. Attitudes on smoking and body weight (derived from family, peers, and advertising) would promote initiation, whereas pharmacology (nicotine effects on body metabolism and food consumption) would promote continued smoking.

Sociodemographic factors that predispose young people to cigarette smoking include low socioeconomic status, low level of parental education, and the individual's developmental stage of adolescence. With respect to the last of these, the transition years from elementary to high school, grades 7-10 (ages 11-16) appear to be a particularly high-risk time for initiation (see Table 8.4).

Ethnic Differences in Nicotine Dependence

Differences in tobacco use by young people are specific to and consistent within ethnic groups. The rates for daily smoking for 12th graders in 1991 were highest among non-Hispanic whites (21%), next highest among Hispanics (12%), and lowest among African Americans (5%); the rates in 1991 for smoking one or more cigarettes in the preceding 30 days were 32% for non-Hispanic whites, 25% for Hispanics, and 9% for African Americans (Johnston, O'Malley, & Bachman, 1992, p. 64). A striking trend of decline in smoking has occurred among African American high school seniors: from 26.8% in 1976 to 4.4% in 1993 for smoking daily during the preceding 30 days (Johnston, O'Malley, & Bachman, 1994b). Differences in the *smoking habits* of various ethnic groups are notable and may influence the addictive process. Compared with whites, African Americans show a consistent preference for menthol brands, higher tar levels, and higher nicotine levels; African Americans also smoke fewer cigarettes per day. These factors influence inhalation patterns and health risks. For instance, because menthol cigarettes "provide a sensation of cooling when smoked," they may "promote deeper and more prolonged inhalation" (Robinson, Pertschuk, & Sutton, 1992, p. 131). Although current initiation rates are lowest for African Americans, there is evidence that adult African Americans are more highly addicted to tobacco than are whites. The cotinine levels of adult African Americans are higher than those of whites, even though they smoke fewer cigarettes (Wagenknecht et al., 1990). African Americans consume higher levels of nicotine from each cigarette than do whites (Perez-Stable, Herrera, Jacob, & Benowitz, 1998). A greater dose of nicotine per cigarette may be explained in part by the smoking of menthol cigarettes, as discussed previously. In addition, this observation is consistent with the generally lower income level of African Americans compared with whites and economic pressure to extract more nicotine per cigarette. Cessation rates for African American adults are lower than those for whites, which seems to indicate a higher level of addiction for African Americans ("Smoking Cessation," 1993). The explanation for the apparent inconsistency between lower current initiation rates and higher levels of addiction in adult African Americans is not clear. Possibly this difference reflects a cohort effect, and in the future fewer adult African Americans will be addicted. Alternatively, it may reflect initiation of cigarette smoking later in life among African Americans compared with whites. Further research is needed to clarify these issues.

Nature of Tobacco Products

Nicotine addiction is maintained through use of tobacco, the only significant source of nicotine. Certain teas and vegetables contain low levels of nicotine, but the amounts available are so low that it is impossible to consume pharmacologically active doses of nicotine from sources other than tobacco. Tobacco is smoked as cigarettes and cigars as well as in pipes, but it can also be *used* without smoking through the application of smokeless tobacco directly to mucous membranes.

Production of Tobacco Products

In the United States, tobacco companies make tobacco products by blending different types of tobacco leaves and adding sugar and other flavorings. Lighter tobaccos, which are found in most American cigarettes, produce acidic smoke when burned. Darker tobaccos, such as those used in cigar and pipe tobacco, produce alkaline smoke. As noted above, the pH of the smoke determines the extent to which nicotine is absorbed through the mouth.

In addition to different types of shredded tobacco leaves, tobacco sheet (reconstituted tobacco) is also blended into many cigarettes. Tobacco sheet uses scraps and stems of the tobacco plant as well as various additives, which are combined into a homogeneous mixture that can then be incorporated into tobacco. The manufacturing of tobacco sheet allows for production of a relatively uniform composition of tobacco, because additives can be used to achieve the end product (Slade, 1993, p. 6).

Reports have been made of evidence that tobacco manufacturers manipulate the nicotine content of cigarettes (American Broadcasting Corporation, 1994; see also Slade, 1993). One way in which manufacturers control the nicotine content of tobacco is by extracting the nicotine from the tobacco and then adding it back in, in controlled amounts, as tobacco extract. Tobacco companies also hold patents on machines designed to spray nicotine solutions onto cigarette tobacco, although it is unclear whether they actually use these devices in the manufacturing of cigarettes. Tobacco manufacturers state that the reason they extract nicotine from tobacco and then reapply it is that nicotine is found in very uneven concentrations in the natural tobacco leaf. By extracting and then reintroducing the nicotine, they can provide tobacco products that deliver consistent amounts of nicotine. It has also been suggested that manufacturers control the amount of nicotine in tobacco so as to ensure a level adequate to maintain nicotine addiction. Supporting this idea is an internal memorandum written by a Philip Morris tobacco company scientist: "The cigarette should be conceived not as a product but as a package. The product is nicotine. . . . smoke is beyond question the most optimized vehicle of nicotine and the cigarette is the most optimized dispenser of smoke" (cited in *Cipollone v. Liggett,* 1992). That the pharmacological actions of nicotine are important determinants of why people smoke is supported by research conducted by both the tobacco industry and nonindustry researchers (Centers for Disease Control, 1988; Robinson & Pritchard, 1992; Robinson, Pritchard, & Davis, 1992).

Modifying Cigarette Yields

Tobacco smoke contains more than 4,000 chemicals, many of which are known toxins. Some of the better-known toxins include carbon monoxide, hydrogen cyanide, nitrogen oxides, ammonia, benzene, formaldehyde, nitrosoamines, vinyl chloride, polycyclic hydrocarbons, polonium-210, arsenic, and lead. Tobacco smoke is an aerosol of droplets containing water, nicotine and other alkaloids, and tar. Tar is what is left in the particulates after water and alkaloids are removed. The particulates are suspended in a gaseous mixture that contains carbon monoxide, nitrogen oxides, and other gases.

To estimate the amounts of various constituents to which smokers are exposed, researchers routinely test cigarettes using a standardized smoking-machine test often referred to as the Federal Trade Commission (FTC) method. The FTC performed and published test results on commercial cigarettes from 1967 to 1985; since that time, the tobacco industry has conducted these tests. The FTC method procedure consists of placing a cigarette into a holder and igniting it; then 35 ml puffs are taken via a syringe over 2 seconds, once every minute, until the cigarette is burned to a specific butt length. The smoke that is collected is passed through a filter, which allows for the collection of the particulate material (tar and nicotine). The gases that pass through the filter are collected and used for determination of the levels of carbon monoxide and other constituents. Thus values for yields of tar, nicotine, and carbon monoxide for each cigarette are reported from this type of testing procedure.

Lowering the yields of tar and other toxic constituents of cigarette smoke makes intuitive sense as a way to reduce the health risks of cigarette smoking. Tobacco companies widely promote cigarettes that are lower in yield, implying that smoking them has health benefits when compared with smoking higher-yield cigarettes. However, the low-yield cigarette concept is in many ways deceptive.

To understand why this is so, it is useful to examine how low-yield cigarettes are engineered. There are several ways in which cigarettes can be engineered to yield low amounts of tar, nicotine, and carbon monoxide in smoking-machine tests. The most obvious way is filtration, in which case a filter is placed at the end of the cigarette. This filter can remove a significant amount of tar. In the United States, 95% of the cigarettes manufactured are filtered. Another way to reduce yields is to reduce the content of nicotine or other toxic substances in tobacco per se. This appears not to be the case with commercial cigarettes. When the nicotine concentration of tobacco in cigarettes of differing yields was measured in one study, it was found that, on average, cigarette tobacco had a nicotine concentration of about 1.6% (Benowitz et al., 1983). There was a significant inverse correlation between concentration of nicotine in tobacco and yield, suggesting that low-yield cigarettes are made with tobacco that contains more, rather than less, nicotine than higher-yield cigarettes. In any case, it is clear that low-yield cigarettes are not low in yield because the contents of nicotine and tar are lower in the tobacco per se. Low-yield cigarettes are engineered to show low yields based on the standardized smoking-machine protocol. This can be done by shortening the cigarette length, increasing the burn rate of the paper, or increasing the length of the filter overwrap so that the machine is able to take fewer puffs before the cigarette is burned to its specified length. Placing less tobacco in each cigarette by using expanded tobacco and/or smaller diameters of cigarettes can also reduce yield. Diluting the mainstream smoke through the use of porous paper or ventilation holes in the filter tipping paper can substantially reduce yields. In the latter case, when the cigarette is inhaled from the tip, considerable room air is drawn in to dilute the tobacco smoke.

Unfortunately, the addicted smoker does not smoke like an FTC smoking machine. Smokers take deeper and more frequent puffs than the machine on average, and can easily alter their smoking behavior as desired. Smokers learn, without realizing what they are doing, that placing their lips or fingers over the cigarette tip improves the draw characteristics of the cigarette. They are actually blocking the ventilation holes so that they are inhaling more tobacco smoke and less room air. Many studies in which the actual intake of nicotine, carbon monoxide, and other constituents of tobacco smoke has been measured in smokers have shown a very weak relationship, if any, to nominal nicotine yield. Thus once smokers become addicted to nicotine, they can easily adapt their smoking behavior to obtain the desired dose of nicotine from any cigarette. It should be noted that ultra-low-yield cigarettes (that is, tar less than 1 mg, nicotine less than 0.1 mg) do seem to make it more difficult for smokers to obtain the levels of nicotine that they can obtain from high-yield cigarettes (Benowitz, Jacob, Yu, et al., 1986). The observation that sales of these ultra-low-yield cigarettes are relatively low suggests that there may be a threshold for nicotine delivery below which nicotine addiction is not easily maintained. As typically smoked, low-yield cigarettes are no less harmful than higher-yield cigarettes. Because smokers take in much more tar and other toxins than estimated by machine yields, the risk of smoking-caused disease is not significantly reduced through the use of low-yield cigarettes.

In summary, people smoke cigarettes largely to obtain the nicotine they desire. They do not smoke in a standardized way as do smoking machines, and therefore machines are poor predictors of actual human exposure. Human exposure can be estimated through direct measures of levels of tobacco smoke constituents in the biological fluids of smokers. Such markers include nicotine; its metabolite, cotinine; carbon monoxide; adducts of various reactive chemicals to hemoglobin or DNA; and tobacco-specific nitrosamine levels and mutagenic activity of the urine.

∽ Conclusions

- Long-term tobacco use is maintained by addiction to nicotine.
- Once addicted, a person finds it difficult to quit using tobacco.
- When children and adolescents begin tobacco use, they rapidly become addicted to nicotine; the addiction maintains their tobacco use in adulthood.
- When young people begin using tobacco, they overestimate the proportion of tobacco use in society, underestimate the addictive nature of tobacco and the risk that they will become addicted over the long term, and underestimate the danger that they will incur tobacco-related disease. Thus children and adolescents be-

come addicted to nicotine before they are able to appreciate fully the consequences of their behavior.

- There is considerable individual variation in susceptibility to nicotine addiction. Environmental, behavioral, personal, socioeconomic, and ethnic factors influence susceptibility to initiation and addiction.

- Among adults, the prevalence of cigarette smoking has declined from 1966 to the present. The prevalence of smoking by young people declined through 1980 but subsequently has been stable, except for among African Americans, for whom there has been a sharp decline.

- Prevention of nicotine addiction among young people is an essential part of any policy aimed at reducing tobacco use in society as a whole.

Chapter 9

A Visceral Account of Addiction

George Loewenstein

I n the past, addiction has been viewed as a sui generis phenomenon (Baker, 1988). Recent theories of addiction, however, draw implicit or explicit parallels between addiction and a wide range of other behaviors. The "disease theory," for example, highlights similarities between addiction and infectious disease (e.g., Frawley, 1988; Vaillant, 1983). Becker and Murphy's (1988) rational choice model of addiction draws a parallel between drug addictions and "endogenous taste" phenomena, such as listening to classical music to attempt to acquire a taste for it, in which current consumption affects the utility of future consumption. In Herrnstein and Prelec's (1992) "garden path" theory, addiction is analogous to bad habits, such as workaholism or compulsive lying, that individuals can acquire gradually due to their failure to notice deterioration in their conduct or situation.

In this chapter, I propose an alternative theoretical perspective that views addiction as one, albeit extreme, example of a wide range of behaviors that are influenced or controlled by *visceral factors* (Loewenstein, 1996). Visceral factors include drive states such as hunger, thirst, and sexual desire; moods and emotions; physical pain; and, most important for addiction, craving for a drug. All visceral factors, including drug craving, are associated with regulatory mechanisms that are es-

AUTHOR'S NOTE: This chapter is an updated version of a chapter by the same title in *Getting Hooked: Rationality and Addiction,* edited by Jon Elster and Ole-Jørgen Skog. Copyright 1999 by Cambridge University Press. Reprinted with permission of Cambridge University Press. I thank Colin Camerer, Donna Harsch, Kalle Moene, and Wiktor Osiatynski for helpful comments.

sential for survival, but all are also associated with behavior disorders—for example, hunger and overeating, fear and phobias, sexual desire and sexual compulsions, anger and spouse abuse, and craving and addiction. At intermediate levels, most visceral factors, including drug craving, produce similar patterns of impulsivity, remorse, and attempts at self-control. At high levels, drug craving and other visceral factors overwhelm decision making altogether, superseding volitional control of behavior.

The defining characteristics of visceral factors are, first, a direct hedonic impact (which is usually negative if the visceral factor remains unmitigated) and, second, an effect on the relative desirability of different goods and actions. The largely aversive experience of hunger, for example, increases the desirability of eating and also affects the desirability of other activities, such as sex. Likewise, fear and pain are both aversive, and each increases the desirability of escape.

The visceral factor perspective (as outlined in Loewenstein, 1996) has two central premises that are especially relevant to addiction: First, immediately experienced visceral factors have a disproportionate effect on behavior and tend to "crowd out" virtually all goals other than that of mitigating the visceral factor; second, people underestimate the impact on their own behavior of visceral factors they will experience in the future.

The disproportionate influence of immediately experienced visceral factors is relevant to an understanding of the force and persistence of addictive behavior. It helps to explain why, once addicted, people have such a difficult time quitting, despite the by-then typically obvious benefits of abstinence. Like extreme hunger, thirst, pain, anger, sleepiness, and a wide range of other visceral sensations, drug cravings limit the scope for volitional control of behavior. Once the addict is "hooked" and subject to intermittent craving, the scope for volition narrows to the point where it may not be useful, either theoretically or practically, to view the addict's behavior as a matter of choice.

The underappreciation of the force of delayed visceral factors is critical to our understanding of why people get addicted in the first place. Underestimating the force of the craving they will experience if they stop taking the drug, people overestimate their own future ability to stop. Early drug-taking behavior, therefore, results from a decision that is distorted by biased expectations.

The visceral account of addiction can be viewed as a hybrid of decision-based and disease perspectives. In the early stages of addiction, drug taking is seen as the product of largely volitional decision making. As an individual becomes addicted to a drug, however, there is a progressive loss of volitional control over drug taking. The visceral account of early drug taking is thus somewhat akin to Herrnstein and Prelec's (1992) in that both view the addict-to-be as engaged in active, but biased, decision making. The models differ, however, in their views about the source of the bias. In Herrnstein and Prelec's model, the bias results from the individual's failure to notice the incremental detrimental effect of engaging in the addictive activity. In the visceral account, it results from the person's failure to appreciate the motivational force of future craving. In its view of the later stages of addiction, the visceral account of addiction is more closely related to the disease perspective. Once addicted, individuals may *recognize* that abstinence is the best course of action, but their ability to abstain is powerfully constrained by the force of intermittent craving.

The feature of the visceral account of addiction that most starkly separates it from other theoretical models proposed by economists and decision theorists is the central role played by cue-conditioned craving—that is, the tendency for cues that become mentally associated with an addictive drug to elicit craving for the drug (for a review of studies that incorporate cue-conditioned craving, see Siegel, Krank, & Hinson, 1988; for a formal model of decision making that incorporates cues, see Laibson, 1994). Cue-conditioned craving needs to be distinguished from the closely related phenomenon of withdrawal—the aversive sensations that addicts experience immediately after ceasing drug taking. The visceral account's emphasis on cue-conditioned craving rather than withdrawal reflects a widespread belief among contemporary addiction researchers that craving rather than withdrawal is the critical impediment to recovery from addiction. Just as it is easier to shed weight than it is to keep it off (National Institutes of Health, 1993), it is easier to withdraw from most drugs than to abstain in the long run (Goldstein, 1994; Shiffman, 1982, p. 72).

In the following section, I present the basic elements of the visceral factor perspective and discuss in detail the two regularities mentioned above: the excessive influence of immediate visceral factors and the insufficient appreciation of delayed visceral factors. I then demonstrate that drug craving exhibits the same characteristics as other visceral factors and present a review of the literature on the determinants and effects of craving. Finally, I present the rudiments of a theoretical account of addiction that incorporates cue-conditioned craving and draws out implications for who gets addicted, the effects of addiction on behavior, quitting and self-binding, relapse, treatment, and the definition of addiction.

∞ The Visceral Factor Perspective

Technically, one can view visceral factors as short-term fluctuations in tastes. However, doing so obscures several crucial differences between visceral factors and tastes. First, visceral factors affect utility directly, even if actual consumption is held constant, and so resemble consumption, not tastes. The effect of a change in tastes on well-being is a largely philosophical issue, but hunger, thirst, pain, and the like have straightforward effects on well-being, holding actual consumption constant.

Second, visceral factors are correlated with external circumstances (stimulation, deprivation, and such) and, as a result, tend to fluctuate, often dramatically, over time.[1] Indeed, the abruptness of such fluctuations may contribute to their potency. Changes in tastes, in contrast, are caused by slow experience and reflection, are typically not anticipated, and do imply a long-term change in behavior. Although tastes change, they tend to be stable in the short run.

Finally, tastes and visceral factors probably draw on different neurophysiological mechanisms. Tastes consist of information stored in memory about the pleasure or discomfort conferred by different forms of consumption. Visceral factors, in contrast, result from neurochemical changes in the reward and motivation centers of the brain. "The core of the brain," Pribram (1984) writes, "uses chemical regulations to control body functions. The configuration of concentrations of these chemicals, although fluctuating around some set point, is sufficiently stable over periods of time to constitute steady 'states.' These states apparently are experienced as hunger, thirst, sleepiness, elation, depression, effort, comfort, and so on" (p. 14).

The Effect of Immediate Visceral Factors

Visceral factors play an important role in the regulation of behavior. They serve as "interrupts" that focus attention on specific high-priority goals. Hunger, for example, signals a current or anticipated nutritional deficit (Toates, 1979). Pain (Fields, 1987) and fear (Janis, 1967) signal the presence of environmental threat. Virtually all visceral factors, including drug craving, focus attention in such a fashion.

Visceral factors also motivate the individual to achieve the goals on which they focus attention. In most cases, this motivation is experienced as an aversive sensation that the individual can mitigate by addressing the need signaled by the visceral factor. Thus hunger, thirst, pain, fear, and drug craving provide motivation for, respectively, eating, drinking, avoidance, flight, and drug consumption. Most visceral factors are aversive, probably because aversion provides a more reliable motivational mechanism than reward. As Damasio (1994) argues: "Suffering puts us on notice. Suffering offers us the best protection for survival, since it increases the probability that individuals will heed pain signals and act to avert their source or correct their consequences" (p. 264).

As the intensity of visceral factors increases, their influence on behavior tends to exhibit a characteristic pattern. At low levels, people seem capable of dealing with visceral factors in a relatively optimal fashion. For example, a person who is mildly frightened by a dog might decide either to tolerate the fear and remain in the dog's proximity or to leave. There is nothing inherently irrational about taking such visceral factors into account, given that they do affect well-being and generally serve important regulatory functions. It makes perfect sense to eat when hungry, drink when thirsty, and withdraw when experiencing pain or fear; to be convinced of this, one need only glimpse the physical conditions of people who are congenitally unable to experience pain (Fields, 1987, pp. 3-5).

When visceral factors become elevated further, they tend to produce internal conflicts between behavior and perceived self-interest. Thus, to continue the above example, as fear toward the dog increases, the individual may begin to experience a tension between how he *wants* to behave and how he thinks he *should* behave. One can imagine the individual thinking: "Get ahold of yourself. The dog is harmless; it has never bitten anyone. It can sense that you are frightened." Such efforts at "self-command" (Schelling, 1984) are characteristic responses to visceral factors in the midrange of intensity.

Finally, at sufficient levels of intensity, visceral factors overwhelm volition altogether. Internal exhortations to do the right thing lose all effectiveness, and the individual is likely to engage in self-destructive behavior such as flight (a dog can run faster than a person) or immobilization (Janis & Leventhal, 1967). Decision making still occurs, in the sense of an *awareness* of the best course of action, but the individual may be unable to act on such awareness.

When visceral factors overwhelm volitional choice, deviations of behavior from perceived self-interest tend to exhibit a characteristic pattern. Not surprisingly, given their attention-focusing function, overwhelming visceral factors tend to narrow an individual's perceptual and motivational focus. Hunger focuses one on food, fear focuses one on options for flight, and so on. At sufficient levels of intensity, individuals make highly skewed trade-offs between goods and activities that alleviate the visceral factor and those that do not. Sex has little appeal to a person who is starving; food has little appeal to a person in the grip of terror.[2]

Visceral factors also produce a second form of attention narrowing—a good-specific collapse of the individual's time perspective to the present. Thus a hungry person makes shortsighted trade-offs between immediate and delayed food, even when expecting tomorrow's hunger to be as intense as today's. This present orientation, however, applies only to goods that are associated with the visceral factor, and only to trade-offs between the present and some other point in time. A hungry person would probably make the same choices as a nonhungry person between immediate and delayed money (assuming that food cannot be purchased) or immediate and delayed sex. A hungry person might also make the same choices as a nonhungry person between food tomorrow versus food on the day after tomorrow. Both of these features differentiate the visceral factor perspective from models that explain addiction on the basis of generalized (across goods and activities) individual differences in time preferences.

Yet a third form of attention narrowing involves the self versus others. Intense visceral factors narrow the individual's focus inwardly and reduce concern for other people. People who are hungry, in pain, angry, or craving drugs tend to be selfish. As torturers understand well, sleep deprivation, hunger, thirst, and pain —indeed, most visceral factors—can cause even the most strong-willed individuals to betray comrades, friends, and family (Biderman, 1960).

Underestimation of Future Visceral Factors

The second important regularity of relevance to addiction is a tendency for people to underappreciate their own susceptibility to visceral influences. Unlike currently experienced visceral factors, which have a disproportionate impact on behavior, delayed visceral factors tend to be ignored or to be severely underweighted in decision making. Today's pain, hunger, anger, and so on are palpable, but the same sensations anticipated in the future receive little weight.

In a series of recent papers dealing with topics other than addiction, various co-authors and I have demonstrated what we call "cold-to-hot empathy gaps"—the tendency for an individual when "cold" (i.e., not experiencing an elevated visceral factor) to mispredict his or her own behavior when "hot" (for reviews, see Loewenstein, O'Donoghue, & Rabin, 1999; Loewenstein & Schkade, 1999). In one study, after showing sexually arousing photographs to one group of male subjects and nonarousing photographs to another, we asked the subjects to predict their own behavior in the context of a typical date-rape scenario. Aroused subjects predicted a much higher likelihood that they would behave in a sexually aggressive manner, as if being aroused made them better able to imagine what they would do when aroused on a date (Loewenstein, Nagin, & Paternoster, 1997).[3]

In another study, my colleagues and I found that people underpredicted the motivational impact of curiosity on their own behavior (Loewenstein, Prelec, & Shatto, 1996).[4] Subjects were given a sample geography question, randomly chosen from a list of 11 such questions, and then were given the remaining 10 questions. All subjects were given a choice between receiving the answers to the 10 questions or receiving a candy bar, but half were given the choice before they took the quiz and the other half were given the choice after they took the quiz. A substantially larger fraction opted for the candy bar before taking the quiz, when they were not curious, than did so after taking the quiz, as if those in the before condition underestimated the force of their own future curiosity.

In a third paper that bears an especially close connection to the phenomenon of addiction, Daniel Adler and I studied people's predictions of how attached they would become to objects they were given (Loewenstein & Adler, 1995). Research on the "endowment effect" (Thaler, 1980) has shown that people become instantly attached to an object they are given, even if they would not have desired the object particularly had they not been endowed with it.[5] The endowment effect can therefore be viewed as a kind of instant "addiction" that is convenient to study in the lab because it is easy to induce and measure. In one study we informed some subjects that they would be endowed with an object, then asked them to predict the price at which they would sell the object back to the experimenter once they had it. These subjects, and others who did not make a prediction, were then given the object and offered the opportunity to sell it back to the experimenter. Much in the same way that addicts-to-be seem to underestimate their own future attachment to drugs, subjects who were not endowed underpredicted substantially their own postendowment selling prices.

The cold-to-hot empathy gap may result from human limitations in the ability to *remember* visceral states. Imagination and memory draw on similar neural resources and invoke similar cognitive processes. Human memory is well suited to remembering visual images, words, and semantic meaning, but seems ill suited to storing information about visceral sensations. Recall of visual images actually activates many of the brain systems that are involved in visual perception (Kosslyn et al., 1993). Thus it appears that to imagine a visual scene in the mind is, in a very real sense, to "see" the scene again, albeit in distorted, incomplete, and less vivid form.

Recall of pain, and probably other visceral factors, however, is qualitatively different. As Morley (1993) observes in an insightful article, we can easily *recognize* pain, but few can *recall* it in the sense of reexperiencing it in imagination or memory. Morley distinguishes among three possible variants of memory for pain: (a) sensory reexperiencing of the pain; (b) remembering the sensory, intensity, and affective qualities of the pain without reexperiencing it; and (c) remembering the circumstances in which the pain was experienced. Most studies of memory for pain have focused on the second of these variants and have obtained mixed results. For example, several studies have examined the accuracy of women's memory of the pain of childbirth, most employing a so-called visual analog scale (basically a mark made on a thermometer scale) (e.g., Rofé & Algom, 1985; Norvell, Gaston-Johansson, & Fridh, 1987). Researchers have reached conflicting conclusions, with some finding accurate estimation, some finding overestimation, and some finding underestimation of past pain.

In contrast to these contradictory findings, most studies on pain memory that have examined the issue are in agreement that subjects possess either Morley's second or third variant of pain memory, but not the first—sensory reexperiencing. For example, Morley (1993) himself, in a survey that elicited pain memories, found that 59% of his subjects were able to recall at least some aspect of the pain sensation, 41% reported that they had no recall of the sensation at all, and not a single subject reported actually reexperiencing the pain. Strongman and Kemp (1991) found that spontaneous accounts of pain tended to fit Morley's third variant of pain memory, remembering the circumstances in which the pain was experienced: "Overwhelmingly, the descriptions were of 'objective' details of the events rather than of the feelings of the respondents" (p. 195). Fienberg, Loftus, and Tanur (1985) conclude their review of the research on pain by asking, "Is it pain that people recall or is it really the events such as injuries and severe illnesses?" (p. 592).

People certainly do become viscerally upset when remembering or recalling certain types of pains, particularly those that evoke vivid images (e.g., those resulting from bloody wounds or dentists' drills; for fuller discussion of this issue, see Loewenstein, 1996; Scarry, 1985). These pains are likely to be exaggerated both in memory and in anticipation (see, e.g., Kent, 1985). Drug craving, as well as other types of pains and discomforts, such as those resulting from cold (Read & Loewenstein, 1999), however, are difficult to imagine and are thus unlikely to evoke visceral reactions when recalled or anticipated. Individuals' failure to recall vividly or anticipate the discomfort of craving can help to explain the postulated underappreciation of future craving.

An additional factor contributes to the underappreciation of future visceral factors: the well-documented tendency for people to overestimate their own abilities. This disposition is evident in the "above average" effect, whereby well over half of survey respondents typically rate themselves in the top 50% of drivers (Svenson, 1981), ethics (Baumhart, 1968), managerial prowess (Larwood & Whittaker, 1977), and a variety of other desirable skills (Dunning & Cohen, 1992; Dunning, Perie, & Story, 1991). The tendency is also evident in a piggyback study conducted in connection with the famous Milgram shock experiment, in which subjects were informed of the methodology and of the high prevalence of shocking behavior and were asked to guess what they personally would have done had they been subjects. Most subjects in the piggyback study did not think that they themselves would have administered powerful shocks to the confederate, as if they underestimated the effect on their own behavior of being exposed to the authoritative and relentless pressure of an experimenter (Milgram, 1965; see also Wolosin, Sherman, & Cann, 1975). It seems plausible that this tendency to overestimate one's own resistance to external influences would also apply to addiction—that is, that people would have exaggerated conceit about their own ability to resist the force of craving.

捠 Craving as a Visceral Factor

There is a widespread, albeit not unanimous, belief among addiction researchers that craving plays a central role in addiction.[6] Craving involves a "strong desire or intense longing" (Kozlowski & Wilkinson, 1987, p. 31). The term *craving* "seems to capture the essence of addiction in terms of its irresistible, compulsive, and anticipatory qualities, . . . has a strong appetitive quality, and is often used to describe intense appetites such as hunger, thirst, or lust" (Marlatt, 1987, p. 42). Craving produces a powerful, often overwhelming, urge to consume a drug. Even cocaine, which at one time seemed to present the anomalous case of an addictive drug that does not produce withdrawal or craving, has been shown to produce intense craving, both in humans and in other animals (Gawin, 1991).

Craving is somewhat different in character from other visceral factors. Whereas most other visceral factors are present from birth, craving arises from a process of neuroadaptation to drug taking. Nevertheless, like other visceral factors, craving plays an important adaptive function. Craving is the by-product of a conditioned association mechanism that acts as an early-warning and defense system to anticipate and protect the organism against the disequilibrating effect of the drug (Eikelboom & Stewart, 1982; Siegel, 1979).

When a pleasure-producing drug is consumed repeatedly, internal defenses or "opponent processes" are activated to neutralize its disequilibrating effect on the organism (Frawley, 1988; Solomon & Corbit, 1974).[7] These processes are triggered by "feedback" mechanisms that signal the drug's presence in the body or its effects, but also by "feedforward"—that is, conditioned anticipation of drug intake (Siegel et al., 1988). The adaptive effect of feedforward is illustrated by a study in which rats that had regularly received dosages of heroin in a specific room were found to overdose when the same dosages were administered in a different room—presumably because the cues necessary for feedforward were missing (Siegel, Hinson, Krank, & McCully, 1982). Craving arises when an individual who is exposed to drug-related cues that produce an adaptive response subsequently does not consume the drug. Although the specific subjective feeling may vary from drug to drug, and perhaps from person to person, craving is invariably unpleasant, and it powerfully increases the desire to take the drug.[8] Note that these two features—the negative hedonic effect and the enhanced desire for the drug—are the defining characteristics of a visceral factor.

Once an individual is addicted to a drug, craving appears to be the main force that keeps him or her taking it. Even mild craving seems to have a profound influence on behavior—an effect equivalent to that exerted by other visceral factors only at extreme levels of intensity. Indeed, a number of researchers have wondered why even mild states of craving can have such a profound influence on behavior. One explanation offered by Berridge and Robinson (1995) is that people can crave drugs with little or no conscious awareness that they are doing so. Another possibility is that craving derives its incentive value not from its intensity, but from its constancy; it simply does not go away until the need that it signals is satisfied. Yet a third, related, possibility is that the motivational power of craving derives not from its intensity, but from the fact that there exists such an effective and instantaneous way of eliminating the discomfort—namely, taking the drug.

Determinants of Craving

As endogenous taste models assume (e.g., Becker & Murphy, 1988; Herrnstein & Prelec, 1992; Koob, Stinus, Le Moal, & Bloom, 1989), craving tends to be positively related to the duration and intensity of prior drug use, and craving sometimes occurs automatically upon cessation of consumption—a phenomenon referred to as *withdrawal*. However, there is a growing consensus that withdrawal itself does not constitute the major impediment to quitting, in part because highly effective therapeutic interventions exist to mitigate withdrawal from many addictive drugs.

Instead, the main impediment to quitting appears to be the problem of craving-induced relapse. As Gawin (1988) comments, "During withdrawal, most cocaine abusers can withstand postcocaine anhedonia (withdrawal)" (p. 12). However, "after . . . the [withdrawal] period ends, episodic craving and the risk for relapse remain because of the continued role of conditioned cues. Relapse is a constant threat because craving can be initiated by almost any environmental cue that becomes associated with the drug—for example, time of day, a particular room or even the color of the room, the presence of specific individuals or paraphernalia associated with drug taking (Siegel, Krank & Hinson, 1988), sounds, and even positive or negative mood states" (Gawin, 1991, p. 1582). As Goldstein (1994) describes the situation with respect to cigarettes:

> A typical addict smokes 10 to 50 cigarettes every day. Each one is linked to a particular time, place, and activity. . . . For example, sitting down to the first morning cup of coffee is a conditioned cue to take out a cigarette and light it. Every meal ends with a cigarette. Sitting down at a desk to work evokes craving for a cigarette. Stepping into the lobby during intermission means light-up time. Just being near other smokers produces an automatic reaching for a cigarette. (p. 114)

    Cue-conditioned craving is similarly important for the more intense and immediately destructive addictions, such as addiction to crack cocaine or heroin. Again Goldstein provides a vivid illustration—the behavior of a heroin addict, Charlie T., who had stabilized on methadone with a regular job, but whose urine test one day showed that he had used heroin:

> He . . . had suddenly been overwhelmed by an irresistible craving and had rushed out of his house to find some heroin. His description was fascinating: it was as though he were driven by some external force he was powerless to resist, even though he knew while it was happening that it was a disastrous course of action for him. (p. 220)

After some discussion, Goldstein and Charlie T. identified the cue that had triggered the relapse. Charlie T. had been watching a TV program about an addict. He recalled:

> They showed an addict fixing, putting the needle into his vein, and suddenly I felt sick, just like needing heroin. I got that craving. I broke out in a sweat. I had that old feeling that only a fix would cure me. (p. 221)

    Theoretical models that view addiction as an endogenous taste phenomenon (e.g., Becker & Murphy, 1988; Herrnstein & Prelec, 1992; Orphanides & Zervos, 1995) assume that decreasing one's taste for the addictive substance is purely a matter of not consuming it. The visceral factor account, in contrast, places much greater importance on cues that are capable of inducing craving. Quitting involves much more than ceasing consumption for a certain interval, because if the addict becomes exposed to sufficiently evocative cues, craving can occur at any time, even years after drug taking has ceased (Gawin, 1988, 1991). Deconditioning—the gradual reduction in a cue's capacity to evoke craving—can be a very slow process. Cues may retain their ability to evoke craving even after years of abstinence (Niaura et al., 1988; Shiffman, 1982), which may help to explain the relatively low rates of successful long-term abstinence from drugs among drug addicts (Hser, Anglin, & Powers, 1993).

    Because addiction "poisons" persons, places, and things associated with it in the sense of imparting them with the ability to induce craving, successful quitting is likely to require a substantial investment in change of environment and lifestyle. As Siegel (1982) observes: "Users will attempt to avoid all contact with cocaine, cocaine paraphernalia and cocaine users when attempting this self-initiated detoxification. Some users report that it is effective to simply avoid dealers or other social users. Others engage in destruction of paraphernalia, and still others employ physical restraint by taking a vacation or even moving to another house or city" (p. 335). However, regardless of such efforts, it is impossible for an individual to eliminate completely the possibility of an encounter with drug-associated cues. Hence the Alcoholics Anonymous expression "Once an alcoholic, always an alcoholic," and Gawin's (1988) pessimistic view that the third, "extinction" phase of addiction to cocaine "persists indefinitely" (p. 14).

Narrowing of Attention

Craving routinely produces each of the three forms of attention narrowing characteristic of all visceral factors. First, it increases the perceived value of the craved substance relative to all other forms of consumption. Frawley (1988) refers to a "process of . . . increasing the behavior that facilitates drug or alcohol use and eliminating behavior that interferes with or does not lead to drug or alcohol use. This leads to a kind of 'tunnel vision' on the part of the addict" (p. 32). This effect is most dramatically evident in the behavior of cocaine addicts, who report that "virtually all thoughts are focused on cocaine during binges; nourishment, sleep, money, loved ones, responsibility, and survival lose all significance" (Gawin, 1991, p. 1581). It is also illustrated vividly by experiments with rats that were given access to cocaine and a wide range of alternative forms of consumption. These animals lost interest in food and other forms of consumption, lost weight, and typically died in a matter of weeks (Pickens & Harris, 1968).[9]

Second, craving seems to shorten the individual's time horizon, particularly when it comes to the drug itself. Addicts are notoriously shortsighted. This is usually viewed as a character trait and, indeed, is often seen as *the* trait that caused them to become addicts in the first place. However, myopia is as much the consequence of as the cause of addiction. Moreover, the visceral factor perspective implies that craving-induced myopia takes a very specific form: It increases the immediate desire for a specific drug but leaves time preferences for other items unchanged and should also not affect time preference for the drug in the future. Consistent with this prediction, Madden, Petry, Badger, and Bickel (1997) found that opioid-dependent individuals' time discount rates for heroin were much higher than those for money. In other words, when delayed, monetary payments lost their incentive value at a much slower rate than did doses of heroin.

Third, craving is notorious for eliciting destructive behavior that belies a lack of concern for the well-being of other people. The literature on drug addiction abounds with horrifying examples of the destructive behavior of drug addicts toward family members, friends, and strangers. Subjected to the miseries of craving, severe addicts tend to classify people into two categories: those who threaten to impede access to the drug and those who can serve as tools for obtaining it (W. Osiatynski, personal communication, 1999).

Imperfect Anticipation of Craving

There are many possible reasons for taking a drug to which one is not addicted: immediate pleasure, peer pressure, relief of depression, and so on. These differ across drugs, situations, and people and undoubtedly account for much of the variance in drug-taking behavior across persons and situations. The main reason for *not* taking a drug, aside from possible immediate negative consequences such as impaired driving or risk of arrest, is the possibility that one will become addicted (that is, not be able to stop) and the negative consequences associated with addiction. Most people view addiction as a negative state of affairs; indeed, due to selective media attention to dramatic cases, stereotypes about the woes of drug addiction may well be exaggerated.

If people truly believed that they would become addicted to a drug—that they would be unable to stop taking it—addiction would almost certainly be less prevalent than it is. However, as noted earlier, people underestimate both the severity of delayed visceral factors and the influence of visceral factors on behavior. Results from the University of Michigan's Monitoring the Future longitudinal study (Johnston, O'Malley, & Bachman, 1993), for example, suggest that high school students underestimate the likelihood of becoming addicted to cigarette smoking. Respondents were asked whether they expected to be smoking cigarettes in 5 years. Among respondents who were occasional smokers (less than one cigarette per day), only 15% predicted that they might be smoking in 5 years, but 5 years later 43% were in fact smoking. Slovic (Chapter 6, this volume) likewise presents findings from diverse studies that indicate that most addicted smokers regret having started smoking but nevertheless hold overly optimistic expectations of their own short-term likelihood of quitting.

There is also evidence for both forms of underestimation on the part of addicts and former addicts. In the study just mentioned, for example, among those who smoked at least one pack a day, only 32% expected to still be smoking in 5 years, but 5 years later 70% still smoked one pack or more per day. More anecdotally, Seeburger (1993) comments that the motivation to stay off a drug

lasts as long as the memory of the undesirable consequences stays strong. But the more successful one is at avoiding an addictive practice on the grounds of such motivation, the less strong does that very memory become. Before long, the memory of the pain that one brought on oneself through the addiction begins to pale in comparison to the anticipation of the satisfaction that would immediately attend relapse into the addiction. Sometimes in AA it is said that the farther away one is from one's last drink, the closer one is to the next one. That is surely true for alcoholics and all other addicts whose only reason to stop "using" is to avoid negative consequences that accompany continuing usage. (p. 152)

Wiktor Osiatynski (1992), in a similar vein, refers to the alcoholic's tendency to underestimate the power of addiction: "After hitting bottom and achieving sobriety, many alcoholics must get drunk again, often not once but a few times, in order to come to believe and never forget about their powerlessness" (p. 128).

These illustrations of the underestimation of visceral factors are particularly disturbing because the people being discussed have had extensive experience with craving. Experience thus does not seem to be sufficient to imprint a memory of the pain of craving. This observation is consistent with research on memory for pain that has found that experiencing a pain repeatedly does not go very far in terms of enhancing an individual's memory for the pain (e.g., Norvell et al., 1987).

෨ A Visceral Account of Addiction

The main features of the visceral account of addiction can be expressed in a series of simple diagrams of the sort often used to illustrate the opponent process perspective (Koob et al., 1989; Solomon & Corbit, 1974). Figure 9.1 highlights the difference between the two accounts.

The opponent process account of addiction posits that, in the early stages of drug taking, the pleasure derived from consuming a drug is gradually neutralized by an opponent process that lingers after the effects of the drug cease, creating a brief period of anhedonia following drug consumption. As drug taking continues, however, the opponent process operates ever more rapidly, reducing the initial period of pleasure associated with drug taking and intensifying and lengthening the subsequent period of anhedonia. The reduction in the drug's effectiveness due to the increasing efficiency of the opponent process produces tolerance (the need for ever-increasing amounts of the drug to achieve the same effect), and the anhedonia that follows in the wake of drug taking produces withdrawal. The opponent process account of drug addiction, therefore, views withdrawal following cessation of drug taking as the mechanism responsible for drug dependence.

As noted earlier, however, it is cue-conditioned craving, and not withdrawal, that appears to be the major impediment to abstinence. As Washton (1988) notes in the context of cocaine addiction, "Most cocaine addicts find it easy to stop using the drug in the short term but very difficult to avoid using it in the long term"

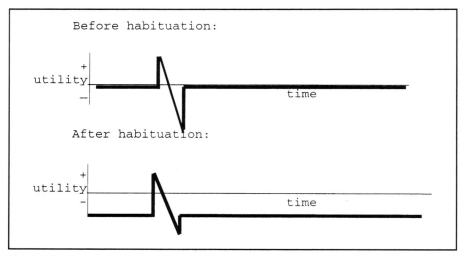

Figure 9.1. Opponent process account.

(p. 34). Indeed, the very ease of stopping in the short run may exacerbate the diffi-culty of stopping in the long run. Washton continues: "After a few weeks or months of abstinence, the patient may have the illusion of being cured. This illu-sion is often the result of ignorance and/or denial about the chronic nature of ad-dictive disease, . . . a tendency to misinterpret one's ability to refrain from drug use as proof that the addiction problem no longer exists" (p. 35).

The visceral account of addiction is depicted in Figure 9.2, the top part of which depicts the time course of utility of a person who is not yet addicted but who is consuming an addictive substance at three points during some relevant period of time. In the case of cigarettes, the diagram might depict cigarettes consumed dur-ing the space of an hour; for coffee or alcohol, it might show cups or glasses con-sumed during the course of a day (e.g., one at lunch and two in the evening); for cocaine, it might show binges occurring during the space of a week (with the larg-est consumption episode occurring on the weekend). It also might be the case that the timing of the episodes is dictated not by clock time, but by other regular or semiregular events, such as meals, routine tasks, or meetings with friends. As the individual continues to consume the addictive substance, either time of con-sumption itself or other cues initiate feedforward mechanisms that neutralize the effect of the drug when it is consumed (second part of Figure 9.2) and produce craving when the drug is not consumed in the presence of the cues (third part of the figure). Thus, over time, the pleasure derived from drug taking declines and the individual experiences ever-worsening levels of craving if he or she fails to take the drug when in the presence of drug-related cues.

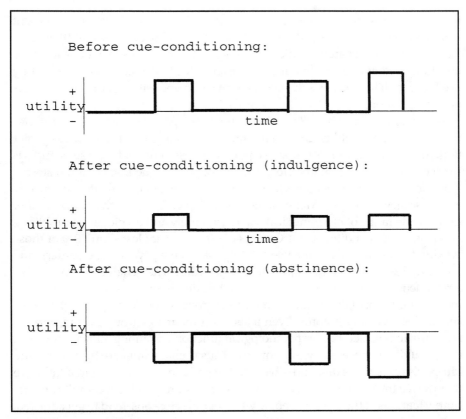

Figure 9.2. Visceral account.

Implications of the Visceral Account of Addiction

Even in this cursory diagrammatic form, the visceral account of addiction provides several testable predictions as well as prescriptions for treatment and policy.

Who Gets Addicted

Each of the major theoretical accounts of drug addiction posits certain causal mechanisms that lead to addiction and that, in turn, suggest that particular types of people will be vulnerable to addiction. The disease model (e.g., Vaillant, 1983), for example, points to genetic susceptibilities to specific types of addictions or classes of addictions, in the same way that people differ in their genetic susceptibility to different types of diseases. There is, indeed, substantial research pointing to genetic bases of addiction, although the heritability findings are at present somewhat unsatisfying at a theoretical level. It is highly unlikely that there is an "alcoholism" or "cigarette addiction" gene, so these studies inevitably raise the question of what underlying traits (e.g., impulsivity? the pleasurableness of drug use? susceptibility to peer influence?) are, in fact, responsible for the observed genetic associations.

Becker and Murphy's (1988) rational choice perspective focuses on low immediate or anticipated utility as the main state or trait that is predictive of drug addiction. Indeed, in this model the whole point of consuming addictive substances is to relieve low states of utility. However, although it is true that common stereotypes depict addicts as people who were miserable to begin with, the evidence is, in fact, somewhat mixed. McLellan et al. (1992, p. 232) report that addicts suffer from a wide range of other medical disorders, family and employment problems, and psychiatric conditions, but Gawin (1988) notes that less than 50% of those seeking treatment for cocaine use exhibit measurable psychiatric disorders, and only 10-15% seem to have major affective disorders. The general issue of psychiatric functioning is complicated by the relative dearth of prospective studies and the resultant lack of an obvious comparison group for evaluating the relative severity of observed symptoms. Even if such a comparison group existed, and the comparison revealed poorer psychological functioning among addicts, however, this would not necessarily support the causal chain implied by Becker and Murphy's model. It is quite possible that the pathologies observed in addicts are themselves the products of addiction, or that they are unrelated causally and are simply features of the types of people who, for other reasons, tend to get addicted. Indeed, as Fischman (1988) notes, the notion that "an organism or a person has to have some prerequisite pathology to find cocaine appealing" is challenged by "the fact that species and conditions of availability seem to be irrelevant to cocaine self-administration" (p. 7).

Finally, there is a class of addiction models that views addiction as the consequence of prediction errors. Herrnstein and Prelec's (1992) "garden path" theory of addiction, for example, assumes that people fail to notice, or for some other reason ignore, the negative effects that consuming addictive substances has on their satisfaction from other activities.[10] Herrnstein and Prelec's model identifies two major traits as critical for addiction: an individual's ability to "handle" the drug (in the sense that the drug has a rapid negative effect on the return from alternative activities) and the individual's failure to notice such effects. According to this scheme, the addiction-prone are those who are unaware that they cannot handle the drug. Becker and Murphy's (1988) model assumes away the latter form of prediction error (unawareness of the drug's effect) and predicts that the first factor—an individual's ability to handle the drug—will be positively rather than negatively related to addiction.

Like the garden-path model, the visceral factor perspective sees addiction as resulting, in part, from an imperfect anticipation of future tastes. However, whereas Herrnstein and Prelec attribute the prediction error to the individual's failure to notice gradual change, the visceral factor perspective attributes it to the individual's underappreciation of the force of future craving. Herrnstein and Prelec's perspective provides a useful account of some forms of addiction—specifically those in which the addiction unfolds very slowly as a result of subtle changes in tastes or in the environment, and in which the threat of addiction is not well publicized. Workaholism is an example; every extra hour one works has an imperceptible negative effect on the quality of one's home life, and the hazards of workaholism are not well publicized. Their model applies less well to drug addictions such as smoking, where the risks are very well publicized, and crack cocaine use, where addiction is quite rapid and the risks are again well-known.

Like other theoretical accounts of addiction, the visceral factor perspective implies that people with specific character traits will be susceptible to addiction. First, the individual must consume the drug initially, because the drug itself is pleasurable, because it satisfies some underlying need, or as a result of social reinforcement of drug use. Second, repeated use of the drug must, in fact, produce cue-conditioned tolerance and craving. Third, and most unique to the visceral account of addiction, the individual must underestimate the aversiveness and force of craving.[11] All three of these characteristics might be general traits that are applicable to a wide range of drugs and also to other visceral factors, or they might be specific to particular drugs and only to drug taking. One individual might find drugs generally pleasurable, tend to experience cue-conditioned craving for a *wide range* of drugs, and underestimate his or her own susceptibility; this would correspond to the case of an "addictive personality." Another person might exhibit these characteristics but only with respect to one drug or a *limited subset* of drugs.

The Effects of Addiction

The visceral account helps to shed light on several common features of addiction that are not addressed by other theoretical perspectives. First, addiction often does not entail continuous, or even highly regular, consumption of a drug. Consumption of many drugs is episodic, and many, if not most, addicts go through periods of abstinence that are typically interrupted by relapse. For some alcoholics, for example, periodic binges are followed by long periods of little or no drinking. Cigarette smokers are notorious for their frequent but rarely successful attempts to quit permanently. Even cocaine addicts alternate between binges and abstinence (Gawin, 1991). Theories that assume addiction results from gradual changes in the returns from different activities, such as Becker and Murphy's and

Herrnstein and Prelec's, have a difficult time dealing with such episodic drug-taking behavior. This type of pattern follows naturally, however, from the visceral factor perspective, because craving, which is assumed to be the major force driving addiction, is as transient as any other type of visceral factor.

Second, the visceral factor perspective helps to shed light on why addiction is so commonly associated with inner conflict and individuals' attempts to control their own behavior—both of which are ruled out by models such as Becker and Murphy's. Such conflicts arise because visceral factors affect behavior much more than they affect cognitive deliberations concerning self-interest (see Loewenstein, 1996). Even when succumbing to their addiction, many addicts are aware that they are not acting in their own self-interest, but find themselves unable to act on this awareness. Other choice-based theories of addiction can explain why addicts wish, ex post facto, that they were not addicted. However, they typically assume that, given the change that has occurred in their tastes, addicts view the current benefits of consuming the drug as justifying the costs.

Third, an important implication of the visceral factor perspective is that there will be a shortening of the time perspective with respect to the addictive substance (or any substance that is directly affected by the visceral factor), but not with respect to other forms of consumption. Drug addicts should make normal, or even farsighted,[12] trade-offs between immediate and delayed food, but look impatient when it comes to trade-offs between immediate and delayed consumption of the drugs to which they are addicted. Other theoretical accounts of addiction either predict no connection between time preference and addiction or assume that the causality runs in the other direction—that is, that addicts become addicted as a result of their generalized impatience.

Finally, the visceral factor perspective predicts extreme fluctuations in the addict's concern for the well-being of other persons, in direct relation to fluctuations in craving. According to the visceral factor perspective, the addict will be extremely self-centered during periods of craving but should be perfectly normal (or even extra-self-sacrificing as a result of guilt) when not experiencing craving. Such a pattern of alternating extreme selfishness and remorse is, of course, characteristic of alcoholics and other drug addicts.

Quitting and Self-Binding

The underestimation of delayed visceral factors can help to explain the prevalence of "self-binding behavior" among addicts—that is, actions that limit their own future access to drugs. The alcoholic who takes Antabuse (assuring him- or herself of miserable withdrawal symptoms), the smoker who ventures off into the wilderness without cigarettes (after a final smoke at the departure point), and the dieter who signs up for a miserable, hungry vacation at a "fat farm" are all imposing future misery on themselves at a point in time much more imminent than when the benefits of abstinence will be enjoyed. To those who view these behavior disorders as manifestations of myopic time preferences, such seemingly far-sighted behavior might seem anomalous. Perhaps, however, the readiness to impose imminent pain on oneself results not from farsighted preferences, but from a failure to appreciate the reality of the near-future pain associated with abstinence in the face of craving. Such a tendency to underestimate craving is, according to the visceral account of addiction, exactly what causes people to become addicted in the first place.

Self-binding, however, requires a special combination of prediction errors. To bind oneself in the first place requires some appreciation for the influence of future craving on one's own *behavior*. Individuals who fail to recognize their own powerlessness in the face of craving will see no need to self-bind. At the same time however, as just noted, self-binding requires a lack of appreciation of the *misery* that one will experience as a result of being unable to mitigate the craving. This condition for self-binding probably explains why addicts rarely self-bind in moments when they are experiencing active craving. Self-binding requires an intellectual appreciation of one's powerlessness in the future combined with a relatively cavalier attitude toward future misery.

Relapse

Relapse is a natural consequence of the visceral factor perspective, because it is virtually impossible to predict perfectly, or to control, one's own exposure to cues that can induce craving. But the problem of relapse is exacerbated by addicts' inadequate appreciation of the force of craving and hence of the riskiness of cue exposure.

First, the abstinent addict may underestimate the risks of taking even a small quantity of the drug. There is substantial evidence that a small quantity of a drug can act as a powerful cue that can reinitiate craving for a drug to which an individual was addicted in the past (Gardner & Lowinson, 1993). Many addicts relapse, even after long periods of abstinence, when, feeling confident because of their lengthy nonuse, they succumb to the temptation to try just a small quantity of the drug.

Second, the addict is likely to underinvest in craving reduction for at least two reasons. First, if people underestimate the power of craving, as seems to be the case, they will also tend to underestimate the benefits of treatment. Second, if they underestimate the ability of environmental cues to elicit craving, they will underinvest in changing their environment. Craving reduction is an expensive proposition, because it is likely to require changes in location, friendships, consumption habits, and other cues associated with drug taking. Addicts are unlikely to incur the enormous costs of such changes if they fail to understand their value. As O'Brien et al. (1988) write: Addicts "often . . . return home after a period of brief treatment feeling well and confident that they will not resume drug use. They are usually surprised to suddenly feel craving, withdrawal, or even 'high' when they encounter people or places associated with their prior drug use" (p. 18). That addicts are caught by surprise by their own craving is not in itself particularly surprising; social scientists themselves have only recently begun to appreciate the potency of conditioned craving and its importance for addiction and relapse.

Willpower

The concept of willpower, which played a central role in 19th-century accounts of the conflict between passion and reason, has only since the end of the 20th century begun to find a place in social science (see, e.g., Baumeister, Heatherton, & Tice, 1994). Despite its prominent role in popular views of addiction, the role of willpower has been dismissed, ignored, or defined in a counterintuitive fashion in recent theoretical accounts of addiction. Disease theorists, for example, tend to view willpower as little more than a code word for the inverse of susceptibility, or to dismiss the role of willpower, as in disease theorists O'Brien et al.'s (1988) comment that "addictive disorders . . . are mistakenly thought to be under the control of 'willpower.' " While not denying the importance of willpower, other researchers view it as an astute application of self-control strategies such as "bunching" and self-binding (e.g., Ainslie, 1992).

In its common usage, the term *willpower* refers to a type of inward exertion, force of concentration, and tolerance of pain or discomfort (Loewenstein, 2000). Thus a runner's exertion of willpower reflects the pain she is able to tolerate to maintain a fast pace; likewise, the willpower that a bored seminar participant mobilizes to remain awake involves inward exertion, in the form of concentration, possibly supplemented by an overt self-infliction of pain, such as biting one's tongue or stabbing one's hand with a pencil. Although such a person might also employ cognitive strategies, such as attempting to scare oneself into waking up, the act of will is much more closely linked with the visceral than with the cognitive.

Willpower could be introduced into the theoretical framework depicted in Figure 9.2 by postulating a short-term constraint in willpower, as depicted in Figure 9.3. The shaded area inside each episode of craving represents willpower. One might postulate that the individual is able to resist, by dint of willpower, a certain total amount (that is, intensity × duration) of craving (see Muraven, Tice, & Baumeister, 1998). Thus, in the diagram, the individual could avoid taking the drug in the first and second episodes of craving, but would find him- or herself de-

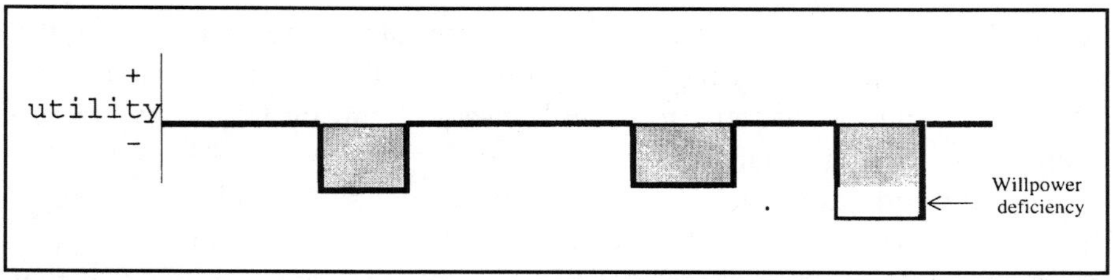

Figure 9.3. Visceral account: after cue conditioning (abstinence).

ficient in willpower, and presumably relapse, when the third, most extreme, episode occurs.

A more realistic model would permit replenishment of willpower over time, which would permit the individual to resist intermittent craving indefinitely, provided that the replenishment rate exceeds the product of frequency and intensity of experienced craving. Such a model might also permit some degree of forward-looking behavior; individuals who recognize that they would ultimately lack the requisite willpower to remain abstinent might decide there is no point in abstaining and might initiate drug use at the first sign of craving (O'Donoghue & Rabin, 1999). Such a pattern of behavior has been observed in studies of dieters who, when told that they will be fed a caloric meal at some point in the future (e.g., an hour hence), tend to lose their resolve and begin eating immediately (Ruderman, 1986).

An additional property of willpower can shed further light on the problem of relapse: It takes time to build up. Salespeople and actors need to "psych themselves up" before they thrust themselves before their customers and audiences, respectively. Athletes "pump themselves up" before entering the track or stepping onto the playing field. Similarly, addicts need to "gird," or "fortify," themselves to resist the urge for drug taking produced by craving. The time it takes to mobilize willpower may help to explain why it is easier to withdraw from drugs in the short run than to resist craving in the long run; withdrawal upon cessation is highly predictable, and one can prepare for it psychologically and sometimes even pharmacologically. Craving, in contrast, typically takes one by surprise.

Treatment

Given the preliminary state of the theoretical perspective proposed here, it would be premature to propose or advocate specific kinds of treatments for addiction. Instead, I will mention some existing treatments of demonstrated effectiveness, the success of which can be understood in terms of the visceral account of addiction. The visceral account implies that successful treatments for drug addiction should (a) alleviate craving so as to promote quitting and (b) maintain vivid memories of the motivational force and misery of craving to prevent relapse among those who have quit.

Many currently available treatments seem to operate by relieving craving. Fluoxetine (Prozac), for example, and other antidepressants have been shown to have some effectiveness in treating a wide range of other behavior disorders that are associated with visceral factors, and may have some benefits when it comes to addiction. It would be interesting to assess whether the effectiveness of antidepressants results from their capacity to mitigate craving, as some have suggested (Gawin, 1991). Deconditioning craving through repeated exposure to drug-related stimuli also seems to be beneficial (O'Brien et al., 1988). Again, the effectiveness of this treatment, in an area where many treatments fail, reinforces the central role in addiction played by craving.

Treatments that do not seem to work can also be understood in these terms. For example, those that block the pleasurable effects of the drug (e.g., administration of opiate antagonists such as naltrexone) appear to be ineffective, perhaps because few people can tolerate their aversiveness.

Keeping memories of the aversiveness and power of craving "alive" involves more subtle interventions than does reducing craving, but it nevertheless seems to be possible to achieve. One method is to expose addicts who have quit to the agonies of people who are still addicted or who have recently quit and are thus engaged in an acute battle against craving. Alcoholics Anonymous currently serves this function by bringing recovering alcoholics into regular contact with people who have just quit or who are struggling with quitting, and by prescribing daily attendance for a year, followed by regular attendance for the duration of the alcoholic's life.

A second method would involve exposing addicts to information that helps them to remember their own agonies while addicted. Innovative research by Gold (1993, 1994) on the sexual behavior of gay men suggests that one means of achieving this might be to persuade addicts to keep daily diaries, both while they are actively addicted and as they go through the early, painful, stages of quitting. Much in the same way that poor memory for craving promotes relapse, according to Gold (1993, 1994), unprotected sex occurs in the heat of the moment (under the influence of a visceral factor), but people cannot remember or predict what the heat felt like, and so enter the next sexual encounter unprepared to deal with it. Based on this intuition, Gold (1994) tested an intervention designed to increase condom use. He had gay men recall as vividly as possible the last sexual encounters in which they had engaged in unprotected anal intercourse and gave them various recall aids. He then compared this intervention to a no-intervention control group and a standard intervention in which subjects were exposed to didactic posters they had not previously seen. The proportions of men in the three groups who subsequently engaged in two or more acts of unprotected anal intercourse differed dramatically—42% and 41% for the control and poster groups, but only 17% for the self-justification group.

What Is an Addiction?

At present, the term *addiction* is used to refer to a multiplicity of behavioral phenomena, to the point where the term is being applied to any compulsion or socially proscribed habit. We speak of "sex addicts" and refer to people as addicted to crossword puzzles and gambling. Should these be considered addictions? My opinion is that conditioned craving should be taken as the defining feature of addiction. In stating that the craving must be conditioned, I side with the endogenous taste theorists—the taste must be acquired in some fashion, a condition that would rule out generic sex as an addictive activity. People are born with a desire to have sex, albeit some more than others, and intense desire often precedes any actual experience. Thus the term *sex addict* is no more appropriate than would be *food addict.* Although it could be argued that some people are, in fact, food addicts, in my opinion this is an error that results from confusing the general term *disorder* with the more specific *addiction.* I suppose, however, that one could become addicted to a particular type of food or particular type of sex due to repeated exposure, as one could to crossword puzzles. Significantly, this definition would exclude gambling from the ranks of addictions because, although once some gamblers begin they may have difficulty stopping, the best evidence seems to be that these individuals do not experience significant craving when they do not gamble (Rosenthal, 1989).

Addiction and Rationality

A critical question about addiction, with significant ramifications for social policy, concerns its rationality. A determination that addiction does not result from rational decision making would undercut two frequently advocated, although opposite, policies aimed at dealing with drug addiction: severely sanctioning drug use and completely legalizing it. On the one hand, if addicts' drug use is not a matter of choice, then it makes no sense, either practically or morally, to sanction it. On the other hand, if initial decisions to use drugs are systematically biased, then legalization has the potential to produce a social catastrophe.

With the exception of Becker and Murphy's (1988) straightforward position on the rationality issue, however, addiction theorists, researchers, and practitioners tend to adopt a somewhat self-contradictory stance. Although most acknowledge the powerful force of addiction on behavior, most also believe that people must be held accountable for their behavior as a matter of policy. The Alcoholics Anonymous literature, for example, exhorts alcoholics to recognize their lack of control over alcohol but at the same time counsels those who come into contact with alcoholics against coddling them and undermining their incentive to quit drinking. The belief that incentives influence behavior contains an implicit assumption that alcoholics do in fact have some control over their drinking behavior. A similarly ambivalent attitude on the rationality issue can be seen in Goldstein's (1994) description of relapse. Despite his self-portrayal as a disease theorist, Goldstein believes that drug users should be held personally accountable for their behavior. Consistent with this policy perspective, he describes relapse as the outcome of a decision: "Relapse is always preceded by a *decision* to use"; but he then continues, "however vague and inchoate that decision may be. It is an impulsive decision, not a rational one; and it is provoked by craving—the intense and overwhelming desire to use the drug" (p. 220; emphasis added). Goldstein's use of adjectives such as "impulsive" and "inchoate" to describe the decision and his depiction of craving as "intense" and "overwhelming" point to severe limitations in the exercise of volition in this "decision."

Like Becker and Murphy's model, the visceral factor perspective provides a straightforward answer to the rationality question. It points to important departures from rationality both in the initial decisions that lead to addiction and in the behavior of the addicted. The decisions that lead to addiction reflect a systematic bias in individuals' ability to predict their own future feelings and behavior. Once addicted, behavior is periodically driven by craving, which overwhelms rational deliberations concerning self-interest.

This does not mean that all addictive behavior is totally irrational, or that addicts (and potential addicts) are not susceptible to incentives, including the price of addictive substances. Addicts are not the mindless, out-of-control, subhuman creatures sometimes depicted in the popular media, which is why policies supporting programs such as needle exchanges can be so effective (Normand, Vlahov, & Moses, 1995). But the behaviors of addicts, and those at risk for addiction, are in some cases distorted by imperfect expectations and in other cases partly or completely overwhelmed by the power of immediate craving. Sensitivity to price and other costs and benefits is a prediction of purely rational theories of addiction, but almost any decision-theoretic model of addiction, including the one proposed here, would predict responsiveness to price.

∞ Concluding Comments

The topic of addiction holds a special fascination for economists. As economists have become increasingly confident in the general applicability of their rational choice paradigm, they have progressively applied it to realms of behavior that are seemingly ever more irrational in character. Addiction is the end of the line in this process because it appears to be so patently irrational. If addiction can be analyzed productively as an instance of rational choice, the argument seems to go, so can every other behavior.

Although the conquest of new areas has produced striking and provocative insights, it has also revealed the constraints of the rational choice perspective. As long as economists trained their sights on such areas as spending/saving, insurance decisions, labor market behavior, bargaining, and investment, the limitations of the reigning theoretical paradigm remained largely hidden. The limitations, however, stand out dramatically as economists have moved down the rationality scale to such patently visceral behaviors as dieting, suicide, and especially addiction.

In contending that addiction is not an entirely rational behavior, I hope to shift the discourse in the opposite direction. My argument is that addiction is only one, albeit extreme, manifestation of the effect of visceral factors on behavior. If one accepts the relatively intuitive argument that addiction is *not* the outcome of a rational choice, and that the irrational aspects of addiction are driven by visceral factors, it follows that behaviors that economists view as rational, such as stock market behavior and labor market behavior, may also be less than fully rational.

The study of addiction may, therefore, shed light not only on addiction itself, but on a wide range of other phenomena that are influenced by visceral factors. Visceral factors are a ubiquitous aspect of everyday life, and they regularly undermine the rationality of decision making, due to both their underestimation in prospect and their disproportional force when they operate in the present. Whereas Becker and Murphy view addiction as one additional illustration of the universal applicability of the rational choice perspective, I view addiction as only one of many types of human behaviors *not* usefully viewed as purely rational.

∞ Notes

1. Although visceral factors themselves tend to fluctuate relatively dramatically, an individual's *proneness* to experiencing different types of visceral factors typically evolves more gradually.

2. In economic parlance, the marginal rate of substitution between goods and activities associated with the visceral factor (e.g., food for hunger) and all other nonassociated goods and activities diminishes.

3. We cannot, of course, rule out the possibility that sexually aroused subjects do not predict their own behavior more accurately but actually overpredict their own likelihood of behaving aggressively.

4. Curiosity is widely viewed as a type of drive or appetite that shares many properties with other drives, such as hunger and, especially, the sex drive (see Loewenstein, 1994).

5. In a typical demonstration of the effect (see, e.g., Kahneman, Knetsch, & Thaler, 1990), one group of subjects (sellers) is endowed with an object and given the option of trading it for various amounts of cash; another group (choosers) is not given the object but given a series of choices between getting the object or getting various amounts of cash. Although the objective wealth positions of the two groups are identical, as are the choices they face, endowed subjects hold out for significantly more money than do those who are not endowed.

6. In the recent past, Wise and others have questioned the importance of craving (conditioned association) for addiction (see, e.g., Wise & Bozarth, 1987). As Wise has noted, animals can become addicted to cocaine and other substances virtually instantly, without prior exposure. Because animals would not seem to have had any chance to habituate to or become conditioned to these substances so quickly, these elements do not appear to be necessary for addiction. However, subsequent research by Wise and his colleagues has shown that cocaine administration results in remarkably quick habituation and conditioned association; animals exhibit physiological signs of distress shortly preceding even the second dose of cocaine, and these distress signs escalate rapidly with subsequent doses (see, e.g., Gratton & Wise, 1994).

7. This is a simplification of reality. Some drugs operate specifically by producing disequilibration such that the organism responds in a pleasure-enhancing fashion—for example, by administering its own opiates (Eikelboom & Stewart, 1982). In these cases, conditioned cues will produce the opposite of craving.

8. A mild example of feedforward and its effects can be seen in the dramatic increase in hunger often experienced right before dinner, especially when one can smell, see, or hear dinner being prepared. If dinner were to be suddenly postponed or canceled after exposure to such cues, the result would be a very mild form of craving that would provide a strong motivation for snacking.

9. It is true that cigarette smokers who quit often overeat, and drug addicts are notorious for substituting other drugs when their drugs of choice are not available; craving can have spillover effects to closely related alternative forms of consumption. But craving favors certain forms of consumption over others. Thus for the former smoker, food has less appeal than a cigarette.

10. Herrnstein and Prelec (1992, p. 333) dismiss Becker and Murphy's model as depicting a process of "self-medication," a charge that Becker and Murphy probably would not deny. They would probably dismiss Herrnstein and Prelec's theory on the basis of its assumption of "irrationality."

11. Although such underestimation seems to be characteristic of all visceral factors (Loewenstein, 1996), there may be unique contributing factors when it comes to drugs. First, people who freely consume a drug in the early stages of an addiction may forestall craving through consumption, and may, therefore, not actually experience full-blown

craving until it has intensified severely. Second, drug users may have the wrong model of drug addiction. People who are unfamiliar with the concept of cue conditioning may point to periods of abstinence (e.g., "I never drink before lunch," or "I'm able to go off coffee when I'm on vacation") as evidence that they are not addicted. Their model of addiction is more akin to the opponent process perspective, which implies relatively constant consumption over time. They infer from the absence of craving or craving-driven consumption during certain time periods that they are in full volitional control of their behavior.

12. The addict may become *more* patient with respect to goods that are substitutes for the drug to which the addict is addicted, because drug consumption will effectively mitigate the visceral factors that would otherwise increase their immediate value. For example, cocaine addicts may be especially *patient* with respect to food because cocaine craving crowds out hunger.

Chapter 10

The Catch-22 of Smoking and Quitting

Daniel Romer
Patrick Jamieson
R. Kirkland Ahern

T his chapter introduces a paradox that traps individuals when they face the decision to start or stop smoking. This paradox, which we call the catch-22 of smoking and quitting, results from the incompatible consequences of the belief that one can quit smoking at any time and by quitting avoid serious health risks. This optimistic belief helps smokers quit the behavior, but it also gives adolescents license to start smoking. By helping young people to start on a smoking habit, the presumption that it is easy to quit creates the addiction that undermines their ability to accomplish the goal.

Figure 10.1 shows the model that summarizes the inherent contradiction in the belief that quitting smoking is easy to do. This optimistic belief leads adolescents to think that the hazards of trying cigarettes are minimal or avoidable and thereby facilitates the initiation of cigarette smoking. This experience opens the door to the development of a smoking habit. Continued smoking leads to addiction, which inhibits the smoker's ability to quit easily and, as a result, reduces the smoker's optimism about being able to quit. Figure 10.1 shows addiction creating a negative feedback loop to beliefs about quitting. This decreases the perceived ease of quitting, which has the effect of reducing plans to quit and thus maintains the smoking addiction. This catch-22 poses challenges to health educators who want to encourage smokers to remain optimistic about their ability to quit but at

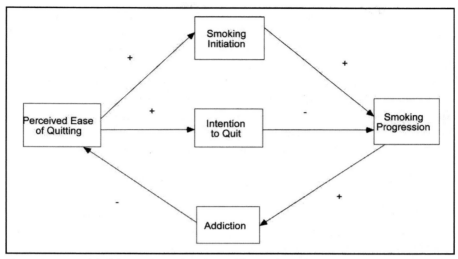

Figure 10.1. Model of the catch-22 of smoking addiction showing the positive effects of optimism about quitting on intention to quit but the damaging effects of optimism on starting to smoke in the first place.

the same time want nonsmokers to recognize the obstacles to quitting so that they never begin.

The belief that one can change one's behavior is recognized as critical in several theories of behavior change, such as social cognitive theory (Bandura, 1986), the transtheoretical model (Prochaska & DiClemente, 1984), and the theory of planned behavior (Ajzen, 1991). Each focuses on either the intention to quit or the belief that quitting is possible as an important precursor to change. Indeed, smokers who want to quit are more likely to plan on doing so if they think they will be able to (Borland, Owen, Hill, & Schofield, 1991; Norman, Conner, & Bell, 1999; Sargent, Mott, & Stevens, 1998). However, smokers who try to quit often relapse. The more often smokers relapse, the more difficult they perceive quitting to be. As a result, the optimism needed to quit may no longer be sufficient to accomplish the goal. In this chapter, we lay out the evidence for the paradox and suggest some strategies for transcending it based on the Annenberg Tobacco Surveys.

⚭ Ease of Quitting as a Factor in Starting and Continuing to Smoke

In the Annenberg samples, we found optimism about quitting to be a major predictor of trial and subsequent progression to heavier smoking among young people. In each of the two surveys, we asked respondents how difficult they thought it would be to quit smoking. In Survey 1, we asked this about a hypothetical smoker who smoked at least two packs of cigarettes a week. In addition, we asked current smokers how difficult it would be to quit if they tried to do it themselves. Although these judgments were correlated ($r = .25$), many smokers who thought they could easily quit did not think others could do so (30%). In addition, many who thought they would have great difficulty quitting thought that other smokers could do so more easily (43%). These discrepancies suggest that it may be important to ask smokers about their own ability to quit when assessing their intentions to do so. Indeed, in Survey 1 we found that smokers' ratings of optimism about their own quitting were more closely related to plans to quit than were ratings of hypothetical smokers' abilities to quit ($r = .12$ versus $.01$).

In Survey 2, we asked all respondents to estimate the difficulty of quitting if they hypothetically smoked a pack of cigarettes a day. We thought this question would be less hypothetical for smokers than for nonsmokers. Analysis of their responses, however, suggested that this was not the case. Smokers' ratings of the ability to quit were still uncorrelated with their plans to quit in Survey 2. As a result, we will rely here on Survey 1 in examining the effects of optimism on the intention to quit. Chapter 4 presents additional findings about optimism and quitting.

As Figure 10.2 indicates, 14- to 22-year-olds in Survey 1 who had tried smoking were more optimistic about their ability to quit than were those who had not tried smoking. A logistic regression analysis indicates that perceived ease of quitting predicts trial even after demographics (age, gender, education, region of country, and race/ethnicity) and perceived risk of smoking are controlled for, OR = 1.57, $p = .01$. A linear regression analysis of actual smoking levels (ranging from never having smoked to smoking a pack of cigarettes a day or more) reveals that perceived ease of quitting also predicts increased levels of smoking, holding constant initial trial and perceived risk of smoking, $t(587) = 2.00, p = .046$. These findings support the contention that optimism about quitting leads to both trial and subsequent progression to a smoking habit.

Figure 10.3 shows results from Survey 2 indicating that optimism about quitting is more related to trial and use among the young than among older respondents. Those over age 39 who currently smoke are less likely to believe that quitting is easy than are younger smokers. In addition, older persons who have tried cigarettes but do not currently smoke are more likely to think that quitting is easy than are those who continue the habit. These patterns suggest that optimism about being able to give up smoking is particularly harmful to adolescents, who are prone to begin smoking if they think that people can quit at any time. Older current and former smokers are far less optimistic (with the possible exception of former smokers over age 70).

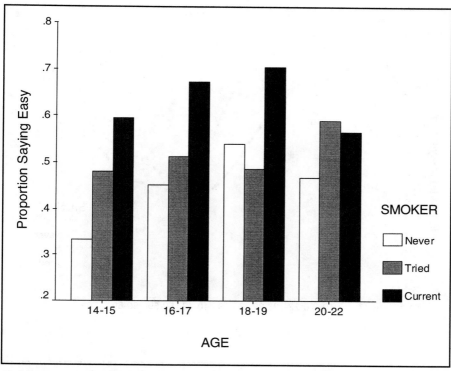

Figure 10.2. Perceived ease of quitting and use of cigarettes at different ages (Survey 1). Respondents who said that quitting smoking would be either "very easy" or "hard, but most people can do it if they really try" were scored as thinking it is relatively easy to quit, whereas those who said it was "very difficult and most cannot do it" or "almost impossible, and only a few will be able to do it" or who did not know were scored as thinking it is relatively difficult.

∞ Perceived Risks of Occasional Smoking Are Low

One of the reasons young people may try smoking without concern about its consequences is the belief that light smoking is relatively harmless. Across all ages (Figure 10.4), respondents in our survey viewed the risk of occasional smoking ("smoking once in a while, say at parties or with friends") as much lower than the risk of daily smoking. Furthermore, as Figure 10.5 indicates, respondents across nearly all age groups who believed it is easy to quit were even less concerned about the risks of occasional smoking. This low level of concern about occasional smoking may also contribute to young people's trial.

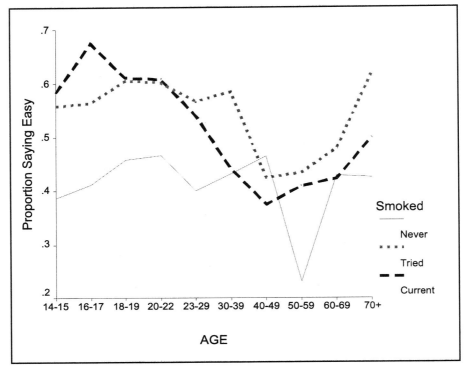

Figure 10.3. Young people who have tried smoking are more likely than older people to say that quitting is easy (Survey 2).

Not only did our respondents perceive occasional smoking as relatively risk-free, they also viewed it as relatively low in risk compared with drug and alcohol use. This conclusion is particularly evident from a survey of a convenience sample of 2,006 urban high school students conducted by the Annenberg Public Policy Center in 1998. Students in these schools had been exposed to considerable education about the hazards of drugs and cigarettes. The Policy Center tested a wide range of antidrug television messages in these schools across the country. Many of the ads produced no effects on perceived risk of drugs or tobacco when those who viewed them were compared with students exposed to a control video. We examined the perceptions of these students concerning the risks of trying and using a variety of drugs, including cigarettes, wine or beer, liquor, chewing tobacco, and marijuana. The trial question was phrased so that it asked whether the student considered each behavior as too risky to try even once (*yes* or *no*). Another question asked how harmful (on a scale from 1 to 5) it would be to engage in each

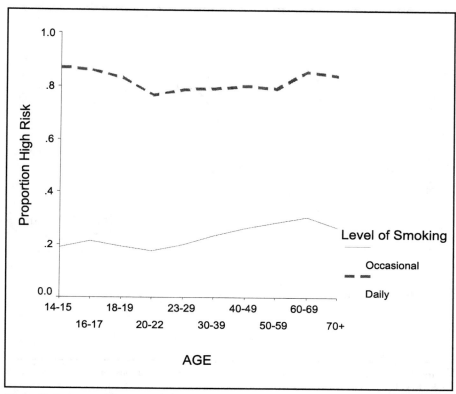

Figure 10.4. Across all ages, people are much less likely to see occasional smoking than daily smoking as "very risky."

behavior twice a week, with 1 indicating that it would not be harmful at all and 5 indicating that it would be very harmful.

The results (Table 10.1) show that the respondents saw smoking a cigarette as about as risky as having a single drink of liquor. They saw it as less risky than smoking marijuana a single time, and as marginally less risky than chewing tobacco. Ratings of harm for engaging in each behavior twice a week (Table 10.2) indicate that both boys and girls regarded cigarettes as the least harmful of the entire set of behaviors.

In summary, we find strong evidence that young people perceive the risks of trying cigarettes as quite low and that optimism about being able to quit at any time reduces the apparent risk even more. As the catch-22 model suggests, optimism about avoiding the harm of cigarettes encourages trial and subsequent progression to heavier smoking.

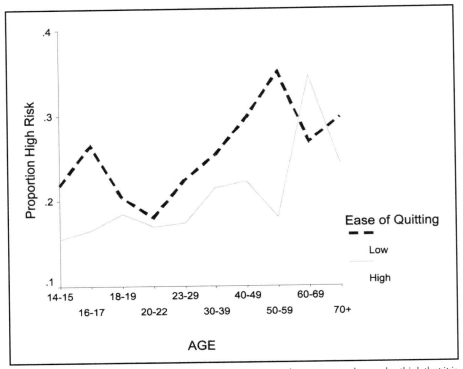

Figure 10.5. The perceived risk of occasional smoking is even lower among those who think that it is easier to quit.

∽ Ease of Quitting and Intentions to Quit

The belief that quitting is possible and within one's capabilities is a form of optimism and self-efficacy that health educators ordinarily would encourage among smokers. An analysis of smokers in Survey 1 ($N = 300$) shows that perceived ease of quitting ("If you were to quit smoking, how difficult do you think it would be?") predicts the intention to quit. A logistic regression analysis controlling for demographic variables and perceived risk of smoking indicated that young smokers who felt they could more easily quit had odds of intending to quit that were two times greater than the odds of those who thought it would be difficult, OR = 2.01, $p = .03$.

To examine effects of continued smoking and attempts to quit on smokers' subsequent optimism about quitting, we tested the causal model in Figure 10.6 for

TABLE 10.1 Percentages Reporting That Various Behaviors Are Too Risky to Try Even Once

Behavior	Boys (N = 1,020)	Girls (N = 926)	Total
Smoke pot	59.0[c]	41.4[b]	50.3[c]
Chew tobacco	53.4[b]	41.6[b]	47.3[b]
Drink beer or wine	43.9[a]	43.0[b]	43.7[a]
Smoke cigarette	51.7[b]	35.0[a]	43.6[a]
Drink liquor	50.2[b]	35.0[a]	42.7[a]

NOTE: Behaviors that do not differ ($p < .05$) have the same superscripts.

TABLE 10.2 Mean Ratings of Harm for Various Behaviors Done Twice a Week

Behavior	Boys (N = 999) (SD)	Girls (N = 854) (SD)	Total (N = 1,913) (SD)
Drink liquor	3.81[d] (1.36)	3.98[e] (1.23)	3.88[d] (1.31)
Smoke pot	3.83[d] (1.45)	3.87[d] (1.33)	3.83[d] (1.40)
Drink beer	3.17[c] (1.46)	3.03[b] (1.40)	3.10[c] (1.43)
Chew tobacco	2.60[b] (1.44)	3.25[c] (1.42)	2.91[b] (1.46)
Smoke cigarettes	2.47[a] (1.42)	2.90[a] (1.48)	2.68[a] (1.40)

NOTE: Behaviors that do not differ ($p < .05$) have the same superscripts. Ratings were reported on a scale of 1 (*not at all harmful*) to 5 (*very harmful*).

the 300 current smokers in Survey 1 (Appendix C provides more detail about this methodology). This model included age and education as predictors of perceived ease of quitting, intention to quit, frequency of current smoking, perception of addiction, perceived personal health risk of smoking, and the number of times the smokers had tried to quit in the past.

The model provided an excellent fit to the data, accounting for nearly all the goodness of fit in the data set (CFI = .999). Weights shown next to each causal path represent standardized path coefficients (*sp*). Age was unrelated to the number of times smokers had tried to quit ($sp = .06, p > .15$), but was positively related to the frequency of current smoking ($sp = .13, p < .05$). Education was negatively related to smoking frequency ($sp = -.24, p < .001$) and positively related to the intention to quit ($sp = .19, p < .01$). Planning to quit smoking was a deterrent to the amount smoked ($sp = -.14, p < .01$), and perceived ease of quitting was positively related to

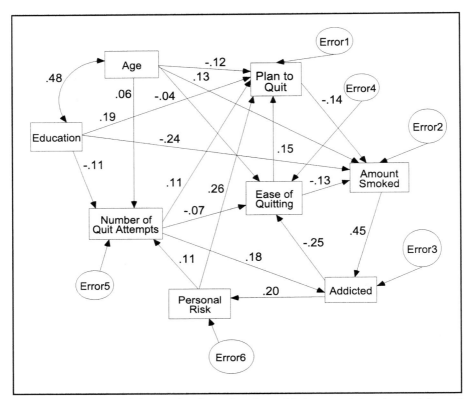

Figure 10.6. Causal model showing the effects of smoking addiction on optimism about quitting and perceived personal risk of smoking (Survey 1). Standardized path weights indicate the strength of the causal relations in the model.

intentions to quit (sp = .15, p < .01). This chain of effects shows that optimism about quitting reduces the amount smoked. Optimism also reduces the amount smoked directly (sp = –.13, p = .05), apart from intentions. With only a single measure of intention, it is difficult to conclude that optimism affects smoking directly. Nevertheless, the results show that optimism is a deterrent to continued smoking, as many theories of behavior change would suggest.

If smoking did not lead to addiction, optimism about quitting would eventually reduce the amount smoked to the point at which smokers quit. However, as the model shows, the more frequently young people smoke, the more addiction to smoking they report (sp = .45, p < .001). Perceived addiction then reduces optimism about quitting (sp = –.25, p < .001), with the result that about 75% of the beneficial effects of optimism on current smoking levels are eliminated and current smoking levels remain largely unchanged. In addition, the more times smokers try to quit and relapse, the more addicted they perceive themselves to be (sp =

.18, $p < .001$). This additional effect further reduces their optimism about quitting. The reduced optimism reported by current smokers (Figure 10.3) is consistent with this finding. Indeed, former smokers are somewhat more optimistic about quitting, perhaps because they managed to do it or were less addicted in the first place.

One possible route out of the catch-22 is the recognition that smoking is hazardous to the smoker's health. As the model shows, an important consequence of perceived addiction is increased recognition of the risk of smoking to the smoker personally ($sp = .20, p < .001$). This recognition motivates attempts to quit ($sp = .11$, $p < .05$), which increase the intention to quit ($sp = .11, p < .05$). In addition, risk perception increases the intention to quit directly ($sp = .26, p < .001$), which also helps to overcome the catch-22. If smokers can sufficiently appreciate the risks of smoking once they have started the habit, they should ultimately be able to reduce their smoking and quit. However, the need for repeated attempts to quit only reinforces the point that young smokers are caught in the catch-22. Furthermore, emphasizing the risks of smoking does not seem to inhibit young people from trying cigarettes (see Chapters 4 and 7 of this volume), so focusing on risk may be helpful only for encouraging quitting.

Mark Twain is reported to have remarked, "Giving up smoking is easy, I've done it hundreds of times." This recognition appears to be a common experience for smokers (see Chapter 4 for a fuller analysis of the predictors of quitting).

∽ Implications for Antismoking Campaigns

Communication programs to discourage smoking should take into account the catch-22 we have described. Adolescents underestimate the addictive properties of cigarettes and overestimate the likelihood that once they start smoking they will be able to quit. Given that the notion that a person can quit before experiencing harm to health increases the likelihood that an adolescent will take up smoking, antismoking campaigns might stress how difficult quitting actually is. However, doing so in a message environment that also reaches existing smokers would be counterproductive, because it would send those smokers the message that there is no reason they should even to try to quit, as such efforts are unlikely to succeed. Because there is no efficient way to place one set of messages with smokers and the other with nonsmokers, antismoking campaigns need to develop messages that will communicate to both while simultaneously diminishing the likelihood that nonsmokers will start and increasing the likelihood that smokers will make the effort to quit. We need message strategies that speak to young non-smokers about the hazards of thinking that quitting is easy while at the same time communicating to all smokers about the benefits of thinking one can quit.

One solution to this paradox is to "reframe" antismoking messages so that both groups can see the trap without falling victim to it. Psychiatrists who have faced this issue when encouraging behavior change in clients inform us that "people are most influenced when they expect a certain message and receive instead a message at a totally different level" (Palazzoli, 1981, p. 45). Reframing is, according to Watzlawick and his colleagues, a process of altering the meaning attributed to a situation by changing the context or frame through which we experience it (Watzlawick, Beavin, & Jackson, 1967; Watzlawick, Weakland, & Fisch, 1974). Reframing empowers the person who is in a paradoxical situation to control the definition of it through greater understanding of the rules of the situation. When reframing succeeds, "it manages to invest a given situation with new meaning that is just as appropriate or even more convincing than the one our client has so far attributed to it" (Watzlawick, 1978, p. 119).

Tversky and Kahneman (1981) have also emphasized the importance of framing in people's decisions to undertake risky behavior. Frames that focus on the gains of a behavior encourage risk taking, whereas frames that focus on the losses encourage risk avoidance. Thinking that one can easily quit smoking frames both decisions to start and decisions to stop in terms of potential gain (e.g., I can try smoking now to see what smoking is like and can quit before suffering serious harm if I don't like it). A more adaptive frame would emphasize the potential cost in each case while leaving optimism about quitting intact.

A reframed message that would accommodate both the smoker who needs to quit and the nonsmoker who should not begin might say, "Each cigarette makes it harder to quit, so don't start, and if you do smoke, stop now." This message acknowledges the importance of control over quitting but places this control in the context of its increasing difficulty the more that one smokes. Instead of focusing on ease, it focuses on progressive difficulty. At the same time, it provides an incentive to quit now rather than later because each cigarette will make quitting that much harder. As a result, the ease of quitting is seen as greatest when one does not begin in the first place.

Part V

LEGAL
AND POLICY
PERSPECTIVES

The Joint Failure
of Economic Theory
and Legal Regulation

Jon D. Hanson and Douglas A. Kysar

Although an overall decline in the adult-age smoking population in the United States has coincided with the advent of various state and federal regulatory efforts, government attempts to curb youth smoking rates have, for the most part, failed. Among persons aged 12-17 years, the incidence of first use of cigarettes per 1,000 potential new users rose continuously during the 1990s and has been steadily higher than it has been for persons aged 18-25 years since the early 1970s ("Incidence," 1998). In addition, evidence provided throughout this book suggests that the adult-age smoking rate, although currently lower than it was in 1965, is nevertheless higher than it ought to be, from both a social cost-benefit perspective and an individual cost-benefit perspective. The puzzle for policy makers, therefore, is why legal regulatory efforts to date have failed to result in, or sometimes even push toward, significantly reduced levels of smoking.

AUTHORS' NOTE: We are grateful to Robbi Miller and David Yosifon for excellent research assistance. One of us has served as a consumer-information expert for plaintiffs on several of the third-wave tobacco cases.

In this chapter, we attempt to solve that puzzle by describing the problem of market manipulation, a problem that emerges due to the existence of both nonrational cognitive tendencies among individuals and self-interested economic behavior among tobacco firms. Put simply, the presence of powerful and ubiquitous cognitive biases among individual consumers creates an opportunity for the manipulation of perceptions and preferences that no profit-maximizing tobacco manufacturer can ignore. Over the past century, tobacco firms' marketing, promotional, and public relations efforts have capitalized on that possibility of manipulation. In the process, they have devised and tested countless manipulative strategies to lower consumer risk perceptions and elevate product demand.

The problem of market manipulation also has important implications for the study of smoking risk perceptions. Because the industry-sponsored survey analyzed by W. Kip Viscusi in his book *Smoking: Making the Risky Decision* (1992b) was not designed to be sensitive to the operation of cognitive biases and market manipulation, it told an inaccurate story of smoking perception and behavior. A fuller story would examine the dispositions of smokers through the more refined and accurate lens of cognitive and social psychology, while bearing in mind the impact of pervasive and subtle manufacturer and industry efforts to create and sustain demand for tobacco products. In this book, the former task is undertaken in Chapters 4 through 6 and 8 through 10, and the latter is aided by reviews of media portrayals of smoking in Chapters 1 and 7.[1]

This chapter demonstrates how those themes converge in a way that helps to explain both the shortcomings of Viscusi's book and the historical failure of tobacco regulation in the United States. Just as surveys about the perceived risks of smoking that are insensitive to the reality of individual cognition reveal little or nothing about how well consumers are informed, legal regulatory efforts that ignore or discount the effects of market manipulation fail to result in socially desirable levels of tobacco product use.

∽ The Behavioralist Decision Maker

Before one can appreciate the problem of market manipulation, one must understand the extent to which people's decision making and behavior deviate from those of the ideal rational utility maximizer.[2] Legal economists have traditionally relied on a simplistic view of human behavior in which individuals are assumed to process available information in a manner that guarantees the maximization of their utility, or pleasure, over time. Under this stylized conception, almost any problem of risk regulation can be understood as a simple matter of ensuring that individuals possess pertinent information regarding the costs and benefits of engaging in a risky behavior. Once such information is disclosed through a legally mandated device, such as product warnings, economists presume that individuals will then make only rational, utility-maximizing choices with respect to the risky behavior. That conception of the human agent is also the one that the cigarette industry promotes and would like to have regulators, courts, and juries adopt (although, as will become clear below, it is not the conception that the industry itself adopts when developing marketing and public relations strategies).

The rational-actor model differs from the model of human behavior that emerges from studies by cognitive psychologists and other researchers whose interest lies in learning how people *actually* behave. For the past few decades, those researchers have been steadily uncovering evidence that human decision-making processes are prone to nonrational, yet systematic, tendencies. These researchers claim not merely that we sometimes fail to abide by rules of logic, but that we fail to do so in predictable ways. In the words of Daniel Kahneman and the late Amos Tversky, two pioneering researchers in the field, we are susceptible to illusions of the mind that are "neither rational nor capricious" (quoted in Piattelli-Palmarini, 1991, p. 28). Cognitive illusions—sometimes referred to as biases—are not limited to the uneducated or unintelligent, and they are not readily unlearned. Instead, they affect us all with uncanny consistency and unflappable persistence. The presence of cognitive biases, therefore, casts considerable doubt on the widely supported policy expedient of providing hazard warnings for products such as cigarettes. Under the influence of persistent nonrational cognitive tendencies, individuals may engage in behavior at odds with their long-term self-interest despite, or even because of, the warning label on the cigarette package.

Below, we review several cognitive biases before accounting in more depth for how they give rise to the problem of market manipulation. The biases are arranged under six headings, reflecting individuals' tendency to behave as faulty scientists, unwarranted optimists, poor statisticians, hasty impressionists, inconsistent preference holders, and constituency-bound politicians.[3]

Faulty Scientists

Psychologists have discovered that individuals often deliberate in a manner that approximates the scientific method—generating and testing causal hypotheses to help make sense of the world. Unlike the ideal practitioner of the scientific method, however, individuals are subject to a variety of cognitive influences that frequently render their conclusions untrustworthy. For instance, a great deal of evidence suggests that individuals tend to begin the deliberative process with a desired belief already in mind. Their "scientific" reasoning then consists of seeking out evidence and constructing explanations to support the desired belief. This cognitive approach—which Ziva Kunda (1990) has called *motivated reasoning*—is dramatically at odds with the classic conception of the scientific method, which of course requires that conclusions follow from observation, not vice versa.

Christopher Hsee (1995) describes a behavioral phenomenon, *elastic justification,* that vividly demonstrates the manner in which motivated reasoning can yield self-interested results. Under the influence of this bias, individuals interpret a range of characteristics in a way that is biased in favor of an outcome that they are privately motivated to reach. For instance, suppose a salesperson desires to go to city A because it is more enjoyable than city B. In city A he can find 40 buyers, whereas in city B he can find between 30 and 90 buyers (so the expected outcome of 60 buyers makes city B the right choice from the perspective of maximizing buyers). The salesperson will subconsciously perceive city B to be on the low end of the scale (say, 35 buyers) in order to justify traveling to city A, even though A is less desirable according to the factor that should matter most, the expected number of buyers.

Following this nonrational genesis, individual beliefs solidify through *perseverance.* This refers to the fact that individuals often simply do not process evidence that contradicts their privately held beliefs in a manner that permits its full and fair consideration (Anderson, Lepper, & Ross, 1980). Psychologists studying the *confirmatory bias* have found that individuals often interpret subsequent evidence as actually providing support for their initial hypotheses, even if the evidence provided is intentionally ambiguous or, indeed, even if it objectively supports the opposite conclusion (Lord, Ross, & Lepper, 1979). Moreover, this process of mental reassurance is self-reinforcing. As Matthew Rabin (1998) has noted, individuals rely on a process of *hypothesis-based filtering,* in which they interpret evidence in a manner that strengthens their belief in their prior hypotheses. That reinforcement, in turn, makes them even more likely to interpret subsequent evidence as supportive of the initial hypotheses. This process can continue in a circular fashion until the individuals' initial beliefs become essentially calcified by evidence that may or may not have provided any actual support.

Finally, in perhaps the most striking finding of all, researchers have discovered that our hypotheses sometimes take on lives of their own; that is, individuals sometimes continue to view their hypotheses as true and accurate even when the evidentiary base that initially gave rise to them is entirely discredited. This phenomenon, which we refer to as the *entity effect,* persists even when individuals know and understand that their beliefs lack an evidentiary foundation. Those under the influence of this bias simply feel that their intuitive views are correct, regardless of whether empirical investigation supports or undercuts them (Anderson et al., 1980; Ross, Lepper, & Hubbard, 1975; Ross, Lepper, Strack, & Steinmetz, 1977).

Unwarranted Optimists

Individuals are subject to a range of biases that reflect an unwarranted level of self-confidence. They all stem from the general tendency of individuals to perceive themselves as above average, regardless of the characteristic upon which they are comparing themselves. For instance, as he details in Chapter 5 of this volume, Neil Weinstein has found many examples of what he has dubbed the *optimism bias*. This refers to the fact that people perceive themselves as less likely than others to experience some negative outcome or, alternatively, more likely than others to experience some positive outcome. Optimism of this sort is remarkably robust, cutting across almost all demographic categories and appearing in a wide variety of contexts (Weinstein, 1980, 1987).

A related false self-confidence bias, the *illusion of control,* causes individuals to believe that they are in control of situations to a greater extent than they actually are. This perception frequently causes people to underestimate the threat of a negative outcome or overestimate their likelihood of avoiding it (Langer, 1975). Because of the *hindsight bias,* individuals also appear to have great difficulty understanding ex post probabilities. For instance, after an outcome occurs, individuals often overestimate both its ex ante likelihood of occurring and the accuracy with which they could have predicted that likelihood (Fischhoff, 1975; Hawkins & Hastie, 1990). Interestingly, many of these false self-confidence biases tend to be exaggerated when they are accompanied by a process of reasoning. That is, self-confidence biases often are more pronounced among scientists and experts who develop elaborate models to predict or explain a probabilistic outcome than among laypersons who simply attempt to hazard a guess (Griffin & Tversky, 1992).

Poor Statisticians

Beginning with the now-classic collection *Judgment Under Uncertainty: Heuristics and Biases* (Kahneman, Slovic, & Tversky, 1982), behavioral researchers have uncovered a wide variety of ways in which individuals improperly perform statistical and probabilistic tasks. Many of those errors result from the tendency of individuals to utilize *heuristics* or mental shortcuts to avoid complex computational or logical analysis. For instance, Tversky and Kahneman (1983) note that, in making decisions about uncertain future events, people tend to ignore more probative statistical data in favor of evidence that is particularly salient, vivid, or easily "available" to them. That is, their probability judgments are driven by the ease with which they can recall previous occurrences of the event or the ease with which they can imagine the event occurring in the future. This *availability heuristic* results in biased judgments whenever the strength of an event's availability is poorly correlated with its actual prevalence (Tversky & Kahneman, 1973). Rabin (1998) describes one of the implications of the availability heuristic for social judgment:

> Our assessment of a given city's crime rate is likely to be too influenced by whether we personally know somebody who has been assaulted, even if we are familiar with much more relevant general statistics. Likewise, dramatic stories by people we know about difficulties with a brand of car are likely to be overly influential even if we are familiar, via Consumer Reports, with general statistics of the reliability of different brands. (p. 30)

Similarly, the *representativeness heuristic* can lead to biased perceptions due to its tendency to emphasize specific data to the exclusion of more general, but often more pertinent, information (Kahneman & Tversky, 1973). Under the representativeness heuristic, individuals judge the frequency or likelihood of something by the degree to which it resembles something else (for instance, its class). Thus individuals might believe that it is very likely that a person is a professional basketball player simply because she is very tall, even if it is known that objectively only a small percentage of tall people are professional basketball players. Moreover, individuals tend to disregard base-rate information when they are given more specific evidence—even if that evidence is irrelevant to the calculus. In the words of Kahneman and Tversky (1972): "People respond differently when given no specific evidence and when given worthless evidence. When no specific evidence is given, the prior probabilities are properly utilized; when worthless specific evidence is given, prior probabilities are ignored" (p. 5).

Two related biases stemming from the representativeness heuristic involve the manner in which individuals attempt to understand chance. The *gambler's fallacy* refers to the fact that "chance is commonly viewed as a self-correcting process in which deviation in one direction induces a deviation in the opposite direction to restore the equilibrium" (Tversky & Kahneman, 1982, p. 7). Thus individuals mistakenly believe that the roulette wheel is necessarily "due" to hit red if previous spins have resulted in a string of hits on black. Relatedly, the *law of small numbers* involves an erroneous assumption that small samples of a population necessarily resemble the population at large (Tversky & Kahneman, 1982). As a result, individuals often are overly confident in their ability to make judgments about an entire population based solely on a small subset of it. In other words, just as gamblers believe that a local sample must represent the global pattern, individuals believe that the global pattern can be predicted from a local sample.

A final example of statistical reasoning shortcuts is *anchoring and adjustment,* or the tendency of individuals to fix or anchor their judgments on an initial estimate and then gradually adjust the estimate up or down in the face of new evidence. As Tversky and Kahneman (1982) have shown, the subsequent adjustment often remains unduly anchored to the initial estimate; that is, individuals do not allow subsequent evidence to influence their judgments as strongly as the evidence might merit. This bias can be understood as a manifestation of the more general tendency of individuals to ignore pertinent evidence through belief perseverance and the confirmatory bias. As one cognitive researcher has put it: "Once we have made an intuitive estimate, even if we are told that we are wrong, we *still* keep the initial rough estimate as an implicit baseline. We are anchored to it. We are unwilling to neglect it completely and start afresh" (Piattelli-Palmarini, 1991, p. 29).

Hasty Impressionists

As Paul Slovic describes in Chapter 6 of this volume, there is substantial evidence that individuals process information using two parallel mechanisms: a primarily rational system or a primarily emotional one. The former is logical, abstract, and deliberate, whereas the latter is intuitive, impressionistic, and nonconscious. Because the rational system is relatively inefficient, it is ill suited for many everyday judgments. Thus individuals rely to a great extent on their emotional system of subtle, nonconscious reactions to external stimuli, which psychologists refer to as *affect.* Significantly, individuals generally feel this experiential mode of thinking as more immediate and intense than the rational system, even when the systems yield conflicting judgments (Epstein, 1994).

The notion that individual behavior is dominated by affective responses has important implications for individuals' perceptions of risk. Behavioral researchers have found that several qualitative characteristics—such as whether a risk is naturally or technologically imposed, whether it threatens individuals or large populations, and whether it is immediate or latent—influence the severity that individuals ascribe to a risk (Slovic, 1987, 1992). Of course, under the strict cost-benefit analysis associated with utility maximization, those characteristics should have no bearing. Contrary to the economist's belief, however, individuals feel that many of the qualitative characteristics not captured by a sterile cost-benefit analysis play significant roles in their understanding and experiencing of risks.

A recent finding justifies an even greater departure from the economist's model. Slovic and his colleagues have discovered that individuals often conflate the concepts of risk and benefit when conducting risk analysis (Alhakami & Slovic, 1994; Finucane, Alhakami, Slovic, & Johnson, 2000). If an individual views something as offering great benefits, he or she will tend to downplay any risks associated with it, and vice versa. The obvious implication of this finding is that if

one can generate a large positive affect in connection with an object of perception, individuals will tend to view the object as less risky than they would otherwise.

Inconsistent Preference Holders

A large and fascinating body of research demonstrates that individuals do not exhibit stable, independent preferences, as economists typically presume; rather, they have preferences that are context dependent, variable, and inconsistent. One important source of such inconsistencies arises from *framing effects,* or the tendency for nonsubstantive alterations in the way information is presented to result in significant differences in interpretation, attitude, and behavior (Tversky & Kahneman, 1981). In one of the earliest experiments involving framing effects, Kahneman and Tversky (1984) discovered that individuals exhibit a strong preference for a scenario that is expressed as a gain (400 lives saved out of 600) over the mathematically equivalent option expressed as a loss (200 lives lost out of 600).

Many other preference-inconsistency biases can be understood as particular instances of framing effects. For instance, the *endowment effect* shows that individuals often value an item more when they perceive that they own or possess it (Kahneman, Knetsch, & Thaler, 1991). It is important to note that research by George Loewenstein and Daniel Adler (1995) suggests that individuals cannot predict the operation of the endowment effect; that is, they underestimate the extent to which their valuation of something will be increased upon possessing it. Similarly, *context effects* involve the tendency for individuals' preferences among choices to shift depending on the overall context in which the choices are presented (Simonson, 1989). Given a choice between a small and a medium-size radio, subjects often choose the small one. Many of those same individuals, however, switch to the medium-size radio when a large option is added to the mix (Simonson & Tversky, 1992).

Researchers studying *attribution theory* have also discovered strong evidence to suggest that people's preferences are not defined strictly according to outcome, as economists typically assume (Croson, 1998). Instead, rather than simply evaluating the costs and benefits of the outcome itself, individuals often care about the conduct or processes that went into the production of a particular outcome (Rabin, 1998). Thus, for instance, if they perceive a bad result as accidental, individuals will often feel less outrage than if they perceive it as resulting from a knowing choice. In the product context, consumers react differently (show more anger and wish for increased retribution) if they believe the cause of product failure is located with a manufacturer and if the risks associated with the unsafe product are a function of the manufacturer's choice. Evidence further suggests that preferences are reciprocal: People willingly sacrifice their material well-being to punish others who act unfairly or selfishly and to reward or assist those who act cooperatively or benignly. To tap into that principle, public relations firms and others engaged in "spin control" employ the teachings of attribution theory to frame public understanding of events in the ways that best suit their clients.

Another bias in this category is the widely studied phenomenon of *intertemporal preference inconsistencies* (Ainslie & Haslam, 1992; Kirby & Herrnstein, 1995). This refers to the fact that, other things being equal, individuals prefer instant gratification and delayed dissatisfaction. Obviously, there is a problem with that pair of preferences. The practice of making shortsighted trade-offs can result in an overwhelming burden of dissatisfaction that must eventually be confronted (for instance, in the form of lung cancer). In related research, George Loewenstein (1996) has examined a variety of behaviors that result from *visceral factors* that encompass the feelings associated with drug addiction—drive states like hunger, thirst, and sexual desire; moods and emotions; and physical pain. Not surprisingly, visceral factors can frequently trump long-term preferences. "At sufficient levels of intensity," notes Loewenstein, "these, and most other visceral factors, cause people to behave contrary to their long-term interest, often with full awareness that they are doing so" (pp. 272-273). In Chapter 9 of this book, Loewenstein applies that insight to explain individual decisions to engage in potentially addictive consumption choices such as cigarette smoking.

Constituency-Bound Politicians

Social psychologists have written extensively on the influence of social context on judgment and choice. As a leading scholar in that area, Philip Tetlock (1995), admonishes:

> The "isolated information processor" image of human nature underlying the cognitive research program is too restrictive as a basis for a comprehensive theory of judgment and decision-making. People typically make up their minds in rule-governed social and organizational settings in which they feel personally accountable or responsible for the stands they take. We need an alternative research program that builds upon the cognitive tradition by placing the information processor in social context. The guiding metaphor I suggest for this alternative research program is that of the politician whose primary goal is to maintain the positive regard of important constituencies to whom he or she feels accountable. A major goal of the politician research program is the identification of the cognitive, social, and political strategies that people use for coping with demands for accountability from significant others in their lives. (p. 299)

TABLE 11.1   Summary of Accountability Research

Has Politician Committed to Position?	Does Politician Know Constituency's Position?	
	Yes	No
Yes	(1) Defensive bolstering	(2) Defensive bolstering
No	(3) Acceptability heuristic	(4) Preemptive self-criticism

Using Tetlock's metaphor, the question becomes: What strategies do we as politicians adopt in order to cope with the demands of accountability imposed upon us by our constituencies?

The evidence that answers that question can be roughly summarized in terms of the two basic questions asked in Table 11.1: First, does the politician know the position that his or her constituency would take on a given issue? Second, has the politician already committed to a particular position on that issue? Numerous studies indicate that when an individual knows the views taken by his or her audience and has not committed to a position regarding a particular issue, that individual will engage in the same sort of mental shortcuts that cognitive theorists explain can make us poor statisticians. That individual/politician will, in other words, adopt the constituency's accepted position in order to save the energy required to examine the pros and cons of any alternative position. Tetlock, Skitka, and Boetter (1989, p. 633) call this tendency the *acceptability heuristic.*

Unfortunately, that cognitively simple option is not always available. When, for example, a person does not know her audience's position and has not previously committed to one herself, she will tend to engage in careful and self-critical analysis of the options. The goal of such a politician is to anticipate the potential criticism of some of her constituents and maintain adequate wiggle room in choosing her own option to avoid offending them. Tetlock et al. (1989, p. 633) refer to this strategy as *preemptive self-criticism.* Finally, when a politician has already committed to a particular position on a given topic, conformity and self-criticism lose much of their effect. Instead, the politician must invest considerable mental energy toward developing a viable defense of her original commitments. Tetlock et al. refer to such efforts to demonstrate the courage of one's convictions as *defensive bolstering* or *retrospective rationalizations.*

Such defensive efforts appear to constitute another form of motivated reasoning. Put differently, politician-constituency dissonance has the same sort of influence on our judgments as does cognitive dissonance. At bottom, therefore, Tetlock's findings are significant not so much in what they teach us about how people think (cognitive psychologists have already shown that human reasoning is highly influenced by heuristics and motivations) but in demonstrating the extraordinary degree to which our cognitive corner cutting and motivations can be influenced by the views of the people to whom we feel accountable.

Summary

The preceding discussion underscores the fact that human beings often render scientific and probabilistic judgments imperfectly. Indeed, we are far from perfect assessors of our own preferences and our own well-being. Rather than accurately processing available information and flawlessly ordering preferences according to expected outcomes, we engage in a variety of behaviors that reflect, variously, rigid belief systems, inflated sense of self, limited computational ability, a reason-trumping set of emotional responses, inadequate capacity for self-control, and underappreciated allegiance to the views of the people around us. This research raises serious doubts about the explanatory power of the rational utility-maximization model on which Viscusi's analysis is largely predicated. Those imperfections are made all the more intractable by the fact that we tend to see ourselves as reasoning and deliberative decision makers. We are strongly inclined, in other words, to accept arguments and evidence that we are independent-minded, thoughtful, rational actors and to reject arguments and evidence to the contrary.

∞ The Problem of Market Manipulation in the Cigarette Market

In light of the fact that consumer risk perceptions may be influenced by, for instance, the contexts within which decision choices are presented, it is not surprising that manufacturers exploit those effects to maximize their profits. In other words, the fact that consumer perceptions and preferences shift depending upon factors within manufacturers' control creates a heretofore unrecognized element of manufacturer market power: the power of perceptual manipulation (see generally Hanson & Kysar, 1999b).

Manufacturers' incentive to engage in such manipulative conduct lies in the opportunity to elevate demand for their products artificially. Other things being equal, it is in manufacturers' interest for consumers to have the lowest estimate of product risks possible. The lower the consumers' risk estimate, the more consumers will be willing to pay for the product, leading to greater sales and increased profits for manufacturers. Generating consumer underestimation of product risks (as well as overestimation of product benefits) in this manner is simply a means of cost externalization, a practice that manufacturers have every incentive to pursue. As we will argue, no consumer product market has demonstrated this possibility more clearly than the market for tobacco products.

There have been several studies of the remarkable campaign of manipulation conducted by tobacco manufacturers over the past century (Glantz, Slade, Bero, Hanauer, & Barnes, 1996; Hilts, 1996; Kluger, 1996). Despite an abundance of widely reported scientific knowledge regarding the dangers of smoking offered by credible government, scientific, and medical authorities, the industry managed for several decades (and perhaps is still managing) to keep alive a "controversy" in public discourse over whether cigarettes do in fact have harmful effects. Using a variety of public relations mechanisms—including (a) creating an industry-sponsored institution to foster seemingly independent research that, in fact, was intended to be favorable (or, at worst, harmless) to the industry; (b) producing health reassurance cigarettes that their designers actually knew to provide little or no health advantages over regular cigarettes; (c) silencing critics through such tactics as employment discharge and spurious litigation; (d) suppressing internal research that was often more damning than that of government and public health authorities; and (e) utilizing marketing and public relations techniques that capitalized on consumer cognitive biases to lower cigarette risk estimates—the tobacco industry perpetrated, and in many respects continues to perpetrate, an unparalleled campaign of misinformation on the American public (Hanson & Kysar, 1999b). The result has been to encourage misperceptions of the health hazards of smoking even today. Here we focus on several examples from the history of tobacco marketing that illustrate the problem of market manipulation. Through this review we attempt to demonstrate just how closely the industry's marketing efforts align with the behavioral vulnerabilities of individuals described in the first part of this chapter.

Faulty Scientists

As noted above, individuals tend to act as lay scientists, adopting and testing hypotheses about the world in a manner that often fails to comport with the rational-actor ideal. Although understandable in light of individual cognitive limitations, this departure from models of scientific and statistical reasoning nevertheless creates an opportunity for tobacco manufacturers to shape, influence, and exploit consumer perceptions.[4] For instance, because individuals tend to disregard evidence that contradicts their initial hypotheses, tobacco manufacturers can seek to create a favorable impression in consumers as soon as possible so that the consumers' initial views interfere with any unfavorable information that subsequently comes to light. A particularly effective tactic might be to aim simplistic positive messages at young people at an age when competing negative information might not be comprehensible. The 6-year-old who recognizes a connection between Joe Camel and cigarettes (Fischer, Schwartz, Richards, Goldstein, & Rojas, 1991) may not recognize the more complex connection between cigarettes and cancer. Likewise, the child whose R. J. Reynolds beach shoes leave behind the word *Camel* in the sand (Solomon, 1996, p. 411) may not comprehend the causal nexus between tobacco and heart disease.

Cigarette manufacturers appear to be well aware of this possibility. To give just a few examples, there is some evidence that as early as 1967 the industry used highly specialized advertising campaigns to boost smoking rates among 12-year-old girls (Hilts, 1996, p. 69). In 1973, Dr. Claude E. Teague, Jr., of R. J. Reynolds (RJR) wrote a now infamous memorandum that discussed many of the marketing themes that would eventually characterize the highly successful Joe Camel campaign (R. J. Reynolds, 1973). Around that time, other tobacco firms engaged in youth-oriented demographic studies with such revealing names as Project Sixteen and Youth Target (Hilts, 1996, p. 80). A 1979 Philip Morris document proclaims that, although the Marlboro brand could claim only 17% of the overall cigarette market, it enjoyed a greater than 50% share of the smokers who were 17 years old and younger (see *Humphrey v. Philip Morris*, 1998, trial exhibit no. 11808). That success was partially the consequence of initiatives such as the Summer Sampling Program, under which 150 samplers visited beaches and other "markets of opportunity," where branded items were "given away at the beach, bars, and other hangouts" (Philip Morris, 1987). More recently, the California Department of Health Services (1995) reported that stores within 1,000 feet of a school had significantly more tobacco advertising than did stores that were not near schools.

Each of these practices reflects the industry's understanding that targeting extremely young and impressionable minds is vital to the future of its business. As Claude Teague observed in his 1973 memo: "Realistically, if [R. J. Reynolds] is to survive and prosper, over the long term, we must get our share of the youth market. In my opinion this will require new brands tailored to the youth market. . . . we need brands designed to be particularly attractive to the young smoker" (R. J. Reynolds, 1973). A decade later, another RJR document explained that "young adults" are the "only source of replacement smokers," and "if younger adults turn away from smoking, the Industry must decline, just as a population which does not give birth will eventually dwindle" (R. J. Reynolds, 1984b). Similarly, a 1981 Philip Morris document admonished that "it is important to know as much as possible about teenage smoking patterns and attitudes. Today's teenager is to-morrow's potential regular customer, and the overwhelming majority of smokers first begin to smoke while still in their teens" (Philip Morris, 1981, p. 1).

Once a favorable product impression is made on a younger smoker, tobacco manufacturers might seek to take advantage of *belief perseverance* and the *confirmatory bias* by providing current smokers with evidence that can be misread by the consumer as additional support for the initial product impression.[5] The benefit to manufacturers of reinforcing a favorable product impression in this manner is that the impression becomes, to a large extent, entrenched. The practice of *hypothesis-based filtering* causes an individual to interpret ambiguous evidence in light of his or her initial hypothesis, which in turn reinforces the individual's conviction about the truth of the hypothesis and induces him or her to interpret further ambiguous evidence as consistent with it. Additionally, the *entity effect* can cause an individual to retain belief in a hypothesis even when it has been thoroughly discredited; that is, an individual's belief in a hypothesis may be completely independent of the veracity of the data underlying it. Relatedly, the unrelenting campaign by tobacco industry groups to create controversy over the question of the health effects of cigarettes seems designed to capitalize on *elastic justification.* By creating doubt about the health risks of smoking, manufacturers create elasticity for the health and safety attributes of their product; that is, they open a plausible spectrum of possibilities within which consumers believe the actual health and safety attributes of cigarettes may fall. Seeking a means to justify their behavior, smokers naturally (and apparently unknowingly) perceive the health risks of smoking to be at the low end of the manufacturer-created spectrum. For those reasons, tobacco manufacturers that are able to create a favorable first impression of cigarettes among young people hold significant sway over such customers when challenges are later raised over the safety or value of their product.

Cigarette manufacturers, again, appear to be well aware of that potential advantage. The R. J. Reynolds marketing principle is nearly explicit in that regard: "Attract a smoker at the earliest opportunity and let brand loyalty turn that smoker into a valuable asset" (R. J. Reynolds, 1984b). In addition, the industry-sponsored and controlled Tobacco Industry Research Council (TIRC) and later the Council for Tobacco Research (CTR) were both established, in significant part, for the purpose of promoting favorable scientific research that could be used in public relations, lobbying, and litigation efforts. Internal industry documents strongly indicate that those research bodies were used less to advance scientific knowledge about the health risks of smoking than to build public trust so that the industry could manipulate the public's perception of those risks (Hanson & Kysar, 1999b). In hindsight, such industry efforts might seem like rather obvious public relations ploys. To smokers at the time, however, they probably appeared as reassuring sources of objective information. Eager to maintain cognitive consistency, smokers who enjoyed the habit but feared possible health consequences quickly adopted the notion that some other factors may cause the observed harms and that cigarettes may not be harmful after all. So it was, for example, that in response to the surgeon general's report in 1964 a Philip Morris executive emphasized that the industry "must in the near future provide some answers in which [it] give[s] smokers a psychological crutch and a self-rationale to continue smoking" (Philip Morris, 1964, p. 1). The influence of those industry tactics should not be underestimated. As one industry executive admitted, "CTR is [the] best [and] cheapest insurance the tobacco industry can buy and without it the Industry would have to invent CTR or would be dead" (Hilts, 1996, p. 16).

Because the confirmatory bias causes individuals to view disconfirming evidence with an unjustifiably jaundiced eye, it also helps to explain why the tobacco industry devoted so much attention to denying that scientists had uncovered a causal link to support the observed correlation between smoking and cancer. Under the influence of the confirmatory bias, individuals eager to maintain their initial hypotheses will latch onto any aspect of disconfirming evidence that appears to offer a less damaging, alternate explanation. The industry's knowledge of this reassuring effect can be seen in a remarkable assertion made by the director of public relations at Brown & Williamson (B&W): "*Doubt is our product* since it is the best means of competing with the 'body of fact' that exists in the mind of the general public. It is also the means of establishing a controversy" (Glantz et al., 1996, pp. 190-191; emphasis added). A TIRC executive made a similarly candid statement in 1972: "In the cigarette controversy, the public—especially those who are present and potential supporters (e.g., tobacco state congressmen and heavy smokers)—must perceive, understand, and believe in evidence to sustain their opinions that smoking may not be the causal factor" (Tobacco Industry Research Council, 1972).

Pursuant to such advice, the industry conducted a decades-long marketing and lobbying campaign emphasizing that "there is no proof that cigarette smoking is one of the causes" of lung cancer (Tobacco Industry Research Council, n.d.); that "after millions of dollars and over 20 years of research: The question about smoking and health is still a question" (Tobacco Institute, 1970); that "cigarette smoking has not been scientifically established to be a cause of chronic diseases, such as cancer, cardiovascular disease, or emphysema" (congressional testimony of Dr. Sheldon Sommers, then scientific director of CTR, quoted in Glantz et al., 1996, p. 20); that "studies which conclude that smoking causes disease have regularly ignored significant evidence to the contrary" (R. J. Reynolds, 1984a); and that "we have looked at the data and [it] has all been statistical data that has not convinced me that smoking causes death" (congressional testimony of Andrew Tisch, CEO of Lorillard, quoted in Hilts, 1996, p. 123). Each of those statements and numerous others made throughout the industry's campaign played into the individual's status as a faulty lay scientist. Seeking evidence and reasons to justify ignoring the cognitive dissonance they felt due to growing awareness of smoking hazards, individual smokers could easily find such evidence and reasons in the industry's far-reaching public relations campaign.

Unwarranted Optimists

Apart from orchestrating the formation and maintenance of product impressions in this manner, tobacco manufacturers have capitalized on the many ways in which individuals display an unwarranted sense of self-confidence. An obvious candidate for exploitation is the *optimism bias*—that is, the tendency for consumers to assume that population risks that they may understand, or even overestimate, do not apply with equal force to themselves. Studies indicate that the optimism bias is stronger for risks not evidenced by present symptoms and for risks that consumers believe can be controlled through behavior modification. Given that the most significant risks of cigarettes are latent, and in light of manufacturers' efforts to give smokers the perceived ability to reduce risks through brand selection, it is hardly surprising that the optimism bias plays a significant role in smokers' perceptions of cigarette risks.

Relatedly, risk analysts have found that when individuals believe they can control whether a risk will occur through their own behavior, they will not adequately account for the risk in making consumption decisions. The proliferation of filter-tipped, low-tar, and low-nicotine cigarettes provided consumers with just such an *illusion of control.* By giving consumers the impression that they can select among levels of safety by choosing different types of cigarettes, tobacco manufacturers contributed to consumer underestimation of the hazards of smoking. This practice has continued with the more recent debut of cigarettes advertised as having "no additives," an introduction that came fresh on the heels of widely publicized state lawsuits against the tobacco companies (Rao, 1997). Indeed, the timing of all such "revolutionary" product design enhancements throughout the past century appears to have coincided with moments of heightened public awareness of smoking risks (Hanson & Kysar, 1999a, pp. 1474-1479).

The very fact that smokers have switched to low-tar and low-nicotine cigarettes provides further support for the idea that individuals are easily led to believe that they have control over risks, a belief that in turn heightens their optimism. It appears, in other words, that smokers have been significantly reassured by the misleading, although often only implicit, health claims of cigarette manufacturers regarding, for example, "filtered," "light," and "low-tar" cigarettes. Although smokers concerned about the health risks of cigarettes likely take some comfort in smoking seemingly safer brands, it is not at all clear that "lights" are any safer in practice than "regulars" (Hanson & Kysar, 1999a, pp. 1474-1479; see also Chapter 8, this volume). It also appears that cigarette manufacturers have long been aware of the potential economic benefits of fostering these misleading perceptions in consumers. Industry documents from a 1968 conference of tobacco company scientists reveal that several participants stressed the difference between creating a "health image" or "health reassurance cigarette," such as "a low tar-low nicotine cigarette which the public accepts as a healthier cigarette," and a "health-oriented" product that is actually designed to be safer (Glantz et al., 1996, p. 129). As a B&W document noted at the time, "The illusion of filtration is as important as the fact of filtration" (Brown & Williamson, 1966, p. 2).

Poor Statisticians

The many ways in which individuals fail to perceive and process probabilistic information accurately have also influenced the market for tobacco products. The *availability heuristic,* for example, may well play a role in consumer failure to fully appreciate smoking-related health hazards. It seems plausible that the availability heuristic has contributed to lowering smokers' estimates of the personal risks of cigarettes, given that smokers rarely experience direct evidence, at least in their day-to-day use of the product, that they are being injured by smoking. Unlike the harms caused by, say, tornadoes, homicides, and airplane accidents, the precise nature of the particular harms caused by smoking is not often depicted in the media or covered by the news (Mattson, Pollack, & Cullen, 1987; Weinstein, 1987). Furthermore, tobacco manufacturers interested in raising public awareness of positive product attributes can easily tap into the availability heuristic by maximizing the frequency and intensity of product-extolling advertisements. Unsurprisingly, manufacturers have inundated public spaces with healthful images of smoking. For several decades, cigarette manufacturers relied heavily on celebrity and medical endorsements. Tennis great Bill Tilden was quoted as saying, "[Camels] don't get my wind or upset my nerves," and actor Henry Fonda noted, "My voice is important to my career. I smoke Camels because they're mild" (both quoted in Kluger, 1996, p. 88). Likewise, countless advertisements featured physicians and tag lines such as "Just what the doctor ordered" and "Doctors recommend Camel" (see Hilts, 1996, p. 2; Kluger, 1996, p. 185). Today, manufacturers rely less on celebrities and explicit health claims. Nevertheless, ubiquitous images of healthy and attractive smokers in advertisements and frequent implicit health messages probably foster the cognitive illusion that smoking is safer than it in fact is.

Smokers subject to the *representativeness heuristic* may also focus on irrelevant factors to the exclusion of important base-rate information about smoking. The willingness of individuals to ignore prior probabilities in favor of new (perhaps worthless) data suggests a clear method for manufacturers to obscure product risk attributes: Confound the consumer with specific, irrelevant information (and all the better if that information is purportedly safety related). Philip Morris employed this tactic in 1930s advertisements trumpeting its use of "diethylene glycol" as a humidifying agent. Although independent tests showed no safety difference in cigarettes produced with the new agent, Philip Morris boldly called its product "the cigarette that takes the fear out of smoking" (see Hilts, 1996, p. 66; Kluger, 1996, pp. 100-102, 131). R. J. Reynolds conducted a similarly meaningless appeal to science in its empty pronouncement that "science advances new data that may completely change your ideas of cigarettes" (see Kluger, 1996, p. 87).

Although these early advertisements may seem transparent in retrospect, the same manipulative use of representativeness likely helped convince legions of smokers to switch to filter-tipped and light cigarettes rather than quit smoking altogether. As we noted earlier, industry scientists apparently understood that a primary mission was to produce the perception (rather than the reality) of a safer cigarette. In the wake of highly publicized scientific announcements during the 1950s and 1960s, tobacco manufacturers believed that smokers needed a dose of new, specific information that could trump public awareness of the health hazards of smoking. Filter-tipped and light cigarettes helped lead consumers to ignore base-rate risks in just that manner.

Hasty Impressionists

The impact of experiential thinking in the consumer context has been stated nicely by an early proponent of the significance of *affect* for decision making:

> We sometimes delude ourselves that we proceed in a rational manner and weigh all the pros and cons of the various alternatives. But this is probably seldom the case. Quite often, "I decided in favor of X" is no more than "I liked X." . . . We buy the cars we "like," choose the jobs and houses we find "attractive," and then justify these choices by various reasons. (Zajonc, 1980, p. 155)

In other words, our affective responses to products often determine our purchasing decisions, regardless of whether we experience these decisions as having resulted from "reasons." Significantly, our affective responses can dominate our consumption choices even when our rational processing systems suggest contrary decisions. Indeed, an individual's affective system can often confound his or her rational system by causing logically distinct categories such as "cost" and "benefit" to become conflated in the individual's mind. Thus a manufacturer that succeeds in generating a positive affective response with respect to its product may gain the added effect of lowering consumer estimates of the product's potential to cause harm.

Consumer product manufacturers clearly strive to cultivate positive affect in relation to their products.[6] This effort can be seen in the omnipresent practice of feel-good advertising that carries little if any information about the product being pitched, but plenty of gushing views of the happiness, wealth, and beauty that allegedly can be gained from its consumption. Tobacco ads are no exception. Indeed, Philip Morris's decades-long "Marlboro Man" campaign might be considered the ultimate in such "lifestyle advertising." By frequently offering depictions of the free and natural cowboy smoker, Philip Morris instilled in many smokers a positive affective association with the product. Consequently, consumers viewed (and still view) subsequent negative information about smoking through the bias of experiential thinking. As Seymour Epstein (1994) explains, "Cigarette advertising agencies and their clients are willing to bet millions of dollars in advertising costs that the visual appeal of their messages to the experiential system will prevail over the verbal message of the surgeon general that smoking can endanger one's life, an appeal directed at the rational system" (p. 712). Given the durability of such practices throughout the 20th century, the bet appears to be a good one.

Apart from their general efforts to generate positive affect for their products, tobacco manufacturers have also capitalized on qualitative characteristics that influence how individuals perceive and respond to risks. To give just one example, consider the recent "natural" marketing campaigns adopted by R. J. Reynolds for its Salem menthol cigarettes and Brown & Williamson for its Kool Natural cigarettes. Both feature content such as forest-green design schemes, Edenesque images of waterfalls and lush foliage, and repeated use of the words *nature* and *natural*. A recent print ad for Kool Natural Lights, for instance, repeats the word *natural* a remarkable 13 times in a single half-page layout. The companies skirt deceptive advertising liability by linking "natural" with the cigarettes' mint leaf-supplied menthol flavor. The overall effect of the campaigns, however, is far more subtle. As behavioral researchers have noted, people respond more favorably to risks that they view as emanating from natural, as opposed to human-made, sources. In other words, people may underestimate a risk simply because it is attributed to nature. R. J. Reynolds has exploited this cognitive bias in the tag line to its Salem ads: "Menthol from nature. Created by plants, not people." Never mind that cigarettes typically contain hundreds of additives, many of which are created by people, not plants (Hanson & Logue, 1998).

Inconsistent Preference Holders

The fact that individuals hold preferences that are context dependent, variable, and inconsistent presents an opportunity for tobacco manufacturers to shape not only consumers' views of the risks of smoking, but also their views of smoking's benefits. The *endowment effect* represents a simple example of this possibility. For many years, as we have mentioned above, tobacco manufacturers distributed free samples of their products, often at places where children were likely to be present (Kessler et al., 1996). Aside from increasing the likelihood of addiction among people who might not otherwise pay for a package of cigarettes, this practice may have played into the endowment effect. Because they now "possessed" packages of cigarettes, recipients of the free samples were more likely to view the product positively. This effect was probably even more pronounced among children, because they could not otherwise lawfully obtain the products.

The fact that tobacco manufacturers have targeted children in their marketing and advertising is unsurprising given that children are, in comparison with nonsmoking adults, relatively open-minded with respect to the perceived harmfulness and addictiveness of smoking. Behavioral researchers have provided some evidence that such fresh thinkers are less likely than others to be influenced by prominent informational cascades, such as the health risk awareness that followed the surgeon general's smoking-related announcements of the 1950s and 1960s (Rabin, 1998, p. 26). The industry's focus on young people is also predictable given that children appear to have more pronounced *time-inconsistent preferences* (that is, less concern for the long-term health consequences of smoking) than do nonsmoking adults (Hanson & Logue, 1998), a phenomenon of which the industry seems aware. Claude Teague, for instance, observed that "the smoking-health controversy does not appear important to the [youth] group because, psychologically, at eighteen, one is immortal" (R. J. Reynolds, 1973). In another RJR document written 15 years later, youth were characterized as similarly myopic: To them "what is critical is today, not tomorrow" (R. J. Reynolds, 1988, Bates No. 507241673).

Unsurprising, too, is the fact that tobacco advertising imagery is ubiquitous in U.S. society and especially intense at convenience stores. Such imagery probably triggers *visceral factors* over which addicted smokers have little control (see Chapter 9, this volume). It is no accident that cigarettes are often displayed for sale (together with other "impulse items") at grocery store checkout stations. Although nonsmokers might not even notice a rack of cigarettes, few smokers will miss it or the opportunity to stock up for the day. Such product placement probably poses additional enticements for smokers attempting to quit, for at every turn they are confronted with reminders of what they are missing and opportunities to make easy purchases.

The tobacco industry also seems to have developed ways to take advantage of *framing effects* by portraying its products in ways that minimize smoker risk perceptions. For instance, although most smokers consume "light" cigarettes, they are not called "regulars," and regulars are not called "heavies." The introduction of "light" and "ultra-light" cigarettes reflected manufacturers' efforts to reassure smokers about the health consequences of smoking rather than efforts actually to improve those consequences. Referring to such cigarettes as "lights" may have survived as an industry custom in part because the denomination also takes advantage of framing effects. Like all other manipulative practices, this use of framing need not be conscious on the part of manufacturers. Because the market rewards manipulation, it will evolve to contain manipulation, regardless of manufacturers' motivations.

Similarly, *context effects* may also play a role in some smokers' decisions to smoke. The very presence of a "regular" and "unfiltered" cigarette may encourage many would-be quitters to smoke the "light" and "filtered" brands—just as the presence of a large radio can cause some individuals to buy a medium radio rather than a small one, even when they prefer the small to the medium radio in other contexts. Some advertising campaigns appear to seize on this tendency explicitly, such as "If you smoke, please smoke Carlton" (see Richards, 1987) and "I thought about all I'd read and said to myself, either quit or smoke True. I smoke True." A Vantage advertisement goes even further:

> To the 3,000,000 people who started smoking this year:
> Despite all the arguments against smoking, one simple fact remains. Last year, three million people started to smoke.
> This year the criticism will continue. And next year too. But after all is said and done, another three million people will probably start smoking.
> Maybe the people who criticize smoking should stare the facts in the face. Then they might recommend that if you've decided to smoke, but are concerned about "tar" and nicotine, you might smoke Vantage. (Lorillard, 1974, Bates No. 03280729)

Finally, *attribution theorists* have shown that consumers can be significantly influenced by their perceptions of a seller's conduct and intentions. The relevance of attribution theory to tobacco policy seems fairly clear.[7] Consumers, to be adequately informed in the sense that they truly have free choice in the market, need to know more than just the information regarding the ill health effects and addictiveness of cigarettes. They also need to understand the extent to which those outcomes are inherent and unavoidable in the product or the result of volitional and even deliberate acts of manufacturers. Such information can have a significant effect on consumers' willingness to pay for a product, an effect of which tobacco manufacturers seem well aware.

With respect to the perceived locus of harm, for instance, manufacturers have gone to great lengths to deny or raise doubts about any causal connection between smoking and disease. Consider, for example, the TIRC's widely distributed documents listing "human ills erroneously attributed to tobacco over the centuries" and the millions of dollars spent by the industry to support the research efforts of those scientists who argued that genetic or environmental factors caused cancer in smokers (Glantz et al., 1996, pp. 291-296; Hilts, 1996, p. 15). Tobacco manufacturers used the work of those scientists in congressional hearings, lawsuits, brochures sent to doctors, and public relations. In other words, the tobacco companies placed the locus of smoking-related harms with the environment and consumers, thus depressing the public's anger toward, and desire for retribution against, manufacturers.[8] As we have explained elsewhere, however, the tobacco industry appears to have long known that cigarettes cause cancer—or, in other words, that locus belongs with the product and its manufacturers (see, e.g., Hanson & Kysar, 1999a, pp. 1496-1500).

In addition, the industry has sought to persuade consumers that it has no control over any risks that cigarettes might pose. With respect to the addictiveness of smoking, for example, tobacco companies have continuously attempted to characterize smoking as a "habit" (tantamount to eating "gummy bears") and to deny that it is an "addiction" (Glantz et al., 1996, pp. 4-5). Responding to the publication of the 1988 surgeon general's report stating that cigarettes are addictive, the industry press release was clear: "Claims that cigarettes are addictive contradict common sense" (Tobacco Institute, 1988). In 1994, six tobacco company CEOs testified before Congress that nicotine is not addictive. Similarly, cigarette manufacturers have defended their position by pointing to misleading statistics, such as the evidence that approximately half of all smokers manage to quit (Hanson & Logue, 1998, pp. 1194-1195). According to the long-term industry view, control lies with smokers.[9] They freely choose to consume a product that they perceive to be risky (even if manufacturers deny those risks); consequently, the public should support unregulated tobacco as a means of "protect[ing] everyone's freedom against an overbearing government" (Glantz et al., 1996, p. 185).

Again, however, internal industry documents indicate that controllability actually rests, to a considerable degree, with manufacturers (Hanson & Kysar, 1999a, pp. 1500-1502). Indeed, the industry has long understood that a key ingredient of its success is the addictiveness of its product. As an internal Philip Morris (1972) document characterized it, "Cigarettes should be conceived not as a product but as a package. The product is nicotine. The cigarette is but one of many package layers. . . . Think of the cigarettes as a storage container for a day's supply of nicotine" (p. i). In similar terms, an R. J. Reynolds (1972) document described the industry as "a specialized, highly ritualized and stylized segment for the pharmaceutical industry"; nicotine is "a potent drug with a variety of physiological effects" and "habit-forming"; cigarettes are "a vehicle for delivery of nicotine, designed to deliver nicotine in a generally acceptable and attractive form" (p. 2). Cigarette manufacturers realized how important this feature was. For example, British American Tobacco (n.d.), in an internal document, emphasized that "high on the list of product requirements is an adequate level of nicotine to sustain the smoking habit" (p. 7; quoted in Wilson & Gillmer, 1999, p. 614).

Finally, the cigarette industry has attempted to assuage consumer fears by portraying itself as motivated primarily by concern for the safety and freedom of consumers. For instance, in 1954, member tobacco manufacturers announced the formation of the TIRC with a full-page advertisement that appeared in 448 newspapers across the country, reaching a circulation of 43,245,000 in 258 cities (Hilts, 1996, p. 12). Headlined "A Frank Statement to Cigarette Smokers," the ad included the following assurances: "We accept an interest in people's health as a basic responsibility, paramount to every other consideration in our business. . . . We always have and always will cooperate closely with those whose task it is to safeguard the public health" (Tobacco Industry Research Council, 1954). As the following examples illustrate, efforts such as these were repeated throughout the second half of the 20th century, each designed to project an appearance of responsibility and concern on the part of cigarette manufacturers (Hanson & Kysar, 1999a, pp. 1484-1489):

> We recognize that we have a special responsibility to the public to help scientists determine the facts about tobacco and health, and about certain diseases that have been associated with tobacco use. We accepted this responsibility in 1954 by establishing the [TIRC], which provides research grants to independent scientists. We pledge continued support of this program of research until the facts are known. (Tobacco Industry Research Council, n.d.)

> We feel a deep sense of responsibility to our cigarette smokers. All of us who work in this industry feel a deep concern over questions raised about cigarettes and health. We will not rest until we learn the scientific facts that will provide solutions to the medical problems in question. We intend to leave no research question unanswered in our quest for the truth. What have we done to help find the truth? This industry has allocated nearly twenty million dollars for the support of research projects by independent scientists, through The Council for Tobacco Research–U.S.A., and through the American Medical Association Education and Research Foundation. If more funds

are needed for this research, I am sure the industry will provide them. (Philip Morris, 1966, p. 10)

We in the industry took a position which is one that we think is probably the only correct or moral one, which is that some very serious charges have been made, and it's up to us morally to find the answers. (Philip Morris, 1976, p. 16)

The smoking and health controversy is a very important question; our industry has been—and is, of course, trying to provide the answer. If there ever should be any component or components, as found in smoke, that can be proven to be, or contribute to be, a cause of any disease in man, we will of course, take them out. (R. J. Reynolds, 1977, p. 1)

The companies fully recognized that the industry has an absolute duty and a heavy obligation to seek to determine what if any part its products play in disease. . . .
    I am utterly secure in saying to you that the tobacco industry recognizes its responsibility and its duty and that it will continue its every effort and at whatever cost to find the answer to the question "What part, if any, does tobacco play in human diseases?" (Brown & Williamson, 1977, pp. 2-9)

This semblance of cooperation and responsibility appears intended to produce affective responses in smokers that not only would have increased their willingness to transact with tobacco manufacturers, but also would have lowered their perception of the risks of smoking.
    Of course, those sorts of strategies made good economic sense given the tort system's sensitivity to such attributional considerations (Hanson & Reyes, 1999), a sensitivity of which the industry was also aware. As David Hardy, a prominent tobacco lawyer, advised Brown & Williamson (in a letter to B. Debaun dated August 20, 1970) with regard to the risk posed by "careless" company employees:

A plaintiff would be greatly benefited by evidence which tended to establish actual knowledge on the part of the defendant that smoking is generally dangerous to health, that certain ingredients are dangerous and should be removed, or that smoking causes a particular disease. This would not only be evidence that would substantially prove a case against the defendant company for compensatory damages, but could be considered as evidence of willfulness or recklessness sufficient to support a claim for punitive damages. The psychological effect on judge and jury would undoubtedly be devastating to the defendant. (quoted in Hanauer, Slade, Barnes, Bero, & Glantz, 1995, p. 235)

Guided by such counsel, tobacco manufacturers appear to have long attempted to manipulate attributional perceptions in order to avoid the outrage that would result from the public's knowing the truth.

Recently, as the legal landscape has changed, and as the industry's credibility has been more seriously challenged, manufacturers have begun to alter their public relations strategies slightly. In their current campaigns, some manufacturers are now making concessions regarding the causal connection between cigarettes and disease and regarding the addictiveness of their products. It is interesting to note, however, that central to their new campaigns are continued efforts to attribute responsibility for those harms to smokers, as illustrated by these quotes from three manufacturers' Web sites:

We agree with the overwhelming medical and scientific consensus that cigarette smoking causes lung cancer, heart disease, emphysema and other serious diseases in smokers. Smokers are far more likely to develop serious diseases, like lung cancer, than non-smokers. There is no "safe" cigarette. . . .

We agree with the overwhelming medical and scientific consensus that cigarette smoking is addictive. (Philip Morris, 2000a)

Brown & Williamson believes that people who choose to smoke are accepting significant health risks, and that, in the most simple and commonly understood sense, smoking is the cause of certain diseases. . . .

Brown & Williamson agrees that, by current definitions of the term "addiction," including that of the Surgeon General in 1988, cigarette smoking is addictive. (Brown & Williamson, 2000)

R. J. Reynolds Tobacco Company manufactures products that have significant and inherent health risks for a number of serious diseases, and may contribute to causing these diseases in some individuals. (R. J. Reynolds, 2000)

Notice that in virtually all cases the manufacturers emphasize that there is nothing that can be done about that causal connection; they treat it as somehow inherent in their product and thus outside their control. "There is," after all, "no 'safe' cigarette." The Brown & Williamson admission goes further, suggesting that it is the consumers who have control, because it is they who "choose to smoke." There is no mention of the possibility of making a "safer" cigarette, the average age of the individual who makes the "choice" to smoke, or the efforts made by the industry to attract people to make that "choice" initially and then re-peatedly thereafter. Those manufacturers who acknowledge the addictiveness of cigarettes attempt to dilute the importance of that fact by adopting watered-down definitions of addiction and say nothing about manufacturers' control over that characteristic. To demonstrate their good motives, those companies continue to emphasize that they are only being responsive to consumer preferences—imply-ing that they have no effect on those preferences—and are interested in selling only to adults. Some go further and highlight their good corporate deeds. Philip Morris (2000b), for instance, describes its charitable conduct and motives as fol-lows:

> The Philip Morris family of companies has been making grants to nonprofit organizations—local, national and international—since 1956, making it one of the nation's oldest corporate giving programs.
>
> Today, we are also one of the largest corporate contributors of monetary grants in the United States, with annual charitable contributions of more than $60 million in 1998.
>
> The reason we continue to give is simple: We want to make a meaningful difference in people's lives. You see, while Philip Morris is well known for being a family of companies, we are also a company of families. And the val-ues and qualities that are important in our homes are also fundamental to our business. Foremost among these is a commitment to community service and lending a hand to others who need our help.

In short, manufacturers who are making slight concessions regarding causation are careful to present themselves as lacking in control and selflessly motivated.[10]

Constituency-Constrained Politicians

As we have summarized above, people (politicians) tend to accept the views of the people to whom they feel accountable (constituents) instead of investing the cognitive resources needed to weigh the pros and cons of alternative views. To-bacco manufacturers appear to take advantage of that tendency in at least two major ways. First, by maintaining a "controversy" about the health effects of smoking, they encourage potential smokers to rely on the acceptability heuristic and thus to save the significant costs of attempting to sort out the risks that they face. Second, individual manufacturers go to great lengths to make consumption of their product appear to be acceptable among potential smokers' constituents. In other words, manufacturers manipulate the acceptability heuristic to attract those groups of individuals who have not committed to a position on smoking.

Consider, in that light, Claude Teague's description in the RJR memo mentioned above of the "psychological effects" (i.e., "the expected or derived gratifications") that "influence a pre-smoker to try smoking and which sustain the beginning smoker during the largely awkward and unpleasant 'learning to smoke' phase." Teague explains:

> Pre-smokers learn to smoke to identify with and participate in shared experiences of a group of associates. If the majority of one's closest associates smoke cigarettes, then there is strong psychological pressure, particularly as a young person, to identify with the group, follow the crowd, and avoid being out of phase with the group's value system even though, paradoxically, the group value system may esteem individuality. This provides a large incentive to begin smoking. If this be true, then the same effect strongly influences the brand chosen, it likely being the popular, "in" brand used by one['s] close associates.
>
> Thus a new brand aimed at the young smoker must somehow become the "in" brand and its promotion should emphasize togetherness, belonging and group acceptance, while at the same time emphasizing individuality and "doing one['s] own thing." (R. J. Reynolds, 1973, p. 6)

Teague's recognition of the significance of peers in motivating young people to begin smoking is not unusual. Indeed, as a Philip Morris executive pointed out, among experts in the tobacco industry, "there is general agreement on [why people begin to smoke]. The 16 to 20 year-old begins smoking for psychosocial reasons. The act of smoking is symbolic, it signifies adulthood, he smokes to enhance his image in the eyes of his peers" (Philip Morris, 1969, p. 6).

To attract young smokers, therefore, companies have regularly and extensively studied youth attitudes toward smoking in order to shed "light on the very vital teenage sector of the market" (R. J. Reynolds, 1968, p. 1). And cigarette companies have devised promotional devices for enhancing the perceived acceptability of their products. For instance, the nearly 1 million hats, T-shirts, towels, and other products that RJR sold in 1975 served not only as "walking billboards" for RJR's products but as advertisements that were implicitly backed by the young people who wore them (R. J. Reynolds, 1974, p. 10). Similarly, the sampling promotions of many manufacturers sought to tap into the power of peer influence. Advertisers for Newport, for example, concluded as follows:

Sampling appears to represent the most viable trial vehicle for Newport. With availability within the peer group ("bumming") as the primary means of trial among Newports' target group, sampling appears to be the "only" acceptable marketing vehicle by which to develop a base. (Ricci, 1978, p. 2)

Cigarette manufacturers do more than simply try to make their products seem acceptable to the peers of potential smokers. They also offer their cigarettes to young people as a means of identifying and joining a peer group to which the potential smoker may otherwise lack access. In explaining the surging success of RJR's "Smooth Character" Camel line (on which RJR spent $75 million per year on billboard advertising, beach recreational merchandise, and print ads; R. J. Reynolds, 1989), an advertising agency for a concerned Philip Morris listed the following factors:

Given a climate of rejection/ostracism

- Smokers want to belong and feel that it is acceptable to smoke (Camel ads)

- Being rebellious and outspoken helps to keep criticism at bay

- Camel gives the smoker a lot of excitement and involvement at a time when they need to feel better about themselves

- Camel offers this age group a peer group which feeds their need to belong. (Eckman & Goldberg, 1992, p. 8)

In sum, in obtaining youth-market dominance, RJR seems to have tapped into the acceptability heuristic in a group that especially craves acceptance and thus is particularly vulnerable to such manipulation.

Often enough, however, the peer group is already well established, and manufacturers seek simply to make their brands the accepted cigarettes within that group. In the 1980s, for example, B&W devoted considerable marketing efforts to leveraging peer pressure within certain racial groups in support of Kool cigarettes:

Clearly, the sole reason for B&W's interest in the black and Hispanic communities is the actual and potential sales of B&W products within these communities and the profitability of these sales. . . . this relatively small and often tightly knit community can work to B&W's marketing advantage, if exploited properly. Peer pressure plays a more important role in many phases of life in the minority community. Therefore, dominance of the marketplace and the community environment is necessary to successfully increase sales share. (Brown & Williamson, 1984, p. 2)

Even some of the manufacturers' public service campaigns offered ostensibly to help curb underage smoking seem quite suspicious in light of the acceptability heuristic as well as evidence that perceptions of peer smoking prevalence are positively correlated with young people's intentions to smoke (Centers for Disease Control and Prevention, 1994a, p. 193). For example, Philip Morris has spent $100 million on its "Think, don't smoke" campaign, which emphasizes to kids that smoking is an adult activity and they should therefore resist peer pressure to smoke (Worth, 1999, p. 4). Such campaigns do not emphasize the dangers and addictiveness of smoking; indeed, they may even encourage kids to smoke by implying that smoking is acceptable among their peers (in part because it is a so-called adult activity).

For confirmed smokers, Tetlock's findings regarding constituency-constrained politicians indicate some of the manipulative consequences of tobacco manufacturer conduct. Indeed, all of the conduct reviewed in previous sections regarding how manufacturers have attempted to assuage the concerns of individual smokers has also been conduct that has enabled those smokers to engage in defensive bolstering in response to concerns raised by those smokers' constituents. And the industry apparently understands that effect. Indeed, if one substitutes the words *defensive bolstering* for *self-justification* in the following quotation, it becomes apparent that the tobacco industry identified the phenomenon well before Tetlock did:

> Presumably, the satisfaction derived from tar and nicotine causes most people who start smoking to want to continue smoking. However, because such large numbers of the institutions and leaders he believes in are against smoking, the average smoker often seeks self-justification for smoking. Good cigarette advertising in the past has given the average smoker a means of justification. (Brown & Williamson, 1976, p. 1)

Summary

Our account of the practices and conduct of the tobacco companies illustrates a multidimensional approach to expanding the industry's reach and profitability. Much of the industry's conduct appears to have been designed to generate positive affect in young smokers and then to maintain those impressions throughout their lives by, among other tactics, suggesting that cigarettes are healthful, emphasizing the non-health-related benefits of smoking, and denying and attempting to discredit the evidence that smoking is harmful. In other words, like any business in a free market, the tobacco industry sought to maintain its existing customers and attract new ones. Because of the substantial health risks posed by the

product and the fact that consumers had some understanding of these risks, cigarette manufacturers had (and still have) particularly strong incentives to manipulate consumer risk perceptions.

There is still some question, however, regarding whether the industry has succeeded in accomplishing its goal. After all, as Viscusi (1992b) emphasizes, consumers have been the recipients of a great deal of publicly provided risk information, and, as his evidence purportedly shows, most consumers do have some
awareness of the potential risks of long-term smoking. That question is addressed
in some of the previous chapters in this volume as well as in our earlier work
(Hanson & Kysar, 1999a, 1999b), in which a great deal of evidence is reviewed and
reported that demonstrates that the tobacco industry's efforts to manipulate consumer risk perceptions have succeeded. In addition, a number of scholars, ourselves included, have argued that close inspection of Viscusi's data and methodology reveals numerous flaws in his analysis, flaws that raise serious doubts about
whether one can reasonably infer from his underlying data that consumers accurately perceive, much less overestimate, the general risks of long-term smoking
(see generally Borland, 1997; Eiser, 1994; Hanson & Kysar, 1999a, pp. 1527-1551;
Hanson & Logue, 1998; Slovic, 1998). In short, Viscusi's survey sheds light on only
a narrow and insignificant slice of the picture, one that is largely irrelevant to the
question of how consumers actually process information and make decisions.

∞ Limitations of Existing Theoretical and Legal Frameworks

The existence of nonrational cognitive tendencies and the related problem of
market manipulation helps to explain the shortcomings of Viscusi's treatment of
tobacco issues, the failure of tobacco regulation, and the success of the tobacco industry in the United States. Because neither Viscusi in *Smoking: Making the Risky
Decision* (1992b) nor the United States in its tobacco policy has taken
behavioralism seriously, neither has recognized tobacco manufacturers' capabil-
ity of exploiting individual cognitive biases for gain. In this section we briefly review the causes and consequences of those oversights.

Limits of Economic Theory

The existence of widespread and persistent nonrational behavior poses a significant threat to the foundations of economic theory. The field of microeconom-

ics is premised on certain assumptions about the nature of individual behavior within the market. If those assumptions turn out to be incorrect for many individuals much of the time, as behavioralism suggests they probably do, economists may suddenly find themselves less relevant to policy makers than they have grown accustomed to being. In order to avoid necessitating a wholesale revision of the discipline, many legal economists have attempted to incorporate the findings of the behavioral research into the neoclassical economic conception of the rational actor. This new brand of economic analysis—which is being referred to as *behavioral economics*—attempts to enhance the predictive capabilities of the economic model without otherwise altering its structure. As three leading commentators have put it, "Behavioral economics allows us to model and predict behavior relevant to law with the tools of traditional economic analysis, but with more accurate assumptions about human behavior" (Jolls, Sunstein, & Thaler, 1998, p. 1474).

One important result of this desire to maintain the overall structure of the traditional economic model has been that commentators tend to view cognitive biases as exogenous influences on individual behavior; that is, legal economic scholars typically assume that the biases will have a fixed influence on behavior, unaffected by other factors within the model. This supposed stability of influence allows those scholars to utilize the standard model of economic behavior with only the (fixed) additional input of a particular cognitive bias. In our view, the full significance of the behavioral research can be seen only when limitations on decision-making abilities are treated as endogenous to the economic model—that is, when it is recognized that in addition to cognitive biases influencing the behavior of individuals, other factors within the model are influencing the presence and force of cognitive biases. This possibility arises from the very same aspect of cognitive biases that has made other scholars quick to incorporate them into the standard economic model: the fact that they are "systematic and can be modeled" (Jolls et al., 1998, p. 1475). Just as the predictability of biases makes them easy to assimilate into economic models, it also makes them easy to exploit by those who seek to influence the behavior of other economic actors. As we have argued above, one finding that emerges from this endogenous analysis is the likelihood that product manufacturers, including tobacco firms, will manipulate perceptions of product risks and benefits in order to increase consumers' willingness to pay for the product.

Some scholars have noted that risk assessments are manipulable in this fashion but have failed to see that *manufacturers* can take advantage of such manipulability. That failing is evident, for example, in various aspects of Viscusi's work on consumer risk perceptions. Viscusi (1992b) attempts to discredit studies that suggest consumers underestimate risks by arguing that the designers of the studies have manipulated survey respondents through framing effects: "Some

observed biases in past studies may be due to the manner in which the risk perception question is framed rather than to any underlying shortcoming in individual behavior" (p. 102). He recognizes that survey respondents, like consumers, are
subject to manipulation, but he fails to see how that vulnerability will play out in
the retail product context. Similarly, Viscusi's (1996, p. 686) proposal for reforming
products liability law generally—imposing a national, uniform warning system—at least implicitly acknowledges that consumer risk perceptions can be manipulated or shaped by the manner in which information is presented. Nevertheless, Viscusi fails to recognize that similar manipulations can be perpetrated by
manufacturers for less benign or paternalistic reasons than his proposal entails.

   Finally, in some of his most famous research, Viscusi (1992a, pp. 234-242) has
gathered evidence suggesting that the addition of child-safety caps on medica-
tions did not actually lower the incidence of child poisonings as regulators expected it would. Instead, through something Viscusi terms the *lulling effect,* consumers overestimated the efficacy of safety caps and responded by lowering their
own parental care levels, a behavioral response that had the effect of offsetting any
safety gains that would have been achieved through the addition of safety caps. In
other words, the fairly insignificant design change of safety caps had the effect of
substantially altering consumer risk perceptions. Ever critical of government regulators for producing such unintended consequences, Viscusi never considers
whether manufacturers could cause similar effects. However, if government regulators can have a significant optimism-producing effect that is both unintentional
and contrary to their goal, then certainly manufacturers can generate similarly
powerful effects when they act deliberately in pursuit of profit.

   The foregoing discussion helps reveal what we believe is the central shortcoming of *Smoking: Making the Risky Decision.* The problem is not that Viscusi completely ignores behavioralism or the possibility of perceptual manipulation. On
the contrary, behavioralist research and the problem of manipulable consumers
are important components of his story. According to Viscusi (1992b, p. 70), the
very reason that consumers supposedly overestimate the risks of smoking is that
the government and the media have manipulated consumers by making those
risks excessively salient to them. However, if he really believes that an
"anti-smoking campaign" by "anti-smoking zealots and the public health community" has led consumers to overestimate the risks of smoking (Viscusi, 1998b,
p. 25), then it is puzzling that he ignores the possibility that a prosmoking campaign has influenced consumer perceptions in the opposite direction or that in-
dustry-provided survey data might reflect such a prosmoking bias. We agree that
there has been an antismoking campaign that has had some, albeit unfortunately
limited, effect. Nevertheless, Viscusi's failure to consider how the industry itself
might have influenced consumers is glaring in light of the evidence of successful
industry efforts to counteract the "antismoking" campaign.

By discounting both the potential for market manipulation and the evidence that the tobacco industry has in fact attempted to manipulate consumer risk estimates, Viscusi essentially takes two irreconcilable positions. The first is that the market should be largely unregulated because of its overwhelming and benign power to ensure social efficiency. In calling for less regulation of cigarettes, Viscusi (1998b) writes, "State and federal governments alike should abandon their combative stance, take a more open-minded approach to the safety of tobacco products, and make advancement of consumer welfare the paramount concern" (p. 19). He claims that "there is tremendous evidence that market forces are enormously powerful, not only with respect to smoking but also with respect to risky choices" (p. 25). Consequently, he calls for greater use of market forces because he believes that market forces are far more powerful and effective than regulators.

Viscusi's second position, however, which is largely implicit, is that government regulators have been more successful than the market in shaping the risk perceptions and preferences of consumers. Specifically, he believes that government regulators have caused an irrational availability cascade among consumers regarding the risks of smoking. If Viscusi were to take behavioralism seriously, however, he would see that there are many other sources of manipulation aside from the government. More important, he would recognize that those sources include the market, the very institution that he vehemently argues is more effective than regulators at accomplishing product safety goals. All the logic of economic theory and all the evidence of tobacco marketing in the past century suggest that the market is likewise more powerful than the government at manipulating consumer perceptions and preferences. Failing to make that recognition, Viscusi is left with a conflicted view of the smoking question; he argues that "enormously powerful" market forces can produce safer cigarettes, but he does not recognize that those same powerful forces can manipulate consumers.

Limits of Legal Regulation

A similar lack of appreciation for the problem of market manipulation has plagued legal regulation of tobacco products in the United States. Three primary areas of legal control—warning requirements, products liability suits, and deceptive advertising regulation—have all failed in various ways to achieve their stated goals. The first two of these mechanisms have failed in part because, at least until recent years, they did not acknowledge the problem of market manipulation. The third has failed in part because, although it expressly seeks to regulate market manipulation, it is ill designed to combat the severity and complexity of manipulative conduct on the part of manufacturers.

Beginning with the Federal Cigarette Labeling and Advertising Act of 1965, product warnings have been the primary policy tool used by the U.S. government in its campaign against smoking (Hanson & Logue, 1998). This focus parallels the consensus that has emerged among legal economics scholars who have studied the problem of products liability generally. Those scholars believe that providing consumers with accurate information eliminates any undue optimism that consumers may have regarding the potential for a product to cause harm. The supposed economic benefit of such a policy is that once consumers are fully informed through hazard warnings, they will demand an optimal level of safety and purchase only those products having marginal benefits that exceed marginal costs. Thus scholars, such as Viscusi, who take this view believe that people who continue to smoke despite cigarette warnings do so out of fully informed and voluntary choice. In other words, smokers make the risky decision and, for them, the right decision.

This conception, however, fails to distinguish between instances in which consumers simply lack product information and instances in which they are subject to the influence of cognitive biases. The many cognitive biases identified in this chapter and elsewhere in this book all remain powerfully at play even when a warning label is placed on the cigarette package. Thus, although product warnings conceivably can remedy deficiencies in consumer information, deficiencies in consumer cognitive processing seem far more subtle and intractable.

Recognizing the force of this reasoning, some recent advocates of product warnings have argued that warnings should be carefully designed by regulators to account for cognitive biases. Viscusi (1991b), for instance, asserts that a regulatory agency charged with constructing and testing the effects of product warnings would provide the best response to the problem of cognitive biases: "The best practical solution to the problem of competing risks of labeling is pretesting the warning—its language and its presentation of information—for its ability to accomplish the intended objective" (p. 137). He reiterates this recommendation in the context of tobacco products in particular (Viscusi, 1992b, p. 150).

As we argue with respect to Viscusi's study of smoking perceptions, however, this solution appears at first to be sensitive to the operation of cognitive biases, but it ultimately fails to take behavioralism to its logical conclusion. The problem is again the failure to recognize the endogenous effects of cognitive biases in consumer product markets. Viscusi's solution discounts completely the impact of manufacturers' efforts to counteract product warnings. For a variety of reasons, the market is far more capable of influencing consumer behavior than is the regulator who devises product warnings, and the market's incentives are squarely to diminish the effects of warnings (Hanson & Kysar, 1999a, pp. 1555-1556). As long as legally adequate warnings are included on product packages, a product's remaining marketing materials can, with impunity, encourage overconsumption. Indeed, a primary goal of the marketing materials may be to undermine the effect of the legally mandated warnings. We suspect that this problem is significant, especially considering that American consumers are exposed to 25,000 commercials each year, and total annual worldwide advertising expenditures now exceed $350 billion (Hanson & Kysar, 1999a, p. 1559).

No product illustrates this possibility more acutely than cigarettes. Tobacco manufacturers have been able to minimize the effect of Congress's warning requirements at every stage in the campaign against cigarettes (Hanson & Logue, 1998, p. 1168, n. 9). The unparalleled marketing expenditures of the industry seem in many cases simply to have overwhelmed the warnings. Inundated with the industry's images, slogans, cartoons, and other "lifestyle" marketing techniques— all of which are backed by an advertising budget several orders of magnitude greater than that of any public health agency—consumers have, unsurprisingly, failed to understand fully the message about cigarette health risks. Moreover, the industry is well aware that warnings may be positioned to have a forbidden-fruit appeal to minors. As one industry insider noted, the "warning label on the package may be a plus" when it comes to recruiting young smokers (R. J. Reynolds, 1973, p. 8). Those are just two examples of the ways in which the hazard warnings of regulators have proven ineffective, or even counterproductive, when combined with the marketing efforts of manufacturers. A recent ad campaign by R. J. Reynolds that openly derides the warning label requirements may represent a third. The campaign features a rotating series of cartoonish scenes, each with a "warning" label, similar in design to the labels mandated by federal legislation, that mockingly warns viewers that the ad may contain suggestive images.

Brown & Williamson has taken this mocking a step further by altering its voice mail message in a way that has attracted thousands of callers—many of whom, we suspect, are underage. By dialing one of the company's toll-free service numbers (800-578-7453), consumers have been able to enjoy a very different sort of corporate message. For instance, one such greeting begins by warning callers under 21 years of age to hang up immediately, and then an anonymous voice (with musical accompaniment) oozes:

> Good. Now that it's just us, there's something that we—Brown & Williamson Tobacco—would like to tell you. It may be a little soon, but . . . well, it just feels right. We, the Brown & Williamson Tobacco Corp., are in love with you. Yup, you heard right. Brown & Williamson is in love. We're a giant corporation, and you make us feel like a little kitten. Thank you, lover! By the way, the other tobacco companies hate you and think you're ugly. They told us so.

More recently, we found the following recording at that number:

> Hello and welcome to the Brown & Williamson Tobacco Corporation. If you've reached this number in error, you're in luck, because we're about to serenade you. If you've dialed correctly, you're in luck, because we're about to serenade you. [music begins]
>
> > Oh, the tobacco plant is a lovely plant with leaves so broad and green,
> > But you shouldn't think about the tobacco plant if you're still a teen.
> > 'Cause tobacco is a big person's plant, and that's the way it should be.
> > So if you're under 21, go and climb a tree.
> > Oh, the tobacco plant is a lovely plant, and that my friends is no yarn.
> > We let it ripen in the field and hang it in the barn.
>
> [over humming] If you think that really sucked, we agree. Write a better song about the tobacco plant and we'll use it.

Although it is difficult to document, it seems fairly clear that such mockery can only undermine the impact of product warnings and other information that young people might receive regarding the hazards of smoking.

The use of private litigation as a means of regulating tobacco markets is also problematic. Until recent years, private plaintiffs suffered a remarkably uniform string of defeats in tort suits brought against tobacco manufacturers. In two successive "waves" of litigation, tobacco firms managed to avoid paying damages (or settling for a substantial payment) in virtually every case brought against them by smoking plaintiffs, notwithstanding the fact that during those years products liability law in general underwent a "revolution" that greatly liberalized recovery for consumer plaintiffs (Hanson & Logue, 1998, p. 1169). The industry achieved that success through a variety of strategies, both procedural and substantive. Procedurally, the industry's scorched-earth litigation strategy often involved exhausting any opposing litigants, both mentally and financially. An attorney for R. J. Reynolds described the strategy as follows: "The aggressive strategy we have taken regarding depositions and discovery in general continues to make these cases extremely burdensome and expensive for plaintiffs' lawyers, particularly sole practitioners. To paraphrase General Patton, the way we won these cases was not by spending all of [R. J. Reynolds's] money, but by making that other son of a bitch spend all of his" (quoted in *Haines v. Liggett Group,* 1993, p. 421).

Substantively, the industry won many of its courtroom battles by focusing juror attention on the plaintiffs' own roles in choosing to smoke and by using the federally mandated warning labels as evidence that the plaintiffs knowingly assumed the risk of harm from smoking. "As a result, jurors tended to blame plaintiffs who had continued to smoke despite health warnings about the link between tobacco use and disease, instead of identifying the tobacco industry as the cause of the innumerable tobacco-induced illnesses" (Kelder & Daynard, 1997). In so criticizing smoking plaintiffs, these jurors may have been exhibiting the *hindsight bias*. That is, they may have overestimated the plaintiffs' ex ante knowledge and awareness of smoking health risks simply because the plaintiffs later contracted terminal diseases caused by cigarettes. Significantly, because the nature and extent of manipulative industry conduct was unknown at the time of the first two waves of litigation, these jurors were not provided any evidence to counteract their intuitive notions that (a) cigarettes are harmful and (b) people know it.

These notions may be true, in a very limited sense, but the more pertinent question is whether people's ability to act on their knowledge of smoking risks is impaired by either (a) the operation of other cognitive influences or (b) the conduct of the tobacco industry. Plaintiffs in a third wave of tobacco litigation have begun offering evidence of an affirmative answer to that more pertinent question, with respect to both the operation of other cognitive influences and the conduct of the tobacco industry. By revealing the extent to which cigarette companies knew that nicotine was pharmacologically active and highly addictive and by demonstrating how those companies manipulated nicotine content to addict smokers, these plaintiffs have begun to transform the juror skepticism that used to greet tobacco plaintiffs into attributive outrage at the industry's deceptive and manipulative conduct. As a result, several verdicts and settlements have been reached in the third wave of tobacco litigation that have been favorable to plaintiffs (Kelder & Daynard, 1997).

Nevertheless, products liability in its current incarnation is an imperfect way to regulate manipulative conduct on the part of tobacco manufacturers. No legal jurisdiction currently allows a products liability plaintiff to recover damages based solely on a showing that the defendant's product caused the plaintiff's harm. Instead, the plaintiff must also demonstrate that the defendant was somehow at fault, either because its product was unreasonably designed or manufactured or because the defendant failed to warn against a foreseeable risk (Croley & Hanson, 1993). In practice, those elements have meant that tobacco litigants must demonstrate manipulative conduct on the part of the industry, such as its knowledge and exploitation of the addictive properties of nicotine. Although the history of tobacco marketing appears to reveal a wide range of conduct that could meet this burden, the requirement of affirmative demonstration of manipulation in court creates informational difficulties that impair the effectiveness of private litigation as a means of regulating the tobacco industry. For many of the same reasons that we discuss below with respect to the enforcement of deceptive advertising regulations, plaintiffs and juries are unable to identify sufficiently and act against manipulative manufacturer conduct in all of its ever-shifting incarnations. To that extent, manipulative conduct on the part of tobacco manufacturers will escape legal control.

Finally, a third primary area of legal regulation has been through the enforcement of the Federal Trade Commission's authority to "prevent persons, partnerships, or corporations . . . from using unfair or deceptive acts or practices in commerce" (Federal Trade Commission Act, 1914, § 45[a][2]). For instance, between 1945 and 1960, the FTC completed seven formal cease-and-desist order proceedings against tobacco manufacturers for making medical or health claims. Similarly, the U.S. Food and Drug Administration has asserted jurisdiction over cases in which manufacturers have made medical claims regarding their tobacco products, such as when Fairfax cigarettes claimed to prevent respiratory disease and Trim Reducing-Aid cigarettes claimed to aid in weight reduction. More generally applicable actions by the FTC have included performing regular tests on the tar and nicotine yields of various cigarette brands and pressuring manufacturers to disclose data on such yields voluntarily, securing a 1972 consent order with six major cigarette companies that required a "clear and conspicuous" health warning in all of their cigarette advertisements, and providing an annual report to Congress on the current state of tobacco marketing and promotional practices (Federal Cigarette Labeling and Advertising Act, 1965).

This deceptive advertising approach differs from both warning requirements and traditional products liability litigation in that it expressly recognizes the problem of manipulative conduct by tobacco manufacturers. However, the effectiveness of FTC and other government regulation of deceptive advertising is necessarily limited by, among other things, the regulator's comparative disadvantages vis-à-vis the market. Because market manipulation is incredibly subtle and slippery, it does not lend itself to traditional command-and-control regulatory solutions. Market manipulation is subtle in the sense that consumers are not the only ones who fail to recognize manipulation. Regulators also fail to see precisely how consumers are being manipulated. It is slippery in the sense that any particular attempt to prevent or to counteract it will often lead to new and unanticipated forms of manipulation. We believe that the many manipulative practices identified in this chapter illustrate just how ingenious the market has been at producing objectionable conduct and just how limited the FTC's success has been in its role as consumer watchdog.

More precisely, we believe that the FTC suffers from a number of institutional limitations that prevent it from fully combating the problem of market manipulation. First, the FTC is a centralized, singular agency that must attempt to monitor the actions of a number of active tobacco firms on the market. The sheer labor cost of gathering and reviewing $6 billion worth of advertising and promotional materials each year (Federal Trade Commission, 1995) is prohibitive given the agency's limited resources. As a result, tobacco manufacturers who contemplate engaging in manipulative conduct face only a percentage chance that they will be subject to FTC enforcement action. Coupled with the fact that FTC penalties are often insubstantial in comparison with the benefits of manipulation, it is fairly clear that cigarette manufacturers face incomplete incentives to abstain from manipulative behavior. Second, in addition to monitoring tobacco marketing activities, the FTC must attempt to discern the precise impact that each piece of advertising has on individual perceptions of smoking risks and benefits. Although one might theoretically glean this information by employing the insights of cognitive psychology, as we have attempted to do in this chapter, a more immediate and trustworthy source of information would be the monetary feedback that tobacco manufacturers receive in response to their advertising campaigns—a source of information that, of course, lies within the exclusive control of the manufacturers. Third, the agency operates in an ex post fashion, seeking out deceptive or manipulative advertising only after it has been introduced to the market. This approach necessarily creates a time lag during which manipulative marketing can influence consumer perceptions. Finally, the FTC must operate under incentives that most commentators agree are weaker than the financial incentives that spur activity within the market. As a result, tobacco manufacturers who face powerful financial incentives to manipulate consumer perceptions may consistently outmaneuver the FTC simply because they have a stronger desire to do so (Hanson & Logue, 1998).

For these reasons, we think it unlikely that current regulation of deceptive trade practices is sufficient to combat market manipulation. Admittedly, much of the industry conduct challenged as manipulative in this chapter might be classified as fraud under existing consumer protection statutes. Nevertheless, we do not believe that the FTC's command-and-control approach could ever equal the resolve of financially motivated market actors. Government agencies do not have the incentives or the resources necessary to identify and act against market manipulation in its many evolving forms. Indeed, the tobacco industry practices actually challenged by the FTC and other regulatory agencies may represent only those practices that have been around long enough or are egregious enough to become transparent. The full extent of market manipulation may be far more insidious and problematic than those transparent examples reveal.

෨ Responding to the Challenge of Market Manipulation

The problem of market manipulation is, at bottom, a problem with the market itself.[11] Manipulation of consumers occurs because it must. To succeed in any reasonably competitive market, sellers must minimize the perceived price of their product. Put differently, the invisible hand of the market guarantees that the most successful sellers will be those who, wittingly or not, are the most successful manipulators. The challenge for those interested in limiting tobacco use, therefore, is to devise a system of regulation that equals the manipulative market in resourcefulness and tireless zeal to influence smoker behavior. We believe that the only institution capable of doing so is the market itself. In other words, the question for policy makers is not how to regulate tobacco markets, but how to make tobacco markets regulate themselves (Hanson & Logue, 1998). Below we provide a few speculative proposals toward that end. Our more general recommendation is for policy makers of all stripes—politicians, regulators, legal scholars, economists, public health advocates, and others—to give serious thought to the possibility that market manipulation actually is as pervasive and problematic as we have described. Only through collective inspection will this problem yield fully to understanding and public control.

Internalizing Product Costs

A crucial first step toward effective legal regulation of smoking would be the institution of a liability mechanism that forces cigarette manufacturers to incorporate the health costs of smoking into product prices (Hanson & Logue, 1998, pp. 1260-1261). One such mechanism would be the long-advocated products liability regime of "enterprise liability" (Calabresi, 1970; Croley & Hanson, 1993; Hanson & Logue, 1998). A properly designed "smoker's compensation" tribunal might also accomplish the same result at a lower administrative cost (Hanson & Logue, 1998, pp. 1283-1286; Hanson, Logue, & Zamore, 1998). Regardless of the chosen mechanism, by imposing liability upon tobacco firms based solely on the causal relationship between smoking and health, the legal system would achieve something that almost all economists agree is prerequisite to the proper functioning of markets: the internalization of product costs.

Currently, smokers behave as if they externalize a large portion of the costs of smoking—which one us has estimated (with Kyle Logue) to be at least $7.00 per pack (Hanson & Logue, 1998, p. 1242). Many of those costs are borne ultimately by public and private insurers, but the majority appear to be borne by long-term smokers, who, because they are ill informed, nevertheless treat those costs as if they were external (Hanson & Logue, 1998). Under the current legal regime, not only are smokers ill informed, but manufacturers have every incentive to keep them that way.

A liability regime that requires tobacco manufacturers to pay for the costs of all smoking-caused harms would force manufacturers to pass those costs on to smokers through product price increases. That pass-through would, as one of us has detailed elsewhere (Hanson & Logue, 1998), have two important and related effects. First, it would dampen much of the tobacco industry's incentive to manipulate consumer risk perceptions. After all, a tobacco manufacturer who persuades consumers to underestimate the health costs of its product gains little given that, roughly speaking, the manufacturer must ultimately bear those costs. Put differently, manufacturers who continued to engage in manipulative practices in such a regime would be, to a significant degree, only fooling themselves. As noted above, under traditional command-and-control regulation, regulators are only able to control the manipulative practices that are egregious enough or have been around long enough to become transparent. Under enterprise liability or smoker's compensation, on the other hand, even those practices that are unknown to regulators (or to manufacturers themselves) become effectively "regulated" in the sense that they are no longer economically attractive for manufacturers to follow. Indeed, manufacturers essentially regulate themselves, avoiding manipulative behavior simply because it is a costly exercise that offers little or no gain (assuming that a market rate of interest is added to future health cost liabilities when they are assessed). In short, while consumer protection agencies, following a command-and-control approach, valiantly attempt to spot and stamp out fires of manipulation as they are identified, enterprise liability combats manipulation by eliminating the touchwood altogether.

The second benefit to be gained from a total-cost liability regime is that consumers would be given a more independent and accurate source of information regarding smoking costs (Hanson & Logue, 1998, pp. 1221-1223). Enterprise liability would force tobacco manufacturers to charge a nominal price that includes the full expected health costs of their products. By internalizing the costs of smoking onto smokers and cigarette manufacturers, a system of enterprise liability or smoker's compensation would operate like an excise tax that forces the price of a package of cigarettes to reflect its full cost. This sticker price information would essentially raise the bar over which tobacco firms must jump in order to manipulate smoker perceptions and preferences. Regardless of what tobacco manufacturers attempted to convey in marketing campaigns, consumers would know that the health risks of smoking were at least the amortized equivalent of, say, $7.00 per package. Consequently, consumers would confront the total costs of cigarette smoking when they made the purchasing decision and would behave *as if* they were well-informed about product risks (even if, as argued throughout this book, they otherwise are unduly optimistic with respect to those risks). Of course, the fact that smoking is addictive complicates the matter with respect to current smokers, who may be fairly price insensitive, at least in the short run. Nevertheless, a great deal of evidence suggests that consumers, especially young ones, are price sensitive even for an addictive product like tobacco (Viscusi, 1992b, pp. 102-105). Thus a significant increase in the price of cigarettes would cause a significant number of people to either stop smoking or not begin smoking when they otherwise might have. This reduction in cigarette use is desirable inasmuch as consumers would simply be reacting to the full costs of a product that they formerly misperceived.

A supplement to this system that might be desirable in light of consumer underestimation of addiction would be an additional tax levied on cigarette brands in accordance with their market share among young consumers. These performance-based standards could be employed to help encourage manufacturers to turn their marketing prowess toward discouraging underage smoking. The economic logic of this policy proposal differs slightly from the above discussion of cost internalization. Although this "youth tax" could be justified as a means of internalizing the unrecognized and poorly understood costs of addiction, a more likely argument in its favor would simply be that such a youth tax is necessary to enforce existing legal prohibitions on the sale of tobacco products to minors.

Managing Perceptions of Product Benefits

Even the implementation of a market-corrective device like enterprise liability would not entirely eliminate the problem of market manipulation. Among other problems, tobacco manufacturers would still manipulate consumer perceptions of cigarette benefits, even if they held far reduced ability and incentive to downplay the costs. In the past, cigarette manufacturers have certainly proven themselves effective at both dulling smoker awareness of the health costs of smoking and increasing smoker estimates of the benefits of smoking. They have accomplished this through the use of ubiquitous "lifestyle" advertising and other promotional techniques that seek to create positive affective responses toward cigarettes in consumers. As noted previously, young people especially have been the targets of such efforts (Pierce & Gilpin, 1995; Pierce, Lee, & Gilpin, 1994).

This possibility of preference manipulation requires a dramatic theoretical departure from the standard view of consumer product markets. Economists typically assume that manufacturers are price takers, meaning that they are able to obtain only a "normal" profit that is factored into the "cost" of the good. Likewise, economists typically assume that consumer preferences are exogenously given. They neither consider nor question the origins of preferences. The task for consumers in most economic models is simply to choose the least costly alternative among comparable goods. Once one admits market manipulation, however, it becomes clear that manufacturers can influence consumer preferences among goods. Thus it is possible for tobacco firms to manipulate consumer preferences even in the face of a legal regime that forces prices up to their full social costs. One therefore must be concerned about the young person who, although accurately perceiving the long-term health costs of smoking through product prices, nevertheless chooses to begin smoking as a result of manipulative advertising campaigns (rather than as a result of some true, unmanipulated preference for cigarettes). Because affective associations between cigarettes and positive attributes may begin as early as age 3 (Fischer et al., 1991), this concern is not overstated, despite its arguable undertone of paternalism. So the question becomes: What else might be done to respond to this side of the market manipulation problem? The possibilities sketched below are intended only as illustrative samples of potential options—icebreakers with which policy analysts and lawmakers might begin.

One means of constraining manipulative industry conduct might be to eliminate the business income tax deduction for tobacco advertising expenses—much as business expense deductions have been disallowed for lobbying activities. This measure would simply make manipulative marketing more costly for tobacco manufacturers to undertake, thereby reducing the volume of such marketing that occurs. A second policy alternative might be to institute a tax on cigarettes that directly funds social marketing campaigns designed to counteract the effects of tobacco advertising. Several states have followed such an approach in their consent agreements with the tobacco industry, earmarking certain funds for health awareness and other social marketing campaigns. Among other activities, those states have hired marketing firms to utilize their expertise in demographic and psychographic marketing for the purpose of reducing youth tobacco use. The resultant campaigns, using sophisticated modern marketing techniques, have demonstrated a significant advantage over the government's traditional, strictly informational approach, which has largely failed with respect to youth perceptions (Hanson & Kysar, 1999a, p. 1483).

The Massachusetts Department of Health, for instance, has developed a campaign around the theme "Get Outraged" that appears designed to incite and channel attributive outrage at the industry's conduct. Featuring such slogans as "Chemicals in cigarette smoke are so toxic you couldn't dump them in a landfill" and "Cigarettes kill the equivalent of two jumbo jets crashing every day," the Massachusetts campaign appeals to the same affective response system in viewers that the industry has long targeted. Rather than idyllic images of Western landscapes and attractive models, however, the campaign features close-up photos of smoke-damaged skin and cancerous lungs. A companion Web site (at http://www.getoutraged.com) further develops this theme by providing links to some of the industry documents that have been unearthed through litigation. Included are such ominous industry snippets as "Goal—Determine the minimum level of nicotine that will allow continued smoking" and "Long after the adolescent preoccupation with self-image has subsided, the cigarette will pre-empt even food in time of scarcity on the smoker's priority list."

The California Department of Health Services has also been a forerunner in the development of sophisticated antitobacco marketing campaigns. Since 1991, for instance, it has funded "Tobacco*Free Challenge Racing," a program that sponsors race cars and conducts educational events at car races (Weinreich, Abbot, & Olson, 1999). Tobacco manufacturers have long used motorsport sponsorship as a key promotional device, funneling some $300 million per year into the automobile racing industry. Although manufacturers publicly claim that such efforts are intended to attract brand switchers, more likely purposes include the following: (a) seeking to connect tobacco products in the minds of consumers with the healthy lifestyle associated with sports; (b) appealing to sports participants and spectators, who are often risk and adventure seekers, characteristics common to tobacco users; and (c) aiming to associate cigarettes with the general positive affect that viewers feel toward sporting events like car races (Duffy, 1996). "Tobacco*Free Challenge Racing" responds to such efforts by competing directly with sponsoring tobacco companies. The advantage of this tactic is that the California Department of Health Services reaches an audience that might not otherwise receive the antitobacco message. Racetrack fans are 30% more likely to smoke than the average Californian, perhaps because they are less likely to receive smoking prevention and cessation messages in their workplaces and schools (Weinreich et al., 1999). Through race and driver sponsorship, however, the California campaign has produced some encouraging results. For instance, the number of children ages 7 to 12 who believe that "few" race car drivers use tobacco has risen from 17% to 41% during the life of the campaign (Weinreich et al., 1999).

"Get Outraged" and "Tobacco*Free Challenge Racing" are representative examples of public health campaigns that actively seek to influence social norms rather than just provide health-related information. Because they are more directly responsive to the practice of market manipulation by tobacco manufacturers, these campaigns are more likely to achieve the desired end of curtailing youth smoking. In essence, the campaigns themselves are a form of market manipulation that mirrors much of the industry's preference-shaping conduct, the only differences being that these campaigns are motivated by public health, not profit, and they are designed to reduce, not raise, cigarette consumption.

Given the potential positive influence of antitobacco social marketing campaigns, some policy steps could be taken to institutionalize their presence in all states. Rather than leaving campaigns to rely on funds from one-time industry settlements with individual states, as many currently must, a social marketing tax might be instituted to expand the campaigns and to make them self-perpetuating. An excise tax could be levied on each package of cigarettes that directly funds the provision of government counterprogramming against industry preference manipulation. The scheme could be designed to be at least partially performance based. That is, a portion of the compensation awarded to marketing firms could be based on the measured effectiveness of their campaigns. At the very least, such a policy would help to level the playing field between the government and the tobacco industry in their ongoing battle for adolescent mindshare. With cigarette firms currently spending $6 billion per year on advertising and promotion expenditures (Hanson & Kysar, 1999a, p. 1480), it seems that a great deal of leveling is needed.

Summary

Because it is subtle and slippery, market manipulation does not admit of an easy policy solution. Nevertheless, the institution of some mechanism to internalize product costs—enterprise liability and smoker's compensation being two strong candidates—constitutes a promising means of reducing the effectiveness of tobacco industry manipulation of smoker risk perceptions. Similarly, the problem of industry preference manipulation might be at least partially addressed through the elimination of the tax deduction for tobacco advertising and promotion. This "sand-in-the-wheels" approach could be well buttressed by the institution of a social marketing tax on cigarettes that would be used to fund countermanipulative public health campaigns and to discourage preference manipulation, particularly of young consumers.

These specific policies should be considered part of a more general effort to raise awareness of the problem of market manipulation, among both policy makers and the public. It is difficult to deny the market's ability to produce and allocate goods efficiently on massive scale. However, our awe at this ability may sometimes cause us to overlook less desirable aspects of the market system. Put differently, the fact that all manner of fresh fruits and vegetables can be purchased year-round at extremely low prices truly is a marvel. The fact that 3,000 children are convinced every day to purchase and ignite a combination of chemicals that may well addict them, enfeeble them, and ultimately kill them is a tragedy. And it remains a tragedy even if it is accomplished "efficiently."

∽ Conclusion

In his role as a consumer information expert for the tobacco industry, Viscusi has displayed a remarkable degree of confidence in his studies. In sworn testimony, he has said the following: "I know of no studies other than my own that have ever done this in a valid manner" (1997b, p. 213); "Nobody else in the literature that's published has asked the questions in a meaningful way" (1997a, pp. 140-141); and "The value I would place on anybody else's studies . . . would be zilch because I already have the studies that have nailed down this effect" (1997a, p. 141). Even before the publication of this book, those statements were misguided. For years, a large and dedicated group of physicians, psychologists, decision theorists, and public health researchers, including some of the contributors to this book, have been studying smoker perceptions and producing results squarely at variance with Viscusi's, through survey techniques far more sensitive to the insights of behavioralism than were the industry-sponsored surveys on which Viscusi relies.

To be fair, it is entirely possible that Viscusi simply overlooked those studies, given his preference for efficiency-oriented scholarship. Still, his assertions strike us as a bit immodest. After all, the tobacco industry seems not to have relied upon Viscusi or his ilk when devising and implementing its marketing strategies. Instead, it has turned to behavioralists, marketing experts, and public relations experts to explain, predict, and alter consumer behavior. The surveys that Viscusi was provided to analyze—surveys that Viscusi concludes help demonstrate, among other things, why people smoke—were commissioned not by the industry itself, but by the industry's lawyers purely for purposes of "proving" to juries, courts, and regulators that there is no cause for concern. We know of no evidence to suggest that the industry's marketers were at all interested in those surveys, or surveys like them, much less that they scrutinized the surveys to help learn more about consumer motivations and the like. In short, the decision-making model that Viscusi assumes explains consumer behavior and the evidence that Viscusi claims is so illuminating appear to be of no interest to the groups who truly have a financial incentive to understand consumer behavior. Given his faith in markets, it is perplexing that Viscusi has nowhere taken *that* market evidence more seriously.

The fact that Viscusi believes that studies contradicting his own either do not exist or do not threaten the conclusions that he draws from the industry-sponsored surveys merely reflects the fact that Viscusi is, after all, human. He is subject to the same cognitive biases that plague us all, including the tendency to be overconfident in one's conclusions. Nevertheless, Viscusi is defending a position about which, it seems to us, the risk of overconfidence may be especially dangerous. The problem of youth smoking is a significant one, and it appears to be only getting worse. The number of adolescents who become daily smokers before the age of 18 increased by 73% from 1988 (708,000) to 1996 (1.226 million)—rising from nearly 2,000 to more than 3,000 persons under the age of 18 years who become daily smokers each day ("Incidence," 1998). That increase in youth smoking is attributable in significant part to the manipulative conduct of cigarette manufacturers, conduct that is not adequately addressed by either Viscusi's model of smoker risk perceptions or the government's current approach to tobacco regulation. Until policy analysts and policy makers take seriously the problem of market manipulation, tobacco manufacturers will continue to manipulate around, through, and in spite of legal regulation, leading many more consumers, especially young ones, to make the risky and, for them, wrong decision.

∾ Notes

1. For interested readers, some of the same territory covered in this book and in this chapter is also covered, although in different ways, in our previous articles on market manipulation (see Hanson & Kysar, 1999a, 1999b).

2. Legal scholars studying the intersection of cognitive psychology and economics have adopted the term *behavioralism* to describe their project (see, e.g., Jolls, Sunstein, & Thaler, 1998). This terminology has caused some confusion due to the fact that cognitive psychology itself emerged largely as a critical response to behavioral psychology. Nevertheless, we use the terminology in this chapter to indicate clearly the legal literature to which we are indebted.

3. Readers interested in a more complete and detailed review of the relevant literature may wish to see Hanson and Kysar (1999a), portions of which we summarize here.

4. The evidence that we highlight in this subsection to indicate how tobacco manufacturers manipulate consumers as faulty scientists could as easily be offered below to indicate how manufacturers manipulate consumers as socially constrained politicians. Both the faulty scientist and the socially constrained politician actively seek reasons to justify their preferred behavior. By providing such reasons, therefore, manufacturers serve both. More generally, much of the evidence provided in each of the subsections in this part of the chapter could as easily have been placed in one or more of the other subsections. Our goal is simply to provide a suggestive sample of the many ways in which tobacco manufacturers have attempted to influence consumer conduct by tapping into numerous sources of consumer manipulability.

5. Of course, a chemical addiction (or any form of addiction) to a product would seem to intensify these biases (and all forms of motivated reasoning). Thus a goal of manufacturers would no doubt be to addict consumers as soon as possible and keep them addicted as long as possible. There is some evidence indicating that tobacco manufacturers were explicitly pursuing these goals. For instance, Teague, in his memo attempting to shed light on the "factors influencing pre-smokers to try smoking, learn to smoke and become confirmed smokers," wrote the following: "For the pre-smoker and 'learner' the physical effects of smoking are largely unknown, unneeded, or actually quite unpleasant or awkward. The expected or derived psychological effects are largely responsible for influencing the pre-smoker to try smoking, and provide sufficient motivation during the 'learning' period to keep the 'learner' going, despite the physical unpleasantness and awkwardness of the period.

"In contrast, once the 'learning' period is over, the physical effects become of overriding importance and desirability to the confirmed smoker, and the psychological effects, except the tension-relieving effect, largely wane in importance or disappear" (R. J. Reynolds, 1973).

6. For a more complete discussion of these efforts and affect generally, see Slovic's contribution to this volume in Chapter 6.

7. For a fuller treatment of this subject, see Hanson and Reyes (1999).

8. For the past half century, as already described, the industry and its spokespersons have denied that smoking is injurious or have argued that there remains considerable scientific controversy regarding the harmful effects of smoking. Despite overwhelming evidence to the contrary, the industry has relinquished those positions only reluctantly and only very recently. Even in 1998, Philip Morris CEO Geoffrey Bible testified under oath at the Minnesota trial that, as to whether smoking causes disease, "I just don't know. It may, but I don't know" (p. 5738).

9. Although tobacco manufacturers have very recently begun to temper this position, as late as 1994 Philip Morris issued a press release containing the following unequivocal language: "Fact: Philip Morris does not believe cigarette smoking is addictive."

10. A segment aired on ABC World News Tonight (Harris, 2001) reported that Philip Morris spent $115 million on charity in year 2000 and spent $150 million on TV ads publicizing its good deeds.

11. For expanded versions of some of the arguments made in this section, see Hanson and Kysar (2000).

Tobacco and
Public Health Policy

A Youth-Centered Approach

Richard J. Bonnie

I n 1994, the U.S. surgeon general issued an important report titled *Preventing Tobacco Use Among Young People* (Centers for Disease Control and Prevention, 1994a) that summarized current scientific knowledge on smoking initiation and the efficacy of preventive interventions. Building on this foundation, an Institute of Medicine (IOM) report published the same year, *Growing Up Tobacco Free* (Lynch & Bonnie, 1994), made a strong case for a youth-centered strategy for preventing tobacco-related disease and death and developed a substantial body of recommendations to implement this approach. In August 1996, the U.S. Food and Drug Administration published regulations effectuating many of the recommendations proposed in the IOM report, including restrictions on the sale of tobacco products to young people and restrictions on advertising and promotion.

As a member of the IOM committee and one of the primary authors of the 1994 report, I supported the FDA's regulatory initiative. However, as the report itself indicates, there was much reason for skepticism about the validity of the FDA's creative assertion of jurisdiction over conventional tobacco products in light of the

AUTHOR'S NOTE: An earlier and substantially different version of this chapter appeared in *Growing Up Tobacco Free: Preventing Nicotine Addiction in Children and Youths,* edited by B. S. Lynch and R. J. Bonnie. Copyright © 1994 by National Academy Press, Washington, DC.

agency's long-settled position of declining to assert jurisdiction and a 30-year history of congressional action and inaction reflecting that understanding (Lynch & Bonnie, 1994, p. 235). I was therefore not surprised when the U.S. Supreme Court invalidated the agency's action, leaving further regulatory judgments in the hands of the Congress and state legislatures. Although the master settlement of the states' Medicaid lawsuits includes a variety of provisions aimed at reducing youth smoking, many of the proposals included in the IOM report remain unimplemented.

In this chapter, I make the case for the youth-centered strategy of prevention embraced by the IOM report and by the FDA's aborted regulatory effort. Building on the portion of *Growing Up Tobacco Free* that articulates the basic rationale for this approach, I then go on to summarize the available evidence regarding the effectiveness of these policies.

∾ The Case for a Youth-Centered Tobacco Control Policy

Use of tobacco products is the nation's deadliest addiction. Smoking cigarettes is the leading cause of avoidable death in the United States. More than 430,000 people die prematurely each year from diseases attributable to tobacco use, representing more than 5 million years of potential life lost ("Cigarette Smoking-Attributable Mortality," 1993). The toll of deaths attributable to tobacco use is greater than the combined toll of deaths from AIDS, car accidents, alcohol abuse, suicides, homicides, fires, and use of illegal drugs (Lynch & Bonnie, 1994). Smoking is the main cause of 87% of deaths from lung cancer, 30% of all cancer deaths, 82% of deaths from pulmonary disease, and 21% of deaths from chronic heart disease (Centers for Disease Control, 1989). Use of smokeless tobacco is a cause of oral cancer (National Cancer Institute, 1992). In a study of women who did not smoke but did use snuff chronically, the risk for oral cancers was found to be 50 times greater than the risk for nonusers (Winn et al., 1981).

The nation has a compelling interest in reducing the social burden of tobacco use. We can accomplish this by preventing people from starting to use tobacco and by getting users to quit. The premise of the IOM report, which is developed in this chapter, is that, in the long run, the prevalence and social costs of tobacco use can be reduced most efficiently and substantially through the adoption of a youth-centered policy aimed at preventing children and adolescents from initiating tobacco use. Moreover, because the prevalence of tobacco use among young people has remained stubbornly fixed for more than 15 years and has been rising in recent years, a youth-centered prevention policy must be aggressively imple-mented if tobacco-related morbidity and mortality are to be significantly reduced. This is not to say that other avenues of tobacco control should be de-emphasized or abandoned; helping addicted users to quit and otherwise reducing the harm from tobacco use are important elements of a comprehensive public health policy. However, in the long run, the social toll of tobacco addiction will remain unac-ceptably high unless young people are diverted from the pathway to addiction.

Tobacco Use and Addiction Begin During Childhood and Adolescence

In 1988, the U.S. surgeon general issued a major report demonstrating that cig-arettes and other forms of tobacco are addicting, that most tobacco users use to-bacco regularly because they are addicted to nicotine, and that most tobacco users find it difficult to quit because they are addicted to nicotine (Centers for Disease Control, 1988). Tobacco use is not a choice like jogging or a habit like eating choc-olate; it is an addiction fueled by nicotine.

Most smokers begin smoking during childhood or adolescence, and nicotine addiction begins during the first few years of tobacco use. Moreover, decades of experience in tracking tobacco use show that if people do not begin to use tobacco as youngsters, they are highly unlikely to initiate use as adults. For any cross sec-tion of adults who smoke daily, 89% began using cigarettes and 71% began smok-ing daily by or at age 18 (Centers for Disease Control, 1994a). In short, decisions that young people make about whether to use tobacco have lifelong conse-quences. On the one hand, if a person reaches the age of 18 without being a user of tobacco products, he or she is highly unlikely to become a tobacco user during adulthood. On the other hand, most children and adolescents who do initiate reg-ular tobacco use become addicted; their addiction persists for many years thereaf-ter, perhaps throughout their lives. This is why a youth-oriented prevention policy should be at the center of any coherent strategy for countering tobacco-related disease and death.

Tobacco Use by Children and Youth Remains Persistently High

Since 1964, when the surgeon general called the nation's attention to the health hazards of cigarettes, the prevalence of smoking has declined substan-tially—from approximately 45% of the adult population in 1963 to 25% in 1997

("Cigarette Smoking," 1999). Among adults, the number of former smokers (43 million) now nearly equals the number of current smokers (46 million). In fact, among men alive today, more are former smokers than current smokers ("Cigarette Smoking," 1993). Adult per capita consumption fell from 4,286 in 1963, the highest level ever attained in the United States, to 2,287 in 1998 (Federal Trade Commission, 2000).

Despite these impressive successes, the nation's progress toward eliminating tobacco-related disease is in jeopardy. The estimated prevalence of smoking among adults appears to have leveled off in 1990 at around 25%. The use of smokeless tobacco, especially snuff, continues to increase, having tripled between 1972 and 1991. The estimated prevalence of use of smokeless tobacco by adults was 2.9% in 1991—5.6% among men and 0.6% among women. Among 18- to 24-year-old men, the rate was 8.2% ("Use of Smokeless Tobacco," 1993). As a result of these recent trends, the nation fell far short of two key Healthy People 2000 objectives—a 15% prevalence of regular smoking among adults and a reduction of smokeless tobacco use by males ages 12-24 to a prevalence of no more than 4% (U.S. Department of Health and Human Services, 1991, pp. 140, 147). Unless these current trends are reversed, the nation will fail to achieve these objectives in 2010 and certainly will not meet the new objectives of reducing the prevalence of any type of tobacco use among adults to 13% (Mendez & Warner, 2000).

Why has the momentum toward reducing tobacco use been stalled? The answer lies in the replenishment of the tobacco-using population with new recruits. Despite the marked decline in adult smoking prevalence and the intensifying social disapproval of smoking, it has been estimated that 3,000 young people become regular smokers every day (Pierce, Fiore, Novotny, Hatziandreu, & Davis, 1989). In 1996, more than 1.8 million people became daily smokers, two-thirds of them (1.2 million) under age 18 ("Response to Increases," 1998). According to data from the University of Michigan's Monitoring the Future Study (Johnston, O'Malley, & Bachman, 1999a), in 1999, 34.6% of the nation's high school seniors were current smokers (that is, they smoked within the past 30 days) and 23.1% smoked daily. Among 8th-grade students, 17.5% were current smokers and 8.1% smoked daily. The number of cigarettes consumed annually by about 3 million children and adolescents in the United States has been estimated conservatively at 516 million packs (Cummings, Pechacek, & Shopland, 1994). The National Youth Tobacco Survey (NYTS), a new youth tobacco survey initiated in 1999 by the American Legacy Foundation, found that the prevalence of current cigarette use (within past 30 days) was 28.4% among high school students (grades 9-12) and 9.2% among middle school students ("Tobacco Use," 2000).

According to the Monitoring the Future Study's data, 8.4% of high school seniors in 1999 were using smokeless tobacco (Johnston et al., 1999a). The NYTS data for 1999 indicate that 6.6% of high school students and 2.7% of middle school students were using smokeless tobacco ("Tobacco Use," 2000). It has been estimated that children and adolescents consume 26 million containers of smokeless tobacco annually (DiFranza & Tye, 1990).

Current use of cigars and novel tobacco products such as bidis and kreteks represent emerging public health problems among U.S. youth. The NYTS survey shows that in 1999, 15.3% of high school students and 6.1% of middle school students had used cigars within the past 30 days ("Tobacco Use," 2000). The 30-day prevalence of use of bidis and kreteks was 5% and 5.8%, respectively, among high school students, and about 2% among middle school students. Overall prevalence of any kind of tobacco use was 34.8% among high school students and 12.8% among middle school students.

The prevalence of all forms of tobacco use by young people, including smoking, has been basically flat since about 1980 and has actually increased in recent years. According to data from the Monitoring the Future Study, among high school seniors, the prevalence of regular smokers (i.e., those who have smoked in the past 30 days) was 30.5% in 1980 and 34.6% in 1999; the prevalence of daily smokers was 21.3% in 1980 and 23.1% in 1999. Small increases and decreases occurred in the rates over the years, but no one was prepared for the substantial increase that occurred in the early 1990s before the figures leveled off (Johnston et al., 1999a). Although little use of smokeless tobacco was seen among adolescents before 1970, the prevalence of its use among older teens (16-19 years old) increased nearly tenfold between 1970 and 1985 (Marcus, Crane, Shopland, & Lynn, 1989) and appears overall to have remained constant since then (Johnston et al., 1999a).

A recent study of adolescent smoking initiation rates from 1940 to 1992 basically tells the same story that can be inferred from the point prevalence trends. Using data from the tobacco use supplement of the U.S. Census's Current Population Survey, Anderson and Burns (2000) showed that initiation rates among male adolescents (12-17) declined between 1945 and 1982 but have increased since 1983. Among females, initiation rates have increased since 1940, catching up with rates for males by the mid-1970s before leveling off. As these trends clearly show, the forces that have been reducing tobacco use by adults—especially getting adults to quit—have not been as effective in reducing the onset of tobacco use among children and adolescents.

Beneath these aggregate prevalence figures lies an intriguing reminder of the ethnic diversity of American society. Since 1980, while daily smoking prevalence has increased markedly among non-Hispanic white high school seniors (from 22% in 1980 to 28.3% in 1998), there has been a dramatic decline in daily smoking among African American seniors (16% in 1980 to 7.4% in 1998; Johnston, O'Malley, & Bachman, 1999b). (The rates for Hispanics are intermediate between these two.) In their study of adolescent smoking initiation rates from 1940 to 1992, Anderson and Burns (2000) showed that initiation rates among non-Hispanic whites have been higher than those for Hispanic and African Americans through-out this period, but that the trends were basically the same (and the curves were parallel) for all three groups until the late 1970s, when the initiation rates for His-panics and African Americans dropped significantly in comparison with those for non-Hispanic whites. Specifically, the initiation rate for non-Hispanic white males has increased since 1978, whereas the rates for Hispanic and African Amer-ican males have continued the 50-year decline. Among females, the initiation rates among African Americans declined during the 1980s, and the rates for His-panics and non-Hispanic whites leveled off.

Public health officials remain uncertain about the reasons for these divergent trends among ethnic subgroups of American youth, and many are hopeful that a tobacco-free norm has taken root among African American young people. The key question is whether this trend will be sustained in the African American pop-ulation. Unfortunately, it appears that these trends will not be sustained, at least among males. Prevalence of smoking among African American males doubled between 1991 and 1999—although it still remains below the rate for other high school students. The NYTS data for 1999 indicate that current smoking preva-lence among middle school black students was about the same as that among white and Hispanic students ("Tobacco Use," 2000).

Aggressive Measures Are Needed

There seems to be general agreement among public health officials that ag-gressive measures will be needed to make a substantial and enduring reduction in the prevalence of tobacco use by America's children and adolescents. Indeed, public health officials are worried that the incidence of youthful consumption will continue to rise unless decisive steps are taken. These concerns are rooted in the economics of the tobacco market. Because of the overall decline in adult con-sumption since 1964, the tobacco companies have been competing for shares of a shrinking market. Declining demand has led to the introduction of generic brands, discount pricing, and other forms of price competition. It has also led to remarkable increases in expenditures for advertising and promotion. Collectively, the tobacco industry spent more than $6.73 billion in 1998 to advertise and pro-mote tobacco products, a 19% increase over 1997 expenditures (Federal Trade Commission, 2000). The population of the United States is exposed to a massive array of protobacco messages every day. Inevitably, these messages "promote" to-bacco use to children and adolescents as well as adults, and to impressionable nonusers of tobacco products as well as users.

Many public health officials and observers are convinced, despite industry claims to the contrary, that the tobacco companies have purposely targeted their promotional activities at young people. The well-rehearsed industry position is that all of this promotional activity is designed to promote brand loyalty and to encourage switching among smokers, not to increase demand by recruiting new smokers or discouraging current smokers from quitting. In a recent analysis of corporate documents produced through discovery in Canadian litigation, Richard Pollay (2000) has convincingly shown that these assertions are contradicted by advertising campaigns targeting "starters" and "concerned smokers." Whatever the intentions of the tobacco companies, however, the ubiquitous display of messages promoting tobacco use, making it seem attractive and associated with independence and personal well-being, clearly fosters an environment in which experimentation by adolescents is expected, if not implicitly encouraged.

An accumulating body of empirical research supports the hypothesis that exposure to advertising and other promotional activities is associated with positive attitudes toward smoking, susceptibility to smoking, and smoking initiation. Although most of the studies are cross-sectional or correlational, two recent longitudinal studies have provided support for a causal link. Pierce, Choi, Gilpin, Farkas, and Berry (1998) found that receptivity to cigarette promotional activity among California adolescents was associated 3 years later with progression along a 4-point smoking initiation continuum. Biener and Siegel (2000) found that Massachusetts adolescents who in 1993 owned a tobacco promotional item and named a brand whose advertisements attracted their attention were more than twice as likely to become smokers 4 years later than adolescents who did neither. Although the empirical evidence is mixed (Chaloupka & Warner, 2000), the weight of this still-developing body of research points to a link between adolescent initiation of tobacco use and promotional activity by tobacco companies. It seems likely that pervasive tobacco marketing for decades, and particularly the large increase in promotional expenditures in recent years, has helped to maintain a constant—and even rising—rate of initiation for the past 20 years and that little progress will be achieved in reversing this pattern as long as these activities remain unabated.

In sum, two trends have raised widespread concern among public health officials regarding the present status of tobacco control efforts. First, the prevalence of smoking and smokeless tobacco use by young people has remained stubbornly high at the same time the prevalence of tobacco use by adults has declined. Second, aggressive marketing by the tobacco companies has increased the volume of protobacco messages at the same time that public health advances seem to have slowed or even come to a halt. These combined concerns have led many public health experts, including the IOM committee and many national health organizations, to conclude that the top strategic priority should be to prevent children and adolescents from using tobacco products and becoming dependent on them. A vigorous effort to prevent initiation of tobacco use by young people must be a core component, if not the centerpiece, of the nation's tobacco control policy and should be among its highest public health priorities. This is not to say that preventing youth initiation should be the exclusive focus of tobacco policy. Helping adults quit, protecting nonsmokers from environmental tobacco smoke, and other measures to reduce tobacco-related harm are clearly essential elements of a comprehensive policy. However, the IOM and many public health leaders have concluded that a youth-centered policy is politically prudent and ethically compelling.

❧ Public Support for a Youth-Centered Tobacco Control Policy

A youth-centered tobacco control strategy has broad public support. In a national survey of adults in 1993—well before the FDA's initiative, the states' Medicaid lawsuits, and the attendant disclosure of the incriminating industry documents—a majority (73%) favored an increase in the tax on cigarettes as a measure to help finance health care reform. Those who were opposed to the tax on cigarettes were asked how their support would change if the money were to be used for various other purposes. A majority of that group (73%) said that they would be more likely to support a tax if the money were used to *discourage smoking among young people.* Of the entire population surveyed, 62% believed that increasing the cigarette tax would discourage young people from starting to smoke, and 76% favored restrictions on cigarette advertising that appeals to children (Gallup Organization, 1993, pp. 3, 10). Another 1993 poll, of U.S. voters, found that the most popular restriction on the sales of tobacco products would be a ban on cigarette vending machines: 73% (including 66% of all smokers) said they favored banning cigarette machines "in order to make it more difficult for kids to obtain cigarettes" (Marttila & Kiley, 1993, p. 26). Two-thirds of the voters surveyed favored banning smoking in all public places, such as restaurants, stores, and government buildings—policies that would promote a tobacco-free social norm for young people. About two-thirds of the voters surveyed agreed with the assertion that tobacco companies "do everything they can to get teenagers and young people to take up smoking." In a third poll of smokers, 70% were concerned that their children would eventually start smoking because the children see them smoking, 93% agreed that more should be done to educate kids about the dangers of cigarettes, and only 17% believed that tobacco manufacturers should be allowed to advertise their products to high school students or to children (7%) (Gallup Organization, 1993, p. 17).

More recent results from the second Annenberg Tobacco Survey also support the claim that a youth-centered tobacco control strategy has broad public support, even among young people. Most adults over age 22 (84%) disagreed with the statement "If teenagers want to smoke, they should be able to because it is their personal choice." A majority of young people ages 14 to 22 (56%) also disagreed with the statement. When asked whether "teenagers should be able to buy cigarettes if they want to," more than 90% of the adults and nearly 80% of the young people surveyed disagreed. In addition, more than 80% of both adults and young people agreed that "advertising to discourage people from smoking is a good idea." This Annenberg survey also asked smokers whether they agreed that they "should have the right to smoke in public places." Despite the self-interest that smokers would be expected to display, more than a third of both adult and young smokers disagreed with this statement.

Growing public support for youth-centered tobacco control measures is also reflected in the activity of local advocacy coalitions and in grassroots political action. Hundreds of localities have enacted local ordinances banning vending machines, establishing smoke-free environments in public places, and otherwise promoting a tobacco-free norm (National Cancer Institute, 1993). Unfortunately, strong grassroots support for tobacco control policies at the local level has too often been neutralized through powerful lobbying by the tobacco industry at the state level, resulting in weak state legislation that preempts more restrictive local measures. Legislative initiatives at local and state levels relating to advertising and promotion have also been stymied by a preemptive provision of federal law that precludes "any requirement or prohibition based on smoking and health." As discussed below, this preemption must be repealed before state and local governments will be able to implement youth-centered tobacco control initiatives and thereby carry out the public will.

∞ Ethical Foundation of a Youth-Centered Tobacco Control Policy

A youth-centered tobacco control policy has a firm ethical foundation. American society ordinarily values and respects the prerogative of adults to decide how to live their own lives as long as they do not endanger anyone else. Adults, if adequately informed, are assumed to be capable of making rational and voluntary choices that involve weighing the risks and benefits of particular behaviors in light of their own preferences and values. The applicability of the rational choice model to tobacco use has been a subject of ongoing controversy in the literature of applied ethics (Goodin, 1989; Rabin & Sugarman, 1993). Although some writers have accepted the possibility that adequately informed adults can make a rational and voluntary choice to use tobacco, thus taking the risk of becoming addicted (e.g., Feinberg, 1986, pp. 128-134; Viscusi, 1992b), others have pointed out that the onset of addiction compromises the voluntariness of subsequent choices, even by adults (e.g., Goodin, 1989; Schelling, 1992). As a practical matter, however, arguments about the rationality of choices by adults to initiate tobacco use are beside the point, because at least 70% of adult daily smokers had already become daily smokers, and presumably had already become addicted, by the time they were 18 years old. Thus the critical issue is whether children and adolescents are in a position to make informed and rational choices about whether to become tobacco users.

No one suggests that preteens have the necessary abilities to make rational choices about tobacco use, yet a significant proportion of adult smokers began using tobacco before they became teenagers. Monitoring the Future data indicate that in 1999, 44% of 8th graders had tried smoking, 8.6% were daily smokers, and 3.3% were already smoking at least half a pack a day.

Some researchers have suggested that adequately informed adolescents (over age 13) exhibit cognitive decision-making skills similar to those used by young adults (through age 25) (Office of Technology Assessment, 1991; Quadrel, Fischhoff, & Davis, 1993). Others have claimed that adolescents are well-informed about some specific health risks of tobacco use and may actually overestimate the various risks (Viscusi, 1992b). Slovic (1998, 2000b) and others have contested these claims. Even if these controversial assertions are accepted, however, they do not show that adolescents are in a position to make sound, "rational," self-interested choices about tobacco use. It is also necessary to take into account other faulty beliefs held by adolescents regarding the consequences of tobacco use and developmentally linked deficiencies in maturity of judgment (Scott, Reppucci, & Woolard, 1995; Steinberg & Cauffman, 1996), including adolescents' tendency to evaluate and weigh risks and benefits within a shortened time frame.

Adolescents' decisions to engage in risky behaviors, including tobacco use, reflect a distinctive focus on short-term benefits and accompanying tendencies to discount long-term risks or dangers and to believe that those risks can be controlled by personal choice. Decision-making deficiencies exhibited by children and adolescents who choose to use tobacco are most evident when the perceptions and reasoning of these young people are compared with the perceptions and reasoning of their peers who choose not to use tobacco. Clearly, those who choose to use tobacco perceive greater benefits relative to risks than do those who choose not to do so (Benthin, Slovic, & Severson, 1993; Eiser, 1983). What is most striking, however, is the nature of the trade-off.

When children and adolescents begin to use tobacco, they tend to do so for transient reasons closely linked to specific stages in their development—to assert independence and achieve perceived adult status, for example, or to establish bonds with peers who use tobacco. Young people who smoke or intend to smoke tend to be heavily influenced by their perception of potential *social* benefits and risks of doing so. Compared with nonsmokers and young people who do not intend to smoke, smokers and likely smokers also tend to exaggerate the social benefits (by overestimating the prevalence and popularity of smoking among peers and adults) and to underestimate the social risks (by underestimating the prevalence of negative attitudes toward smoking held by their peers) (Leventhal, Glynn, & Fleming, 1987).

The evidence also shows that adolescents who have begun to smoke tend to ignore or discount long-term health risks. The issue is not one of general knowledge. Adolescent smokers seem to be aware of the link between tobacco use and various diseases, but data consistently show that young smokers, compared with nonsmokers, systematically give less weight to the long-term risks. Indeed, established smokers report that they did not actually think about the health risks when they decided to become smokers (Slovic, Chapter 6, this volume), tending to confirm (through recollection) what the etiological literature on adolescent smoking shows—that the perceived psychosocial benefits provide the major impetus for smoking, and that the health risks—although recognized—do not weigh very heavily in the decision. Another way of describing this phenomenon is to say that the perceived social attractions of smoking (probably reinforced by the lifestyle messages embedded in tobacco advertising) establish a positive attitude (affect) toward the behavior that tends, in turn, to diminish the salience of the risks, reflecting an inverse and reciprocal relationship between perceived benefit and perceived risk (Alhakami & Slovic, 1994; Finucane, Alhakami, Slovic, & Johnson, 2000).

Adolescents' decision making is plagued especially by their difficulty in envisioning long-term consequences and appreciating the personal relevance of those consequences (recognizing that "this *could* happen to me"). Abundant evidence demonstrates that young people who begin to use tobacco do not understand the nature of addiction and, as a result, believe that they will be able to avoid the harmful consequences of tobacco use. They recognize, cognitively, that a lifetime of smoking is dangerous, but they also tend to believe that smoking for a few years will *not* be harmful, a belief that is less common among nonsmokers (Slovic, 1998, 2000a). Among 12- to 18-year-olds in the 1989 Teenage Attitudes and Practices Survey, 21% of smokers (compared with 3% of those who never smoked) said they believed that it is safe to smoke for only a year or two (Allen, Moss, Giovino, Shopland, & Pierce, 1993). Giving up smoking after a few years certainly is less risky than smoking for a lifetime, but smoking for a few years significantly increases the risk that one will end up smoking for a lifetime. The key is that many young people who smoke do not expect to smoke over a lifetime and, in fact, expect to smoke only for a few years. They believe, in short, that they can escape the harmful consequences of an admittedly risky practice. What they do not appreciate, of course, is the grip of nicotine addiction.

Adolescents' failure to appreciate the long-term consequences of decisions to smoke is explicitly revealed by a longitudinal track of the University of Michigan's Monitoring the Future Study. As high school seniors, the subjects were asked, "Do you think you will be smoking cigarettes 5 years from now?" As Neil Benowitz summarizes in Chapter 8 of this volume, 85% of respondents who were occasional smokers (less than one cigarette per day) predicted that they probably or definitely would *not* be smoking in 5 years, as did 60% of those who smoked one to five cigarettes per day and 32% of those who smoked one pack per day. However, at follow-up 5-6 years later, of those who had smoked one pack per day as seniors, only 13% had quit, and 69% still smoked one pack or more per day. Of those who smoked one to five cigarettes per day as seniors, only 30% had quit, and 44% had increased their consumption. Even among those who had been only occasional smokers (less than one cigarette per day), only 58% had quit and 37% had actually increased their cigarette consumption (Centers for Disease Control and Prevention, 1994a; Johnston, O'Malley, & Bachman, 1994a).

If a young person decides to begin smoking at the age of 12 or 13, the deficit in his or her ability to appreciate the long-term risks of doing so is even more pronounced and disturbing than it is at 16 or 17. Indeed, it is clear that the grip of nicotine addiction is most powerful and most enduring for those who begin smoking at the youngest ages. Unfortunately, the age of onset of tobacco use has decreased significantly over the past 20 years, especially for girls (Centers for Disease Control and Prevention, 1994a).

Most young people regret their choices to start smoking and report difficulty quitting *even during adolescence.* The 1989 Teenage Attitudes and Practices Survey data show that 74% of 12- to 18-year-old smokers reported that they had seriously thought about quitting, 64% had tried to quit, and 49% had tried to quit in the previous 6 months (Allen et al., 1993). Among high school seniors (1985-1989), of those who had smoked at all in the past 30 days, 43% reported a desire to stop smoking. Of this group and of the subgroup who smoked daily, 28% and 39%, respectively, stated that they had tried unsuccessfully to stop (Centers for Disease Control and Prevention, 1994a). In the 1991 Youth Risk and Behavior Survey of more than 12,000 adolescents in grades 9-12, a majority of self-reported smokers (54% of boys and 62% of girls) reported that they had tried to quit smoking in the previous 6 months (Centers for Disease Control and Prevention, 1994b). Annenberg's national telephone survey in 1999-2000 found that, among the 478 smokers in the youth sample, 84% said that they planned to quit within a year and 93% predicted that they would succeed (see Jamieson & Romer, Chapter 2, this volume). Optimism about quitting was expressed even by 80% of the young respondents who had already been smoking for more than 5 years. Most telling was the response of all smokers to the "regret" question: "If you had it to do over again, would you start smoking?" More than 85% of adult smokers and 80% of youth smokers answered no.

In sum, when children and adolescents begin to use tobacco, they are putting their health at risk without considering or giving any significant weight to the long-term consequences of their actions. They simply do not appreciate the personal relevance of the long-term statistical risks of multiple diseases, and they suffer from a profound inability to understand the powerful grip of nicotine addiction. These deficiencies of risk perception (and the tendency also to exaggerate the perceived social benefits of using tobacco) justify concerted social action to prevent children and adolescents from starting to use tobacco in the first place.

⟶ Elements of a Youth-Centered Tobacco Control Policy

The traditional focus of primary prevention in tobacco policy has been school-based instruction. Such programs play an important role, especially if they are part of broader, communitywide initiatives. However, model tobacco prevention programs have not been widely disseminated or adopted and, as a result, most school-based instruction appears to have only modest impact (Lynch & Bonnie, 1994). Experts in the field generally agree that these programs cannot be expected to have an impact commensurate with the scope of the problem. More aggressive measures are needed to counteract the social forces that continue to induce a quarter of the nation's young people to use tobacco products.

A successful strategy for preventing nicotine dependence in children and adolescents must encompass measures for reducing the accessibility of tobacco products to young people and for increasing their cost, for strengthening the social factors that tend to discourage consumption, and for erasing or mitigating social factors that tend to encourage consumption. Such measures typically require legislative or regulatory action. Reports issued by the IOM and the National Cancer

Policy Board in 1994, 1998, and 2000 have summarized what is known about the potential utility of various preventive measures, offering specific recommendations for action grounded in existing knowledge.

During the course of their studies, the IOM committees and boards have reviewed a wide range of activities: federal efforts, state government programs, the actions of advocacy and health professional organizations, and policies of several foreign nations where tobacco control has been pursued successfully. *Growing Up Tobacco Free* addresses research and policy questions surrounding the addictive process, the setting of social norms concerning tobacco use, preventive and cessation interventions, the advertising and promotion of tobacco products as well as their pricing and taxation, the reduction of youth access to tobacco products, and the regulation of tobacco products.

During its deliberations, the IOM committee assessed a variety of possible recommendations in terms of extent of potential impact, practicality of implementation, and likelihood of adoption. Model programs in Canada, Australia, New Zealand, California, and Massachusetts have implemented multiple program and policy components at the same time, rendering analysis of the impacts of specific measures methodologically difficult. However, the composite effects have been substantial, and there is strong reason to believe that a multipronged attack is far more likely to produce results than any single measure taken alone. The National Cancer Policy Board's 2000 report, *State Programs Can Reduce Tobacco Use,* reviews the evidence concerning the impact of multipronged state interventions and concludes that these programs are effective in reducing tobacco use among both adults and young people.

Growing Up Tobacco Free concludes that several measures should be the subjects of immediate attention at the state, federal, and local levels of government and in the private sector, and that several other major initiatives will be required to sustain long-term progress. Despite all the public debate, legislation, and litigation that has occurred over the years since that report was published, these basic conclusions still seem warranted.

Actions That Should Be Taken Immediately

In *Growing Up Tobacco Free,* the IOM identifies three priorities for immediate action, with a particular focus on the Congress: (a) raising the price of tobacco products, with a target increase of $2.00 per pack; (b) repealing the federal preemption of state and local regulation of advertising and promotion; and (c) building the capacity of states to implement comprehensive tobacco control programs (Lynch & Bonnie, 1994). Although the report does not identify enforcing youth access restrictions as a priority, I include it here, not because cutting off supply is a promising strategy for curbing youthful tobacco use, but because reversing the traditional practice of lax enforcement is an essential element of a comprehensive plan, and it is a step that is relatively easy to take.

Raising the Price

In *Growing Up Tobacco Free*, the IOM urges Congress to "enact substantial increases in the federal tax on tobacco products to increase their price and to raise revenues for tobacco control, health care, and other uses" (Lynch & Bonnie, 1994, p. 17). The report emphasizes the federal tax in order to set a floor across the country and to prevent the cross-state smuggling that typically accompanies substantial disparities in state excise taxes. Subsequent National Cancer Policy Board (1998, 2000) reports have taken note of the improbability of significant federal action and have correspondingly emphasized the importance of increasing state excise taxes.

The weight of the evidence indicates that children and adolescents are more price sensitive than adults, and that a significant price increase has a strong and immediate impact on overall sales of tobacco products. Whereas a 10% increase in the price would reduce adult consumption by about 4%, economists believe that such an increase would reduce smoking among young people by about twice as much. Increasing the price would reduce the amount of smoking by adolescent users, promote cessation, and, according to the predominant view, reduce the number of new tobacco users (Warner et al., 1995). The IOM (Lynch & Bonnie, 1994) and the National Cancer Policy Board (1998) recommend that the price of tobacco products be raised to a level comparable with that in other major industrialized countries and suggest that a reasonable target would be to increase the price of cigarettes (largely through federal and state excise taxes) by $2.00 per pack, with proportional increases for smokeless tobacco products.

Wholesale prices have increased an average of 65 cents per pack since the master settlement agreement was signed in 1998, the federal excise tax was raised to 24 cents per pack in 1997 (with a phased-in 15-cent increase), and six states now have excise taxes of more than 75 cents per pack. Even the high-tax states, however, remain far below the recommended $2.00 target, and 20 states have excise taxes below 20 cents per pack (National Cancer Policy Board, 2000).

Repealing Federal Preemption

Growing Up Tobacco Free urges Congress "to repeal the federal law that precludes state and local governments from regulating tobacco promotion and advertising occurring entirely within the state's borders" (Lynch & Bonnie, 1994,

p. 17). The National Cancer Policy Board reiterates this recommendation in *Taking Action to Reduce Tobacco Use* (1998).

Many states and local governments have signaled a willingness to experiment with stronger measures to control the messages projected about tobacco use, particularly those to which children and adolescents are exposed. California, Massachusetts, and Maryland, for example, have strong antitobacco media programs in place. Yet, currently, state and local governments are impeded by federal law from regulating promotion and advertising of tobacco products in various visual media, including billboards, and at the point of sale. Federal preemption of this nature limits the ability of local communities to effectuate the public will and to restrict the protobacco messages to which young people are regularly exposed. As a result, the effectiveness of public education and public health efforts in reducing tobacco use is also limited.

Although the multistate settlement agreement between the state attorneys general and the tobacco industry bans billboards altogether (see National Association of Attorneys General, 1998), point-of-sale advertising is unaffected, and the definition of billboards leaves some gaps in the prohibition. The states ought to be free to complete the job.

Building State Capacity for Tobacco Control

Growing Up Tobacco Free urges Congress "to increase the capacity of state and local governments and coalitions of interested organizations to pursue youth-centered tobacco control policies" (Lynch & Bonnie, 1994, p. 17) and *Taking Action to Reduce Tobacco Use* reiterates that "the federal government must support state and local infrastructure for tobacco control" (National Cancer Policy Board, 1998, p. 10). Although there is a continuing need for federal guidance and financial support for state capacity building, increases in state excise taxes and the master settlement have made additional revenues available and have shifted the focus of attention to state legislatures. Settlements of the state Medicaid suits in Florida, Minnesota, Mississippi, and Texas resulted in industry payments to those states, and the master settlement will establish revenue streams for the remaining states. Overall, these agreements could transfer as much as $246 billion to the states over the next 25 years.

For the past decade, most of the major initiatives on tobacco control have taken place in states and in local communities. California, Massachusetts, and Michigan, for example, have increased tobacco taxes, dedicating a fraction of the revenues to tobacco control, and have implemented targeted programs that provide promising models for other states. Many local governments have established innovative programs to enforce youth access laws that have become models for other states and localities. The National Cancer Institute cultivated state initiatives in the 17 states participating in its pioneering American Stop Smoking Intervention Study (ASSIST). The Centers for Disease Control and Prevention has initiated programs in the non-ASSIST states, although funding for individual states under this program (IMPACT) is very low. In addition, the Robert Wood Johnson Foundation is collaborating with the American Medical Association to mount the Smokeless States program. In 1999, the Centers for Disease Control and Prevention issued guidelines for best practices for funding and implementing comprehensive tobacco control programs. Even as the states allocate their own funds for tobacco control, the federal government must provide technical assistance, grants, and cooperative agreements to enable all interested states, local governments, and community coalitions to undertake comprehensive tobacco control programs and to implement them effectively.

In *State Programs Can Reduce Tobacco Use,* the third in a series of periodic reports on tobacco, the National Cancer Policy Board (2000) addresses the effectiveness of state tobacco control initiatives and concludes that these programs have been effective in reducing tobacco use. Reducing youth smoking is a key measure of effectiveness of these programs, even though they also aim to promote cessation and reduce smoking among adults. In a review and synthesis of data bearing on the effects of programs in California, Massachusetts, Arizona, Oregon, and Florida, Wakefield and Chaloupka (2000) have found evidence that these programs have affected teenage smoking. For example, although Massachusetts adolescents had a higher smoking prevalence than those in the rest of the country before the start of the tobacco control program, the gap narrowed over the first 3 years of implementation, and smoking prevalence among high school students did not grow as much as it did elsewhere in the country. Siegel and Biener (2000) conducted a longitudinal survey of 592 Massachusetts respondents ages 12 to 15 at baseline in 1993 and examined the effects of exposure to antismoking messages. They found that the television component of the Massachusetts media campaign may have reduced the rate of progression to established smoking among young adolescents.

Improving Enforcement
of Youth Access Restrictions

One of the essential components of a youth-centered strategy, and of a comprehensive state tobacco control program, is a meaningful effort to enforce restrictions on youth access to tobacco. It has long been illegal—in every state—to sell tobacco products to minors, but until recently, enforcement was virtually nonexistent. In 1992, Congress included a provision in the Substance Abuse and Mental Health Services Administration (SAMHSA) reauthorization bill (the Synar Amendment) that ties federal block grant moneys to improved compliance with state laws proscribing such sales. States risk reduced payments from SAMHSA if they fail to meet compliance targets. The federal government has not yet withheld state funds based on the Synar Amendment, but such action is under consideration for several states that have not met Synar targets. A federal ban on youth sales, with mandatory ID-card inspection of those 26 and younger, was the central thrust of the 1996 FDA tobacco regulation eventually struck down by the U.S. Supreme Court in May 2000. The effect of the Court's decision was to return full responsibility for promulgating and enforcing youth access bans to the states.

With federal encouragement, assistance, and financial support, many states have beefed up their enforcement of these laws, including licensing systems for vendors, bans on vending machines, and many other components recommended in *Growing Up Tobacco Free* and included in the FDA's Tobacco Rule. As a result, compliance with the law has increased considerably in some jurisdictions (DiFranza, 1999), although enforcement remains lax and merchant compliance remains low (in relation to the Synar targets) in many states (DiFranza & Rigotti, 1999).

A key question raised by the Synar Amendment and the emphasis on enforcing youth access restrictions is whether increased enforcement can achieve a meaningful reduction in access, and, if so, whether reduced access will lead to reduced consumption. Will, for example, fewer children and adolescents experiment with tobacco products and become dependent on them? Even if underage access to tobacco products in commercial channels is significantly reduced, to what extent will underage consumers still be able to obtain tobacco products through other channels, from, for example, older consumers or a "gray" market?

Some studies suggest that making it more difficult for minors to purchase tobacco may substantially reduce consumption. In Woodridge, Illinois, 2 years after the passage of successfully enforced youth access legislation, the number of seventh- and eighth-grade students surveyed who reported having experimented with cigarettes had decreased from 46% to 23%. The number of students surveyed who described themselves as smokers had decreased from 16% to 5%. These effects persisted after 5 years (Jason, Katz, Vavra, Schnop-Wyatt, & Talbot, 1999). In Leominster, Massachusetts, after active law enforcement of local age restrictions on tobacco sales, the number of students who identified themselves as smokers decreased from 22.8% at pretest to 15.8% at posttest 2 years later. It is not known whether these effects have persisted.

Despite these apparent successes, caution about the potential effects of limiting access is warranted. Other studies have failed to find effects on consumption, but they have also found that vendor compliance was low (Rigotti et al., 1997; Stead & Lancaster, 2000). Enforcement of youth access laws can be expected to have a significant direct effect on consumption only if, as in Woodridge and

Leominster, the commercial accessibility of tobacco to minors is significantly reduced (DiFranza, 2000). Furthermore, the reductions in consumption witnessed in Woodridge and Leominster followed enforcement efforts of an intensity that may be impossible to achieve in urban settings. The public health experience with restrictions on youth access to alcohol has had mixed results. Progress has been made, especially in reducing traffic fatalities, but alcohol remains widely available to underage young people, both through commercial sources and through parents, siblings, and friends. Data from the University of Michigan's Monitoring the Future Study for 1999 show that 74% of 8th graders and 89% of 10th graders said that alcohol is fairly easy or very easy to get.

Critics of a youth-centered strategy have argued that an excessive focus or exclusive reliance on youth access restrictions can siphon resources and political will away from more powerful tobacco control measures (Glantz, 1996). I agree that an exclusive focus on youth access restrictions is a mistake. Enforcement of youth access restrictions is difficult and is unlikely to have a major impact on youth smoking if it is the main element of local tobacco control. However, failure to enforce these laws in a meaningful manner could undermine whatever other steps are taken to establish a tobacco-free norm.

In the long run, the real public health benefit of a reinvigorated youth access policy lies not in its direct effect on consumer choices but in its declarative effects—that is, in the capacity of such a policy to symbolize and reinforce an emerging social norm that disapproves of tobacco use. Legal restrictions often have important educative effects and thereby help to shape attitudes and beliefs. They do this best when they are congruent with an emergent social norm accompanied by a strong social consensus, precisely the conditions that now exist in the context of tobacco control. The level of public support for youth access restrictions is high among young people as well as adults and among smokers as well as nonsmokers. This tobacco-free norm can be fostered through carefully coordinated, multidimensional programs as part of an integrated approach, both legal and nonlegal. Conversely, overt failure to implement youth access restrictions actually undermines the tobacco-free norm; an unenforced restriction is probably worse than no restriction at all. Unenforced laws convey the message that the intent is not to be taken seriously and thereby undermine school and community attempts to educate youth regarding the serious health consequences of tobacco use. In the context of the emerging norm, contradictory messages should no longer be tolerated. Coupled with advertising images that convey the message that tobacco use is desirable, unenforced restrictions on sales to minors contribute to the web of psychosocial influences that lead children to begin using these products. The message should be strong and unequivocal that tobacco use is unhealthful and socially disapproved. Youth access laws are an essential part of that message.

Actions Required to Sustain
Progress in the Long Term

Growing Up Tobacco Free characterizes the priorities for immediate action listed above as first steps in a long-term strategy for preventing nicotine dependence in children and adolescents and thereby reducing the adverse health consequences of tobacco use. The report identifies four key components of such a strategy: (a) federal regulation of tobacco products, (b) restriction of tobacco advertising and promotion, (c) promotion of a tobacco-free norm, and (d) monitoring of, and research on, policy effectiveness.

Regulation of Tobacco Products

Tobacco products have been consistently exempted from coverage under consumer safety, food, and drug legislation, and as a result have been largely unregulated. This lack of regulation stands in stark contrast to other products that have far less disastrous long-term health implications than the use of tobacco products. In *Growing Up Tobacco Free,* the IOM recommends that the U.S. Congress enact a comprehensive regulatory statute delegating to an appropriate agency "the necessary authority to regulate tobacco products, for the dual purpose of discouraging consumption and reducing the morbidity and mortality associated with use of tobacco products" (Lynch & Bonnie, 1994). The report recommends that this agency be authorized to regulate the design and constituents of tobacco products—as well as their labeling and packaging—emphasizing the ways in which these interventions could be expected to discourage youth smoking. The report specifically discusses the concept of plain packaging as well as the possibility of setting and gradually reducing ceilings on the nicotine content of tobacco products.

A year after the release of the IOM report, the FDA formally proposed to regulate tobacco products using its existing authority under the Food, Drug, and Cosmetics Act. The FDA's Tobacco Rule regulated the advertising and marketing of tobacco products and the distribution of these products to minors, but did not address the design and constituents of tobacco products. If the Supreme Court had upheld the FDA's assertion of jurisdiction over tobacco products, the agency would have had broad authority to move beyond the current rule to regulate the design and content of tobacco products as well.

Now that the U.S. Supreme Court has ruled that the FDA does not have jurisdiction over conventional tobacco products, Congress must fill the regulatory gap by enacting a specific regulatory statute for tobacco products, as recommended in the 1994 IOM report. Congress and the executive branch should take the necessary steps to ensure that possible strategies for regulating the design and constituents of tobacco products are given careful and systematic study. The FDA's authority must be broad enough—and its budget large enough—to allow the agency to protect the public health on the basis of scientific knowledge as that knowledge accumulates. An adequate scientific foundation already exists for some regulatory initiatives. Studies clearly indicate, for example, that smokers adapt to cigarettes labeled and machine tested as low in nicotine by inhaling more often or more deeply. Informational requirements regarding tar and nicotine yields could be changed in light of actual human exposures from tobacco products (e.g., cigarette labeling that takes account of smoking behavior and not just machine-determined yields). On some issues, such as nicotine reduction, regulation must await new research or access to the results of studies now available only to private tobacco firms. In other areas, new information should be available in the coming years. Proposals for harm reduction through modified tobacco products and other forms of long-term nicotine maintenance will require further research, but these modified tobacco products are already being introduced into the marketplace. It is imperative that Congress establish a suitable framework for regulating these novel products that purport to reduce the risks of smoking, and particularly for policing the health claims that are made in promoting them, whether express or implied.

Restriction of Advertising and Promotion

Children and adolescents believe that adults and even their peers smoke and use tobacco products far more than they actually do. Ubiquitous messages that associate tobacco use with images of youthfulness, athletic prowess, and sexuality reinforce a social norm that encourages tobacco use. Once initiated on a regular basis, tobacco use becomes further reinforced by the physiological and psychological processes of nicotine addiction. The protobacco messages in advertising and promotion are particularly difficult to combat among children and adolescents. *Growing Up Tobacco Free* therefore concludes that advertising and promotion of tobacco products should be severely curtailed and recommends that advertising be restricted to text-only formats and that various forms of promotional activities attractive to young people be banned.

Although the FDA's proposed Tobacco Rule tracked these recommendations very closely, these portions of the rule never went into effect because the federal district court held that the FDA lacked statutory authority to regulate advertising and marketing of conventional tobacco products. Fortunately, the master settlement agreement bans the use of cartoon characters in magazine advertising, the use of brand names on merchandise (such as T-shirts and hats), product sampling, product placement in movies and other media, and sponsorship of team sports; it also limits other forms of brand-name sponsorship to one per year. Federal regulation is still needed, however, because print advertising remains substantially unrestricted, even in media targeted to youth, and other gaps remain as well in the billboard restriction and at the point of sale. Perhaps the most important part of the master settlement is a provision for the creation of a foundation (the American Legacy Foundation) responsible for developing a strong anti-tobacco campaign. Together, comprehensive restrictions on advertising and promotion by the tobacco companies (as envisioned by the detailed recommendations set forth in *Growing Up Tobacco Free*) and a well-funded counteradvertising effort might fundamentally reshape the messages about tobacco to which young Americans are exposed.

Promotion of a Tobacco-Free Norm

Growing Up Tobacco Free urges governments and voluntary organizations at all levels to sustain and reinforce the continued evolution of a tobacco-free norm in American society. Only a few decades ago, smoking was the social norm; now it is approaching a status of social deviance. The continued evolution of a tobacco-free norm is the core component of a long-term strategy for reducing the prevalence of tobacco use among children and adolescents. Legal tools have been used successfully to undergird and reinforce the emerging tobacco-free norm by banning smoking in places of public accommodation (public buildings, restaurants, and so on) and enabling private organizations to do the same. Public smoking bans also protect the health of nonsmokers, including children, by reducing their exposure to environmental tobacco smoke. It is therefore important for governments and private organizations to implement smoke-free policies in schools, workplaces, fast-food restaurants, and all other places where children and adolescents spend their time. As mentioned earlier, meaningful enforcement of youth access restrictions is an essential component of the effort to nurture and sustain a tobacco-free norm.

Monitoring and Research

The recommendations in *Growing Up Tobacco Free* (Lynch & Bonnie, 1994) and in subsequent reports by the National Cancer Policy Board (1998, 2000) set forth a blueprint for preventing youth initiation as part of a comprehensive tobacco control program. These recommendations are based on the knowledge at hand. Research to improve prevention and cessation interventions can help improve those efforts over time. Understanding the reasons for the remarkable decline in smoking prevalence among African American young people, particularly girls, is a major research priority. A better understanding of the molecular and cellular corre-lates of nicotine addiction and the factors that mediate the adverse health effects of tobacco use can also provide helpful clues to guide future efforts. Moreover, im-proving smoking cessation treatments to help the 49 million Americans who smoke will benefit the smokers and foster knowledge about nicotine addiction as well.

For purposes of the topic discussed in this chapter, however, data and research are most needed to monitor the effects of policy interventions. Some of the data most useful to the IOM committee came from studies of tobacco control policy, such as epidemiological studies and risk-factor analyses that monitor the effects of policy change. For example, decisions about which policies are most likely to succeed were aided by assessments of the large-scale programs undertaken in Canada and California, measurements of the effects in local jurisdictions where youth access laws have been rigorously enforced, and studies describing the polit-ical influences that shape tobacco policy. The state of California and the Robert Wood Johnson Foundation have been leaders in promoting such policy research; they have been joined recently by the National Cancer Institute.

∞ Conclusion

Arguments concerning a youth-centered approach to tobacco control have domi-nated political debates about tobacco policy in the United States since 1994, spurred in part by the IOM report *Growing Up Tobacco Free.* Unfortunately, all the talk has produced too little effective action, especially at the federal level, and in the meantime, tobacco use among young people has both increased and diversi-fied. Both ethically and politically, a youth-centered approach is a sound strategy for achieving comprehensive regulatory action in the Congress and in state legis-latures. Being convinced of the powerful case for a youth-centered approach, I want to take note of the criticisms that have been levied against such an approach, both by the tobacco control community and by critics holding a libertarian per-spective.

Many tobacco control leaders have been severely critical of the youth-centered approach. I was particularly taken aback by a statement attributed to Richard Peto, a revered figure in tobacco epidemiology. In an August 2000 press briefing, at the time of the release of results of a long-term study of smoking and lung cancer that demonstrated that quitting significantly reduces the risk of cancer in a more or less linear fashion tied to age at time of quitting, Peto said: "This idea that adults can't stop, that all you can do is prevent young people from starting smoking is just really wrong. That is one of the great strategic mistakes in tobacco control, I think" (quoted in Brown, 2000, p. A3). As I have noted a number of times above, strong steps to prevent initiation are not meant to be taken in lieu of actions aimed at helping people to quit or reduce the harm from tobacco use. We ought to try to find effective measures to help people quit. However, I think Peto is mistaken when he says that a youth-centered approach has been a strategic mistake. Quite the contrary—strong regulatory measures will not be embraced, in the face of deeply rooted libertarian traditions, unless they are tied persuasively to a youth-centered argument. Tobacco control has many important domains, many of which are not coercive. However, the paternalistic features of tobacco control rest most securely on a platform of reducing initiation among children and adolescents who lack sufficient maturity to make rational judgments in their own long-term interests.

Not surprisingly, the strong regulatory interventions described above—and justified on a youth-centered basis—have been criticized from the other direction because they unduly interfere with the liberty of adults. During the course of its deliberations, the IOM committee was mindful that many youth-centered policy recommendations will also tend to reduce tobacco use by adults. From an ethical standpoint, it is important to emphasize that coercive or restrictive measures to suppress smoking by adults are more controversial than equivalent measures taken to prevent initiation by young people. At the same time, however, otherwise justified youth-centered interventions (or measures taken to protect nonsmokers from environmental tobacco smoke, for that matter) should not be weakened simply because they will make tobacco use more costly or inconvenient for adults. After all, the ultimate public health goal of tobacco control policy is to reduce the health toll associated with tobacco use, and the government is fully justified in taking noncoercive measures to discourage tobacco use by adults and encouraging them to quit. From this perspective, the relationship between a youth-centered prevention strategy and a broader tobacco control policy is a reciprocal one. On the one hand, reducing the onset of tobacco use among young people is an essential element of a successful strategy of long-term tobacco control. On the other hand, successful tobacco control initiatives aimed at adults in the society as a whole—such as the widespread adoption of tobacco-free policies, establishing a normative climate unfavorable to smoking—play an important role in preventing nicotine addiction among young people. In both respects, a successful youth-centered prevention policy is an integral and indispensable feature of a comprehensive tobacco control agenda.

Appendix A

Survey 1: Youth Perception of Tobacco Risk, Summer 1999

Selection Interview

Hello, my name is _____, calling for Princeton Survey Research. We are conducting a national opinion survey about some important health care issues. May I please speak with an adult age 18 or older who lives in this household?

N1.   First, in order to be sure we are representing the opinions of people in different kinds of households, could you please tell me how many people age 45 or older currently live in this household?

   [Record number: 0-98]
   99   (Refused)

N2.   How many people between the ages of 23 and 44 now live in this household?

   [Record number: 0-98]
   99   (Refused)

N3.   How many people between the ages of 14 and 22 now live in this household?

   [Record number: 0-98; **terminate if 0**]
   99   (Refused) **[Terminate]**

N4.   ([**If N3 > 1:**] Which of these people age 14 to 22 had the most recent birthday?) Is this person a male or female?

    1   Male
    2   Female
    9   (Refused) **[Terminate]**

N5.   How old is this person?

    [Record number: 14-22]
    98 (Other) **[Terminate]**
    99 (Refused) **[Terminate]**

Ask N6-N7 if selected child is 14-15 [N5 = 14-15]:

N6.   May I please speak with the parent or legal guardian of this (**Insert age [from N5]**)-year-old ([**N4 = 1:**] boy | [**N4 = 2:**] girl)?

    1   Yes
    2   No **[Terminate]**

N7.   We are conducting this study for a large university interested in health care issues facing young people today. This survey is completely confidential. We would like to interview your (**Insert age**)-year-old (son | daughter). Would it be possible to talk with (him | her) now for a short interview?

    1   Yes
    2   No **[Terminate]**

Ask N8 if selected child is 16-22 [N5 = 16-22]:

N8.   May I please speak with this (**Insert age**)-year-old (male | female)?

    1   Yes
    2   No [Terminate]

[Ask all:]

(If new respondent:) Hello, my name is _____, calling for Princeton Survey Research. We are conducting a national opinion survey about some important health care issues. This survey is completely confidential.

N9.   Just to confirm, what is your age?

           [Record number: 14-22]

                    14-15
                    16-17
                    18-20
                    21-22
           98   (Other) **[Terminate]**
           99   (Refused) **[Terminate]**

N9A.   As I mentioned before, your responses to this survey will be kept
           completely confidential. Have you ever smoked a cigarette, even
           one or two puffs?

           1   Yes
           2   No
           9   (Refused) **[Terminate]**

N10.   During the past 30 days, have you smoked any cigarettes?

           1   Yes **[Select Smoker]**
           2   No **[Select Nonsmoker]**
           9   (Refused) **[Terminate]**

Main Interview

D1.   Respondent's sex:

           1   Male
           2   Female

D2.   On another subject, are you currently in school?

           1   Yes
           2   No
           9   (Refused)

Ask D3 if currently in school [D2 = 1]:

D3.   What grade or level of school are you in? (Do not read responses)

           1   Grade 8 or lower
           2   High school freshman

3   High school sophomore
4   High school junior
5   High school senior
6   Technical or vocational school after high school
7   Junior college
8   Four-year college
9   Graduate or professional school
99 (Refused)

Ask D4 if not currently in school [D2 = 2-9]:

D4.   What is the last grade or level of school you completed?
        (Do not read responses)

        1   Grade 8 or lower
        2   High school freshman
        3   High school sophomore
        4   High school junior
        5   High school senior
        6   Technical or vocational school after high school
        7   Junior college
        8   Four-year college
        9   Graduate or professional school
        99 (Refused)

[Ask all:]

Q1.   Now I would like you to think about people who smoke cigarettes.
        Out of every 100 cigarette smokers, how many do you think will
        (Insert)?

        [Randomize items:]

        a.   get lung cancer because they smoke
        b.   have heart problems, like a heart attack, because they smoke
        c.   die from a smoking-related illness

        [Record number: 0-100]

        998   (Don't know)
        999   (Refused)

Q2.   I just asked you about smokers. Now I would like you to think about nonsmokers. Out of every 100 nonsmokers, how many do you think will get lung cancer?

[Record number: 0-100]

998   (Don't know)
999   (Refused)

Q3.   Some people say that cigarette smoking (Insert). Have you heard this?

a.   will most likely shorten a person's life
b.   is dangerous to a person's health
c.   is bad for a person's health but not dangerous
d.   is not bad for a person's health
e.   makes it easier for some people your age to keep their weight down makes it easier for some people your age to relax and have a good time with friends

1   Yes
2   No
8   (Don't know)
9   (Refused)

Q4.   In your opinion, is (Insert) very risky for a person's health, somewhat risky, only a little risky or not at all risky?

a.   smoking
b.   smoking every day
c.   smoking only once in a while, say at parties or with friends

1   Very risky
2   Somewhat risky
3   A little risky
4   Not at all risky
8   (Don't know)
9   (Refused)

Q5.   Please tell me how much you agree or disagree with the following statements. Here is the (first | next) statement: (Insert) Do you strongly agree, somewhat agree, somewhat disagree or strongly disagree?

[Randomize items:]

a. If someone wants to smoke, they should be able to because it is their personal choice.
b. The harmful effects of cigarettes have been exaggerated.

1 Strongly agree
2 Somewhat agree
3 Somewhat disagree
4 Strongly disagree
8 (Don't know)
9 (Refused)

Q6. In your opinion, is it true or false that smoking two or more packs of cigarettes a week (Insert), or don't you know enough to say?

[Randomize items:]

a. will most likely shorten a person's life
b. increases a person's chances of getting lung cancer

1 True
2 False
8 (Don't know)
9 (Refused)

[Randomize Q7-Q8:]
Ask Q7 if think smoking increases lung cancer risk [Q6b = 1]:

Q7. On average, how much does smoking two or more packs a week increase a person's chances of getting lung cancer? Would you say smokers are about twice as likely to get lung cancer, five times as likely, 10 to 20 times or 50 times as likely?

1 Twice
2 Five times
3 10 to 20 times[1]
4 50 times
8 (Don't know)
9 (Refused)

Ask Q8 if think smoking shortens life expectancy [Q6a = 1]:

Q8.　　On average, by how many years does smoking two or more packs a week shorten a person's life? Would you say a few months, one year, five to 10 years or 20 years?

    1　Few months
    2　One year
    3　Five to 10 years[2]
    4　20 years
    8　(Don't know)
    9　(Refused)

[Ask all:]

Q9.　　For each of the following statements, please tell me if you think it is true or false or if you don't know enough to say.

[Randomize items:]

    a.　Women who smoke while pregnant increase the chances their baby will be born with health problems.[3]
    b.　Each year thousands of nonsmokers die from breathing other people's smoke.[4]
    c.　Each year more people die from gunshots and car accidents than die from smoking.[5]

    1　True
    2　False
    8　(Don't know)
    9　(Refused)

Q10.　　On another subject, would you say (Insert) is very risky for a person's health, somewhat risky, only a little risky or not risky at all?

[Randomize items:]

    a.　getting drunk regularly
    b.　smoking marijuana regularly

    1　Very risky
    2　Somewhat risky
    3　A little risky
    4　Not at all risky
    8　(Don't know)
    9　(Refused)

[No Q11]

Q12.   Which of these two statements comes closer to what you think?
         You can just tell me the letter of the statement. (Read responses 1-2:)

    1   A—People your age who smoke can damage their lungs by
         smoking for just a few years.[6]
    2   B—People your age cannot damage their lungs from smoking
         because you have to smoke for many years for that to happen.
    8   (Don't know)
    9   (Refused)

Q13.   For each of the following statements, please tell me if you think it is
         true or false or if you don't know enough to say.

    [Randomize items:]

    a.   Smoking makes it harder for people your age to participate in
         athletics.[7]
    b.   Smoking makes it easier for some people your age to keep their
         weight down.
    c.   Smoking makes it easier for some people your age to relax and
         have a good time with friends.

    1   True
    2   False
    8   (Don't know)
    9   (Refused)

Q14.   In your opinion, once someone is smoking two or more packs a
         week, how easy or hard is it for them to quit and never smoke again?
         Is it . . . (Read responses 1-4:)

    1   A—Very easy, and anyone who wants to can
    2   B—Hard, but most people can do it if they really try
    3   C—Very difficult, and most cannot do it
    4   D—Almost impossible, and only a few will be able to do it
    8   (Don't know)
    9   (Refused)

Q15.   In your opinion, is it true or false that a chemical in cigarettes makes smoking addictive, or don't you know enough to say?

    1   True[8]
    2   False
    8   (Don't know)
    9   (Refused)

[No Q16]

Q17.   I would like you to imagine four people your age. Each now smokes two or more packs a week but says they want to quit and will do so sometime in the next five years. Of these four people, how many do you think will actually quit in the next five years?

[Record number: 0-4]

    0   None
    1   1[9]
    2   2
    3   3
    4   All 4
    8   (Don't know)
    9   (Refused)

Q18.   Of all the deaths in one year, do you think more people die from (Insert)?

[Randomize items:]

    a.   A—smoking or from B—not exercising[10]
    b.   A—smoking or B—abusing alcohol and drugs[11]

    1   A
    2   B
    8   (Don't know)
    9   (Refused)

Q18A.   As I read you the names of some movie actors and actresses, tell me if they smoke in their personal lives, do not smoke in their personal lives or if you don't know enough to say.

[Randomize items:]

       a.   Winona Ryder

       b.   Leonardo DiCaprio

       c.   Sylvester Stallone

       1   Smoke

       2   Do not smoke

       3   (Never heard of person)

       8   (Don't know if smoke)

       9   (Refused)

Ask Q19-Q21 if smoked in past month [N10 = 1]:

Q19.   Next I have some questions about you and your behavior. Some people say that by smoking you are increasing the chances you will get lung cancer when you are older. Do you agree or disagree, or don't you know enough to say?

       1   Agree

       2   Disagree

       8   (Don't know)

       9   (Refused)

Q20.   Do you think smoking is very risky for your personal health, somewhat risky, not too risky or not at all risky?

       1   Very risky

       2   Somewhat risky

       3   A little risky

       4   Not at all risky

       8   (Don't know)

       9   (Refused)

Q21.   If you decided you wanted to quit smoking and never start again, how easy or hard do you think it would be for you to do? Would it be . . . (Read responses 1-4:)

       1   A—Very easy

       2   B—Hard, but you could do it if you tried

       3   C—Very difficult, and you might not be able to do it

       4   D—Almost impossible

       8   (Don't know)

       9   (Refused)

[Ask all:]

Q22.   Do your parents or any of the adults you live with smoke?

    1   Yes
    2   No
    8   (Don't know)
    9   (Refused)

Ask Q23 if parents smoke [Q22 = 1]:

Q23.   How would you rate their health? Very good, good, poor or very poor?

    1   Very good
    2   Good
    3   Poor
    4   Very poor
    8   (Don't know)
    9   (Refused)

[Ask all:]

Q24.   Have you ever known someone who (Insert)?

    a.   died of lung cancer or another disease because they smoked
    b.   once smoked but quit and never smoked again

    1   Yes
    2   No
    8   (Don't know)
    9   (Refused)

[No Q25]

Ask Q26-Q26A if smoked in past month [N10 = 1]:

Q26.   How frequently did you smoke cigarettes in the past 30 days? (Read responses 1-5:)

    1   A—Less than one cigarette a day
    2   B—One to five a day
    3   C—A half a pack a day
    4   D—A pack a day
    5   E—More than a pack a day
    9   (Refused)

Q26A.   What brand of cigarettes do you smoke the most? (Do not read responses)

    1 Benson & Hedges
    2 Camel
    3 Kool
    4 Marlboro
    5 Merit
    6 Newport
    7 Salem
    8 Vantage
    9 Winston
    97 (Other) **[Record verbatim]**
    98 (Don't know)
    99 (Refused)

Ask Q27 if did not smoke in past month but have smoked [N10 = 2 and N9A = 1]:

Q27.   Which of the following best describes you? If you want, you can just tell me the letter. (Read responses 1-4:)

    1   A—You tried smoking just once or twice.
    2   B—You smoke occasionally.
    3   C—You smoke regularly, that is, two or more packs a week.
    4   D—You used to smoke two or more packs a week but now smoke less.
    9   (Refused)

Ask Q28 if smoked in past month but less than a half a pack or more a day [Q26 = 1,2,9]:

Q28.   Have you ever smoked two or more packs of cigarettes a week?

    1   Yes
    2   No
    9   (Refused)

Ask Q29-Q33 if smoked in past month [N10 = 1]:

Q29. Do you plan to quit smoking?

  1 Yes/(Already have)
  2 No
  8 (Don't know)
  9 (Refused)

Q30. About how many times, if any, have you quit smoking?

  [Record number: 0-97]

  0   None
  1-2   1-2
  3-5   3-5
  6-10   6-10
  11-97   More than 10
  98   (Don't know)
  99   (Refused)

Q31. How long have you smoked? For a few months or less, for about a year, for a few years or for more than a few years?

  1 Few months or less
  2 A year
  3 Few years
  4 More than a few years
  8 (Don't know)
  9 (Refused)

Q32. Do you consider yourself addicted to cigarettes or not?

  1 Yes
  2 No
  8 (Don't know)
  9 (Refused)

Q33. Which of these statements comes closer to what you think? (Read responses 1-2:)

  1 A—You might have damaged your health by smoking.
  2 B—You have not smoked long enough to do damage to your health.
  8 (Don't know)
  9 (Refused)

[Ask all:]

D5.   I have just a few more questions to help us understand the people who took part in our survey. Are you yourself of Hispanic origin or descent, such as Mexican, Puerto Rican, Cuban or some other Spanish background?

        1   Yes
        2   No
        8   (Don't know)
        9   (Refused)

D6.   What is your race? (**If Hispanic [D5 = 1]:**) Are you white Hispanic, black Hispanic or some other race? (**Else:**) Are you white, black, Asian or some other race?

        1   White
        2   Black
        3   Asian
        4   Other
        8   (Don't know)
        9   (Refused)

That completes our survey. Thank you very much for taking time to answer our questions. We really appreciate your time. Have a nice (day | evening).

ɶ Notes

1. "Men who smoke increase their risk of death from lung cancer by more than 22 times. . . . Women who smoke increase their risk of dying from lung cancer by nearly 12 times" (Centers for Disease Control and Prevention, 1996, citing "Cigarette Smoking-Attributable Mortality," 1993).

2. "On average, smokers die nearly seven years earlier than nonsmokers" (Centers for Disease Control and Prevention, 1996, citing unpublished data from the CDC Office on Smoking and Health, 1994).

3. "Women who use tobacco during pregnancy are more likely to have adverse birth outcomes, including babies with low birth weight, which is linked with an increased risk of infant death" (Centers for Disease Control and Prevention, 2000b).

4. "Annually, exposure to secondhand smoke . . . causes an estimated 3,000 deaths from lung cancer" (Centers for Disease Control and Prevention, 1996, citing U.S. Environmental Protection Agency, 1992).

5. Smoking kills more people each year than gunshots and car accidents combined (McGinnis & Foege, 1993, as cited in Centers for Disease Control and Prevention, 2000b).

6. "Cross-sectional and longitudinal data show that smoking also adversely affects lung function in children and adolescents" (Centers for Disease Control and Prevention, 1994a, p. 17).

7. "Even among young people trained as endurance runners, smoking appears to compromise physical fitness in levels of both performance and endurance" (Centers for Disease Control and Prevention, 1994a, p. 28).

8. "Tobacco-delivered nicotine can be highly addictive. Each year, nearly 20 million people try to quit smoking in the United States, but only about 3 percent have long-term success" (Centers for Disease Control and Prevention, 1994a, p. 31).

9. "Of daily smokers who think that they will not smoke in five years, nearly 75 percent are still smoking five to six years later" (Centers for Disease Control and Prevention, 2000a).

10. Smoking kills more people each year than lack of exercise (McGinnis & Foege, 1993, as cited in Centers for Disease Control and Prevention, 2000b).

11. Smoking kills more people each year than abuse of alcohol and drugs combined (McGinnis & Foege, 1993, as cited in Centers for Disease Control and Prevention, 2000b).

Appendix B

Survey 2: Perception of Tobacco Risk, Fall 1999, Age 14-22 Version

Selection Interview

Hello, my name is _____, calling on behalf of the University of Pennsylvania. We are conducting a national opinion survey about some important health issues. May I please speak with an adult age 18 or older who lives in this household?

N1.   First, in order to be sure we are representing the opinions of people in different kinds of households, could you please tell me how many people age 45 or older currently live in this household?

[Record number: 0-97]

98 (Don't know)
99 (Refused)

N2.   How many people between the ages of 23 and 44 now live in this household?

[Record number: 0-97]

98 (Don't know)
99 (Refused)

N3.   How many people between the ages of 14 and 22 now live in this household?

[Record number: 0-97]

   0 None **[Screen out: QN3: No teens age 14-22]**
98 (Don't know) **[Screen out: QN3: No teens age 14-22]**
99 (Refused) **[Screen out: QN3: No teens age 14-22]**

IF N1 = 1-97 OR N2 = 1-97 CONTINUE INTERVIEW, ELSE THANK & TERMINATE (S/O NO ONE AGE 23+ INHH)

N4.   (**[If (N3 > 0:]** Which of the people age 23 or older had the most recent birthday?) Is this person male or female?

1   Male
2   Female
9   (Refused) **[Refused Information QN4 = Terminate]**

N5.   How old is this person?

14-22   **[Screen out: QN5: Ineligible Age]**
23-97
98   (Don't know) **[DK/Refused Age QN5 = Terminate]**
99   (Refused) **[DK/Refused Age QN5 = Terminate]**

Ask N6-N7 if selected child is 14-15 [N5 = 14-15]:

N6.   May I please speak with the parent or legal guardian of this (**Insert age [from N5]**)-year-old (**[N4 = 1:]** boy | **[N4 = 2:]** girl)?

1   Yes
2   No **[N6 refused—CB for conversion—if refuse again then terminate]**

N7.   We are conducting this study on behalf of the University of Pennsylvania about some important health issues facing young people today. This survey is completely confidential. We would like to interview your (**Insert age**)-year-old (son | daughter). Would it be possible to talk with (him | her) now for a short interview?

1   Yes
2   No **[N7 refused—CB for conversion—if refuse again then terminate]**

Ask N8 if selected child is 16-22 [N5 = 16-22]:

N8.   May I please speak with this (**Insert age**)-year-old (male | female)?

        1   Respondent already on phone [**Continue with N9**]
        2   Respondent coming to phone
        3   Schedule callback
        9   (Refused) [**N8 refused—CB for conversion—if refuse again then terminate**]

[Ask all:]

(If new respondent:) Hello, my name is _____, calling on behalf of the University of Pennsylvania. We are conducting a national opinion survey about some important health issues. This survey is completely confidential.

N9.   Just to confirm, what is your age?

        [Record number:]

14-22   **[Screen out: ineligible age]**

CONTINUE INTERVIEW

98   (Don't know) [**Terminate**]
99   (Refused) [**Terminate**]

Main Interview

D1.   Respondent's sex:

        1   Male
        2   Female

D2.   On another subject, do you currently attend school either part-time or full-time?

        1   Yes
        2   No
        9   (Refused)

Ask D3 if currently attend school [D2 = 1]:

D3.   What grade or level of school are you in? (Do not read responses)

    1   Grade 8 or lower
    2   High school freshman
    3   High school sophomore
    4   High school junior
    5   High school senior
    6   High school degree
    7   One year of technical or vocational school after high school
    8   Two or more years of technical or vocational school after high school
    9   One year of college
    10 Two years of college, no degree
    11 Two years of junior college, associate's degree
    12 Three years of college, no degree
    13 Four-year college degree
    14 Graduate or professional school after college, no degree
    15 Graduate or professional school degree
    98 (Don't know)
    99 (Refused)

Ask D4 if not currently in school [D2 = 2-9]:

D4.   What is the last grade or level of school you completed?
       (Do not read responses)

    1   Grade 8 or lower
    2   High school freshman
    3   High school sophomore
    4   High school junior
    5   High school senior
    6   High school degree
    7   One year of technical or vocational school after high school
    8   Two years of technical or vocational school after high school
    9   One year of college
    10 Two years of college, no degree
    11 Two years of junior college, associate's degree
    12 Three years of college, no degree
    13 Four-year college degree
    14 Graduate or professional school after college, no degree
    15 Graduate or professional school degree
    98 (Don't know)
    99 (Refused)

Now on another topic . . .

[Randomly read-in "smoking" or "cigarette," CATI identify in the data whether "smoking" or "cigarette" was inserted]

QS1.   When you hear the word (smoking | cigarette), what is the first thought or image that comes to mind?

[Record verbatim-coding, do not code this OE]

QS2.   How would you describe this image? Is it something very good, somewhat good, somewhat bad, or very bad?

1   Very good
2   Somewhat good
3   Somewhat bad
4   Very bad
8   (Don't know)
9   (Refused)

QS3.   Next, please try to form an image in your mind of a person smoking a cigarette. Do you have an image of a person smoking? Tell me about this person. Is the person (Insert)?

[Randomize items:]

a.   Alone?
b.   Eating a good meal?
c.   Drinking?
d.   Just finishing something satisfying?
e.   Attractive?
f.   Sick?
g.   Relaxed?
h.   Happy?
i.   Anxious?
j.   Popular?
k.   A celebrity or famous person?

1   Yes
2   No
8   (Don't know)
9   (Refused)

QS4. As I mentioned before, your responses to this survey will be kept completely confidential. Have you ever smoked a cigarette, even one or two puffs?

1 Yes
2 No
8 (Don't know)
9 (Refused)

QS5. Now I want to ask about the last 30 days. In the last 30 days, have you:

a. Smoked cigarettes of any kind? **[Assign to smoking version]**
b. Smoked cigars of any kind?
c. Used chewing tobacco of any kind?

1 Yes
2 No
8 (Don't know)
9 (Refused)

QS6. Have you ever heard of flavored cigarettes called Bidis (Beedeez)?

1 Yes
2 No
8 (Don't know)
9 (Refused)

QS7. **[If yes to QS6:]** Have you ever tried one?

1 Yes
2 No
3 (Don't know)
4 (Refused)

QS8. **[If yes to QS7:]** Have you smoked one in the past 30 days?

1 Yes **[Assign to smoking version]**
2 No
8 (Don't know)
9 (Refused)

QS9.   [If yes to QS7:] How would you compare the experience to smoking regular cigarettes? More enjoyable, less enjoyable or about the same?

    1   More enjoyable
    2   About the same
    3   Less enjoyable
    8   (Don't know)
    9   (Refused)

[Ask QS10 of "smokers" (QS5a = 1 OR QS8 = 1) *or* those who have smoked cigars in past 30 days (QS5b = 1)]

QS10.   Do you consider yourself a smoker?

    1   Yes
    2   No
    8   (Don't know)
    9   (Refused)

QZZ.   DUMMY QUESTION TO CLASSIFY SMOKER/NONSMOKER:

    1   Smoker (QS5a = 1 OR QS8 = 1 OR QS10 = 1)
    2   Nonsmoker (everybody else)

Q1.   To the best of your knowledge, what, if any, are the illnesses caused by smoking cigarettes? (Probe:) Anything else? (Probe until no further ideas come to mind.)

    1   Lung cancer
    2   Emphysema
    3   Heart disease
    4   Stroke
    5   Throat cancer
    6   Mouth cancer
    7   Diabetes
    8   Bronchitis
    93-97   Other (specify)
    98   (Don't know)
    99   (Refused)

Q1A.   Now I would like you to imagine 100 cigarette smokers, both men
and women, who smoked cigarettes for their entire adult lives. How
many of these 100 people do you think will die from lung cancer?

[Record number: 0-100]

998   (Don't know)
999   (Refused)

Q2.   I just asked you about smokers. Now I would like you to imagine
100 *nonsmokers*, both men and women, who never smoked and don't
live with smokers. How many do you think will die from lung
cancer?

[Record number: 0-100]

998   (Don't know)
999   (Refused)

Q3.   Now I would like you to think again about 100 people who smoke
cigarettes for their entire adult lives. All of these smokers will
eventually die of something. Now consider the following 5 possible
causes of death: automobile accidents, heart disease, stroke, lung
cancer, and all other causes combined. Please tell me how many of
the 100 cigarette smokers you think will die from (Insert)? OK.
Now, how many of the (Insert remaining number) smokers will die
from (Insert)? **[Keep a running total to help R get to 100 by
item e.] [For item e:]** OK, you now have (Number remaining)
smokers left. By your estimates, these smokers will die from all other
causes not mentioned already. Is that about right? **[If R wants to
re-estimate earlier numbers, then allow to go back.]**

[Randomize items a through c; always ask d then e last]

a.   automobile accidents
b.   heart disease
c.   stroke
d.   lung cancer
e.   all other causes combined

[Record number: 0-100]

998   (Don't know)
999   (Refused)

Q3A.   In your opinion, [IF SMOKER (QZZ = 1) read "is your smoking,"
        if NONSMOKER (QZZ = 2) read "if you were a smoker, would
        your smoking"] (be) very risky for your health, somewhat risky,
        a little risky or not at all risky for your health?

        1   Very risky
        2   Somewhat risky
        3   A little risky
        4   Not at all risky
        8   (Don't know)
        9   (Refused)

Q4.   In your opinion, would (Insert) be very risky for your health,
        somewhat risky, a little risky or not at all risky for your health?

        a. your smoking every day
        b. your smoking only once in a while, say at parties or with friends

        1   Very risky
        2   Somewhat risky
        3   A little risky
        4   Not at all risky
        8   (Don't know)
        9   (Refused)

[No Q4A-Q4B]

Q4C.   Please imagine how you would feel smoking a cigarette.
        [IF SMOKER (QZZ = 1) read "Does smoking a cigarette,"
        IF NONSMOKER (QZZ = 2) read "If you were to smoke a
        cigarette, would it"] make you feel . . . (Read list)

        1   Very good
        2   Somewhat good
        3   Somewhat bad
        4   Very bad
        8   (Don't know)
        9   (Refused)

Q4D.   How tense or relaxed would smoking a cigarette make you feel . . .
        (Read)

      1 Very tense
      2 Somewhat tense
      3 Neither tense nor relaxed
      4 Somewhat relaxed
      5 Very relaxed
      8 (Don't know)
      9 (Refused)

Q4E.   Thinking about your best friend, does he or she smoke? **[If no best
        friend:]** Then think of the person who you would like to have as a
        best friend.

      1 Yes
      2 No
      3 Can't think of anyone
      8 (Don't know)
      9 (Refused)

Q4F.   Thinking about everyone you have contact with in a typical day, how
        many would you say currently smoke? More than half, between a
        half and a quarter, less than one-quarter or just about no one?

      1 More than half
      2 Between a half and a quarter
      3 Less than one-quarter
      4 Just about no one
      8 (Don't know)
      9 (Refused)

Q4G.   Thinking about your friends and the people you spend time with,
        how many would you say currently smoke? More than half, between
        a half and a quarter, less than one-quarter, or just about no one?

      1 More than half
      2 Between a half and a quarter
      3 Less than one-quarter
      4 Just about no one
      8 (Don't know)
      9 (Refused)

[IF SMOKER (QZZ = 1) read "do," "about your smoking," if NONSMOKER (QZZ = 2) read "would," "if you smoked"]

Q4H.　How (do | would) your friends feel (about your smoking/if you smoked)? (Do | Would) they mostly approve, mostly disapprove, or about the same of both?

　　　1　Mostly approve
　　　2　About the same of both
　　　3　Mostly disapprove
　　　4　(Don't care)
　　　5　(Don't know)
　　　6　(Refused)

Q5.　Imagine someone who starts to smoke a pack of cigarettes a day at age 16. How much do you agree with the following statements about this person? The first one is (Insert). Do you strongly agree, somewhat agree, somewhat disagree, or strongly disagree?

　　[Randomize items:]

　　　1.　There is usually no risk to the person at all for the first few years.
　　　2.　Although smoking may eventually harm this person's health, there is really no harm to him or her from smoking the very next cigarette.
　　　3.　If someone wants to smoke, they should be able to because it is their personal choice.

　　　1　Strongly agree
　　　2　Somewhat agree
　　　3　Somewhat disagree
　　　4　Strongly disagree
　　　8　(Don't know)
　　　9　(Refused)

[Randomize order of Q6-Q7, within Q6 randomly ask Q6-1 or Q6-2, same for Q7, randomly ask Q7-1 or Q7-2]

Q6-1 (Alternative 1).　If you smoked a pack of cigarettes a day, how much do you think it would increase your chances of getting lung cancer? Would you say you would be no more likely to get lung cancer than if you did not smoke at all, twice as likely, five times as likely, 10 to 20 times or 50 times as likely?

1   No more likely
2   Twice as likely
3   Five times
4   Ten to 20 times
5   50 times
8   (Don't know)
9   (Refused)

Q6-2 (Alternative 2). If you smoked a pack of cigarettes a day, how much do you think it would increase your chances of getting lung cancer? Would you say you would be no more likely to get lung cancer than if you did not smoke at all, twice as likely, three times as likely, five times as likely, or 10 or more times as likely?

1   No more likely
2   Twice as likely
3   Three times
4   Five times
5   Ten or more times
8   (Don't know)
9   (Refused)

Q7-1 (Alternative 1). If you smoked a pack of cigarettes a day, how much do you think it would shorten your life? Would you say not at all, by one year, five to 10 years, 15 years, or 20 years or more?

1   Not at all
2   One year
3   Five to 10 years
4   15 years
5   20 years or more
8   (Don't know)
9   (Refused)

Q7-2 (Alternative 2). If you smoked a pack of cigarettes a day, how much do you think it would shorten your life? Would you say not at all, by a few months, by one year, two or three years, or five to 10 years?

1   Not at all
2   A few months
3   One year
4   Two to three years

5   Five to 10 years
8   (Don't know)
9   (Refused)

Q8.   How long, if ever, do you think it takes for smoking to seriously harm the health of a new smoker: A few minutes of smoking, a few weeks of smoking, one year, 5 years, more than 5 years of smoking, or does smoking not affect one's health?

1   Does not affect health
2   A few minutes of smoking
3   A few weeks of smoking
4   One year of smoking
5   Five years of smoking
6   More than five years of smoking
8   (Don't know)
9   (Refused)

Q9.   For each of the following statements, please tell me if you think it is true or false or if you don't know enough to say.

[Randomize items:]

a.   Each year thousands of nonsmokers of all ages die from breathing other people's smoke.
b.   Each year more people of all ages die from gunshots and car accidents than die from smoking.

1   True
2   False
8   (Don't know)
9   (Refused)

Q10.   On another subject, if you (Insert), do you think it would be very risky for your health, somewhat risky, a little risky or not risky at all for your health?

[Randomize items:]

a. got drunk regularly
b. smoked marijuana regularly
c. never wore a seat belt when riding in a car
d. ate a lot of foods that are high in fat

1 Very risky
2 Somewhat risky
3 A little risky
4 Not at all risky
8 (Don't know)
9 (Refused)

[No Q11–Q12]

[IF SMOKER (QZZ = 1) read "makes," if NONSMOKER (QZZ = 2) read "would make"]

Q13. For each of the following statements, please tell me if you think it is true or false or if you don't know enough to say.

[Randomize items:]

a. Smoking (would) make(s) it harder for me to participate in athletics.
b. Smoking (would) make(s) it easier for me to keep my weight down.
c. Smoking (would) make(s) it easier for me to relax and have a good time with friends.

1 True
2 False
8 (Don't know)
9 (Refused)

Q14. In your opinion, if you were to smoke a pack of cigarettes a day, how easy would it be for you to quit and never smoke again?
(Read responses 1–4:)

1 Very easy; you could quit with no trouble
2 Hard, but you could do it if you really tried
3 Very hard, you don't know that you could do it
4 Almost impossible, you doubt that you could do it
8 (Don't know)
9 (Refused)

[No Q15-Q16]

Q17.   I would like you to imagine ten people your age who smoke a pack of cigarettes a day. All ten of these people SAY that they would like to quit in the next five years. How many of them do you think would actually quit permanently in the next five years?

[Record number: 0-10]

98   (Don't know)
99   (Refused)

Q18.   Of all the deaths in one year to people of all ages, do you think more people die from (A) smoking or (B) abusing alcohol and drugs?

1   A—Smoking
2   B—Abusing alcohol and drugs
8   (Don't know)
9   (Refused)

Q18A.   Thinking about a cigarette advertisement you have seen recently, what brand was advertised in the ad?

1   Benson & Hedges
2   Camel
3   Kool
4   Marlboro
5   Merit
6   Newport
7   Salem
8   Vantage
9   Winston
96   (Other) **[Record verbatim]**
97   (VOL) None seen
98   (VOL) Don't know
99   (VOL) Refused

Q18B.   Have you been to a bar, pub or microbrewery in the past six months?

1   Yes
2   No
8   (Don't know)
9   (Refused)

Q18C.   **[If yes to Q18B:]** When you have been to a bar, pub or microbrewery in the past six months, has there been any entertainment sponsored by a cigarette company? **[Note: Entertainment includes bands or acts]**

   1   Yes
   2   No
   8   (Don't know)
   9   (Refused)

Q18D.   For each of the following statements, please tell me if you strongly agree, somewhat agree, somewhat disagree, or strongly disagree.

   [Randomize items:]

   a.   If teenagers want to smoke, they should be able to because it is their personal choice.
   b.   I can control how much of other people's cigarette smoke I am exposed to.
   c.   Teenagers should be able to buy cigarettes if they want to.
   e.   Advertising to discourage people from smoking is a good idea.
   f.   The harmful effects of cigarettes have been exaggerated.

   1   Strongly agree
   2   Somewhat agree
   3   Somewhat disagree
   4   Strongly disagree
   8   (Don't know)
   9   (Refused)

Q18E.   Some groups are running ads telling people why they shouldn't smoke. In the past month, do you remember hearing or seeing many, some or none of these ads?

   1   Many
   2   Some
   3   None
   8   (Don't know)
   9   (Refused)

Ask Q19–Q21 if smoked in past month [QZZ = 1]:

Q19.   When you first started to smoke, how much did you think about (Insert)? Did you think about this a lot, a little, or not at all?

    a.   How smoking might affect your health?
    b.   How smoking might affect the health of others around you?

    1   A lot
    2   A little
    3   Not at all
    8   (Don't know)
    9   (Refused)

[No Q19A-Q19B]

Q19C.   How much do you think about the health effects of smoking now?

    1   A lot
    2   A little
    3   Not at all
    8   (Don't know)
    9   (Refused)

Q19D.   Since you started smoking, have you heard of any health risks of smoking that you didn't know about when you started?

    1   Yes
    2   No
    8   (Don't know)
    9   (Refused)

Q19E.   When you first started smoking, did you think more about how smoking would affect your future health or about how you were trying something new and exciting?

    1   Thought about future health
    2   Thought about trying something new and exciting
    3   Other
    8   (Don't know)
    9   (Refused)

Q19F.   When you first started smoking, how long did you think you would continue to smoke? A few days, a few months, less than a year, one to five years, longer than five years or didn't you think about it?

    1   A few days
    2   A few months
    3   Less than a year
    4   One to five years
    5   Longer than five years
    8   Didn't think about it
    9   (Refused)

Q19G.   If you had it to do over again, would you start smoking?

    1   Yes
    2   No
    8   (Don't know)
    9   (Refused)

Q20.   Compared to the average smoker, do you think you are more likely to get sick from smoking, less likely to get sick from smoking, or that your chance of getting sick from smoking is about the same as the average smoker?

    1   More likely
    2   About the same
    3   Less likely
    8   (Don't know)
    9   (Refused)

Q21.   Compared to the average smoker, do you (Insert)?

[Randomize items:]

    a.   Smoke more cigarettes per week, fewer cigarettes per week, or about the same number?
    b.   Smoke cigarettes with higher tar and nicotine levels, lower tar and nicotine levels, or about the same levels?
    c.   Inhale more when you smoke, inhale less, or inhale about the same amount?
    d.   Think you could quit smoking more easily, less easily, or about as easily?

    e.   Think you are more addicted to cigarettes, less addicted to cigarettes, or about the same?

    f.   Think your lifestyle is more healthy, less healthy, or about the same?

    g.   Think you are more influenced by cigarette ads, less influenced by cigarette ads, or about the same?

    1   More than the average smoker
    2   Same as the average smoker
    3   Less than the average smoker
    8   (Don't know)
    9   (Refused)

[Ask all:]

Q22.   **[If under 23:]** Do your parents or any adults you live with smoke? **[If 23 or older:]** Do your parents smoke?

    1   Yes
    2   No
    3   Parents no longer living
    8   (Don't know)
    9   (Refused)

Ask Q23 if parents smoke [Q22 = 1]:

Q23.   How would you rate their health? Very good, good, poor or very poor?

    1   Very good
    2   Good
    3   Poor
    4   Very poor
    8   (Don't know)
    9   (Refused)

[Ask all:]

Q24.   Have you ever known someone who (Insert)?

    a.   died of lung cancer or another disease because they smoked
    b.   really wanted to quit smoking but couldn't
    c.   was a regular smoker who quit and never started again

1 Yes
2 No
8 (Don't know)
9 (Refused)

[No Q25]

Ask Q26-Q26F if smoked in past month [QZZ = 1]:

Q26.   How frequently did you smoke cigarettes in the past 30 days? Just tell me when I get to the right amount. (Read responses 1-7:)

1 Less than one cigarette a day
2 One to five a day
3 Six to ten a day
4 Eleven to fourteen a day
5 Fifteen to nineteen a day
6 Twenty a day
7 More than twenty a day
8 (Don't know)
9 (Refused)

Q26A.   What brand of cigarettes do you smoke the most? (Do not read responses)

1 Benson & Hedges
2 Camel
3 Kool
4 Marlboro
5 Merit
6 Newport
7 Salem
8 Vantage
9 Winston
97 (Other) **[Record verbatim]**
98 (Don't know)
99 (Refused)

Q26B.   Where do you get most of your cigarettes?

1 Vending machines
2 Convenience stores like 7-11 or gas stations
3 Supermarkets
4 On the Internet

    5   From friends
    6   From relatives
    7   Other
    8   (Don't know)
    9   (Refused)

Q26C.   How much does a pack of Marlboro cigarettes cost in your city or town? Are they about $1, $2 to $3, $3 to $4, or more?

    1    $1
    2    $2 to $3
    3    $3 to $4
    4   More
    8   (Don't know)
    9   (Refused)

Q26D.   How much do you spend per week on cigarettes? Just tell me when I get to right amount. $1 or less, $2 to $5, $6 to $12, $13 to $20, $21 to $30, or more than $30.

    1    $1 or less
    2    $2 to $5
    3    $6 to $12
    4    $13 to $20
    5    $21 to $30
    6   More than $30
    8   (Don't know)
    9   (Refused)

Q26E.   Suppose the price of cigarettes went up $1 per pack. Would the amount you smoked go down or would it stay the same?

    1   Go down
    2   Stay the same
    3   Other
    8   (Don't know)
    9   (Refused)

Q26F.   For each of the following statements, please tell me if you strongly agree, somewhat agree, somewhat disagree, or strongly disagree.

    a.   Smokers should have the right to smoke in public places.
    b.   I try to avoid smoking near people who think smoke is harmful.

c. **[If under age 23:]** I don't expect to live long enough for smoking to hurt me.

1 Strongly agree
2 Somewhat agree
3 Somewhat disagree
4 Strongly disagree
8 (Don't know)
9 (Refused)

Ask Q27 if did not smoke in past month but have smoked [QS5a = 2 and QS4 = 1]:

Q27. You said earlier that you had not smoked cigarettes in the past month. Which of the following best describes you? If you want, you can just tell me the letter. (Read responses 1-3:)

1 A—You have tried smoking but never continued.
2 B—You smoke occasionally but not in the past month.
4 C—You used to smoke regularly but now smoke less.
8 (Don't know)
9 (Refused)

Ask Q28 if smoked in past month but less than 11 cigarettes a day [Q26 = 1,2,3,8,9]:

Q28. Have you ever smoked a pack or more of cigarettes a day?

1 Yes
2 No
8 (Don't know)
9 Refused

Ask Q29-Q33 if smoked in past month [QZZ = 1]:

Q29. Do you plan to quit smoking?

1 Yes/(Already have)
2 No
8 (Don't know)
9 (Refused)

Ask Q29A if planning to quit [Q29 = 1]

Q29A. When are you planning to quit? Is it in the next six months, six months to a year, or more than a year from now?

1   Next 6 months
2   6 months to a year
3   More than a year from now
8   (Don't know)
9   (Refused)

Ask Q29B if planning to quit in next year [Q29A = 1 or 2]

Q29B.   If we called you again in a year, would you guess you would have successfully quit smoking?

1   Yes
2   No
8   (Don't know)
9   (Refused)

Q30.   About how many times, if any, have you tried to quit smoking?

[Record number: 0-97]

98 (Don't know)
99 (Refused)

Q31.   How long have you smoked? For a few months or less, for about a year, for one to five years or for more than five years?

1   Few months or less
2   About a year
3   One to five years
4   More than five years
8   (Don't know)
9   (Refused)

Q32.   Do you consider yourself addicted to cigarettes or not?

1   Yes, addicted
2   No, not addicted
8   (Don't know)
9   (Refused)

[Ask all:]

Q33.   Imagine that you had smoked a pack of cigarettes each day for ten years. If you were then to quit permanently and not smoke again for the next ten years, would your lungs recover completely, recover somewhat or not recover at all?

1   Recover completely
2   Recover somewhat
3   Not recover at all
8   (Don't know)
9   (Refused)

D5.   I have just a few more questions to help us understand the people
who took part in our survey. Are you yourself of Hispanic origin or
descent, such as Mexican, Puerto Rican, Cuban or some other
Spanish background?

1   Yes
2   No
8   (Don't know)
9   (Refused)

D6.   What is your race? (**If Hispanic [D5 = 1]:**) Aside from being
Hispanic, do you consider yourself white, black or some other race?
(**Else:**) Are you white, black, Asian or some other race?

1   White
2   Black
3   Asian
4   Other
8   (Don't know)
9   (Refused)

D7.   Are you married, living as married, widowed, divorced, separated,
or have you never been married?

1   Married
2   Living as married
3   Widowed
4   Divorced
5   Separated
6   Never been married
8   (Don't know)
9   (Refused)

D8.   With which religious group do you identify? Would you describe
yourself as Protestant, Catholic, Jewish, Muslim, some other
non-Christian religion, or don't you have a religious preference?

01 Protestant
02 Catholic
03 Jewish
04 Muslim
05 Some other non-Christian religion
06 No religious preference
97 Other (SPECIFY)
98 (Don't know)
99 (Refused)

D9.   Last year, that is in 1998, what was your household's total income before taxes? Just stop me when I get to the right category: (Read categories)

01 Less than $15,000
02 $15,000-$30,000
03 $30,001-$40,000
04 $40,001-$50,000
05 $50,001-$60,000
06 $60,001-$75,000
07 $75,001-$100,000
08 $100,000-$150,000
09 Over $150,000
98 (Don't know) (DO NOT READ)
99 (Refused)

D10.   Do you live with your parents?

1 Yes
2 No
9 Don't know/Refused

That completes our survey. Thank you very much for taking time to answer our questions. We really appreciate your time. Have a nice (day | evening).

Appendix C

Causal Modeling Methodology

Several chapters in this volume report on analyses of the Annenberg Tobacco Surveys using causal modeling methodology. This methodology is quite common in the social sciences and is particularly helpful for understanding how responses to surveys are related to one another. One feature of the method is the use of causal diagrams to represent these relationships. In this book, these diagrams are used to summarize how people's beliefs and experiences about cigarettes affect their use of cigarettes. For example, the diagrams in Chapter 7 show the relationships between exposure to cigarette advertising and various effects of the advertising. There are three types of relationships or causal paths in the diagrams. The first type of path is from external factors such as age and advertising to mediators such as the perceived risk of smoking. The second type is from mediators to outcomes (e.g., perceived risk to trying smoking). If perceived risk mediates the effects of age or advertising, then paths between age and advertising to risk will be different from zero, and the path from risk to smoking trial will also be nonzero. There is also a direct path from age to trial that represents effects of age not mediated by perceived risk.

A third type of path relates errors of measurement or other sources of unexplained response in the mediators, outcomes, or measures of these concepts. For example, Figure 7.15 has an error in the risk mediator that corresponds to those parts of risk not explained by the external factors (such as age). There is also error in the two measures of risk that is not explained by the risk.

Causal diagrams are called *models* because they represent both theory and knowledge about smoking. In Figure 7.15, age is shown as a cause of cigarette trial (not the other way around) because we know that trying to smoke will not affect one's age. This path represents all of the experiences as young people grow older that increase their chances of smoking cigarettes. The goal of the analysis is to identify some of these experiences.

Theories of the effects of cigarette advertising suggest that exposure to ads should encourage young people to try smoking by influencing imagery, feelings, and possibly risk perceptions. If the survey results support this prediction, then the paths in Figure 7.17 between advertising exposure and the mediators of influence (imagery, feelings, and risk perception) will be different from zero. The mediators should also directly affect trial. A statistical procedure that combines factor analysis and regression analysis is used to estimate the strength of the paths between the potential causes and their effects. We used a program called AMOS to estimate these paths (see Arbuckle & Wothke, 1999). The paths we present are standardized (*sp*) and typically range between plus and minus one. It is possible to follow the paths leading from a cause to its effects and to multiply the path weights along the way to measure the size of the causal relation. For example, if the path weight from A to B is .5 and the weight from B to C is .5, then the relation between A and C is .5 × .5, or .25.

The results of our causal analyses suggest that our models are consistent with the survey data. In addition, the statistical program provides various goodness-of-fit indices that allow one to evaluate the adequacy of a causal model. We present the comparative fit index (CFI) for all models. This index varies between zero and one, with values greater than .90 considered to indicate an adequate fit (Bentler, 1990). Nevertheless, even if a model fits the data and the paths have values that are consistent with theory, the findings do not prove that the causes in the model actually caused the outcomes. They only indicate that the model may be correct.

Whenever possible, we present alternative models to see if other explanations of the results are as consistent with the data as the preferred model. In judging the adequacy of alternative models, we look to measures of fit that take into account the complexity of the model as well as its ability to explain the data. We present two measures of fit: the root mean square error of approximation (RMSEA; Browne & Cudeck, 1993) and the Akaike (1987) information criterion (AIC). Values less than .05 for the RMSEA are considered acceptable, and the lower the value, the better the fit. The AIC only has a lower bound of zero, and values closer to zero indicate better fits.

Daniel Romer
Patrick Jamieson

References

Achievements in public health, 1900-1999: Tobacco use—United States, 1900-1999. (1999). *Morbidity and Mortality Weekly Report, 48,* 986-993.

Ainslie, G. (1992). *Picoeconomics.* Cambridge: Cambridge University Press.

Ainslie, G., & Haslam, N. (1992). Hyperbolic discounting. In G. Loewenstein & J. Elster (Eds.), *Choice over time* (pp. 57-92). New York: Russell Sage Foundation.

Aitken, P. P., Leathar, D. S., & Squair, S. I. (1986). Children's awareness of cigarette brand sponsorship of sports and games in the UK. *Health Education Research, 1,* 203-211.

Ajzen, I. (1991). The theory of planned behavior. *Organizational Behavior and Human Decision Processes, 50,* 179-211.

Akaike, H. (1987). Factor analysis and AIC. *Psychometrica, 52,* 317-332.

Alhakami, A. S., & Slovic, P. (1994). A psychological study of the inverse relationship between perceived risk and perceived benefit. *Risk Analysis, 14,* 1085-1096.

Allen, K. F., Moss, A. J., Giovino, G. A., Shopland, D. R., & Pierce, J. P. (1993). Teenage tobacco use: Data estimates from the Teenage Attitudes and Practices Survey, United States, 1989. *Advance Data From Vital and Health Statistics, 224.*

American Broadcasting Corporation. (1994, February 28). *Day one.*

American Psychiatric Association. (1994). *Diagnostic and statistical manual of mental disorders* (4th ed.). Washington, DC: Author.

Anda, R. F., Croft, J. B., Felitti, V. J., Nordenberg, D., Giles, W. H., Williamson, D. F., & Giovino G. A. (1999). Adverse childhood experiences and smoking during adolescence and adulthood. *Journal of the American Medical Association, 282,* 1652-1658.

Anda, R. F., Williamson, D. F., Escobedo, L. G., Mast, E. E., Giovino, G. A., & Remington, P. L. (1990). Depressions and the dynamics of smoking: A national perspective. *Journal of the American Medical Association, 264,* 1541-1545.

Note: Many of the tobacco industry documents cited in this volume are identified by their "Bates numbers"; these represent a citation convention developed to organize industry documents revealed to the public through litigation. Most of these documents are now available to the public at the Minnesota Tobacco Document Depository in Minneapolis and can be obtained there through the use of Bates numbers. Many industry documents are also available through various World Wide Web archives, which can be accessed at http://www.tobaccoarchives.com.

Anderson, C., & Burns, D. M. (2000). Patterns of adolescent smoking initiation rates by ethnicity and sex. *Tobacco Control, 9*(Suppl. 2), ii4-ii8.

Anderson, C. A., Lepper, M. R., & Ross, L. (1980). Perseverance of social theories: The role of explanation in the persistence of discredited information. *Journal of Personality and Social Psychology, 39*, 1037-1049.

Arbuckle, J. L., & Wothke, W. (1999). *AMOS 4.0 user's guide.* Chicago: SPSS.

Armstrong, B. K., deKlerk, N. H., Shean, R. E., Dunn, D. A., & Dolin, P. J. (1990). Influence of education and advertising on the uptake of smoking by children. *Medical Journal of Australia, 152,* 117-124.

Ary, D. V., & Biglan, A. (1988). Longitudinal changes in adolescent cigarette smoking behavior: Onset and cessation. *Journal of Behavioral Medicine, 11,* 361-382.

Auerbach, O., Hammond, E. C., & Garfinkel, L. (1970). Histologic changes in the larynx in relation to smoking habits. *Cancer, 25,* 92-104.

Auerbach, O., Hammond, E. C., & Garfinkel, L. (1979). Changes in bronchial epithelium in relation to cigarette smoking, 1955-1960 vs. 1970-1977. *New England Journal of Medicine, 300,* 381-386.

Australian National Health and Medical Research Council. (1997). *The health effects of passive smoking: A scientific information paper* [On-line]. Available Internet: http://www.health. gov.au/nhmrc/advice/nhmrc/forward.htm

Ayanian, J. Z., & Cleary, P. D. (1999). Perceived risks of heart disease and cancer among cigarette smokers. *Journal of the American Medical Association, 281,* 1019-1021.

Baker, T. B. (1988). Models of addiction: Introduction to the special issue. *Journal of Abnormal Psychology, 97,* 115-117.

Bandura, A. (1986). *Social foundations of thought and action: A cognitive social theory.* Englewood Cliffs, NJ: Prentice Hall.

Baron, J. A. (1996). Beneficial effects of nicotine and cigarette smoking: The real, the possible and the spurious. *British Medical Bulletin, 52*(1), 58-73.

Bauer, U. E., Johnson, T. M., Hopkins, R. S., & Brooks, R. G. (2000). Changes in youth cigarette use and intentions following implementation of a tobacco control program: Findings from the Florida Youth Tobacco Survey, 1998-2000. *Journal of the American Medical Association, 284,* 723-728.

Baumeister, R. F., Heatherton, T. F., & Tice, D. M. (1994). *Losing control: How and why people fail at self-regulation.* San Diego, CA: Academic Press.

Baumhart, R. (1968). *An honest profit.* Englewood Cliffs, NJ: Prentice Hall.

Becker, G., & Murphy, K. (1988). A theory of rational addiction. *Journal of Political Economy, 96,* 675-700.

Benowitz, N. L. (1996). Biomarkers of cigarette smoking. In National Cancer Institute, *The FTC cigarette test method for determining tar, nicotine, and carbon monoxide yields for U.S. cigarettes: Report of the NCI Expert Committee* (Smoking and Tobacco Control Monograph 7; Publication No. NIH 96-2789). Washington, DC: U.S. Department of Health and Human Services.

Benowitz, N. L., Hall, S. M., Herning, R. I., Jacob, P., III, Jones, R. T., & Osman, A. L. (1983). Smokers of low-yield cigarettes do not consume less nicotine. *New England Journal of Medicine, 309,* 139-142.

Benowitz, N. L., Jacob, P., III, Kozlowski, L. T., & Yu, L. (1986). Influence of smoking fewer cigarettes on exposure to tar, nicotine, and carbon monoxide. *New England Journal of Medicine, 315,* 1310-1313.

Benowitz, N. L., Jacob, P., III, Yu, L., Talcott, R., Hall, S., & Jones, R. T. (1986). Reduced tar, nicotine, and carbon monoxide exposure while smoking ultralow- but not low-yield cigarettes. *Journal of the American Medical Association, 256,* 241-246.

Benthin, A., Slovic, P., Moran, P., Severson, H. H., Mertz, C. K., & Gerrard, M. (1995). Adolescent health-threatening and health-enhancing behaviors: A study of word association and imagery. *Journal of Adolescent Health, 17,* 143-152.

Benthin, A., Slovic, P., & Severson, H. H. (1993). A psychometric study of adolescent risk perception. *Journal of Adolescence, 16,* 153-168.

Bentler, P. M. (1990). Comparative fit indices in structural equation models. *Psychological Bulletin, 107,* 238-246.

Berridge, K. C., & Robinson, T. E. (1995). The mind of an addicted brain: Neural sensitization of wanting versus liking. *Current Directions in Psychological Science, 4,* 71-76.

Bible, G. (1998, March 2). [Testimony]. In *Minnesota v. Philip Morris, Inc., et al. (Minn. Dist. Ct.).*

Biderman, A. D. (1960). Social-psychological needs and "involuntary" behavior as illustrated by compliance in interrogation. *Sociometry, 23,* 120-147.

Biener, L., & Siegel, M. (2000). Tobacco marketing and adolescent smoking: More support for a causal inference. *American Journal of Public Health, 90,* 407-411.

Black, W. C., Nease, R. F., Jr., & Tosteson, A. N. A. (1995). Perceptions of breast cancer risk and screening effectiveness in women younger than 50 years of age. *Journal of the National Cancer Institute, 87,* 720-731.

Boney-McCoy, S., Gibbons, F. X., Reis, T. J., Gerrard, M., Luus, C. A. E., & Sufka, A. V. W. (1992). Perceptions of smoking risk as a function of smoking status. *Journal of Behavioral Medicine, 15,* 469-488.

Borland, R. (1997). What do people's estimates of smoking-related risk mean? *Psychology and Health, 12,* 513-521.

Borland, R., Owen, N., Hill, D., & Schofield, P. (1991). Predicting attempts and sustained cessation after the introduction of work-place smoking bans. *Health Psychology, 10,* 336-342.

Bornstein, R. F. (1989). Exposure and affect: Overview and meta-analysis of research, 1968-1987. *Psychological Bulletin, 106,* 265-289.

Boyle, C. M. (1968, December 14). Some factors affecting the smoking habits of a group of teenagers. *Lancet, 2,* 1287-1289.

Brandt, A. M. (1990, Fall). The cigarette, risk, and American culture. *Daedalus, 119,* 155-174.

Breslau, N., Kilbey, M., & Andreski, P. (1991). Nicotine dependence, major depression, and anxiety in young adults. *Archives of General Psychiatry, 48,* 1069-1074.

Brickman, P., Coates, D., & Janoff-Bulman, R. (1978). Lottery winners and accident victims: Is happiness relative? *Journal of Personality and Social Psychology, 36,* 917-927.

British American Tobacco. (n.d.). [Internal document]. Bates No. 102690342.

Brown, D. (2000, August 3). Study shows smokers' risks. *Washington Post,* p. A3.

Brown, R. A., Lewinsohn, P. M., Seeley, J. R., & Wagner, E. F. (1996). Cigarette smoking, major depression, and other psychiatric disorders among adolescents. *Journal of the American Academy of Child and Adolescent Psychiatry, 35,* 1602-1610.

Brown & Williamson. (1966, June). *Market potential of a health cigarette* (Special Report No. 248, by M. E. Johnston). Bates No. 2040452500-2040452523.

Brown & Williamson. (1976, November 29). *Re: Cigarette advertising history* (Memorandum from F. E. Latimer to B. L. Broecker & M. J. McCue). Bates No. 680086039-680086044.

Brown & Williamson. (1977, June 6). *Remarks by Addison Yeaman at Maxwell Associates Biannual Tobacco Seminar.* Bates No. 682338629-682338637.

Brown & Williamson. (1984, September 7). *Total minority marketing plan limited* (M.A.B., discussion paper, attachment 3). Bates No. 531000141-531000144.

Brown & Williamson. (2000). *Hot topics: Smoking and health issues* [On-line]. Available Internet: http://www.brownandwilliamson.com/1_hottopics.html

Browne, M. W., & Cudeck, R. (1993). Alternative ways of assessing model fit. In K. A. Bollen & J. S. Long (Eds.), *Testing structural equation models* (pp. 136-162). Newbury Park, CA: Sage.

Bruine de Bruin, W., Fischhoff, B., Halpern-Felsher, B., & Millstein, S. (2000). Expressing epistemic uncertainty: It's a fifty-fifty chance. *Organizational Behavior and Human Decision Processes, 81,* 115-131.

Bruvold, W. H. (1993). A meta-analysis of adolescent smoking prevention programs. *American Journal of Public Health, 83,* 872-880.

Burns, D. M., Garfinkel, L., & Samet, J. M. (1997). [Introduction, summary, and conclusions]. In National Cancer Institute, *Changes in cigarette-related disease risk and their implications for prevention and control* (Smoking and Tobacco Control Monograph 8; Publication No. NIH 97-4213). Washington, DC: U.S. Department of Health and Human Services.

Bush, P. J., & Iannotti, R. J. (1993). Alcohol, cigarette, and marijuana use among fourth-grade urban schoolchildren in 1988/89 and 1990/91. *American Journal of Public Health, 83*, 111-115.

Calabresi, G. (1970). *The costs of accidents.* New Haven, CT: Yale University Press.

California Department of Health Services. (1995). *Operation Storefront: Youth against tobacco advertising and promotion.* Sacramento: Author.

California Environmental Protection Agency, Office of Environmental Health Hazard Assessment. (1997). *Health effects of exposure to environmental tobacco smoke.* Sacramento: Author.

Cameron, P. (1967). The presence of pets and smoking as correlates of perceived disease. *Journal of Allergy, 67*, 12-15.

Cameron, P., Kostin, J. S., Zaks, J. M., Wolfe, J. H., Tighe, G., Oselett, B., Stocker, R., & Winton, J. (1969). The health of smokers' and nonsmokers' children. *Journal of Allergy, 69*, 336-341.

Camp, D. E., Klesges, R. C., & Relyea, G. (1993). The relationship between body weight concerns and adolescent smoking. *Health Psychology, 12*, 24-32.

Carmelli, D., Swann, G. E., Robinette, D., & Fabsitz, R. R. (1992). Genetic influence on smoking: A study of male twins. *New England Journal of Medicine, 327*, 829-833.

Centers for Disease Control. (1988). *The health consequences of smoking: Nicotine addiction. A report of the surgeon general* (DHHS Publication No. CDC 88-8406). Washington, DC: Government Printing Office.

Centers for Disease Control. (1989). *Reducing the health consequences of smoking: 25 years of progress. A report of the surgeon general* (DHHS Publication No. CDC 89-8411). Washington, DC: Government Printing Office.

Centers for Disease Control and Prevention. (1994a). *Preventing tobacco use among young people: A report of the surgeon general* (Publication No. S/N 017-001-004901-0). Washington, DC: U.S. Department of Health and Human Services.

Centers for Disease Control and Prevention. (1994b). [Youth Risk Behavior Survey, Division of Adolescent and School Health]. Unpublished raw data.

Centers for Disease Control and Prevention. (1996). *Cigarette smoking-related mortality* [On-line]. Available Internet: http://www.cdc.gov/tobacco/research_data/health_consequences/mortali.htm

Centers for Disease Control and Prevention. (1999). *Best practices for comprehensive tobacco control programs.* Washington, DC: U.S. Department of Health and Human Resources.

Centers for Disease Control and Prevention. (2000a). *Incidence of initiation of cigarette smoking among U.S. teens* [On-line]. Available Internet: http://www.cdc.gov/tobacco/research_data/youth/initfact/htm

Centers for Disease Control and Prevention. (2000b). *Targeting tobacco use: The nation's leading cause of death* [On-line]. Available Internet: http://www.cdc.gov/tobacco/overview/oshaag.htm

Chaloupka, F. J., & Warner, K. E. (2000). Economics of smoking. In A. J. Culyer & J. P. Newhouse (Eds.), *Handbook of health economics* (2 vols.). New York: North-Holland.

Changes in the cigarette brand preferences of adolescent smokers—United States, 1989-1993. (1994). *Morbidity and Mortality Weekly Report, 43*, 577-581.

Chapman, S., & Fitzgerald, B. (1982). Brand preference and advertising recall in adolescent smokers: Some implications for health promotion. *American Journal of Public Health, 72*, 491-494.

Chapman, S., Wong, W. L., & Smith, W. (1993). Self-exempting beliefs about smoking and health: Differences between smokers and ex-smokers. *American Journal of Public Health, 83*, 215-219.

Charlton, A. (1986). Children's advertisement-awareness related to their views on smoking. *Health Education Journal, 45*, 75-78.

Charlton, A. (1996). Children and smoking: The family circle. *British Medical Bulletin, 52*(1), 90-107.

Chassin, L., Presson, C. C., Sherman, S. J., & Edwards, D. A. (1990). The natural history of cigarette smoking: Predicting young-adult smoking outcomes from adolescent smoking patterns. *Health Psychology, 9,* 701-716.

Cigarette advertising—United States, 1988. (1990). *Morbidity and Mortality Weekly Report, 39,* 261-265.

Cigarette smoking among adults—United States, 1991. (1993). *Morbidity and Mortality Weekly Report, 42,* 230-233.

Cigarette smoking among adults—United States, 1997. (1999). *Morbidity and Mortality Weekly Report, 48,* 993-996.

Cigarette smoking-attributable mortality and years of potential life lost—United States, 1990. (1993). *Morbidity and Mortality Weekly Report, 42,* 645-649.

Cipollone v. Liggett Group, Inc., 112 S. Ct. 2608 (1992).

Cohen, J., & Davis, R. G. (1991). Third-person effects and the differential impact in negative political advertising. *Journalism Quarterly, 68,* 680-698.

Cohen, J., Mutz, D., Price, V., & Gunther, A. C. (1988). Perceived impact of defamation: An experiment on third-person effects. *Public Opinion Quarterly, 52,* 161-173.

Cohn, L. D., Macfarlane, S., Ynez, C., & Imai, W. K. (1995). Risk-perception: Differences between adolescents and adults. *Health Psychology, 14,* 217-222.

Colley, J. R., & Holland, W. W. (1967). Social and environmental factors in respiratory disease. A preliminary report. *Archives of Environmental Health, 67,* 157-161.

Comparison of the cigarette brand preferences of adult and teenaged smokers—United States, 1989, and 10 US communities, 1988 and 1990. (1992). *Morbidity and Mortality Weekly Report, 41,* 169-173, 179-181.

Conrad, K. M., Flay, B. R., & Hill, D. (1992). Why children start smoking cigarettes: Predictors of onset. *British Journal of Addiction, 87,* 1711-1724.

Croley, S. P., & Hanson, J. D. (1993). Rescuing the revolution: The revived case for enterprise liability. *University of Michigan Law Review, 91,* 683-797.

Croson, R. T. A. (1998). *Theories of altruism and reciprocity: Evidence from linear public goods games.* Unpublished manuscript.

Cummings, K. M., Pechacek, T., & Shopland, D. (1994). The illegal sale of cigarettes to U.S. minors: Estimates by state. *American Journal of Public Health, 84,* 300-302.

Damasio, A. R. (1994). *Descartes' error: Emotion, reason, and the human brain.* New York: Avon.

Damasio, A. R., Tranel, D., & Damasio, H. C. (1990). Individuals with sociopathic behavior caused by frontal damage fail to respond autonomically to social stimuli. *Behavioural Brain Research, 41,* 81-94.

Dappen, A., Schwartz, R. H., & O'Donnell, R. (1996). A survey of adolescent smoking patterns. *Journal of the American Board of Family Practice, 9,* 7-13.

Dawber, T. R. (1980). *The Framingham study: The epidemiology of atherosclerotic disease.* Cambridge, MA: Harvard University Press.

Denissenko, M. F., Pao, A., Tang, M., & Pfeifer, G. P. (1996). Preferential formation of benzo[a]pyrene adducts at lung cancer mutational hotspots in P53. *Science, 274,* 430-432.

Diefenbach, M. A., Weinstein, N. D., & O'Reilly, J. (1993). Scales for assessing perceptions of health hazard susceptibility. *Health Education Research, 8,* 181-192.

DiFranza, J. R. (1999). Are the Federal and state governments complying with the Synar Amendment? *Archives of Pediatrics and Adolescent Medicine, 153,* 1089-1097.

DiFranza, J. R. (2000). Youth access: The baby and the bath water. *Tobacco Control, 9,* 120-121.

DiFranza, J. R., & Rigotti, N. A. (1999). Impediments to the enforcement of youth access laws. *Tobacco Control, 8,* 152-155.

DiFranza, J. R., Rigotti, N. A., McNeill, A. D., Ockeen, J. K., Savageau, J. A., St. Cyr, D., & Coleman, M. (2000). Initial symptoms of nicotine dependence in adolescents. *Tobacco Control, 9,* 313-319.

DiFranza, J. R., & Tye, J. B. (1990). Who profits from tobacco sales to children? *Journal of the American Medical Association, 263*, 2784-2787.

Doll, R. (1996). Cancers weakly related to smoking. *British Medical Bulletin, 52*(1), 35-49.

Doll, R. (1998). The first reports on smoking and lung cancer. In S. Lock, L. Reynolds, & E. M. Tansey (Eds.), *Ashes to ashes: The history of smoking and health.* Amsterdam/Atlanta, GA: Rodopi.

Doll, R., & Hill, A. B. (1950). A study of the aetiology of carcinoma of the lung. *British Medical Journal, 2*, 740-748.

Doll, R., & Hill, A. B. (1954). The mortality of doctors in relation to their smoking habits: A preliminary report. *British Medical Journal, 1*, 1451-1455.

Doll, R., Peto, R., Wheatley, K., Gray, R., & Sutherland, I. (1994). Mortality in relation to smoking: 40 years' observations on male British doctors. *British Medical Journal, 309*, 901-911.

Dozois, D. N., Farrow, J. A., & Miser, A. (1995). Smoking patterns and cessation motivations during adolescence. *International Journal of the Addictions, 30*, 1485-1498.

Duffy, M. (1996). Econometric studies of advertising, advertising restrictions and cigarette demand: A survey. *International Journal of Advertising, 15*, 1-23.

Dunning, D., & Cohen, G. L. (1992). Egocentric definitions of traits and abilities in social judgment. *Journal of Personality and Social Psychology, 63*, 341-355.

Dunning, D., Perie, M., & Story, A. L. (1991). Self-serving prototypes of social categories. *Journal of Personality and Social Psychology, 61*, 957-968.

Eckman, B., & Goldberg, S. (1992, March). *The viability of the Marlboro Man among the 18-24 segment.* Bates No. 2024462266-2024462292.

Edwards, G., Arif, A., & Hodgson, R. (1982). Nomenclature and classification of drug- and alcohol-related problems: A shortened version of a WHO memorandum. *British Journal of Addiction, 77*, 3-20.

Eikelboom, R., & Stewart, J. (1982). Conditioning of drug-induced physiological responses. *Psychological Review, 89*, 507-528.

Eiser, J. R. (1983). Smoking, seat-belt use and perception of health risks. *Addictive Behaviors, 8*, 75-78.

Eiser, J. R. (1994). Risk judgments reflect belief strength, not bias. *Psychology and Health, 9*, 197-199.

Eiser, J. R., Reicher, S. D., & Podpadec, T. J. (1995). Smokers' and non-smokers' estimates of their personal risk of cancer and of the incremental risk attributable to cigarette smoking. *Addiction Research, 3*, 221-229.

Eiser, J. R., Sutton, S. R., & Wober, M. (1979). Smoking, seat belts and beliefs about health. *Addictive Behaviors, 4*, 331-338.

Ennett, S. T., & Bauman, K. E. (1994). The contribution of influence and selection to adolescent peer group homogeneity: The case of adolescent cigarette smoking. *Journal of Personality and Social Psychology, 67*, 653-663.

Epstein, S. (1994). Integration of the cognitive and the psychodynamic unconscious. *American Psychologist, 49*, 709-724.

Ernst L. Wynder, M.D. [Obituary]. (1999). *Morbidity and Mortality Weekly Report, 48*, 987.

Ershler, J., Leventhal, H., Fleming, R., & Glynn, K. (1989). The quitting experience for smokers in sixth through twelfth grades. *Addictive Behaviors, 14*, 365-378.

Escobedo, L. G., Marcus, S. E., Holtzman, D., & Giovino, G. A. (1993). Sports participation, age at smoking initiation, and the risk of smoking among U.S. high school students. *Journal of the American Medical Association, 269*, 1391-1395.

Eskenazi, B., & Castorina, R. (1999). *Association of prenatal maternal or postnatal child environmental tobacco smoke exposure and neurodevelopmental and behavioral problems in children* (Publication No. WHO/NCD/TF1/99.11). Geneva: World Health Organization.

Federal Cigarette Labeling and Advertising Act, 15 U.S.C. § 1331-1340 (1965).

Federal Trade Commission. (1995). *Report to Congress for 1995 pursuant to the Federal Cigarette Labeling and Advertising Act.* Washington, DC: Author.

Federal Trade Commission. (2000). *Report to Congress for 1998 pursuant to the Federal Cigarette Labeling and Advertising Act.* Washington, DC: Author.

Federal Trade Commission Act, 15 U.S.C. § 41-58 (1914).

Feinberg, J. (1986). *Harm to self* (Vol. 3). New York: Oxford University Press.

Fields, H. L. (1987). *Pain.* New York: McGraw-Hill.

Fields, T. (1998, October 20). Trial begins in smokers' class action suit against tobacco industry. *Philadelphia Inquirer,* p. A16.

Fienberg, S. E., Loftus, E. F., & Tanur, J. M. (1985). Recalling pain and other symptoms. *Health and Society, 62,* 582-597.

Finucane, M. L., Alhakami, A. S., Slovic, P., & Johnson, S. M. (2000). The affect heuristic in judgments of risks and benefits. *Journal of Behavioral Decision Making, 13,* 1-17.

Fischer, P. M., Schwartz, M. P., Richards, J. W., Jr., Goldstein, A. O., & Rojas, T. H. (1991). Brand logo recognition by children ages 3 to 6 years: Mickey Mouse and Old Joe the Camel. *Journal of the American Medical Association, 266,* 3145-3148.

Fischhoff, B. (1975). Hindsight foresight: The effect of outcome knowledge on judgment under uncertainty. *Journal of Experimental Psychology: Human Perception and Performance, 1,* 288-299.

Fischhoff, B., & Bruine de Bruin, W. (1999). Fifty-fifty = 50%. *Journal of Behavioral Decision Making, 12,* 149-163.

Fischhoff, B., Slovic, P., Lichtenstein, S., Reid, S., & Coombs, B. (1978). How safe is safe enough? A psychometric study of attitudes towards technological risks and benefits. *Policy Sciences, 9,* 127-152.

Fischman, M. W. (1988). Behavioral pharmacology of cocaine. *Journal of Clinical Psychiatry, 49,* 7-10.

Fishbein, M. (1977). Consumer beliefs and behavior with respect to cigarette smoking: A critical analysis of the public literature. In Federal Trade Commission, *Report to Congress pursuant to the Public Health Cigarette Smoking Act for the year 1976.* Washington, DC: Federal Trade Commission.

Fisher, L. A., & Bauman, K. E. (1988). Influence and selection in the friend-adolescent relationship: Findings from studies of adolescent smoking and drinking. *Journal of Applied Social Psychology, 18,* 289-314.

Flay, B. R. (1985). Psychological approaches to smoking prevention: A review of findings. *Health Psychology, 4,* 449-488.

Flay, B. R., Ockene, J., & Tager, I. B. (1992). Smoking: Epidemiology, cessation, and prevention. *Chest, 102*(Suppl.), 277S-301S.

Fletcher, C., & Peto, R. (1977). The natural history of chronic airflow obstruction. *British Medical Journal, 1,* 1645-1648.

Flynn, B. S., Worden, J. K., Secker-Walker, R. H., Pirie, P. L., Badger, G. J., Carpenter, J. H., & Geller, B. M. (1994). Mass media and school interventions for cigarette smoking prevention: Effects 2 years after completion. *American Journal of Public Health, 84,* 1148-1150.

Frawley, P. J. (1988). Neurobehavioral model of addiction: Addiction as a primary disease. In S. Peele (Ed.), *Visions of addiction: Major contemporary perspectives on addiction and alcoholism.* Lexington, MA: Lexington.

French, S. A., Perry, C. L., Leon, G. R., & Fulkerson, J. (1994). Weight concerns, dieting behavior, and smoking initiation among adolescents: A prospective study. *American Journal of Public Health, 84,* 1818-1820.

Gallup Organization. (1993). *The public's attitudes toward cigarette advertising and cigarette tax increase* (Study conducted for the Coalition on Smoking or Health). Princeton, NJ: Author.

Gardner, E. L., & Lowinson, J. H. (1993). Drug craving and positive/negative hedonic brain substrates activates by addicting drugs. *Seminars in the Neurosciences, 5,* 359-368.

Gawin, F. H. (1988). Chronic neuropharmacology of cocaine: Progress in pharmacotherapy. *Journal of Clinical Psychiatry, 49,* 11-16.

Gawin, F. H. (1991). Cocaine addiction: Psychology and neurophysiology. *Science, 251*, 1580-1586.

Gerrard, M., Gibbons, F. X., Benthin, A. C., & Hessling, R. M. (1996). A longitudinal study of the reciprocal nature of risk behaviors and cognitions in adolescents: What you do shapes what you think, and vice versa. *Health Psychology, 15*, 344-354.

Gibbons, F. X., & Buunk, B. P. (1997). *Health, coping, and social comparison*. Hillsdale, NJ: Lawrence Erlbaum.

Gibbons, F. X., McGovern, P. G., & Lando, H. A. (1991). Relapse and risk perception among members of a smoking cessation clinic. *Health Psychology, 10*, 42-45.

Glantz, S. A. (1996). Preventing tobacco use: The youth access trap [Editorial]. *American Journal of Public Health, 86*, 156-158.

Glantz, S. A., & Jamieson, P. (2000). Attitudes towards secondhand smoke, smoking, and quitting among young people. *Pediatrics, 106*, 82-84.

Glantz, S. A., & Parmley, W. W. (1995). Passive smoking and heart disease: Mechanisms and risk. *Journal of the American Medical Association, 273*, 1047-1053.

Glantz, S. A., Slade, J., Bero, L. A., Hanauer, P., & Barnes, D. E. (1996). *The cigarette papers*. Berkeley: University of California Press.

Glassman, A. H., Helzer, J. E., Covey, L. S., Cottler, L. B., Stetner, F., Tipp, J. E., & Johnson, J. (1990). Smoking, smoking cessation, and major depression. *Journal of the American Medical Association, 254*, 1546-1549.

Gold, D. R., Wang, X., Wypij, D., Speizer, F. E., Ware, J. H., & Dockery, D. W. (1996). Effects of cigarette smoking on lung function in adolescent boys and girls. *New England Journal of Medicine, 335*, 931-937.

Gold, R. (1993). On the need to mind the gap: On-line versus off-line cognitions underlying sexual risk-taking. In D. Terry, C. Gallois, & M. McCamish (Eds.), *The theory of reasoned action: Its application to AIDS preventive behavior*. New York: Pergamon.

Gold, R. (1994, July). *Why we need to rethink AIDS education for gay men*. Plenary address to the Second International Conference on AIDS' Impact: Biopsychosocial Aspects of HIV Infection, Brighton, England.

Goldstein, A. (1994). *Addiction: From biology to drug policy*. New York: Freeman.

Goldstein, A. O., Fischer, P. M., Richards, J. W., Jr., & Creten, D. (1987). Relationship between high school student smoking and recognition of cigarette advertisements. *Journal of Pediatrics, 110*, 488-491.

Goodin, R. E. (1989). *No smoking: The ethical issues*. Chicago: University of Chicago Press.

Grant, A. M., & Job, R. F. S. (2000). *Comparisons between smokers', nonsmokers', and ex-smokers' smoking-related and smoking-unrelated unrealistic optimism*. Unpublished manuscript, University of Sydney, Department of Psychology.

Gratton, A., & Wise, R. A. (1994). Drug- and behavior-associated changes in dopamine-related electrochemical signals during intravenous cocaine self-administration in rats. *Journal of Neuroscience, 14*, 4130-4146.

Greening, L., & Dollinger, S. J. (1991). Adolescent smoking and perceived vulnerability to smoking-related causes of death. *Journal of Pediatric Psychology, 16*, 687-699.

Griffin, D., & Tversky, A. (1992). The weighing of evidence and the determinants of confidence. *Cognitive Psychology, 24*, 411-435.

Gritz, E. H., Carr, C. R., & Marcus, A. C. (1991). The tobacco withdrawal syndrome in unaided quitters. *British Journal of Addiction, 86*, 57-69.

Gunther, A. C. (1995). Overrating the X-rating: The third-person perception and support for censorship of pornography. *Journal of Communication, 45*(1), 21-39.

Gunther, A. C., & Thorson, E. (1992). Perceived persuasive effects of product commercials and public service announcements: Third-person effects in new domains. *Communication Research, 19*, 574-596.

Hahn, A., Renner, B., & Schwarzer, R. (1998). Perception of health risk: How smoker status affects defensive optimism. *Anxiety, Stress and Coping, 11*, 93-112.

Haines v. Liggett Group, Inc., 814 F. Supp. 414 (D. N.J. 1993).

Hajek, P., Jackson, P., & Belcher, M. (1988). Long-term use of nicotine chewing gum: Occurrence, determinants, and effect on weight gain. *Journal of the American Medical Association, 260*, 1593-1596.

Hanauer, P., Slade, J., Barnes, D. E., Bero, L. A., & Glantz, S. A. (1995). Lawyer control of internal scientific research to protect against products liability lawsuits: The Brown and Williamson documents. *Journal of the American Medical Association 274*, 234-240.

Hansen, W. B., & Malotte, C. K. (1986). Perceived personal immunity: The development of beliefs about susceptibility to the consequences of smoking. *Preventive Medicine, 15*, 363-372.

Hanson, J. D., & Kysar, D. A. (1999a). Taking behavioralism seriously: Some evidence of market manipulation. *Harvard Law Review, 112*, 1420-1572.

Hanson, J. D., & Kysar, D. A. (1999b). Taking behavioralism seriously: The problem of market manipulation. *New York University Law Review, 74*, 630-749.

Hanson, J. D., & Kysar, D. A. (2000). Taking behavioralism seriously: A response to market manipulation. *Roger Williams University Law Review, 6*(1).

Hanson, J. D., & Logue, K. D. (1998). The costs of cigarettes: The economic case for ex post incentive-based regulation. *Yale Law Journal, 107*, 1163-1361.

Hanson, J. D., Logue, K. D., & Zamore, M. S. (1998). Smokers compensation: Toward a blueprint for federal regulation of cigarette manufacturers. *Southern Illinois University Law Journal, 22*, 519-600.

Hanson, J. D., & Reyes, A. C. (1999). *Law and attribution: A critique of and alternative to positive law and economics.* Unpublished manuscript.

Harris, D. (2001, February). Corporate goodwill or tainted money? Retrieved from the World Wide Web March 5, 2001, from http://abcnews.go.com/sections/wnt/WorldNewsTonight/wnt010208_philipmorris_feature.html

Havik, O. E., & Maeland, J. G. (1988). Changes in smoking behavior after a myocardial infarction. *Health Psychology, 7*, 403-420.

Hawkins, S. A., & Hastie, R. (1990). Hindsight: Biased judgments of past events after the outcomes are known. *Psychological Bulletin, 107*, 311-327.

Herrnstein, R., & Prelec, D. (1992). A theory of addiction. In G. Loewenstein & J. Elster (Eds.), *Choice over time.* New York: Russell Sage Foundation.

Hilts, P. J. (1996). *Smoke screen: The truth behind the tobacco industry cover-up.* Reading, MA: Addison-Wesley.

Hirayama, T. (1981). Passive smoking and lung cancer. *British Medical Journal, 282*, 1393-1394.

Hirschman, R. S., Leventhal, H., & Glynn, K. (1984). Development of smoking behavior: Conceptualization and supportive cross-sectional survey data. *Journal of Applied Social Psychology, 14*, 184-206.

Hoorens, V. (1996). Unrealistic optimism in social comparison of health and safety risks. In L. D. Rutter & L. Quine (Eds.), *The social psychology of health and safety: European perspectives* (pp. 153-174). Aldershot, England: Avebury/Ashgate.

Hsee, C. K. (1995). Elastic justification: How tempting but task-irrelevant factors influence decisions. *Organizational Behavior and Human Decision Processes, 62*, 330-337.

Hser, Y., Anglin, M. D., & Powers, K. (1993). A 24-year follow-up of California narcotics addicts. *Archives of General Psychiatry, 50*, 577-584.

Hughes, J. R. (1988). Dependence potential and abuse liability of nicotine replacement therapies. In O. F. Pomerleau & C. S. Pomerleau (Eds.), *Nicotine replacement: A critical evaluation* (pp. 261-277). New York: Alan R. Liss.

Hughes, J. R., Gulliver, S. B., Fenwick, J. W., Valliere, W. A., Cruser, K., Pepper, S., Shea, P., Solomon, L. J., & Flynn, B. S. (1992). Smoking cessation among self quitters. *Health Psychology, 11*, 331-334.

Hughes, J. R., & Hatsukami, D. K. (1986). Signs and symptoms of tobacco withdrawal. *Archives of General Psychiatry, 43*, 289-294.

Humphrey v. Philip Morris Inc., No. C1-94-8565 (Minn. Dist. Ct., 1998).

Hunt, W. A., Barnett, L. W., & Branch, L. G. (1971). Relapse rates in addiction programs. *Journal of Clinical Psychology, 27,* 455-456.

Hunter, S. M., Croft, J. B., Burke, G. L., Parker, F. C., Webber, L. S., & Berenson, G. S. (1986). Longitudinal patterns of cigarette smoking and smokeless tobacco use in youth: The Bogalusa Heart Study. *American Journal of Public Health, 76,* 193-195.

Hurt, R. D., Croghan, G. A., Beede, S. D., Wolter, T. D., Croghan, I. T., & Patten, C. A. (2000). Nicotine patch therapy in 101 adolescent smokers: Efficacy, withdrawal symptom relief, and carbon monoxide and plasma cotinine levels. *Archives of Pediatrics and Adolescent Medicine, 154,* 31-37.

Hurt, R. D., & Robertson, C. R. (1998). Prying open the door to the tobacco industry's secrets about nicotine: The Minnesota tobacco trial. *Journal of the American Medical Association, 280,* 1173-1181.

Hussain, S. P., & Harris, C. C. (1998). Molecular epidemiology of human cancer: Contribution of mutation spectra studies of tumor suppressor genes. *Cancer Research, 58,* 4023-4037.

Incidence of initiation of cigarette smoking—United States, 1965-1996. (1998). *Morbidity and Mortality Weekly Report, 47,* 837-840.

International Agency for Research on Cancer, Working Group on Cancer. (1986). *Tobacco smoking* (Monographs on the Evaluation of the Carcinogenic Risk of Chemicals to Humans, Vol. 38). Lyon, France: World Health Organization.

Jamieson, P. (1999). *Risk perception and the 14-22 smoker and nonsmoker.* Unpublished master's thesis, University of Pennsylvania.

Janis, I. L. (1967). Effects of fear arousal on attitude change: Recent developments in theory and experimental research. In L. Berkowitz (Ed.), *Advances in experimental social psychology* (Vol. 3, pp. 167-224). New York: Academic Press.

Janis, I. L., & Leventhal, H. (1967). Human reactions to stress. In E. F. Borgatta & W. Lambert (Eds.), *Handbook of personality theory and research.* Chicago: Rand McNally.

Jason, L. A., Katz, R., Vavra, J. Schnop-Wyatt, D. L., & Talbot, B. (1999). Long-term follow-up of youth access laws' impact on smoking prevalence. *Journal of Human Behavior in the Social Environment, 2,* 1-13.

Johnston, L. D., O'Malley, P. M., & Bachman, J. G. (1992). *Smoking, drinking, and illicit drug use among American secondary school students, college students, and young adults, 1975-1991: Vol. 1. Secondary school students* (NIH Publication No. 93-3480). Washington, DC: National Institute on Drug Abuse.

Johnston, L. D., O'Malley, P. M., & Bachman, J. G. (1993). *National survey results on drug use from the Monitoring the Future Study* (NIH Publication No. 93-3598). Rockville, MD: National Institute on Drug Abuse.

Johnston, L. D., O'Malley, P. M., & Bachman, J. G. (1994a). [Monitoring the Future Study]. Unpublished raw data supplied by the Centers for Disease Control and Prevention, Office on Smoking and Health, Atlanta, GA.

Johnston, L. D., O'Malley, P. M., & Bachman, J. G. (1994b). [Monitoring the Future Study]. Unpublished raw data supplied by the University of Michigan, Institute for Social Research.

Johnston, L. D., O'Malley, P. M., & Bachman, J. G. (1999a). *Monitoring the Future Study* [Press release]. Ann Arbor: University of Michigan.

Johnston, L. D., O'Malley, P. M., & Bachman, J. G. (1999b). *National survey results on drug use from the Monitoring the Future Study, 1975-1998: Vol. 1. Secondary school students* (NIH Publication No. 99-4660). Rockville, MD: National Institute on Drug Abuse.

Jolls, C., Sunstein, C. R., & Thaler, R. (1998). A behavior approach to law and economics. *Stanford Law Review, 50,* 1471-1550.

Kahneman, D. (1997). New challenges to the rationality assumption. *Legal Theory, 3,* 105-124.

Kahneman, D., Knetsch, J. L., & Thaler, R. H. (1990). Experimental tests of the endowment effect and the Coase theorem. *Journal of Political Economy, 98,* 1325-1348.

Kahneman, D., Knetsch, J. L., & Thaler, R. H. (1991). The endowment effect, loss aversion, and the status quo bias. *Journal of Economic Perspectives, 5,* 193-206.

Kahneman, D., Slovic, P., & Tversky, A. (Eds.). (1982). *Judgment under uncertainty: Heuristics and biases.* New York: Cambridge University Press.

Kahneman, D., & Snell, J. (1992). Predicting a changing taste. *Journal of Behavioral Decision Making, 5,* 187-200.

Kahneman, D., & Tversky, A. (1972). Subjective probability: A judgment of representativeness. *Cognitive Psychology, 3,* 430-454.

Kahneman, D., & Tversky, A. (1973). On the psychology of prediction. *Psychological Review, 80,* 237-251.

Kahneman, D., & Tversky, A. (1984). Choices, values, and frames. *American Psychologist, 39,* 341-364.

Kann, L., Kinchen, S. A., Williams, B. I., Ross, J. G., Lowry, R., Hill, C. V., Grunbaum, J. A., Blumson, P. S., Collins, J. L., Kolbe, L. J., & State and Local YRBSS Coordinators. (1998). Youth risk behavior surveillance—United States, 1997. *Morbidity and Mortality Weekly Report, 47,* 1-17.

Kelder, G. E., & Daynard, R. A. (1997). The role of litigation in the effective control of the sale and use of tobacco. *Stanford Law and Policy Review, 8,* 63-98.

Kent, G. (1985). Memory of dental pain. *Pain, 21,* 187-194.

Kessler, D. A., Witt, A. M., Barnett, P. S., Zeller, M. R., Natanblut, S. L., Wilkenfeld, J. P., Lorraine, C. C., Thompson, L. J., & Schultz, W. B. (1996). The Food and Drug Administration's regulation of tobacco products. *New England Journal of Medicine, 335,* 988-994.

King, C., Siegel, M., & Celebucki, C. (1998). Adolescent exposure to cigarette advertising in magazines: An evaluation of brand-specific advertising in relation to youth readership. *Journal of the American Medical Association, 179,* 516-520.

Kirby, K. N., & Herrnstein, R. J. (1995). Preference reversals due to myopic discounting of delayed rewards. *Psychological Science, 6,* 83-89.

Klintzner, M., Gruenewald, P. J., & Bamberger, E. (1991). Cigarette advertising and adolescent experimentation with smoking. *British Journal of Addiction, 86,* 287-298.

Kluger, R. (1996). *Ashes to ashes: America's hundred-year cigarette war, the public health, and the unabashed triumph of Philip Morris.* New York: Alfred A. Knopf.

Koob, G. F., Stinus, L., Le Moal, M., & Bloom, F. E. (1989). Opponent process theory of motivation: Neurobiological evidence from studies of opiate dependence. *Neuroscience and Behavioral Reviews, 13,* 135-140.

Kosslyn, S. M., Alpert, N. M., Thompson, W. L., Maljkovic, V., Weise, S. B., Chabris, C. F., Hamilton, S. E., Rauch, S. L., & Buonanno, F. S. (1993). Visual mental imagery activates topographically organized visual cortex: PET investigations. *Journal of Cognitive Neuroscience, 5,* 263-287.

Kottke, T. E., Brekke, M. L., Solberg, L., & Hughes, J. R. (1989). A randomized trial to increase smoking intervention by physicians: Doctors helping smokers, round 1. *Journal of the American Medical Association, 261,* 2101-2106.

Kozlowski, L. T., & Wilkinson, D. A. (1987). Uses and misuses of the concept of craving by alcohol, tobacco, and drug researchers. *British Journal of Addiction, 82,* 31-36.

Kozlowski, L. T., Wilkinson, D. A., Skinner, W., Kent, C., Franklin, T., & Pope, M. (1989). Comparing tobacco cigarette dependence with other drug dependencies: Greater or equal "difficulty quitting" and "urges to use," but less "pleasure" from cigarettes. *Journal of the American Medical Association, 261,* 896-901.

Kristiansen, C. M., Harding, C. M., & Eiser, J. R. (1983). Beliefs about the relationship between smoking and causes of death. *Basic and Applied Social Psychology, 4,* 253-261.

Kunda, Z. (1990). The case for motivated reasoning. *Psychological Bulletin, 108,* 480-498.

Laibson, D. I. (1994). *A cue-theory of consumption* (Working paper). Cambridge, MA: Harvard University, Economics Department.

Langer, E. J. (1975). The illusion of control. *Journal of Personality and Social Psychology, 32,* 311-328.

Larwood, L., & Whittaker, W. (1977). Managerial myopia: Self-serving biases in organizational planning. *Journal of Applied Psychology, 62*, 194-198.

Lasorsa, D. L. (1989). Real and perceived effects of Amerika. *Journalism Quarterly, 66*, 373-380.

Law, M. R., & Hackshaw, A. K. (1997). A meta-analysis of cigarette smoking, bone mineral density and risk of hip fracture: Recognition of a major effect. *British Medical Journal, 315*, 841-846.

Lee, C. (1989). Perceptions of immunity to disease in adult smokers. *Journal of Behavioral Medicine, 12*, 267-277.

Leventhal, H., Glynn, K., & Fleming, R. (1987). Is the smoking decision an "informed choice"? *Journal of the American Medical Association, 257*, 3373-3376.

Levin, M. L., Goldstein, H., & Gerhardt, P. R. (1950). Cancer and tobacco smoking: A preliminary report. *Journal of the American Medical Association, 143*, 336-338.

Lippman-Hand, A., & Fraser, F. C. (1979). Genetic counseling: Provision and reception of information. *American Journal of Medical Genetics, 3*, 113-117.

LoConte, J. S. (1995). *Optimistic risk perceptions and external risk attributions among smokers: Identifying dimensions of risk-minimization and their correlates.* Unpublished doctoral dissertation, Rutgers University, Department of Psychology.

Loewenstein, G. (1994). The psychology of curiosity: A review and reinterpretation. *Psychological Bulletin, 116*, 75-98.

Loewenstein, G. (1996). Out of control: Visceral influences on behavior. *Organizational Behavior and Human Decision Processes, 65*, 272-292.

Loewenstein, G. (1999). A visceral account of addiction. In J. Elster & O.-J. Skog (Eds.), *Getting hooked: Rationality and addiction* (pp. 235-264). Cambridge: Cambridge University Press.

Loewenstein, G. (2000). Willpower: A decision-theorist's perspective. *Law and Philosophy, 19*, 51-76.

Loewenstein, G., & Adler, D. (1995). A bias in the prediction of tastes. *Economic Journal, 105*, 929-937.

Loewenstein, G., Nagin, D., & Paternoster, R. (1997). The effect of sexual arousal on predictions of sexual forcefulness. *Journal of Research in Crime and Delinquency, 34*, 443-473.

Loewenstein, G., O'Donoghue, T., & Rabin, M. (1999). *Projection bias in predicting future utility* (Working paper). Pittsburgh, PA: Carnegie Mellon University.

Loewenstein, G., Prelec, D., & Shatto, C. (1996). *Hot/cold intrapersonal empathy gaps and the prediction of curiosity* (Working paper). Pittsburgh, PA: Carnegie Mellon University.

Loewenstein, G., & Schkade, D. (1999). Wouldn't it be nice? Predicting future feelings. In E. Diener, N. Schwartz, & D. Kahneman (Eds.), *Well-being: The foundations of hedonic psychology* (pp. 85-105). New York: Russell Sage Foundation.

Lord, C. G., Ross, L., & Lepper, M. R. (1979). Biased assimilation and attitude polarization: The effects of prior theories on subsequently considered evidence. *Journal of Personality and Social Psychology, 37*, 2098-2109.

Lorillard. (1974). *A special presentation for Lorillard Division Loews Theatres, Inc. cigarette advertising 1974-1975.* Bates No. 03280729, 03280646-03280964.

Lynch, B. S., & Bonnie, R. J. (Eds.). (1994). *Growing up tobacco free: Preventing nicotine addiction in children and youths.* Washington, DC: National Academy Press.

MacGregor, D. G., Slovic, P., Dreman, D., & Berry, M. (2000). Imagery, affect, and financial judgment. *Journal of Psychology and Financial Markets, 1*(2), 104-110.

Madden, G. J., Petry, N. M., Badger, G. J., & Bickel, W. K. (1997). Impulsive and self-control choices in opioid-dependent subjects and non-drug using controls: Drug and monetary rewards. *Experimental and Clinical Psychopharmacology, 5*, 256-262.

Mahajan, V., & Peterson, R. A. (1985). *Models for innovation diffusion.* Beverly Hills, CA: Sage.

Marcus, A. C., Crane, L. A., Shopland, D. R., & Lynn, W. R. (1989). Use of smokeless tobacco in the United States: Recent estimates from the Current Population Survey. *NCI Monographs, 8*, 17-23.

Marlatt, G. A. (1987). Craving notes. *British Journal of Addiction, 82*, 42-43.

Marlatt, G. A., & Gordon, J. R. (1985). *Relapse prevention: Maintenance strategies in the treatment of addictive behaviors.* New York: Guilford.

Marttila & Kiley, Inc. (1993). *Highlights from an American Cancer Society survey of U.S. voter attitudes toward cigarette smoking.* Boston: Author.

Mattson, M. E., Pollack, E. S., & Cullen, J. W. (1987). What are the odds that smoking will kill you? *American Journal of Public Health, 77,* 425-431.

McCaul, K. D., & O'Donnell, S. M. (1997). *Naive beliefs about breast cancer risk.* Unpublished manuscript, North Dakota State University, Department of Psychology.

McGinnis, J. M., & Foege, W. H. (1993). Actual causes of death in the United States. *Journal of the American Medical Association, 270,* 2207-2212.

McKenna, F. P., Warburton, D. M., & Winwood, M. (1993). Exploring the limits of optimism: The case of smokers' decision making. *British Journal of Psychology, 84,* 389-394.

McLellan, A. T., O'Brien, C. P., Metzger, D., Alternman, A. E., Cornish, J., & Urschel, H. (1992). How effective is substance abuse treatment—compared to what? In C. P. O'Brien & J. H. Jaffe (Eds.), *Addictive states.* New York: Raven.

McLeod, D. M., Eveland, W. P., & Nathanson, A. I. (1997). Support for censorship of violent and misogynic rap lyrics: An analysis of the third-person effect. *Communication Research, 24,* 153-174.

McNeill, A. D., Jarvis, M. J., Stapleton, J. A., West, R. J., & Bryant, A. (1989). Nicotine intake in young smokers: Longitudinal study of saliva cotinine concentrations. *American Journal of Public Health, 79,* 172-175.

McNeill, A. D., Jarvis, M. J., & West, R. J. (1985). Brand preferences among school children who smoke. *Lancet, 2*(8449), 271-272.

McNeill, A. D., Jarvis, M. J., & West, R. J. (1988). Subjective effects of cigarette smoking in adolescents. *Psychopharmacology, 92,* 115-117.

McNeill, A. D., West, R. J., Jarvis, M. J., Jackson, P., & Bryant, A. (1986). Cigarette withdrawal symptoms in adolescent smokers. *Psychopharmacology, 90,* 533-536.

Mendez, D., & Warner, K. E. (2000). Smoking prevalence in 2010: Why the Healthy People goal is unattainable. *American Journal of Public Health, 90,* 401-403.

Milam, J. E., Sussman, S., Ritt-Olson, A., & Dent, C. W. (2000). Perceived invulnerability and cigarette smoking among adolescents. *Addictive Behaviors, 25,* 71-80.

Milgram, S. (1965). Liberating effects of group pressure. *Journal of Personality and Social Psychology, 1,* 127-134.

Miller, B. A., Ries, L. A. G., & Hankey, B. F. (Eds.). (1993). *SEER cancer statistics review 1973-1990* (NIH Publication No. 93-2789). Washington, DC: National Cancer Institute.

Miller, K. S. (1992). Smoking up a storm: Public relations and advertising in the construction of the cigarette problem, 1953-1954. *Journalism Monographs, 136.*

Morley, S. (1993). Vivid memory for "everyday" pains. *Pain, 55,* 55-62.

Moss, A. J., Allen, K. F., Giovino, G. A., & Mill, S. L. (1992). Recent trends in adolescent smoking, smoking-uptake correlates, and expectations about the future. *Advance Data From Vital and Health Statistics, 221.*

Mowrer, O. H. (1960a). *Learning theory and behavior.* New York: John Wiley.

Mowrer, O. H. (1960b). *Learning theory and the symbolic processes.* New York: John Wiley.

Muraven, M., Tice, D. M., & Baumeister, R. F. (1998). Self-control as limited resource: Regulatory depletion patterns. *Journal of Personality and Social Psychology, 74,* 774-789.

National Association of Attorneys General. (1998, November 16). *Tobacco settlement announcement* [Press release]. Available Internet: http://www.naag.org/tobac/npr.htm

National Cancer Institute. (1992). *Smokeless tobacco or health: An international perspective* (Smoking and Tobacco Control Monograph 2; Publication No. NIH 92-3461). Washington, DC: U.S. Department of Health and Human Services.

National Cancer Institute. (1993). *Major local tobacco control ordinances in the United States* (Smoking and Tobacco Control Monograph 3; Publication No. NIH 93-3532). Washington, DC: U.S. Department of Health and Human Services.

National Cancer Institute. (1996). *The FTC cigarette test method for determining tar, nicotine, and carbon monoxide yields of U.S. cigarettes: Report of the NCI Expert Committee* (Smoking and Tobacco Control Monograph 7; Publication No. NIH 96-2789). Washington, DC: U.S. Department of Health and Human Services.

National Cancer Institute. (1997). *Changes in cigarette-related disease risks and their implications for prevention and control* (Smoking and Tobacco Control Monograph 8; Publication No. NIH 97-4213). Washington, DC: U.S. Department of Health and Human Services.

National Cancer Institute. (1998). *Cigars: Health effects and trends* (Smoking and Tobacco Control Monograph 9). Washington, DC: U.S. Department of Health and Human Services.

National Cancer Policy Board, Institute of Medicine, & National Research Council. (1998). *Taking action to reduce tobacco use.* Washington, DC: National Academy of Sciences.

National Cancer Policy Board, Institute of Medicine, & National Research Council. (2000). *State programs can reduce tobacco use.* Washington, DC: National Academy of Sciences.

National Institutes of Health, Technology Assessment Conference Panel. (1993). Methods for voluntary weight loss and control. *Annals of Internal Medicine, 199,* 764-770.

National Research Council. (1989). *Improving risk communication.* Washington, DC: National Academy Press.

National Research Council, Committee on Passive Smoking. (1986). *Environmental tobacco smoke: Measuring exposures and assessing health effects.* Washington, DC: National Academy Press.

Nelkin, B. D., Mabry, M., & Baylin, S. B. (1998). Lung cancer. In B. Vogelstein & K. W. Kinzler (Eds.), *The genetic basis of human cancer.* New York: McGraw-Hill.

Niaura, R. S., Rohsenow, D. J., Blinkoff, J. A., Monti, P. M., Pedraza, M., & Abrams, D. B. (1988). Relevance of cue reactivity to understanding alcohol and smoking relapse. *Journal of Abnormal Psychology, 97,* 133-152.

Niewoehner, D. E., Kleinerman, J., & Donald, B. R. (1974). Pathologic changes in the peripheral airways of young cigarette smokers. *New England Journal of Medicine, 291,* 755-758.

Norman, P., Conner, M., & Bell, R. (1999). The theory of planned behavior and smoking cessation. *Health Psychology, 18,* 89-94.

Normand, J., Vlahov, D., & Moses, L. E. (1995). *Preventing HIV transmission: The role of sterile needles and bleach* (Report of the Panel on Needle Exchange and Bleach Distribution, Commission on Behavioral and Social Sciences and Education, National Research Council, and Institute of Medicine). Washington, DC: National Academy Press.

Norvell, K. T., Gaston-Johansson, F., & Fridh, G. (1987). Remembrance of labor pain: How valid are retrospective pain measurements? *Pain, 31,* 77-86.

O'Brien, C. P., Childress, A. R., Arndt, I. O., McLellan, A. T., Woody, G. E., & Maany, I. (1988). Pharmacological and behavioral treatments of cocaine dependence: Controlled studies. *Journal of Clinical Psychiatry, 49,* 17-22.

Ochsner, M., & DeBakey, M. (1939). Primary pulmonary malignancy: Treatment by total pneumonectomy; analyses of 79 collected cases and presentation of 7 personal cases. *Surgical Gynecology and Obstetrics, 68,* 435-451.

O'Donoghue, T., & Rabin, M. (1999). Doing it now or later. *American Economic Review, 89,* 103-124.

Office of Technology Assessment. (1991). Consent and confidentiality in adolescent health care decisionmaking. In Office of Technology Assessment, *Adolescent health: Vol. 3. Cross-cutting issues in the delivery of health and related services* (Publication No. OTA-H-467) (pp. 111.141-111.150). Washington, DC: Government Printing Office.

Orphanides, A., & Zervos, D. (1995). Rational addiction with learning and regret. *Journal of Political Economy, 103,* 739-758.

Osiatynski, W. (1992). *Choroba kontroli* [The disease of control]. Warsaw: Instytut Psychiatrii I Neurologii.

Palazzoli, S. (1981). Comments. *Family Practice, 20,* 44-45.

PDAY Research Group. (1990). Relationship of atherosclerosis in young men to serum lipopro-
tein cholesterol concentrations and smoking: A preliminary report from the Pathobiological
Determinants of Atherosclerosis in Youth (PDAY) Research Group. *Journal of the American
Medical Association, 264,* 3018-3024.

Pearl, R. (1938). Tobacco smoking and longevity. *Science, 87,* 216-217.

Pechmann, C. (1997). Does antismoking advertising combat underage smoking? A review of past
practices and research. In M. E. Goldberg, M. Fishbein, & S. E. Middlestadt (Eds.), *Social marketing: Theoretical and practical perspectives* (pp. 189-216). Mahwah, NJ: Lawrence
Erlbaum.

Perez-Stable, E., Herrera, B., Jacob, P., III, & Benowitz, N. L. (1998). Nicotine metabolism and intake in black and white smokers. *Journal of the American Medical Association, 280,* 152-156.

Perloff, R. M. (1989). Ego involvement and the third-person effect of televised news coverage.
Communication Research, 16, 236-262.

Perry, C. L., & Silvis, G. L. (1987). Smoking prevention: Behavioral prescriptions for the pediatri-
cian. *Pediatrics, 79,* 790-799.

Peters, E., & Slovic, P. (1996). The role of affect and worldviews as orienting dispositions in the
perception and acceptance of nuclear power. *Journal of Applied Social Psychology, 26,*
1427-1453.

Peterson, J. E., & Stewart, R. D. (1970). Absorption and elimination of carbon monoxide by inac-
tive young men. *Archives of Environmental Health, 21,* 165-171.

Peto, R., Lopez, A., Boreham, J., Thun, M. J., & Heath, C., Jr. (1994). *Mortality from smoking in
developed countries, 1950-2000: Indirect estimates from national vital statistics.* Oxford: Oxford University Press.

Philip Morris. (1964, January 29). *Re: Surgeon general's report* (Memorandum from G.
Weissman to J. F. Cullman). Bates No. 1005038559-1005038561.

Philip Morris. (1966, June 7). *Remarks of Joseph F. Cullman, 3rd to the South Carolina Tobacco
Warehouse Association, Inc.* Bates No. 0002600012-0002600023.

Philip Morris. (1969, Fall). *Philip Morris Research Center Board presentation.* Bates No.
2023063286-2023063296.

Philip Morris. (1972). *Motives and incentives in cigarette smoking* (Memorandum from W. L.
Dunn of Philip Morris Research Center). Bates No. 2023193285-2023193303.

Philip Morris. (1976, August 16). [Transcript of Thames Broadcasting interview of James C.
Bowling]. Bates No. 0002410318-0002410351.

Philip Morris. (1981, March 13). *Young smokers: Prevalence, trends, implications and related demographic trends* (Report by M. E. Johnson). Bates No. 1003636640-1003636688.

Philip Morris. (1987). *Marlboro summer sampling manual* (Program manual). Bates No.
2045223244-2045223249.

Philip Morris. (1994). *Facts you should know* [Press release].

Philip Morris. (2000a). *Cigarette smoking: Health issues for smokers* [On-line]. Available
Internet: http://www.philipmorrisusa.com/displaypagewithtopic.asp?ID=60

Philip Morris. (2000b). *Making a difference in our communities* [On-line]. Available Internet:
http://www.philipmorris.com/pmcares

Piattelli-Palmarini, M. (1991, March-April). Probability blindness: Neither rational nor capricious. *Bostonia,* pp. 28-35.

Pickens, R., & Harris, W. C. (1968). Self-administration of d-amphetamine by rats. *Psychophar-
macologia, 12,* 158-163.

Pierce, J. P., Choi, W., Gilpin, E. A., Farkas, A. J., & Berry, C. C. (1998). Tobacco industry promotion of cigarettes and adolescent smoking. *Journal of the American Medical Association, 279,*
511-515.

Pierce, J. P., Fiore, M. C., Novotny, T. E., Hatziandreu, E. J., & Davis, R. M. (1989). Trends in cigarette smoking in the United States. *Journal of the American Medical Association, 261,* 61-65.

Pierce, J. P., & Gilpin, E. A. (1995). A historical analysis of tobacco marketing and the uptake of
smoking by youth in the United States: 1890-1977. *Health Psychology, 14,* 500-508.

Pierce, J. P., Gilpin, E. A., Burns, D. M., Whalen, E., Rosbrook, B., Shopland, D., & Johnson, M. (1991). Does tobacco advertising target young people to start smoking? *Journal of the American Medical Association, 266,* 3154-3158.

Pierce, J. P., Lee, L., & Gilpin, E. A. (1994). Smoking initiation by adolescent girls, 1944 through 1988: An association with targeted advertising. *Journal of the American Medical Association, 271,* 608-611.

Pollay, R. (2000). Targeting youth and concerned smokers; Evidence from Canadian tobacco industry documents. *Tobacco Control, 9,* 136-147.

Pomerleau, O. F., & Pomerleau, C. S. (1984). Neuroregulators and the reinforcement of smoking: Towards a biobehavioral explanation. *Neuroscience Biobehavioral Reviews, 8,* 503-513.

Popham, W. J., Muthen, L. S., Potter, L. D., Duerr, J. M., Hetrick, M. A., & Johnson, M. D. (1994). Effectiveness of the California 1990-1991 tobacco education media campaign. *American Journal of Preventive Medicine, 10,* 319-326.

Pribram, K. H. (1984). Emotion: A neurobehavioral analysis. In K. R. Scherer & P. Ekman (Eds.), *Approaches to emotion.* (pp. 13-38). Hillsdale, NJ: Lawrence Erlbaum.

Price, V., Tewksbury, D., & Huang, L. (1998). Third-person effects in publication of a Holocaust-denial advertisement. *Journal of Communication, 48*(2), 3-26.

Prochaska, J. O., & DiClemente, C. C. (1984). *The transtheoretical approach: Crossing traditional boundaries of change.* Homewood, IL: Irwin.

Proctor, R. N. (1995). *Cancer wars: How politics shapes what we know and don't know about cancer.* New York: Basic Books.

Quadrel, M. J., Fischhoff, B., & Davis, W. (1993). Adolescent (in)vulnerability. *American Psychologist, 48,* 102-116.

Rabin, M. (1998). Psychology and economics. *Journal of Economic Literature, 36,* 11-46.

Rabin, R., & Sugarman, S. D. (1993). *Smoking policy: Law, politics, and culture.* New York: Oxford University Press.

Rao, R. M. (1997, December 8). All natural killers: RJR's controversial additive-free cigarettes. *Fortune, 136,* 40.

Read, D., & Loewenstein, G. (1999). Enduring pain for money: Decisions based on the perception of memory of pain. *Journal of Behavioral Decision Making, 12,* 1-17.

Reppucci, J. D., Revenson, T. A., Aber, T. A., & Reppucci, N. D. (1991). Unrealistic optimism among adolescent smokers and non-smokers. *Journal of Primary Prevention, 11,* 227-236.

Resnicow, K., Smith, M., Harrison, L., & Drucker, E. (1999). Correlates of occasional cigarette and marijuana use: Are teens harm reducing? *Addictive Behaviors, 24,* 251-266.

Response to increases in cigarette prices by race/ethnicity, income, and age groups—United States, 1976-1993. (1998). *Morbidity and Mortality Weekly Report, 47,* 605-609.

Ricci, E. (1978, August 31). *Re: Newport focus groups* (Letter to R. Davis). Bates No. 85043204-85043211.

Richards, J. I. (1987). Clearing the air about cigarettes: Will advertisers' rights go up in smoke? *Pacific Law Journal, 19,* 1-70.

Rigotti, N. A., DiFranza, J. R., Chang, Y., Tisdale, T., Kemp, B., & Singer, D. E. (1997). The effect of enforcing tobacco-sales laws on adolescents' access to tobacco and smoking behavior. *New England Journal of Medicine, 337,* 1044-1051.

R. J. Reynolds. (1968, April 9). *Re: Teenage and adult smoking attitudes* (Memorandum from T. P. Haller to R. A. Blevins). Bates No. 500484343-500484344.

R. J. Reynolds. (1972, April 14). *Research planning memorandum on the nature of the tobacco business and the crucial role of nicotine therein* (Memorandum from C. E. Teague, Jr.). Bates No. 501877121-501877129.

R. J. Reynolds. (1973, February 2). *Some thoughts about new brands of cigarettes for the youth market* (Research planning memorandum from C. E. Teague, Jr.). Bates No. 502987357-502987368. Available Internet: http://www.rjrtdocs.com/rjrtdocs/frames.html

R. J. Reynolds. (1974, September 30). *1975 marketing plans presentation, Hilton Head* (Presentation by C. A. Tucker). Bates No. 501421310-501421335.

R. J. Reynolds. (1977, February 11). *Smoking and health update: Scientific and medical aspects of the smoking and health controversy—some paradoxes and fallacies* (Report by Dr. F. G. Colby). Bates No. 500273365-500273420.

R. J. Reynolds. (1984a, January 30). Can we have an open debate about smoking? *New York Times*, p. A11.

R. J. Reynolds. (1984b, April 13). *Strategies and segments* (Memorandum from R. C. Nordine). Bates No. 501928471. Available Internet: http://www.rjrtdocs.com/rjrtdocs/frames.html

R. J. Reynolds. (1988). *Camel Y&R orientation* (Analysis of marketing strategies to reach "younger adult smokers"). Bates No. 507241613-507241838.

R. J. Reynolds. (1989). [Handwritten notes and advertisements, "Gambler"]. Bates No. 506940160-506940167.

R. J. Reynolds. (2000). *Tobacco issues: Health issues* [On-line]. Available Internet: http://www.rjr.com/ti/pages/tihealth_issues.asp

RJR-MacDonald. (1982). *Export—family strategy* [Internal document].

Robinson, J. H., & Pritchard, W. S. (1992). The role of nicotine in tobacco use. *Psychopharmacology, 108*, 397-407.

Robinson, J. H., Pritchard, W. S., & Davis, R. A. (1992). Psychopharmacological effects of smoking a cigarette with typical tar and carbon monoxide yields but minimal nicotine. *Psychopharmacology, 108*, 166-172.

Robinson, R. G., Pertschuk, M., & Sutton, C. (1992, May). Smoking and African Americans. In R. G. Samuels, M. Pertschuk, & C. Sutton (Eds.), *Improving the health of the poor: Strategies for prevention*. Menlo Park, CA: Henry J. Kaiser Family Foundation.

Rodgers, J. L., & Rowe, D. C. (1993). Social contagion and adolescent sexual behavior: A developmental EMOSA model. *Psychological Review, 100*, 479-510.

Rofé, Y., & Algom, D. (1985). Accuracy of remembering post-delivery pain. *Perceptual and Motor Skills, 60*, 99-105.

Rojas, N. L., Killen, J. D., Haydel, F., & Robinson, T. N. (1998). Nicotine dependence among adolescent smokers. *Archives of Pediatrics and Adolescent Medicine, 152*, 151-156.

Romer, D., & Jamieson, P. (in press). Do adolescents appreciate the risks of smoking? Evidence from a national survey. *Journal of Adolescent Health*.

Rooney, B. L., & Murray, D. M. (1996). A meta-analysis of smoking prevention programs after adjustment for errors in the unit of analysis. *Health Education Quarterly, 23*, 48-64.

Rosenthal, R. J. (1989). Pathological gambling and problem gambling: Problems of definition and diagnosis. In H. Shaffer, S. Stein, B. Gambino, & T. Cummings (Eds.), *Compulsive gambling: Theory, research, and practice*. Lexington, MA: Lexington.

Ross, L., Lepper, M. R., & Hubbard, M. (1975). Perseverance in self-perception and social perception: Biased attributional processes in the debriefing paradigm. *Journal of Personality and Social Psychology, 32*, 880-892.

Ross, L., Lepper, M., Strack, F., & Steinmetz, J. (1977). Social explanation and social expectation: Effects of real and hypothetical explanations on subjective likelihood. *Journal of Personality and Social Psychology, 35*, 817-829.

Rothman, K. J. (1986). *Modern epidemiology*. Boston: Little, Brown.

Rowe, D. C., Chassin, L., Presson, C. C., Edwards, D., & Sherman, S. J. (1992). An "epidemic" model of adolescent cigarette smoking. *Journal of Applied Social Psychology, 22*, 261-285.

Ruderman, A. J. (1986). Dietary restraint: A theoretical and empirical review. *Psychological Bulletin, 99*, 247-262.

Russell, M. A. H. (1990). The nicotine addiction trap: A 40-year sentence for four cigarettes. *British Journal of Addiction, 85*, 293-300.

Saad, L. (1998, August-September). A half-century of polling on tobacco: Most don't like smoking but tolerate it. *Public Perspective*, pp. 1-4.

Samet, J. M. (1996). The changing cigarette and disease risk: Current status of the evidence. In National Cancer Institute, *The FTC cigarette test method for determining tar, nicotine, and carbon monoxide yields for U.S. cigarettes: Report of the NCI Expert Committee* (Smoking and Tobacco Control Monographs; NIH Publication No. 96-2789). Washington, DC: U.S. Department of Health and Human Services.

Samet, J. M., & Wang, S. S. (2000). Environmental tobacco smoke. In M. Lippmann (Ed.), *Environmental toxicants: Human exposures and their health effects.* New York: Van Nostrand Reinhold.

Sandman, P. M., Weinstein, N. D., & Miller, P. (1994). High risk or low: How location on a "risk ladder" affects perceived risk. *Risk Analysis, 14,* 35-45.

Sargent, J. D. (1998). Growth in tobacco promotion overstated. *Archives of Pediatrics and Adolescent Medicine, 152,* 513.

Sargent, J. D., Mott, L. A., & Stevens, M. (1998). Predictors of smoking cessation in adolescents. *Archives of Pediatrics and Adolescent Medicine, 152,* 388-393.

Scarry, E. (1985). *The body in pain: The making and unmaking of the world.* Oxford: Oxford University Press.

Schelling, T. C. (1984). Self-command in practice, in policy, and in a theory of rational choice. *American Economic Review, 74,* 1-11.

Schelling, T. C. (1992). Addictive drugs: The cigarette experience. *Science, 255,* 430-433.

Schoenbaum, M. (1997). Do smokers understand the mortality effects of smoking? Evidence from the Health and Retirement Survey. *American Journal of Public Health, 87,* 755-759.

Schwarzer, R. (1994). Optimism, vulnerability, and self-beliefs as health-related cognitions: A systematic review. *Psychology and Health, 9,* 161-180.

Scientific Committee on Tobacco and Health. (1962). *Smoking and health: Summary of a report of the Royal College of Physicians of London on smoking in relation to cancer of the lung and other diseases.* London: Pitman Medical.

Scientific Committee on Tobacco and Health. (1998). *Report of the Scientific Committee on Tobacco and Health* (Publication No. 011322124x). London: Her Majesty's Stationery Office.

Scott, E., Reppucci, N. D., & Woolard, J. (1995). Evaluating adolescent decision making in legal contexts, *Law and Human Behavior, 19,* 221-244.

Seeburger, F. F. (1993). *Addiction and responsibility: An inquiry into the addictive mind.* New York: Crossroads.

Segerstrom, S. C., McCarthy, W. J., & Caskey, N. H. (1993). Optimistic bias among cigarette smokers. *Journal of Applied Social Psychology, 23,* 1606-1618.

Sen, A. K. (1977). Rational fools: A critique of the behavioral foundations of economic theory. *Philosophy and Public Affairs, 6,* 317-344.

Sherman, D. A., Kim, H., & Zajonc, R. B. (1999). *Affective perseverance: Cognitions change but preferences stay the same.* Unpublished manuscript.

Shiffman, S. (1982). Relapse following smoking cessation: A situational analysis. *Journal of Consulting and Clinical Psychology, 50,* 71-86.

Shiffman, S. (1989). Tobacco "chippers": Individual differences in tobacco dependence. *Psychopharmacology, 97,* 539-547.

Shiloh, S., & Saxe, L. (1989). Perception of risk in genetic counseling. *Psychology and Health, 3,* 45-61.

Siegel, M., & Biener, L. (2000). The impact of an anti-smoking media campaign on progression to established smoking: Results of a longitudinal youth study. *American Journal of Public Health, 90,* 380-386.

Siegel, R. K. (1982). Cocaine free base abuse: A new smoking disorder. *Journal of Psychoactive Drugs, 14,* 321-337.

Siegel, S. (1979). The role of conditioning in drug tolerance and addiction. In J. D. Keehn (Ed.), *Psychopathology in animals: Research and treatment implications.* New York: Academic Press.

Siegel, S., Hinson, R. E., Krank, M. D., & McCully, J. (1982). Heroin "overdose" death: Contribution of drug-associated environmental cues. *Science, 216,* 436-437.

Siegel, S., Krank, M. D., & Hinson, R. E. (1988). Anticipation of pharmacological and nonpharmacological events: Classical conditioning and addictive behavior. In S. Peele (Ed.), *Visions of addiction: Major contemporary perspectives on addiction and alcoholism.* Lexington, MA: Lexington.

Sieving, R. E., Perry, C. L., & Williams, C. L. (2000). Do friendships change behaviors, or do behaviors change friendships? Examining paths of influence in young adolescents' alcohol use. *Journal of Adolescent Health, 26,* 27-35.

Simonson, I. (1989). Choice based on reasons: The case of attraction and compromise effects. *Journal of Consumer Research, 16,* 158-174.

Simonson, I., & Tversky, A. (1992). Choice in context: Tradeoff contrast and extremeness aversion. *Journal of Marketing Research, 29,* 281-295.

Slade, J. (1993). Nicotine delivery devices. In C. T. Orleans & J. Slade (Eds.), *Nicotine addiction: Principles and management.* New York: Oxford University Press.

Slovic, P. (1987). Perception of risk. *Science, 236,* 282-295.

Slovic, P. (1992). Perception of risk: Reflections on the psychometric paradigm. In S. Krimsky & D. Golding (Eds.), *Social theories of risk* (pp. 117-152). Westport, CT: Praeger.

Slovic, P. (1998). Do adolescent smokers know the risks? *Duke Law Journal, 47,* 1133-1141.

Slovic, P. (2000a). What does it mean to know a cumulative risk? Adolescents' perceptions of short-term and long-term consequences of smoking. *Journal of Behavioral Decision Making, 13,* 259-266.

Slovic, P. (2000b). Rejoinder: The perils of Viscusi's analyses of smoking risk perceptions. *Journal of Behavioral Decision Making, 13,* 273-276.

Slovic, P., Finucane, M., Peters, E., & MacGregor, D. G. (in press). The affect heuristic. In T. Gilovich, D. Griffin, & D. Kahneman (Eds.), *Intuitive judgment: Heuristics and biases.* Cambridge: Cambridge University Press.

Slovic, P., Layman, M., Kraus, N., Flynn, J., Chalmers, J., & Gesell, G. (1991). Perceived risk, stigma, and potential economic impacts of a high-level nuclear waste repository in Nevada. *Risk Analysis, 11,* 683-696.

Slovic, P., Monahan, J., & MacGregor, D. G. (2000). Violence risk assessment and risk communication: The effects of using actual cases, providing instruction, and employing probability versus frequency formats. *Law and Human Behavior, 24,* 271-296.

Smoking: A high decline in rates. (1998, August-September). *Public Perspective,* p. 7.

Smoking-attributable mortality and years of potential life lost—United States, 1984. (1999). *Morbidity and Mortality Weekly Report, 48,* 131-138.

Smoking cessation during previous year among adults—United States, 1990 and 1991. (1993). *Morbidity and Mortality Weekly Report, 42,* 504-507.

Solomon, M. R. (1996). *Consumer behavior: Buying, having, and being* (3rd ed.). Upper Saddle River, NJ: Prentice Hall.

Solomon, R. L., & Corbit, J. D. (1974). An opponent-process theory of motivation. *Psychological Review, 81,* 158-171.

Stead, L. F., & Lancaster, T. (2000). A systematic review of interventions for preventing tobacco sales to minors. *Tobacco Control, 9,* 169-176.

Steinberg, L., & Cauffman, E. (1996). Maturity of judgment in adolescence: Psychosocial factors in adolescent decision making. *Law and Human Behavior, 20,* 249-272.

Stone, S. L., & Kristeller, J. L. (1992). Attitudes of adolescents toward smoking cessation. *American Journal of Preventive Medicine, 8,* 221-225.

Strecher, V. J., Kreuter, M. W., & Kobrin, S. C. (1995). Do cigarette smokers have unrealistic perceptions of their heart attack, cancer, and stroke risks? *Journal of Behavioral Medicine, 18,* 45-54.

Strongman, K. T., & Kemp, S. (1991). Autobiographical memory for emotion. *Bulletin of the Psychonomic Society, 29,* 195-198.

Sutton, S. R. (1995a). *Are smokers unrealistically optimistic about the health risks?* Unpublished manuscript, University College, London, Department of Epidemiology and Public Health.

Sutton, S. R. (1995b). *Unrealistic optimism in smokers: Effect of receiving information about the average smoker.* Unpublished manuscript, University College, London, Department of Epidemiology and Public Health.

Sutton, S. R. (1998). How ordinary people in Great Britain perceive the health risks of smoking. *Journal of Epidemiology and Community Health, 52,* 338-339.

Sutton, S. R. (1999). How accurate are smokers' perceptions of risk? *Health, Risk and Society, 1,* 223-228.

Svenson, O. (1981). Are we all less risky and more skillful than our fellow driver? *Acta Psychologica, 47,* 143-148.

Swann, G. E., Carmelli, D., Rosenman, R. H., Fabsitz, R. R., & Christian, J. C. (1990). Smoking and alcohol consumption in adult male twins: Genetic heritability and shared environmental influences. *Journal of Substance Abuse, 2*(1), 39-50.

Tailoi, E., & Wynder, E. L. (1991). Effect of the age at which smoking begins on frequency of smoking in adulthood. *New England Journal of Medicine, 325,* 968-969.

Taylor, A. E., Johnson, D. C., & Kazemi, H. (1992). Environmental tobacco smoke and cardiovascular disease: A position paper from the council on cardiopulmonary and critical care, American Heart Association. *Circulation, 86*(2), 1-4.

Terre, L., Drabman, R. S., & Speer, P. (1991). Health-relevant behaviors in media. *Journal of Applied Social Psychology, 21,* 1303-1318.

Tetlock, P. (1985). Accountability: The neglected social context of judgment and choice. *Research in Organizational Behavior, 7,* 297-332.

Tetlock, P., Skitka, L., & Boetter, R. (1989). Social and cognitive strategies for coping with accountability: Conformity, complexity, and bolstering. *Journal of Personality and Social Psychology, 57,* 632-640.

Thaler, R. (1980). Toward a positive theory of consumer choice. *Journal of Economic Behavior and Organization, 1,* 39-60.

Thun, M. J., Day-Lally, C. A., Calle, E. E., Flanders, W. D., & Heath, C. W. J. (1995). Excess mortality among cigarette smokers: Changes in a 20-year interval. *American Journal of Public Health, 85,* 1223-1230.

Toates, F. M. (1979). Homeostasis and drinking. *Behavioral and Brain Sciences, 2,* 95-139.

Tobacco Industry Research Council. (1954, January 4). A frank statement to cigarette smokers. *Boston Globe,* p. 13.

Tobacco Industry Research Council. (1972, May 1). [Memorandum from F. Panzer to H. R. Kornegay].

Tobacco Industry Research Council. (n.d.). *A statement about tobacco and health.* Bates No. 2015069234.

Tobacco Institute. (1970, December 1). After millions of dollars and over twenty years of research: The question about smoking and health is still a question. *Washington Post,* p. A10.

Tobacco Institute. (1988, May 16). *Claims that cigarettes are addictive contradict common sense* [Press Release No. 0125189]. Available Internet: http://www.tobaccoinstitute.com

Tobacco use among middle and high school students—United States, 1999. (2000). *Morbidity and Mortality Weekly Report, 49,* 49-53.

Townsend, J., Wilkes, H., Haines, A., & Jarvis, M. (1991). Adolescent smokers seen in general practice: Health, lifestyle, physical measurements, and response to antismoking advice. *British Medical Journal, 303,* 947-950.

Trichopoulos, D., Kalandidi, A., Sparros, L., & MacMahon, B. (1981). Lung cancer and passive smoking. *International Journal of Cancer, 27*(1), 1-4.

Tversky, A., & Kahneman, D. (1973). Availability: A heuristic for judging frequency and probability. *Cognition Psychology, 4,* 207-232.

Tversky, A., & Kahneman, D. (1974). Judgment under uncertainty: Heuristics and biases. *Science, 185,* 1124-1131.

Tversky, A., & Kahneman, D. (1981). The framing of decisions and the psychology of choice. *Science, 211,* 453-458.

Tversky, A., & Kahneman, D. (1982). Judgment under uncertainty: Heuristics and biases. In D. Kahneman, P. Slovic, & A. Tversky (Eds.), *Judgment under uncertainty: Heuristics and biases* (pp. 3-23). New York: Cambridge University Press.

Tversky, A., & Kahneman, D. (1983). Extensional versus intuitive reasoning: The conjunction fallacy in probability judgment. *Psychological Review, 90,* 293-315.

Tversky, A., & Koehler, D. J. (1994). Support theory: A nonextensional representation of subjective probability. *Psychological Review, 101,* 547-567.

Tye, J. B., Warner, K. E., & Glantz, S. A. (1987). Tobacco advertising and consumption: Evidence for a causal relationship. *Journal of Public Health Policy, 8,* 492-508.

U.S. Department of Health and Human Services. (1981). *The health consequences of smoking: The changing cigarette. A report of the surgeon general.* Washington, DC: Government Printing Office.

U.S. Department of Health and Human Services. (1982). *The health consequences of smoking: Cancer. A report of the surgeon general* (DHHS Publication No. PHS 82-50179). Washington, DC: Government Printing Office.

U.S. Department of Health and Human Services. (1984). *The health consequences of smoking: Chronic obstructive lung disease. A report of the surgeon general.* Washington, DC: Government Printing Office.

U.S. Department of Health and Human Services. (1986). *The health consequences of involuntary smoking: A report of the surgeon general* (DHHS Publication No. CDC 87-8398). Washington, DC: Government Printing Office.

U.S. Department of Health and Human Services. (1990a). *The health benefits of smoking cessation: A report of the surgeon general.* Washington, DC: Government Printing Office.

U.S. Department of Health and Human Services. (1990b). Smoking, tobacco, and cancer program, 1985-1989 status report (NIH Publication No. 90-3107). Washington, DC: Government Printing Office.

U.S. Department of Health and Human Services. (1991). *Healthy People 2000: National health promotion and disease prevention objectives* (DHHS Publication No. PHS 91-50212). Washington, DC: Government Printing Office.

U.S. Department of Health and Human Services (USDHHS). (1994). Preventing tobacco use among young people: A report of the surgeon general. Washington, DC: U.S. Government Printing Office.

U.S. Department of Health and Human Services. (2000). *Reducing tobacco use: A report of the surgeon general.* Washington, DC: Government Printing Office.

U.S. Department of Health, Education, and Welfare. (1964). *Smoking and health: Report of the Advisory Committee to the Surgeon General* (DHEW Publication No. PHS 64-1103). Washington, DC: Government Printing Office.

U.S. Department of Health, Education, and Welfare. (1979). *Smoking and health: A report of the surgeon general.* Washington, DC: Government Printing Office.

U.S. Environmental Protection Agency. (1992). *Respiratory health effects of passive smoking: Lung cancer and other disorders* (Publication No. EPA 600/006F). Washington, DC: Government Printing Office.

Use of smokeless tobacco among adults—United States, 1991. (1993). *Morbidity and Mortality Weekly Report, 42,* 263-266.

Vaillant, G. E. (1983). *The natural history of alcoholism: Causes, patterns, and paths to recovery.* Cambridge, MA: Harvard University Press.

Valente, T. W. (1995). *Network models of diffusion of innovations.* Cresskill, NJ: Hampton.

Viscusi, W. K. (1983). *Risk by choice: Regulating health and safety in the workplace.* Cambridge, MA: Harvard University Press.

Viscusi, W. K. (1990). Do smokers underestimate risks? *Journal of Political Economy, 98,* 1253-1269.

Viscusi, W. K. (1991a). Age variations in risk perceptions and smoking decisions. *Review of Economics and Statistics, 73,* 577-588.

Viscusi, W. K. (1991b). *Reforming products liability.* Cambridge, MA: Harvard University Press.

Viscusi, W. K. (1992a). *Fatal tradeoffs: Public and private responsibilities for risk.* New York: Oxford University Press.

Viscusi, W. K. (1992b). *Smoking: Making the risky decision.* Oxford: Oxford University Press.

Viscusi, W. K. (1996). Individual rationality, hazard warnings, and the foundations of tort law. *Rutgers Law Review, 48,* 625-671.

Viscusi, W. K. (1997a). [Deposition in *Florida v. American Tobacco Co.,* Fla. Cir. Ct., 1996, No. 95-1466AH].

Viscusi, W. K. (1997b). [Deposition in state of Mississippi tobacco litigation 213, No. 94-1429].

Viscusi, W. K. (1998a). *Perception of smoking risks.* Paper presented at the International Conference on the Social Costs of Tobacco, Lausanne, Switzerland.

Viscusi, W. K. (1998b). *Public perceptions of smoking risks.* Unpublished manuscript.

Viscusi, W. K., & Magat, W. A. (1987). *Learning about risk: Consumer and worker responses to hazard information.* Cambridge, MA: Harvard University Press.

Wagenknecht, L. E., Cutter, G. R., Haley, N. J., Sidney, S., Manolio, T. A., Hughes, G. H., & Jacobs, D. R. (1990). Racial differences in serum cotinine levels among smokers in the Coronary Artery Risk Development in (young) Adults Study. *American Journal of Public Health, 80,* 1053-1056.

Wagner, S. (1971). *Cigarette country: Tobacco in American history and politics.* New York: Praeger.

Wakefield, M., & Chaloupka, F. J. (2000). Effectiveness of comprehensive tobacco control programmes in reducing teenage smoking in the USA. *Tobacco Control, 9,* 177-186.

Warner, K. E. (1989). Effects of the antismoking campaign: An update. *American Journal of Public Health, 79,* 144-151.

Warner, K. E., Chaloupka, F. J., Cook, P. J., Manning, W. G., Newhouse, J. P., Novotny, T. E., Schelling, T. C., & Townsend, J. (1995). Criteria for determining an optimal cigarette tax: The economist's perspective. *Tobacco Control, 4,* 380-386.

Washton, A. M. (1988). Preventing relapse to cocaine. *Journal of Clinical Psychiatry, 49,* 34-38.

Watzlawick, P. (1978). *The language of change.* New York: Basic Books.

Watzlawick, P., Beavin, J. H., & Jackson, D. D. (1967). *Pragmatics of human communication: A study of interaction patterns, pathologies, and paradoxes.* New York: W. W. Norton.

Watzlawick, P., Weakland, J. H., & Fisch, R. (1974). *Change.* New York: W. W. Norton.

Wechsler, H., Rigotti, N. A., Gledhill-Hoyt, J., & Lee, H. (1998). Increased levels of cigarette use among college students. *Journal of the American Medical Society, 280,* 1673-1678.

Weinreich, N. K., Abbot, J., & Olson, C. K. (1999, July). *Social marketers in the driver's seat: Motorsport sponsorship as a vehicle for tobacco prevention.* Paper presented at Fifth Annual Innovations in Social Marketing Conference, Montreal. Available Internet: http://www.commerce.ubc.ca/ism/ism-prog.htm

Weinstein, N. D. (1980). Unrealistic optimism about future life events. *Journal of Personality and Social Psychology, 39,* 806-820.

Weinstein, N. D. (1987). Unrealistic optimism about susceptibility to health problems: Conclusions from a community-wide sample. *Journal of Behavioral Medicine, 10,* 481-500.

Weinstein, N. D. (1998a). Accuracy of smokers' risk perceptions. *Annals of Behavioral Medicine, 20(2),* 135-140.

Weinstein, N. D. (1998b). *References on perceived invulnerability and optimistic biases about risk or future life events.* Unpublished manuscript, Rutgers University, Department of Human Ecology. (Available from N. D. Weinstein via e-mail: neilw@aesop.rutgers.edu)

Weinstein, N. D. (1999). What does it mean to understand a risk? Evaluating risk comprehension. *NCI Monographs, 25,* 15-20.

Weinstein, N. D., & Klein, W. M. (1995). Resistance of personal risk perceptions to debiasing interventions. *Health Psychology, 14,* 132-140.

Willett, W. C., Green, A., Stampfer, M. J., Speizer, F. E., Colditz, G. A., Rosner, B., Monson, R. R., Stason, W., & Hennekens, C. H. (1987). Relative and absolute excess risks of coronary heart disease among women who smoke cigarettes. *New England Journal of Medicine, 317,* 1303-1309.

Wilson, G. L., & Gillmer, J. A. (1999). Minnesota's tobacco case: Recovering damages without individual proof of reliance under Minnesota's consumer protection statutes. *William Mitchell Law Review, 25,* 566-625.

Windschitl, P. D., & Wells, G. L. (1996). Measuring psychological uncertainty: Verbal versus numeric methods. *Journal of Experimental Social Psychology: Applied, 2,* 343-364.

Winkielman, P., Zajonc, R. B., & Schwarz, N. (1997). Subliminal affective priming resists attributional interventions. *Cognition and Emotion, 11,* 433-465.

Winn, D. M., Blot, W. J., Shy, C. M., Pickle, L. W., Toledo, A., & Fraumeni, J. F., Jr. (1981). Snuff dipping and oral cancer among women in the southern U.S. *New England Journal of Medicine, 304,* 745-749.

Wise, R. A., & Bozarth, M. A. (1987). A psychomotor stimulant theory of addiction. *Psychological Review, 94,* 469-492.

Wistuba, I. I., Lam, S., Behrens, C., Virmani, A. K., Fong, K. M., Leriche, J., Samet, J. M., Srivastava, S., Minna, J. D., & Gazdar, A. F. (1997). Molecular damage in the bronchial epithelium of current and former smokers. *Journal of the National Cancer Institute, 89,* 1366-1373.

Wolosin, R. J., Sherman, S. J., & Cann, A. (1975). Predictions of own and other's conformity. *Journal of Personality, 43,* 357-378.

World Bank. (1999). *Curbing the epidemic: Governments and the economics of tobacco control.* Washington, DC: International Bank for Reconstruction and Development.

World Health Organization. (1999). *International consultation on environmental tobacco smoke (ETS) and child health* (Consultation report). Geneva: Author.

Worth, R. (1999). Making it uncool. *Washington Monthly, 31*(3). Available Internet: http://www.washingtonmonthly.com/features/1999/9903.worth.cigs.html

Wynder, E. L., & Graham, E. A. (1950). Tobacco smoking as a possible etiological factor in bronchiogenic carcinoma: A study of six hundred and eighty-four proved cases. *Journal of the American Medical Association, 143,* 329-336.

Wynder, E. L., Graham, E. A., Croninger, A. B. (1953). Experimental production of carcinoma with cigarette tar. *Cancer Research, 13,* 855-864.

Zajonc, R. B. (1968). Attitudinal effects of mere exposure. *Journal of Personality and Social Psychology Monograph, 9*(2, Pt. 2), 1-27.

Zajonc, R. B. (1980). Feeling and thinking: Preferences need no inferences. *American Psychologist, 35,* 151-175.

Index

About the Contributors

R. Kirkland Ahern is a doctoral student at the University of Pennsylvania's Annenberg School for Communication. Her training and research center on cognitive and social psychological influences on the processing of media messages. Her dissertation research explores how selective attention, selective exposure, and emotional priming affect information search in an interactive media environment.

Neal L. Benowitz is Professor of Medicine and Chief, Division of Clinical Pharmacology and Experimental Therapeutics, University of California, San Francisco. He is trained in internal medicine, clinical pharmacology, and medical toxicology. His research has focused on understanding the effects of nicotine in people, including how nicotine maintains tobacco use and the pharmacology of nicotine addiction.

Richard J. Bonnie is the John S. Battle Professor of Law and Director of the Institute of Law, Psychiatry and Public Policy at the University of Virginia. He is an expert on public health ethics and law. As a member of the Institute of Medicine of the National Academy of Sciences, he played a substantial role in the writing of the 1994 IOM report *Growing Up Tobacco Free* as well as subsequent IOM reports on tobacco.

Jon D. Hanson is Professor of Law at Harvard University. He teaches courses on tort law, tort theory, corporate law, and "law and behavioralism." Much of his research focuses on consumer behavior and, more specifically, understanding the interactions and net effects of market, regulatory, and other institutional influences on consumer conduct.

377

Patrick Jamieson is a doctoral student at the Graduate School of Education at the University of Pennsylvania. His areas of interest include tobacco surveys, adolescent mental health, and media contagion and suicide.

Douglas A. Kysar will be Assistant Professor of Law at Cornell Law School beginning in spring 2001. His writing and research have focused on nontraditional economic approaches to understanding consumerism and their attendant effects on social welfare and environmental health. He graduated magna cum laude from Harvard Law School in 1998 and currently practices corporate law in Boston.

George Loewenstein is Professor of Economics and Psychology at Carnegie Mellon University. His research focuses on applications of psychology to economics, and his specific interests include the impact of emotions on decision making, decision making over time, bargaining and negotiations, law and economics, the psychology of adaptation, the psychology of curiosity, and the psychology and economics of "out of control" behaviors, including addiction.

Daniel Romer is a Senior Researcher in the Annenberg Public Policy Center at the University of Pennsylvania. He studies adolescent risk behavior and the influence of both peers and the media on adolescents. He has published extensively on risks to healthy development and interventions that might avert those outcomes, especially among young people living in high-poverty urban neighborhoods.

Jonathan M. Samet, M.D., M.S., is Professor and Chairman of the Department of Epidemiology of the Johns Hopkins University School of Hygiene and Public Health. He is trained as a clinician in the specialty of internal medicine and in the subspecialty of pulmonary diseases. His research has addressed the effects of inhaled pollutants in the general environment and in the workplace. He has written widely on the health effects of active and passive smoking and has served as consultant editor and senior editor for reports of the U.S. surgeon general on smoking and health.

Paul Slovic is President of Decision Research in Eugene, Oregon, and Professor of Psychology at the University of Oregon. He studies human judgment, decision making, and risk analysis. He and his colleagues worldwide have developed methods to describe risk perceptions and to measure the effects of those perceptions on individuals, industry, and society.

Neil D. Weinstein is Professor of Human Ecology and Psychology at Rutgers–The State University of New Jersey. He has published extensively in the fields of risk perception, risk communication, and health-protective behavior. He is particularly well-known for his research on optimism bias in the assessment of personal risks.